Strategic Management Accounting

Keith Ward

BUTTERWORTH
HEINEMANN

Butterworth-Heinemann Ltd
Linacre House, Jordan Hill, Oxford OX2 8DP

 PART OF REED INTERNATIONAL BOOKS

OXFORD   LONDON   BOSTON
MUNICH   NEW DELHI   SINGAPORE   SYDNEY
TOKYO   TORONTO   WELLINGTON

First published 1992
Reprinted 1992

British Library Cataloguing in Publication Data
A catalogue record for this book is
available from the British Library

ISBN 0 7506 0110 8

Composition by Genesis Typesetting, Laser Quay, Rochester, Kent
Printed and bound in Great Britain by M & A Thomson Litho, East Kilbride, Scotland

Contents

Part Five Information Requirements for Strategic Management Accounting

Preface

The objective of this book is to place management accounting clearly within the context of the strategic management of a business, and to provide a practical, yet academically rigorous, framework for applying management accounting techniques and concepts in this environment.

The book starts with an introduction to business strategy and strategic management, and an overview of both competitive and corporate strategic issues. The management accounting implications and associated financial control issues are then examined in these contexts. This is done by considering how management accounting can aid the selection and implementation of the most appropriate competitive strategies, particularly by providing financial information on competitors, customers and individual products. The impact of different types of organization structure, and the consequent overall corporate strategies, on the management accounting requirements of the business is then examined. During these parts of the book, the need to tailor the financial control measure to the stage of development of the business is raised and this is dealt with in detail in Part Four. The final part of the book draws together all the issues involved in collecting, analysing and disseminating the relevant financial supporting information so that a decision oriented strategic management accounting system can be developed, and tailored to the needs of any type of organization.

The book uses a vast range of examples and mini cases to illustrate the main issues; however, it is deliberately not filled with numbers or sophisticated mathematics. The main objective is to convey the important concepts and ideas and to show how management accounting can, and must, be integrated into the strategic decision-making process.

As a result, the material should be relevant to qualified, as well as training, management and financial accountants, and to other managers with interests in financial decision-making in the context of strategic management. It is of particular relevance to advanced MBA courses, having been successfully tested on my strategic management accounting elective at Cranfield.

The style of the book is deliberately challenging and provocative as I believe this area of management accounting represents the greatest challenge to the profession for the foreseeable future.

I wish to thank my secretary, Sheila Hart, and her colleagues, Marjorie Dawe and Aileen Tracey, for typing the manuscript, and Natalie Thomas for producing the computer generated figures, all against completely unreasonable deadlines. I am also grateful to my family, Angela, Samantha and Robert, for putting up with me while I have been writing this book. Apparently I have been getting more bad-tempered as the time has passed; I hope this is not reflected in the resulting text and that you, the reader, feel that the effort, particularly on the part of my family, has been worthwhile.

Keith Ward

Part One

Linking Strategy and Management Accounting

1

Introduction and overview

The title of this book, Strategic Management Accounting, can be restated as 'accounting for strategic management' or, somewhat more specifically, as 'management accounting in the context of the business strategies being planned and implemented by an organization'. In order to make either of these restated wordings usable, it is necessary to define business strategy, strategic management, and also management accounting.

Strategic management

Strategic management is normally regarded as an integrated management approach drawing together all the individual elements involved in planning, implementing and controlling a business strategy. Thus it clearly requires an understanding of the long-term goals and objectives of the organization ('where it wants to go'). There must also be a comprehensive analysis of the environment in which the business both is and will be operating ('where it is'). This analysis must include all the internal operations and resources (both existing and potential) of the organization but, equally importantly, must cover the external aspects of its environment. This includes competitors, suppliers, customers, the economy, governmental changes, as well as legal and other regulatory changes, etc.

This need to include, and indeed concentrate on, these many factors which are external to the organization is a major element which separates strategic management accounting from the other, more traditional, areas of accounting. These have all tended to focus almost exclusively on the internal operations of the organization and only incorporate its specific transactions with the outside world.

The combination of 'where the organization is' and 'where it wants to go' will normally identify the need for a series of actions to bridge the gaps between the two, or even merely to maintain the same position if the external environment is changing adversely. These 'business strategies' must be developed in the context of the internal and external environments so as to ensure that they are practical; if not the goals and objectives of the organization will remain a theoretical 'wish list' rather than an achievable plan for the business. For many large organizations it is also important that business strategies are developed at the appropriate levels within the organization: thus an overall corporate strategy is needed for the organization in total, with separate but linked competitive strategies for each subdivision of the business which is competing in different markets with different products. However so far these business

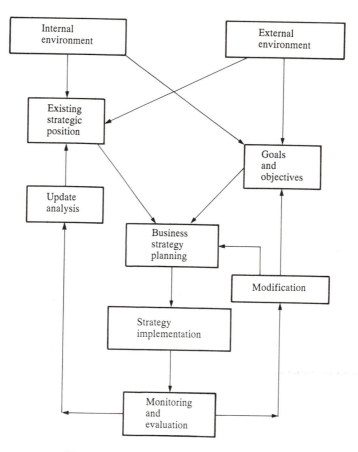

Figure 1.1 Strategic management process

strategies are only plans and the full process of strategic management includes the implementation of the selected strategies.

Some of the goals and objectives are long term, and the relevant strategies will be implemented in a dynamic and continually changing external environment. Therefore it is most unlikely that all the predicted outcomes from these action plans will be achieved. There is a need within any truly comprehensive framework of strategic management for a process of evaluation and control and also modification where necessary. Any such modifications may result in changes to the selected strategies but in some circumstances the organization may be forced to admit that its original goals and objectives are not attainable in the actual external business environment or with its available set of internal resources. Some of the objectives may have to be modified unless some way can be found of either making the environment more attractive or increasing available resources. Thus strategic management is a continual, iterative process, as illustrated in Figure 1.1 and discussed in more detail in Chapter 2. Accounting for strategic management must operate successfully in this changing, evolving environment if it is to make a positive contribution to the financial aspect of this strategic analysis, planning and control process. It is therefore necessary to select which aspects of the finance and accounting function are relevant for this strategic role.

The role of management accounting

In most businesses it is normal to separate the financial function into three main roles which are primarily concerned with:

1 Recording the financial transactions of the business and externally reporting to shareholders and other interested groups the historic financial results of these transactions; ie financial accounting.
2 Raising the funds required by the business in the most appropriate manner: ie financial management (or corporate finance).
3 Supporting the managers of the business in their financial decision-making process and being part of that management team; ie management accounting.

Given the previous discussion on the role of strategic management it is obvious that the most appropriate area for involvement in this strategic role is management accounting. This separation of management accounting from financial accounting is fundamental in that it highlights that management accounting does not concentrate on recording past events or on presentation of externally published financial statements (and hence neither does this book!). However this should not be taken to indicate that strategic management accounting is not very closely concerned with the interests (ie goals and objectives) of shareholders (the owners of the business) and the other important stakeholders in the business (who are now normally considered to include debtholders, customers, suppliers, employees, government and the community, which may be represented by consumer groups and environmentalists).

Different stakeholders

As indicated in Figure 1.2, all the relevant stakeholders in a business will influence the business strategy selected and implemented by the managers (who themselves form only one such group of stakeholders). The relative power of these constituent groups is very important

Figure 1.2 Stakeholders impacting on business strategies

and may change significantly over time or because of the particular strategic issue which is dominant at any particular time. Hence the selection of business strategies is not simply the province of the managers. It is also possible for conflicting sub-strategies to be imposed on a business by different stakeholder groups with differing and incompatible sets of priorities, as is illustrated below and in Chapter 2. In a company all these stakeholders have as their major source of financial information the legally required, published financial statements, but these indicate only the past financial performance and financial position of their business (as the statements only cover historic financial accounting periods and are published a considerable time after these accounting periods have ended). Most of this published information is only produced in summary form for the whole of each legal entity. In the case of very large, well-diversified, publicly quoted groups of companies, this summarized format may not be very informative to many of the interested stakeholders, who may prefer much more detailed information about a particular aspect of the business.

However, for most of today's companies the shareholders have delegated any immediate and detailed involvement to their 'agents', or more accurately in this case 'stewards', who are supposed to use their best efforts on behalf of their principals. Under this extremely important, and well documented, concept of 'agency theory' the 'corporate stakeholders agents' are the senior managers of the business, or directors of the company, who have complete day to day control, subject only to periodic reviews (primarily triggered by the external publication of financial results). Therefore managers should be taking into account the interests of shareholders and the other stakeholders when they are deciding on the long-term strategy of the business, and in the continuous implementation and updating of that strategy. The substantial role of management accounting in this strategic decision-making process also requires that the needs and wishes of outsiders to the management team are always borne in mind – particularly with respect to the risks associated with any specific decision and whether the corresponding level of expected return is acceptable. How this is practically done in the strategic planning process is considered in Chapter 2 and some of the financial implications are considered in Chapters 3 and 4. If managers forget their agency responsibilities to their key stakeholders (ie their principals), the ultimate sanction from any form of efficient financial markets is for the managers to lose their jobs. This may happen either because they are voted out of office by existing shareholders, or these existing shareholders become so dissatisfied that they sell their shares and so pass ultimate ownership control to another set of shareholders, who are quite likely to make significant changes in management. The sanctions available to all the other, non-owning stakeholders are generally more indirect, but their pressure can still have an ultimate impact on the financial results of the business and now they can apply more explicit legal constraints to managers. Even such indirect pressure can prove effective in the long-term, should management seriously abuse their delegated powers of authority.

These different stakeholder groups will have very varied, and possibly conflicting, areas of interest in the organization, and will wish to become involved in the business strategy in very different ways and to differing levels of detail. For example, the shareholders in a large, international, well-diversified conglomerate may have very little knowledge about, or even interest in, the specific businesses, products, markets and countries in which the group is involved. They may principally be concerned with the financial return which they receive in the form of dividends and capital gains, from what would probably be regarded as a low risk investment due to its well-diversified spread of interests. If the previously successful business strategy had involved acquisitions and disposals of businesses, even on a substantial scale, or large scale investments in new manufacturing facilities, it is likely that any new similar proposals would automatically be approved by these shareholders. This would appear to leave the business strategy clearly in the hands of the managers as long as they continue to perform well financially.

However, the attitude of employees to proposals regarding any potential acquisition and disposal of business units may be very different and in some cases could be critical to the actual strategy which is selected or to its ultimate level of success. Also suppliers and customers may pay particular attention to any strategic threats which could lead to the company becoming involved in their existing areas of trading, eg by vertical integration. Any significant competitors may also become important stakeholders who would try to influence the strategy decisions. This could happen if the company proposed strategic moves which were likely to upset an existing balance of power or equilibrium in the industry, eg by a large increase in capacity which could not be absorbed by expected future growth in industry demand. Where the strategy calls for large scale new investments or downsizing through closure of facilities, local and sometimes national governments will suddenly emerge as very interested stakeholders and try to influence the decisions taken by the managers. One of the problems which will be continually returned to throughout the book is that people, not organizations, take decisions. Consequently this issue of how decisions are taken can be critical, and the relative power of pressure groups can significantly influence the ultimate strategic decision.

In an ideal, theoretically sound world the application of agency theory would ensure that all managers made decisions in line with the goals and objectives of all the relevant stakeholders. These would have to be weighted by some appropriate factors reflecting the influence of the stakeholders and the strength, ie the degree of importance, attached by them to the particular objective under consideration. In the imperfect reality of strategic business decisions, it is important that due consideration is given to the interests of all significant stakeholder groups and that as many as possible of the potential implications are evaluated prior to implementing the strategic decision. Thus managers should aim to reflect the objectives of stakeholders. However, if the personal goals of the managers happen to concur with these stakeholder objectives, they are much more likely to be motivated to implement the strategy wholeheartedly.

Aim of goal congruence

As an example, the shareholders of a particular focused company may wish the managers to adopt a very high risk, high growth strategy which, if successful, will give very big financial returns to these shareholders, relative to their possibly quite small initial investment. If the strategy fails and the company is put out of business as a consequence, the shareholders may be able to offset their financial loss against gains made elsewhere in their investment portfolio. In other words they can diversify, and hence reduce, **their** risk, and should do so if individual investments are following high risk focused strategies. However if this high risk strategy fails, the managers may well find themselves out of a job and it is difficult for the managers to diversify their employment portfolios and thus reduce their own risks. The potential extra financial returns available to the managers from the complete success of this high risk strategy may be much smaller than are available to the shareholders and may therefore be insufficient to motivate them to take the risk involved in such a high growth focused strategy. This problem of goal congruence will also be addressed throughout the book but in particular in Part Three, which considers in depth the problems caused by different organizational structures.

In the simplest form of business where the owners are also directly involved as senior managers there should be no such conflict of interest, but for most medium and large enterprises, this has long since ceased to be the case. Indeed in the case of very large businesses, the problem is often increased due to another potential gap in goals and objectives between the top managers of the total business (eg the group board of directors) and the actual divisional and operating managers who, in a hierarchical sense, are the agents of the top managers. The achievement of this required goal congruence all the way through a large multi-tiered business is obviously very difficult and requires a clear focus on the key strategic issues at each level when developing the strategic management accounting system. The need for careful selection of individual management performance measures at all relevant levels which are in accord with the total business strategy is therefore a major task for any good management accounting system, and again indicates the interaction between management accounting and strategic issues, as shown diagrammatically in Figure 1.3.

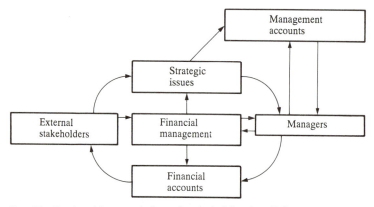

Note: The direction of the arrows indicates the principal direction of influence or not of communication of information

Figure 1.3 Strategic issues and management accounting

Management accounting was also distinguished from financial management, which is primarily concerned with obtaining the required funding for the business in the most appropriate manner. Within the finance and accounting organizations of most large businesses, these roles are normally fulfilled by different people and, for operational day-to-day functions, this separation can be seen to be sensible as it builds on specific skill requirements. However, when the role of financial managers is considered in the context of the business strategy, a vital element is clearly the ability of the business to raise or retain the required funds to implement the desired strategy. If this proves to be impossible, the overall strategy will need to be modified to come into line with the available funding (now normally referred to as the concept of 'affordability') or the continued existence of the total business may be placed in jeopardy. This means that any sensible definition of strategic management accounting must include some aspects of ensuring that adequate funding can be made available as required by any new strategic moves of the business, as is shown in Figure 1.3. This more pro-active forward-looking form of financial management is part of what should be more accurately described as financial strategy. This is really a subject in its own right due to its ability to add considerably to the total value of the business. Consequently only some key, particularly relevant, issues from the subject will be addressed in this book.

Thus the role of strategic management accounting is very definitely not that of a passive, financial score-keeper or 'bean-counter' and is also not restricted to the more normally used definition of 'management accounting', with its concentration on supporting internally based financial decisions. It is a much more positive role of supporting the financial needs of management in their task of directing and controlling the business in the best interests of its owners and the other relevant stakeholders, and in Chapter 3 this role is considered in more detail.

Analysis, planning and control

Strategic management has already been characterized as an iterative process of analysis, planning and control, and management accounting can also be described in these terms, as is shown in Figure 1.4.

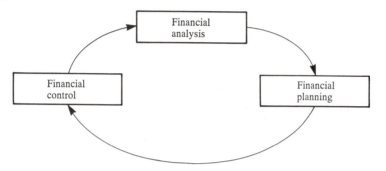

Figure 1.4 Management accounting process

It would be helpful if strategic management accounting could also be analysed into the same three-stage process. It would enable the match between strategic management and its financial support system to be as close as possible. It is quite possible to break the process down into these stages although, as with strategic management itself, the dividing lines become somewhat blurred in practice.

Financial analysis is required to establish where the business is and to ensure that the strategic objectives are realistic and meaningful. Since the business strategy is very concerned with the external environment, a large part of the required financial analysis focuses on external issues and particularly competitors and customers, rather than the more traditional areas, such as internal performance compared against last year or even compared against this year's budgets. Also, instead of concentrating on the financial performance of the business as a whole, the relevant strategic financial analysis breaks the total business down into its main components and provides information on relevant sub-groups, eg product profitability analysis and customer group profitability analysis. These areas of strategic management accounting are considered in Part Two.

The strategic planning exercise is carried out to devise action plans which should achieve the corporate objectives. These plans normally require significant management accounting input as many of these corporate objectives are expressed in financial terms. The business strategy has to be designed and then implemented by the managers in the organization and thus the organizational structure will have a significant impact on the way the strategic plan is developed and implemented. The relevance of different types of organizational structure are considered in Part Three but it should be remembered that the organization can, and should, change its structure if the strategy is being unnecessarily constrained. Many organizations operate in a fast-changing environment and therefore the most appropriate organization structure may also change rapidly as the environment develops. Unfortunately, many businesses seem incapable of rapid structural change and hence maintain an outmoded management structure which is no longer suitable for their current strategic needs, and their financial performance suffers as a result.

Once the strategic plan has been developed and implementation has begun, the role of management accounting becomes that of monitoring the degree of achievement of the financial objectives and of providing appropriate feedback to the relevant decision-makers. This feedback should be used to make correcting decisions to put the plan back on course or to aim for modified objectives (either improved or reduced) where relevant. Financial monitoring and reporting, ie control, should therefore be regarded as a positive tool of management, acting as a much-needed learning process for the difficult task of strategic planning. Far too often, as is considered in Part Five, the financial control process is seen as a way of apportioning blame for what went wrong, or as a means of claiming the credit for what went right. It is also vitally important that the method of financial control is appropriate to the particular business strategy being employed and thus that it is suitably tailored. Unfortunately most organizations use only one major method of monitoring financial performance (some form of Return on Investment being by far the most common) irrespective of the particular stage of development of the business or particular strategic thrusts. In Part Four, following a more detailed justification in Chapter 3, an alternative approach is considered which attempts to select financial controls which are appropriate to different stages of business development.

Decision support system

There is a real danger that, as control of information in an organization creates power, management accountants and other senior financial managers see their primary roles as strategic decision-makers. This is an abuse of their real role which should be as an important and integral part of the strategic management team but they are not, in most cases, the ultimate decision-maker. Accounting is the common business language which enables varied resources and conflicting priorities to be compared and evaluated, and a key role of the financial manager should be that of an expert translator. There is a further role which, as a full member of the management team, requires the financial manager to participate in formulating business objectives and strategies, but this control over financial information should not be used to create an autocratic, unsupportable power base.

Strategic management accounting should be a decision support system and this involves the provision of relevant information to the appropriate strategic decision-maker. This area is covered in Part Five where the specific information requirements for strategic decisions are considered in detail, but the basic requirements are the same as for any area of management accounting. Decision support systems require that the right information is provided to the right people at the right time, but this simplistic statement requires some further explanation.

Need for information

The 'right people' refers fairly obviously to the strategic decision-maker but this can lead to confusion in many organizations. It is often assumed that strategic decisions are only taken at the top of the organization, ie by the very senior managers, and that consequently these are the only managers who require strategic management accounting information. Key decisions may be made by the chief executive or even by the whole board of directors but a business strategy has to be implemented all the way through the organization. It therefore contains a multitude of sub-strategies, all of which require to be planned, and this means that strategic decisions have to be taken at all levels in the organization and the required supporting accounting analysis has to be supplied to the appropriate manager. Also it is impossible for any single manager to monitor the implementation of the complete strategic plan and this will be delegated to various managers at differing levels in the business, who will need to receive appropriately formatted monitoring and control information.

The broad scope of most strategic decisions implies a need for a vast amount of supporting financial analysis but too much information can, in fact, be worse than too little. All managers must be supplied with information, not raw, unprocessed data. A good strategic management accounting system can add tremendous value to a strategic decision-maker by intelligently analyzing the historic information to provide predictions of the probable outcomes of forthcoming decisions. In many repetitive decisions, it can be relatively easy to develop a statistically sound forecasting system by using the outcomes of the multitude of previous decisions. Unfortunately most strategic issues fall into the category of non-repetitive, one-off decisions for which no easy forecast of outcomes can be made. Also the potential range of outcomes is normally wide and more sophisticated decision modelling techniques, such as linear programming techniques and simulations, are required to cope with this complexity. Unless the management accounting system processes this information and presents the output to the decision-maker in an intelligible form, it is possible that the strategic decision may be fatally delayed or not taken at all. This can be caused by the manager trying to analyse the mass of information supplied and to reconcile the almost inevitably conflicting results which will be included. Alternatively a critically important decision may be taken without reference to any of the mass of available information because there was no time to do this analysis to discover which bits were relevant.

Therefore 'the right time' refers both to the time-scale of the decision and the amount of time needed to assimilate the information provided. Clearly, if the financial analysis can be carried out intelligently and the information is then presented in a summarized and appropriately tailored format, this assimilation period can be reduced to a minimum. The decision-maker's time and effort can then be concentrated more productively on selecting the best strategic option. This is one of the great challenges facing strategic management accounting and is discussed in detail in Chapters 19 and 20.

It is still essential to balance the cost of providing this financial information against the benefit to be obtained by the organization from making a better strategic decision. These costs are themselves reducing dynamically with increasing computer power available at lower real prices. It is therefore continually becoming more economic to provide better financial information faster. This should not be interpreted as simply providing more reports, more regularly and more quickly, although it often appears that this is how the opportunity is actually being treated. It should enable management accounting to analyse and model the critically important relationships and to provide predicted outcomes for the relevant combinations of internal and external factors which significantly impact the success of the business strategy. This would enable management accounting to make a very strongly positive contribution to strategic management and this is developed fully in Chapter 3, after techniques of strategic management have been considered in Chapter 2.

However, it is important to place strategic management accounting in a business context as early as possible and so a deliberately stylized and whimsical illustration is given below which shows how strategic financial decisions can only be taken with a good understanding of the overall business strategy involved.

Rudolph and the elves

Rudolph was beginning to regret his rapid rise up the managerial ladder; this time last year he had been head chauffeur but a continuing severe head-cold had made him ask SC (as he was known in the business) for an indoor job. He had started as assistant stores controller, but his skills and elf-motivation had led to his promotion to Head of Production Scheduling and Controller of the Corporate Headcount (HOPSCOTCH for short). One of his main roles was obviously to plan the production of the year's requirements and to recruit the labour necessary to achieve this level of output. He had instantly identified one key problem, seasonality in sales, and had approached the marketing department regarding ways in which this peak could be reduced. However, they felt that customers would be very averse to a change in delivery patterns, even if it were geographically organized. They had been trying for many years to generate additional purchase opportunities so that some spreading would take place but this had not really reduced the peak volume.

They did accept that Rudolph's problems were increasing because their market research was becoming less reliable and was also being received later (very few letters now seemed to come down their chimney until October at the earliest). The lack of reliability and hence very late upsurges in demand for certain products were apparently due not only to the increasing sophistication of customers, but also to the greater product range availability which created shorter product life cycles than they had been used to in the past.

Thus, in recent years, they had been left with large unusable stocks of certain items. One possible reaction to this problem was to produce only low volumes of 'fashion' items early in the year and concentrate on making mainly the 'low risk' products in this period – this was complicated as fewer and fewer products could be classified as low risk. Such a seasonably based system did enable production to be matched more closely with demand, as the demand could be more accurately assessed, but it also increased production costs significantly. Not only was overtime working required, but temporary labour was also hired. This meant increased training for short-term assistants. In spite of this training, Rudolph knew that wastage and rework costs would be significantly higher through the temporary labour and through tiredness on the part of the permanent employees.

Offsetting this, of course, Rudolph had savings arising from not having to rent vast outside warehouses and also in interest costs because he didn't have to finance the higher inventory which would result from an even level of production throughout the year.

There seemed to be significant disadvantages to either seasonal matching or even production, and Rudolph had thought of one option. If he invested in automated production facilities (in particular flexible manufacturing systems) then he could cope with the increased seasonal demand by running the machines for longer hours and he wouldn't need to have more labour with all of its associated problems. If he didn't need the output he could turn the machines off and since the labour element involved would not be very great it wouldn't waste much money. Was this the answer to the problem?

Discussion of problem

Rudolph, in his employment for Santa Claus, has a number of unusual competitive advantages which include an incredibly powerful brand name, a unique distribution system which enables all his customers to be serviced on the same night of the year, plus the not unimportant fact that the products are all given away! Therefore if the problem is placed in the more realistic setting of the toy industry generally, the strategic alternatives can be analysed quite easily.

	Even production	**Seasonally variable production**
Advantages of system	Lowest unit costs	Low inventory – production matched to orders
	Efficient production • stable work force • low wastage	Low financing and storage costs
		Low risk of stock obsolescence
	Good machine utilization	
Disadvantages of system	High inventory levels • physical storage costs • financing costs • risk of stock obsolescence	Higher unit costs
		Increased wastage and rework
		Poor machine utilization

Figure 1.5 Rudolph's initial options

There are two existing strategies in use and a third, flexible manufacturing systems, has been proposed. Figure 1.5 summarizes the advantages and disadvantages of the existing options and it is clear, but not surprising, that the advantages of one system are the main disadvantages of the other.

At first sight, flexible manufacturing systems would appear to have most of the advantages of both current strategies, and hence avoid their disadvantages. However, if the required output can be produced in a very short period of the year (ie the run up to the pre-Christmas sales periods), it is obvious that the machines will be dramatically under-utilized during the rest of the year. The major flaw in Rudolph's argument is 'that turning off these machines when they weren't needed wouldn't waste much money'. The last thing that a company wants to do is to leave expensive plant and machinery idle as the return on investment will rapidly reduce. Also the cost of acquiring really flexible machines is normally much greater than traditional single function equipment, and these flexible machines should consequently be kept running for the maximum possible period (eg 24 hours per day, 7 days per week).

In order to select the best alternative, each toy company should review its business strategy and then identify the critical success factors for that strategy. Only then can a decision be made as to whether even production, seasonally variable production or the extra investment in flexible manufacturing systems should be selected.

If the toy company's strategy was to concentrate on the more stable segment of the market (eg plastic toys for 0–5 years category) then it could logically implement an even production strategy. The risk of stock obsolescence is lower than in the high fashion segment of the market where a strategy of seasonally variable production is more sensible. Also in the more stable product groups it may be more difficult to command any price premium against competition and so efficiency of production is a key success factor. Again, even production should give the lowest unit cost levels which makes it the attractive option, whereas branded fashion products can often achieve a substantial price premium so that any relative cost inefficiencies can be recovered in the higher selling prices. Should the company decide to implement flexible manufacturing processes, it may need to increase its product range so as to utilize fully the expensive new investment in sophisticated plant and machinery. This move could result in a fundamental change in its business strategy as toys would only be one part of the enlarged product range and the main emphasis could become that of manufacturing a varied range of plastic products, rather than being a focused toy company.

These strategic decisions should only be taken after a full evaluation of the financial implications, which requires that strategic management accounting operates within, and is compatible with, the specific business strategy. Far too frequently, businesses make financial decisions without considering their full strategic consequences and by reference only to their short-term impact on profitability or, even worse, cost levels. Thus a proposed change in investment policy or in the method of organizing production may appear to reduce costs but it may have severe adverse repercussions on the marketing strategy of the business. Throughout this book, techniques and concepts are discussed which aim to make management accounting more able to take account of all the potential impacts of these types of strategic decisions. Hopefully, by the end of the book, the reader will be able to carry out a much more exhaustive analysis of Rudolph's problems and suggest the optimum strategic solution.

To send any suggested solution to Rudolph – write it out and then burn it in an open fire, so that the smoke goes up the chimney.

2

Strategic planning

Business strategy encompasses a wide area of management issues and many approaches and techniques have been developed as aids to practising managers. Indeed, particular aspects of business strategy have been made the sole subject of many long books. It would be ridiculous to attempt, in one chapter, to review all of these conceptual models and techniques; therefore, no apology is made for the inclusion of only certain aids to strategic planning which are of particular relevance to strategic management accounting. Some of these techniques are described, in summary form, in this chapter while others are integrated into the context of strategic management accounting in Chapter 3.

From the introductory discussion in Chapter 1, it is clear that the strategic planning process should be much more than a series of five or seven annual budgets which are added together sequentially to form what is termed 'the long range plan' of the organization. As already stated, strategic management is an iterative process of analysis, planning and control in order to achieve the long term strategic aims of the organization but the organization first has to establish what these long term strategic aims are. Subsequently it has to decide at what level in the business this iterative strategic planning process will be carried out.

Mission, goals and objectives

An essential prerequisite for a meaningful strategic plan is the establishment of a set of goals and objectives for the organization. These terms have already been used in Chapter 1 and it is advisable to clarify their meanings before becoming too deeply involved in considering their relevance and applications. The terms 'mission, vision, goals and objectives' are sometimes used interchangeably by organizations, whereas other businesses attribute very specific meanings to the different titles. Unfortunately there does not appear to be universal agreement on the differences but, at least in this book, they will be applied consistently in accordance with their most literal interpretations.

Under this categorization the organization's vision statement is the most general and vague, and encompasses the way in which the organization would like to impact its environment. In other words it is often used to express how the world will become a better place due to the existence of the organization or some other form of lofty and possibly altruistic aim. A more useful way of using the vision statement is to set out what the long-term general aims of the organization are; by keeping the statement general and the time-scale imprecise, the stated vision can be unachievable in practical terms but can still provide a target for the business to keep heading towards.

Figure 2.1 Hierarchy of business aims

Many organizations seem to regard a vision statement as too vague to be helpful, and select the mission statement as their most general expression of purpose. A mission statement should reflect the specific role that the organization plans to fulfil within society over the long term, and therefore limits the scope of its operations by the implicit exclusion of areas outside its stated mission. The mission does not necessarily have to be prescriptive in terms of the goods and services supplied by the business as these may change over time (throughout the book the term 'products' will be used to refer to both goods and services). It could define the customer groupings that will be targetted but, again as the market place changes, new channels of distribution may develop which require new marketing strategies.

The mission statement should however indicate the sectoral focus of the organization (eg fast-moving consumer goods; added-value convenience food products; industrial services, etc) or else it will convey no meaning to any of the stakeholders involved. This communication of organizational purpose is possibly the major benefit of having a mission statement because it should enable every person (eg employee, shareholder, customer, supplier) dealing with or interfacing with the business in any way to understand clearly what the main aims are. [Thus it is very surprising to find businesses where senior managers have taken considerable trouble to develop a mission statement and then fail to tell anyone what it is. Other companies put their mission statement, albeit an abbreviated version, on all their communications, both internal and external, and even hang it on their office walls.]

If a principal benefit is communication, the mission statement must be clear as to the critical, long-term positioning of the business, eg with regard to quality, service, price, etc. It is now common to include statements regarding 'corporate values' and 'guiding business principles', which are indicators of how the organization will conduct its business, and often cover attitudes to employees and their working environment, customers and suppliers, as well as shareholders. The mission statement need not contain quantified financial objectives as these will change over time, but any relative adjectives included (such as leading, largest, pre-eminent, best) should be placed in a context where the method of assessment is incontrovertible. Does 'being the largest company in the washing powder industry' refer to sales revenue, assets employed, profits made or the size of the actual packets of washing powder, and is the industry in question global, national or regional?

As mentioned in Chapter 1, every organization will have a broad range of stakeholders and each group will have distinct and possibly conflicting aims from their involvement with any particular business. The mission statement should indicate whether this particular organization will provide an acceptable fit of the combined aims. Statements on corporate values and guiding business principles can be very important in this area. For example, some investment funds have been established to invest only in 'ethical' businesses. Thus many industries and some markets are excluded from their potential investment portfolio, but they have attracted quite substantial funds from individual investors who feel that these 'ethical' business principles are attractive. A much more specific example is 'Body Shop' where the founder, Anita Roddick, has very explicitly stated that none of their products are developed by being tested on animals; again a range of stakeholders (eg shareholders, customers, employees and environmentalists) are attracted to this guiding business principle.

The mission statement should, therefore, initially be established on the basis of the aims of the key original stakeholders, but once the business is established it should assist new stakeholders in deciding whether to become associated with the organization or not. Therefore to be of continuing value the mission statement really needs to provide a long-term reason for the existence of the organization. Any business that has constantly to redefine its mission so that its strategic moves fit with the mission statement, either is not implementing a well thought through business strategy or has not properly defined its mission in the first place.

Alternatively it may be that it has no real reason to continue as a business and this raises an important question about the continued existence of organizations. Many managers seem to base their strategic decision making on an essential, but implicit, assumption of infinite life for their businesses, irrespective of their original missions. This often means that over time the organization moves into completely unrelated areas where it has no competitive advantages. These moves seem to be justified by management on the arguments that 'they had to do something, otherwise the business would have eventually died!' The original mission of the organization may have been well expressed and clearly understood but has either been achieved or has been superseded and hence made irrelevant by changing circumstances. In such cases the justifiable life of the organization, as originally conceived, is finite and the key stakeholders should be consulted before the managers unilaterally extend their role in society by adding to or fundamentally rewriting the mission statement. This can often be an example of a conflict between the desires of managers to prolong and even enhance their careers, and their duty to act, as agents, in the best interests of the other key stakeholders.

If the mission statement describes 'what the business is' and specifies 'what the business wants to be' in overall terms, the goals of the organization should interpret the mission statement into more understandable statements for the different groups of stakeholders. Thus separate 'goals' may be established for customers, employees and suppliers, as well as for shareholders.

It is at this level of establishing aims and targets that the organization may come up against other examples of conflicting desires. All the different groups of stakeholders may be quite happy with the organization's overall mission statement, but they may have very different emphases which only become highlighted when separate goals are developed for each group. For example if the mission statement referred to the 'development and marketing of high quality products' in a specified sector, the shareholders would probably, quite naturally, assume that the 'high quality' of the products would result in high relative selling prices and consequently good financial returns. The customers may interpret this statement as implying 'good value for money' and resent any attempt to charge above average selling prices. Employees may interpret this 'high quality' as enabling the business to build a large share of the market, with a resulting positive impact on employment prospects. The organization has to try to develop goals for each of these separate groups of stakeholders which are in line with the mission statement so that these potential internal conflicts are minimized, but without creating communication problems which will cause further problems in the future. Clearly the managers will weight their decisions in line with the perceived relative importance of the stakeholders, but as these can change quite dramatically over time, the goals of the organization may also need to be modified appropriately. Therefore goals are often established for shorter time-frames than is the case for the more overall and continuing mission statement, but they are still normally kept general and unquantified.

This means that the strategic planning process needs yet another, more measurable set of aims, and these are normally provided by the objectives of the organization. These objectives will normally provide a quantified statement of the goals of the business or at least some of the shorter term goals. Strategies can be defined as alternative courses of action which can be implemented to try to achieve some specific objectives and thus more specifically appropriate strategies can be selected and implemented if clearly quantified objectives are established. It also enables more meaningful and objective monitoring to be carried out, as it can be more difficult to assess whether the financial performance is getting 'better' than it is to tell if profits have improved by more than 20%, year on year.

However this raises a key problem of setting objectives which is that they have to be realistic and achievable, if they are to be meaningful and worth monitoring actual performance against. This is not so important in the case of a vision statement as an idealistic target can still be worth having, but as the aims of the organization are made more definitive they should also become more practical. In order to achieve this level of practicality, the objectives should be set in the context of the actual environment in which the business is operating and this requires that both internal and external constraints are taken into account. Before considering how this is achieved slightly later in this chapter, the level in the organization at which these goals and objectives are required should be established.

Multi-layered strategic planning process

It is clear that each organization should have an overall vision or mission statement or both. For simple tightly focused organizations, this statement can be developed into a series of appropriate goals. These goals can themselves be quantified into corporate objectives so that the most suitable options can be selected and implemented. However even for such a well-defined business these overall objectives will prove to be inadequate because organizations do not normally function as total entities. In order to achieve the corporate objectives, the required strategic decisions may have to choose among alternative marketing strategies, operational changes, different personnel policies and potentially innovative methods of financing the business. Thus appropriate functional strategies have to be selected. This requires the overall corporate objectives to be broken down into a compatible set of functional objectives if conflicts are to be avoided among these separate functional strategies. Potential problems could arise where, for example, the marketing strategy requires rapid, short-term growth in sales volumes to achieve market share dominance while the market is still itself rapidly growing. This could be important to the long-term overall corporate objectives but could cause dramatic short-term problems for other functions, eg operations (expanding output substantially), personnel (recruiting and training large numbers of new people) and finance (raising the funding for the increased marketing and operational activity). In addition this marketing strategy could be in conflict with these areas' long-term functional goals [eg operations – become the low cost producer in the industry; personnel – develop a stable, well-motivated and efficient workforce; finance – develop good relations with sources of long-term capital so as to access low cost long term funding]. This hierarchical structure of inter-dependent objectives is illustrated in Figure 2.2 and, as is shown, these functional objectives and strategies may indicate that the overall business objectives and strategies are unachievable or inappropriate. A feedback loop is necessary to allow the required modifications to be made to the overall plan. These subsequent revisions should establish an internally consistent set of functional objectives and strategies.

In the case of a large, diversified organization the problem of turning a corporate mission statement into specific objectives can be much greater. While it is possible to set out, for the organization as a whole, goals and objectives which are appropriate for the corporate mission, this may be a meaningless exercise if the business is actually carried out by a group of smaller business units.

There are several different ways for large organizations to subdivide themselves into smaller controllable units. Common methods are to break the business down into functional areas of responsibility or into geographic areas, where managers are made responsible for all the

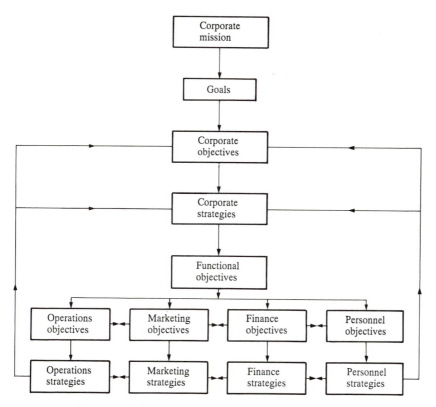

Figure 2.2 Need for functional objectives and strategies

functions carried out within their regions. Another way is to subdivide the organization into separate divisions which are given control over all the functions they need to make them almost autonomous businesses. Normally the central management of the organization retains control of some key elements, such as funding, which stops the divisions being truly independent but allows a good degree of managerial discretion. It is also quite common to create divisions which only provide internal support services (eg information technology), or where one type of process (eg manufacturing) is grouped together to gain economies of scale (eg production efficiencies) but where all the output is sold within the group. Operational control may be greatly enhanced by these organizational structures but they may not be helpful to the strategic planning process.

The most logical and relevant divisions for strategic planning purposes are, not surprisingly, called strategic business units (SBUs). SBUs are normally defined as being divisions of an organization where the managers have control over their own resources, and discretion over the deployment of these resources within specified boundaries (ie their own mission statement and set of goals). Indeed some businesses have even renamed the aims statements of their SBUs (eg as 'divisional charters') thereby clearly distinguishing the reason for existence of the division from that of the organization as a whole. It is usual for SBUs to have external customers and each SBU will normally focus on a particular market segment or product group (or preferably both). It is likely to face specific competitors which may not be shared with any other SBUs within the organization.

For this type of diversified group, the role of corporate strategic planning is to define the overall corporate values and guiding business principles and to set out the limits of the businesses which can be undertaken by the subsidiary units. A further role, which will be considered in more detail in Chapter 3, is to allocate corporate resources to the various operating businesses in accordance with the set of priorities indicated by the overall corporate mission and goals.

Other functions of overall corporate planning will depend upon the degree of diversification among the various SBUs, as unnecessary competition is normally unproductive and should be avoided by the centre acting in a co-ordinating role. More positively this role can ensure that commonly required resources are provided in the most cost-effective manner so that economies of scale are attained wherever possible and that duplications of costs are removed. While this may generate a cost saving by the pooling or grouping together of business support functions (eg research or information technology), it is important to ensure that the cost saving is not more than outweighed by the loss in effectiveness of the activity. This can easily be caused by the transfer of these resources out of the specific market-facing business units into a more centralized staff-type support function, where the previous high degree of focus and concentration on the objectives of specific business units can become blurred or lost altogether. If the resources are left in one of the SBUs and shared by others, a new problem is created. What price should be charged to the sharing partners for the commonly needed resource and who should receive the cost saving achieved? This question of transfer pricing is considered in Part Three.

The individual business units will need to undertake the vast majority of the detailed strategic planning function in diversified groups because only at this level can the managers identify business objectives and select strategies to achieve them. However it can be strongly argued that business objectives and strategies are really all about products and markets/customers in terms of the strategic decisions regarding which products are offered to which markets. If a business unit has a range of either products or market segments then the strategic planning process should be still further subdivided to identify specific objectives and

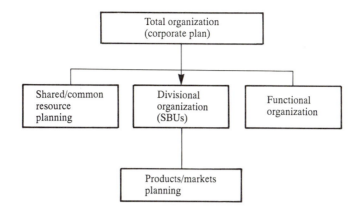

Figure 2.3 Strategic planning levels

strategies for each combination thereof. One of the major managerial judgements needed in strategic planning is how far to take these subdivisions because, as will be seen below, each new level requires a substantial amount of analysis to provide supporting information for the required strategic decisions.

This complex hierarchy of strategic planning levels may well bear little, if any, resemblance to the legal structure of the organization or even to the way the business is organized for day-to-day operations (eg where a geographic/regional structure is used for operational control but where strategic planning is carried out by reference to product groups and market segments). It is important that the planning process can obtain the analytical information which it requires in an appropriate format and the important role played by strategic management accounting in achieving this is discussed in Chapter 3, and the practical issues involved in designing and implementing such systems are considered in Part Five.

Analytical information requirements

The logical start point for the strategic planning process is to review the current situation of the organization in terms of its internal resources and the external environment. However, in the light of the preceding discussion on the many levels of strategic planning, even this simple statement requires clarification. For many organizations there is a large degree of commonality in the external environment for all its operating units and therefore this external part of the analysis can and should be done on an organization-wide basis. Carrying out this situation review at the highest common level not only avoids duplication of effort but also ensures that all levels of the organization are basing their strategic decisions on the same view of the outside world. Even though this common view may be wrong, it should reduce the chances of completely opposite strategies being adopted by different parts of the business. For example, in a multinational organization, it would normally be sensible for one forecast of future exchange rates to be used throughout the divisions. If each division was allowed to make their own forecast it is quite possible that their individual teams of economists would come to completely opposite conclusions (after all, the collective term for economists should be 'a disagreement'). This could have ludicrous consequences for the business whereby if the US based division expected the dollar to strengthen against the Deutsche Mark they would plan on an increased level of imports from Germany. If the German-based division forecast the dollar to weaken relatively to the Deutsche Mark they might expect a lower level of sales to the USA as a consequence. The implications for capacity planning and conflicting marketing strategies within the organization could be horrendous and in many cases will ensure that the business is put at a competitive disadvantage whatever the actual outcome of the particular external environmental factor.

The internal part of this strategic analysis will have to be conducted at the level which has control over the resources concerned, and which can really make decisions over their effective deployment. Normally this will be at different levels in the group organization for different areas and the strategic planning process must allow for this complexity of analysis and decision making.

A major objective of this situation review is to highlight constraints and opportunities which need to be taken into account when planning for the future. Consequently an out of date analysis is of no value. Information is needed on the present, and on likely changes over the planning time horizon. However the historical perspective can often provide the best basis for assessing these likely future developments. It is also important that this situation review is done in the relative context of competition as absolute value statements are unhelpful; eg describing the existing products as being of 'good quality' does not identify whether their relative quality is better or worse than the competition. This relative grading is most easily achieved by carrying out the situation review in the form of a SWOT analysis. SWOT stands for strengths, weaknesses, opportunities and threats, and is normally displayed in a 2×2 matrix as shown in Figure 2.4. The strengths and weaknesses refer to the internal aspects of

Figure 2.4 SWOT analysis

the organization compared both to the competition and to the expectations of the market place; ie what the business is relatively good and bad at doing. This analysis of the existing state of the business has to be done realistically and honestly: fooling oneself is a stupid and often fatal mistake! It must also be done against the aims of the organization as set out in the mission statement and goals, as these will indicate which areas of strength or weakness are likely to prove important in the future. This highlights the differences between the longer term, unchanging mission statement and the more definitive and practically achievable corporate objectives because some objectives will often need to be modified in the light of the SWOT analysis.

This may be particularly true as a consequence of the analysis of the external environment, which aims to highlight external threats (ie potential constraints) and opportunities for the business. Previously established objectives may be clearly seen as unachievable in the light of

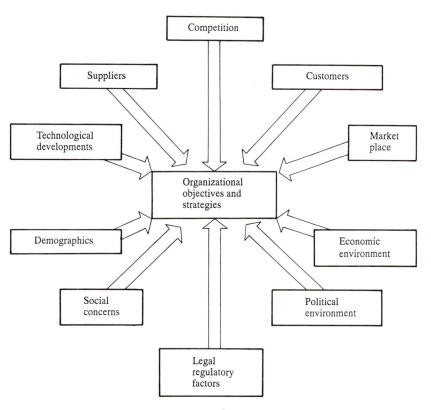

Figure 2.5 External environmental factors

this analysis, or the identification of new future opportunities may reveal that the existing objectives are set at far too low a level. It is important that these opportunities and threats take account of all the relevant external environmental factors and of the inter-relationships among them. As illustrated in Figure 2.5 there are a broad range of such external factors and a similarly large group of internal characteristics can be drawn up. There is a danger that the SWOT analysis becomes an unmanageably long list of unweighted factors, all of which can appear to be of equal significance. If the situation review is to be of assistance to strategic planning, these factors must be ranked in order of importance and priority so that only the main issues are included in the matrix. It is also vital that a balanced matrix is developed, including both strengths and weaknesses, opportunities as well as threats. When an organization carries out this type of analysis for the first time it is not unusual for the initial draft of the matrix to be very unbalanced. If a broad range of strengths has been identified but no weaknesses can be thought of, complacency and arrogance can immediately be added. Alternatively, a long list of weaknesses with no strengths should lead to humility and modesty being inserted into the matrix.

More seriously, where the organization has good relative strengths against existing competition, at least the potential threat from new entrants coming into the industry should be evaluated. This type of linked analytical process will normally result in a fairly well-balanced SWOT matrix.

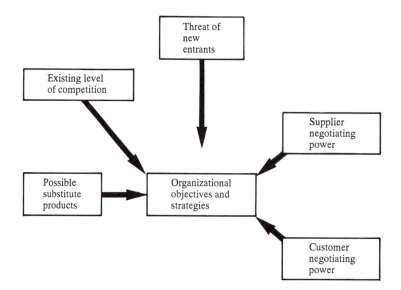

Figure 2.6 Porter's five factors affecting current level of competition

There are several other techniques which can be used to provide a comprehensive analysis of the current position. Michael Porter, in his books[1], uses a five-part model of the existing competitive position. This helps to highlight the key factors which will affect the future achievement of the goals and objectives. The elements of this model are shown in Figure 2.6 and it can usefully be applied with his later technique, a development of the added value concept, which he has called the 'value chain'. The value chain, which is shown in Figure 2.7 looks at the total value added by the industry and by the particular organization within that industry, and then the contribution of each primary and support activity carried out by the organization is separated. The objective of this analysis is to highlight the activities which contribute most significantly to the total value added and to develop strategies to improve on or defend the current share of that value added which is gained by the organization.

The rationale for this positional analysis is easy to say but much more difficult to do in practice. The selected strategies should build on and develop the organization's strengths so that they eliminate or minimize the impact of the potential external threats, and the externally identified opportunities should be used to reduce the significance of the weaknesses while the organization improves its performance in these areas.

If looked at in this way, the situation review should highlight those areas of the business and its environment which are critical to the achievement of its goals and objectives. The available analytical and planning resources should be concentrated on these critical success factors, and the business strategies should be selected accordingly. Many organizations seem to forget that their relative competitive position can change considerably over time and that the external environment can be extremely volatile. Consequently, the critical success factors will also change and this may require a corresponding adjustment to the main strategic thrusts of the organization and to its strategic positioning.

[1]Porter, Michael E., *Competitive Strategy*, Free Press, 1980 and *Competitive Advantage*, Free Press, 1985

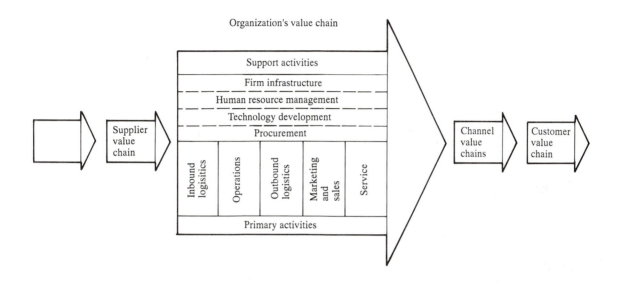

Figure 2.7 Value chains (Source: Porter, Michael, *Competitive Advantage*, Free Press, 1985)

Strategic planning process

The SWOT analysis should be seen as an aid to strategic planning and not as an end in itself. This is true of all the other techniques described in this chapter and they need to be used intelligently, with the exercise of considerable managerial judgement. The situation review will highlight constraints and opportunities for the organization with regard to its goals and overall mission, but it will not provide a specific set of solutions as to what the organization should do. Neither can it give guaranteed, accurate forecasts of how competitors, etc, will respond to any moves made by the business. [As stated above, for large or diversified organizations, separate situation reviews will need to be done at appropriate levels within the organizations, so that specifically tailored strategies can be developed at the business unit and functional levels.] This analytical process will allow the modification and refinement of the previously developed objectives to ensure that they are still practical and achievable given the available internal resources and the currently assessed external environment.

However the main reason for carrying out the analysis is to facilitate the identification of the appropriate courses of action required to achieve these goals and objectives. Given the changing nature of the critical success factors, these strategies will need to change appropriately but must still fit within the overall framework of the organization.

One technique which tries to aid this fit has been developed by Tregoe and Zimmerman[2], in which they designate the main thrust of the business as the 'driving force'. This is seen as the principal agent for changing the nature of the organization, and in their book they separate out nine 'driving forces' which can be sub-grouped into product/market driven, competitive advantage driven, and results driven. They argue that the main driving force, which may change over time, will have a significant impact all the way down the organization in terms of the appropriate sub-strategies that should be implemented, provided that it is clearly communicated to, and understood by, all levels of management. For example, if the business is driven by 'products offered', most of the organization's future growth will be achieved by either launching similar products to those already produced or improving the performance of the existing products. This may require strategic moves into new markets for both these existing and the new products, as well as having significant implications for research and development strategies. A similar but shorter term idea is to identify the main 'strategic thrusts' of the organization which should be dictated by the identified critical success factors. Strategic thrusts are defined by Hax and Majluf[3] as the 'primary issues the firm has to address during the next 3 to 5 years to establish a healthy competitive position in the key markets in which it participates'. This should automatically link them closely to addressing the critical success factors identified by the situation review, while aiming to achieve the goals set for this time period.

However, as has already been discussed, the strategic plan has to be developed in a co-ordinated manner at several different levels in the organization and it is quite possible that different strategic thrusts could be identified for different levels. It is important that this approach does not confuse managers when the apparently conflicting strategies are implemented. Another model for describing generic business strategies has been developed by Porter in his 1980 book, 'Competitive Strategy', and this splits successful strategies into three broad categories, as shown in Figure 2.8. To be successful across its chosen industry, an organization must either be able to supply the product from the lowest cost case in the industry or be able to command a higher price in the market by differentiating its product in the minds of its customers. The business may not be able to sustain either of these strategies across the whole industry. It should then adopt the third strategic category which is to focus on a particular segment of the industry ('niche') where it can command a sustainable competitive advantage. Logically, this sustainable competitive advantage can only be achieved in this niche by either being the low cost supplier or differentiating the product so as to achieve a higher selling price.

[2]Tregoe, B. B. and Zimmerman, J. W., *Top Management Strategy*, Kepner-Tregoe Inc., 1980
[3]Hax, A. C. and Majluf, N. S., *Strategic Management*, Prentice-Hall, 1985

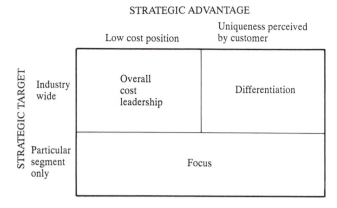

Figure 2.8 Porter model of generic strategies

These models highlight the differences in strategic planning required at the corporate level and at the product/market level. High level corporate planning in widely diversified organizations concentrates on identifying key driving forces and major company-wide strategic thrusts where shared resources and common concerns can assist in the achievement of overall corporate goals and more widely drawn objectives. At the SBU level the concerns should be more tightly focused and functional objectives should be defined which are very closely in line with the overall objectives of the SBU. These overall SBU objectives may not specifically match with the objectives of the total organization as the business units may form part of a business portfolio. Here the separate elements have complementary objectives so as to achieve an optimum result for the group (this is discussed in detail in Chapter 3). Even at the SBU level it may not be possible to define a single competitive strategy, if a group of products is produced or a range of markets is serviced by the business unit. Consequently, competitive strategies have to be developed at the lowest appropriate base of the business whereas corporate mission statements are prescribed at the highest level. Thus strategies are needed, not surprisingly, at the same multi-levels for which objectives are stated (for confirmation refer back to Figure 2.3).

Competitive strategies

Competitive strategies can be defined as specific courses of action which are designed to create sustainable competitive advantages in particular products or identified markets in the pursuit of identified objectives. Consequently, competitive strategies should be the most precise level of strategic planning since they relate to actions regarding products and markets which are to be implemented to achieve the most specific (ie lowest level) objectives of the organization. The apparent combinations for enhancing the sales and marketing performance of the business are fortunately very few and fairly obvious. (Unfortunately, when the main objective for the business is expressed in terms of financial performance, the possible ways of enhancing performance become almost limitless, but this is considered later in the book.) A business can improve its sales of existing products either by selling more to its existing customers (ie increasing market share by improved penetration) or by finding new customers/markets in which to sell these products (ie market development). Alternatively the organization could

Figure 2.9 Ansoff Matrix

acquire or develop new products to sell to its existing customers (product development) and these possibilities have been neatly encapsulated diagrammatically in the Ansoff matrix as is shown in Figure 2.9.

The matrix indicates the appropriate types of strategy which should be implemented depending on which box the organization decides to select as its preferred method of growth. The matrix also suggests a fourth alternative – new products for new customers. This can be described as a diversification strategy or more critically as a questionable strategy (the author often refers to it as 'the wally box') because it does not build on any obvious existing competitive advantage of the business. (This diversification strategy is considered in detail in Chapter 3.) The choice among the other three strategies should be made by examining the relevant strengths and weaknesses identified for the business. These should be placed in the context of the main strategic thrusts of the business and ranked by reference to the driving force or generic strategy of the organization as a whole.

Practical examples of these three strategic options, as they could apply to a clearly defined business, may make this clearer. A supermarket retailer with a chain of stores providing national coverage could choose to increase its market share. If the market is mature and slow-growing, and major competitors are also well-established and highly committed to this market, this option will not look very attractive. It could take its retailing expertise and move into new markets, ie internationally, but it may feel that a lot of its competitive advantages are not readily transferable into these international markets where customer habits and expectations are significantly different. The more attractive alternative may be to use its well-established retail image and loyal customers as a base to expand its product range, ie new products to existing customers. If the new products are reasonably compatible to the current range, economies of scale may be obtainable by selling them through the existing stores. Alternatively, new store outlets may be desirable but this increases the risk that existing customers will not travel to the new stores to try out the new product range. As the retailer has no background in this product area, it may feel the combined product and location risk is unacceptably high. This could be reduced by launching the expansion as a joint venture, with someone who has the product expertise but who is not currently in this market (ie for them the potential expansion would be seen as new markets for existing products). This was the route chosen by Sainsbury's for the launch of their do-it-yourself chain, Homebase, which is 75% owned by them and 25% owned by GB-INNO-BM, the leading Belgian DIY retailer.

A high technology company, such as a volume car manufacturer like Fiat, might view a similar set of alternatives rather differently. If it had spare production capacity, despite a dominant share of its domestic market (Fiat historically has had approximately 60% of the Italian car market), it may feel that its best strategic option was to expand internationally. This attempt to gain new customers for existing products would be stimulated by the high contribution made by any incremental sales, due to the high level of fixed costs in this type of automated production, and the very high costs of new product development in the industry. Fiat may believe that its production technologies would also give it a competitive advantage in manufacturing other complex, durable, high technology products. Ideally, these new products should be developed and produced by managers who are not, at the same time, supposed to be focussing on the drive to increase market share of international car markets. This is indeed how they and most other successful multinational conglomerates are organized.

It is therefore not necessarily true that the three base strategies from the Ansoff matrix are mutually exclusive. Even at the business unit level, managers may believe that they should try to achieve their objectives by implementing all three, or even all four strategies at once. One of the most frequent reasons for breaking a large organization down into divisions is to avoid managers having to implement several strategies at the same time, as this may result in managerial lack of focus, confusion over priorities and ultimately failure of some or all of the strategies. If the SBUs are properly defined the managers should need to focus on one main strategic thrust (eg market or product development, but not both) at one time. The critical strategic focus will change as the environment develops (eg the markets mature) and relative strengths and weaknesses alter (eg competition achieves a technological breakthrough). If the SBU has a range of products or markets under its control, these changes may well take place at different rates for each element in the group. Consequently, although all the products had the same strategic priorities when the SBU was established, over time they will develop different needs and management will become less single-minded. It may be a sensible solution to change the structure of the SBUs to re-establish the strategic focus, even though there may be no reason to change the organizational structures for operational control purposes.

If divisions are changed for strategic planning purposes but not for operational control issues, the organization will inevitably become increasingly complex as, over time, the two structures will have less common elements. Some large and already complex groups have started to accept that the benefits of creating and maintaining tightly defined management strategic focus are worth the complications of having two reporting structures for some of the managers involved – one for operational/tactical issues and a different structure for strategic planning decisions. (After all, managers have coped for many years with the complexity of the line and functional reporting systems which are required by matrix systems of management.) These groups are now defining SBUs, as far as possible, in the ideal way for tight strategic focus and control.

Many other businesses are leaving their organizational structures the same for all planning and control purposes so as to avoid this complex level of managerial reporting. This can often mean that an individual business unit is required to implement several competing, and sometimes conflicting, strategies at the same time. Indeed this has led to a very common way of incorporating the Ansoff matrix into the strategic planning process. This is by using it to compute the gap between the business unit's objectives and what should be achieved by the continuation of the existing business, plus the implementation of the appropriate parts of the three base strategies. In most cases the remaining gap is supposed to be filled by the fourth strategy, ie diversification, and the technique of 'gap' analysis is illustrated graphically in Figure 2.10.

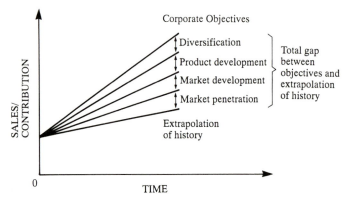

Figure 2.10 Gap analysis

Interactive and iterative process

This technique indicates the normal stages of strategic planning. The situation review shows not only where the business is, but where it is likely to go if no changes are made to the current strategies. A good SWOT analysis should highlight the critical success factors for the business and hence where changes in the strategy are likely to have the most beneficial effect. The managers involved in strategic planning should therefore focus on choosing among the alternative courses of action which could improve the likelihood of achieving the business objectives.

Information is required on the range of probable outcomes for these alternative courses of action and on the risks associated with each. Risk and return are, of course, positively correlated so that an increased level of risk requires a compensatingly higher level of return. However, this relationship can become more complicated than usual when dealing with strategic decisions, because the perception of risk may be in one area of the organization while the return is achieved in another. For example operations may be asked to consider increasing the level of automation in a production process in order to reduce operating costs and to improve product quality on a consistent basis. Operations managers may perceive risks in this strategy, such as increasing the fixed cost base of the business, reducing operational flexibility and causing potential labour disruption if redundancies are required. The benefits are likely to be felt in the sales and marketing and after-sale service areas of the business, so these managers may not perceive the risks as being significant. Another common example that will be considered in detail in Part Five is where additional information is required to support strategic decisions. Quite often, the employees who are required to take on additional work in order to enable this information to be made available, receive none of the benefit of using this information. This creates a risk that the base data will not be accurately recorded, in which case the information may be substantially flawed with a consequent risk of the wrong decision being taken.

It is very important that the strategic planning process draws together all these cross-functional conflicts regarding different views of the same decision. Thus the process must be interactive and consultative so that all appropriate managers have the opportunity to give their input, but the ultimate decision has to be based on an objective view of the business risks and returns. This requires a high level of communication not only of corporate goals and objectives, but also of the subsidiary goals and objectives established by the business subdivisions. It has already been established that strategic decisions need to be taken at many different levels of an organization. Therefore, strategic planning should not be regarded as a top-down process. The situation review and strategic alternatives for one SBU may mean that the overall objectives for the business need to be changed, and this must happen if the strategic plan is to be meaningful and worth the considerable effort involved.

Equally, this means that strategic planning is not a bottom-up planning exercise as this is unlikely to lead to the achievement of any long-term corporate goals. The process is interactive and iterative with the impact of each decision being checked against the overall goals and objectives.

The inevitable conflicts in many of the required strategic decisions will mean that some managers will be unhappy with the direction in which the business is moving. The commitment of all managers to the business strategy is of fundamental importance, because if only a few managers implement directly opposing sub-strategies, the chances of corporate success are dramatically reduced. However, this commitment is almost impossible to achieve through genuine consensus as the business would almost never make any meaningful strategic decision: if the managers could not agree in which direction to move, the only acceptable compromise would be to stand still! What is required is a process of full communication and consultation prior to taking the key strategic decisions at each level, followed by a clear communication of the decision and its implications. If this process is followed, the organization should then expect, and require, that all managers accept the strategy which is to be implemented (even though they may not all agree with it) and are fully committed to its success.

One of the most difficult aspects of this in practice is when the minority originally against the strategy are subsequently proved to be right. Many businesses have continued for far too long with inappropriate strategies because senior managers did not want to admit they were wrong, particularly if the original decision had been heatedly debated.

Changes to strategies and/or objectives will almost inevitably be required and should be implemented in a dynamic rather than static framework. Therefore strategic planning should not be regarded as a one-off exercise but should be seen as a continuous style of management. A long range plan is not something engraved on a tablet of stone which must be mindlessly adhered to no matter how many changes have occurred in the internal and external environment. Managers need to adopt an approach of thinking strategically about the business continuously rather than from time to time going away 'to plan the future of the organization'.

Strategic management has already been defined as an integrated management approach which is concerned with long-term, fundamental decisions about the mission, goals and objectives of the organization. This implies a continuous interest and involvement in strategic planning and implementation, and therefore strategic management is a better description of the desired process than is normally conveyed by strategic planning.

The techniques considered in this chapter are placed in the context of strategic management accounting in the next chapter, and then particular aspects are developed in detail in the subsequent parts of the book. However it may be helpful to illustrate the essential complexity of the strategic planning process by reference to one particular business.

A large firm of insurance brokers had, some years ago, made a conscious decision to centralize the majority of its administrative services and had in fact set this up as a separate division of the group. Thus the group contained some operating divisions which were organized according to particular product areas (eg aviation insurance, marine insurance, etc), while other operating divisions were organized according to customer groupings (eg UK retail broking, which was geographically segmented). All of these divisions were provided centrally with their administrative support, which included accounting, personnel function, computer systems and building services. In order to ensure that operating divisions did not wastefully employ central administrative resources, the costs incurred were apportioned out to the users via a transfer pricing mechanism.

As with most businesses, the charging system led to frequent and violent complaints from the operating divisions, who claimed that they were being overcharged and could do a better job themselves at a considerably lower cost. This issue came to a head as a result of their latest strategic planning exercise. The single key strategic issue for the group, which was identified by the group board, was to improve the relative profitability of the business. This had been volatile in recent years, and at current levels did not justify the level of future investment which was considered desirable on non-financial grounds. The senior management of the centralized management services division had to consider how they should plan their activities in the light of this clear group focus on enhancing profitability.

Their division's expenditure represented over 20% of the group's sales revenues and consequently any cost savings which they could achieve would have a significant impact on group profitability. It was relatively easy to identify a number of areas where considerable savings could be made over the period of the strategic plan, but all of these savings would have a detrimental impact on the level of service provided to the separate operating divisions. For example, the computer systems development budget could be reduced, but it was known that competitors were already investing more heavily in this area, and technology was expected to have a dramatic impact on the way their business was done over the next 10 years. Alternatively cheaper offices could be rented but these would be further from the main business centres and might affect the attitude of some customers towards which insurance broker they used.

It was clear that this support division could not make sensible strategic decisions in isolation of the operating divisions, even though it had deliberately been set up as a separate business in order to obtain the benefits of economies of scale and expertise, etc. Consequently, its strategic planning exercise necessitated a very close involvement from its 'customers' (ie the operating divisions), with respect to both the level of service which they required to achieve their own divisional strategic objectives and the level which they could afford. This question of affordable cost meant that administrative services were split into two types:

1 a group 'standard' which was considered essential for all operating divisions to adhere to, if the group image was to be maintained, eg group-wide conditions of employment;
2 discretionary levels of service which were negotiable between each operating division and the centralized administration division.

With the discretionary areas, the operating division had the right to opt out if it felt the service was too expensive or not necessary for its type of business. This obviously made the centralized administration division much more customer-focused with a greater emphasis on adding value to the group rather than just reducing its cost base. Indeed, as a result of this iterative planning process, the centralized systems development budget was not only significantly increased but also refocused on the areas of strategic competitive advantage which the operating divisions highlighted.

3

Management accounting in the context of strategic management

Strategic management has already been depicted as a continuous management style consisting of an iterative process of analysis, planning and control. It has also been shown that sound strategic decision-making requires the support of a large amount of very varied information. These decision support systems are made more complicated by the involvement of strategic planning at many levels of the organization, and by the common occurrence of cross-functional impacts from strategic decisions. Strategic decisions are also often non-recurring and can be required in response to a dynamic, unexpected change in the external environment.

If management accounting is to be of value to this strategic management process, it must be capable of providing the required information within the available time to the right level of decision-maker. However the type of strategic decisions which face the organization differ depending on the strategic thrusts or driving forces which are dominant, and on the level within the organization at which the particular decision is being taken. The strategic management accounting system has to be tailored to provide the appropriate financial information to support these specific requirements, which will themselves change as the strategy is adjusted in line with movements in the external environment.

Strategic options also change according to the stage of development of the industry and degree of diversification of the organization. Understanding the role of management accounting in this area, and its interaction with strategic management techniques, will highlight many of the essential requirements for a practical system of strategic management accounting.

Product life cycles

It has been a well-established idea for many years that products follow a 'life cycle' which affects the current rate of sale and more importantly has significant implications for the strategic options for the future. Product life cycles have been the subject of much debate recently, but the concept is still of great value to strategic decision-making if it is sensibly applied.

The theory breaks the economic life of a product into a number of stages (four or five being most common) and these are shown Figure 3.1. The model product is developed and launched into the market where it takes time to gain acceptance and thus the initial sales growth is slow. The launch period is clearly a time of high business risk as it is quite possible that the product will fail completely.

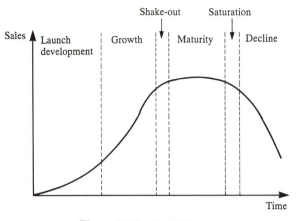

Figure 3.1 Product life cycle

It is a fundamental economic rule that risk and return are positively correlated, ie if the risk increases, the potential return must increase in order to compensate for the increased risk. This rule can be applied at all levels of investment decision from the individual investor looking at alternatives in the capital market, through to the business which is facing a decision as to which projects to undertake. In financial terms the best indicator of risk is volatility of return. A guaranteed level of return to an investor would be regarded as a low risk investment. As the downside range increases, the potential upside from the investments must improve appropriately, and this is shown graphically in Figure 3.2. The chart also shows that even for a no-risk investment (if such an investment can be found!) an investor will demand a postiive return. This is to compensate for giving up the opportunity to use the funds for consumption immediately and for tying their capital up in this project (often referred to as the liquidity preference concept).

If the product is accepted by the market, and achieves a critical mass of sales, the growth phase starts during which sales growth is normally rapid. The ultimate demand for any product will not be infinite and therefore in time the rate of growth will slow as all potential customers have entered the market and a normal rate of usage has been established. It is quite common during the growth phase for a number of late-entrant companies to come into the market due

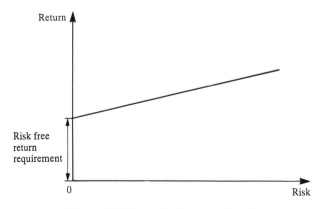

Figure 3.2 Risk and return relationship

to the rapid expansion in demand, and the consequent apparent opportunity to make a good return for a more limited risk.

When a number of new companies enter an industry, they will expand the total capacity of the industry. If they expect sales to continue to grow rapidly, this increase in capacity will probably be substantial, particularly if existing players in the market are also expanding their production facilities in response to this expected future growth demand. Unfortunately, this dramatic explosion in capacity often occurs just before the rate of market growth starts to slow down and sales increases will become more difficult to achieve. Many of the businesses involved will find themselves with substantial spare capacity and there may be a short, sharp shake-out period during which several competitors leave the industry or are taken over and capacity is rationalized – this position is shown graphically in Figure 3.3. Once a more stable position has been established with sales demand relatively balanced by available capacity, the industry can be described as having passed into the maturity stage of the life cycle. Any residual excess capacity will influence the competitive strategies which will be implemented by the players in the industry and this is considered in detail in Chapter 17.

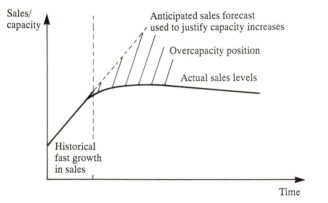

Figure 3.3 Shake-out period

Eventually the demand for the product will start to decline because alternative substitute products have been introduced or customer tastes have changed. With some long-lasting products, the market may simply become saturated and the need for replacement products is insufficient to sustain demand at previous levels. The decline phase of the life cycle ends with the death of the product, although this may take a very long time and this gives rise to one of the main criticisms of the product life cycle concept.

Even if the idea of a life cycle is accepted it is impossible to predict with any precision the length of the different phases and some products seem to pass through one or more phases almost instantaneously. If this is so, the detractors argue that the product life cycle is of little value as a planning aid because it lacks certainty of outcome. By now, it should have been made clear that none of the strategic planning aids or even the simplest of the decisions involved in the process have any degree of certainty regarding their outcome: that is why a strategic planning process is needed. Another criticism is that the product life cycle does not work for all products because there may be substitute products with very similar characteristics which suddenly become available and confuse the transition through the phases. Again this is based on a lack of understanding of the multiple levels at which strategic planning has to be carried out, and consequently the product life cycle may need to be applied at the industry level rather than the individual product level. In some cases the industry may need to be defined in terms of the satisfaction of particular customer needs, rather than the less useful, but more easily identifiable, attributes of the product. For example the product life cycles of many countries' railway systems become much more rational if they are considered as part of the life cycles of customers' demands for transportation rather than as the physical product of a train running on a set of tracks. As previously argued, strategic management aids need the exercise of intelligent managerial judgements to maximize their benefits in the complex area of strategic decision-making, and the product life cycle is a classic illustration of such an aid.

The various stages of the life cycle raise a number of important issues regarding the input of strategic management accounting. The requirement for increased return to compensate for higher risk has already been raised but it is also possible to break risk down into various components and to select sub-strategies which incorporate the most appropriate levels of component risk. For example, the stages of development of the product life cycle have different intrinsic levels of risk, and the business has little control over this fundamental component of total risk as it is determined by the external environment. The risk of a product is clearly at its highest level at the time of development and launch, but the risk is still high during the growth phase because the ultimate size of the industry is still unknown and the level of market share which can be gained and retained is also uncertain. As the market matures and stabilizes, this risk decreases and is concentrated on the length of the maturity phase before the product moves into the decline stage of its life cycle. Interestingly this final phase should be regarded as low risk because the business knows that the product is dying and its strategy should be tailored accordingly.

If this analysis of the developing risk profile of the product is compared to the financial risk profiles of various strategic options for the business, it is much easier to select appropriate combinations, and to highlight unacceptably high or low total risk strategies. The basis for this is shown in matrix form in Figure 3.4 where the product/industry risk is put on one axis and the financial risk on the other. Normally an organization will reject a high product risk with a high financial risk as being an unacceptably high risk combination (mathematically these individual risks compound each other and hence are multiplied together, not added, to give the total risk for the strategy). Only businesses with a very strong appetite for risk will find such a strategy appealing. They will be either very successful or fail completely and go out of business before the product becomes firmly established – the basic determinant of the risk being volatility of outcome which for a new product is normally very high.

However, as indicated in Figure 3.4, most organizations should also reject a low financial risk when combined with a low product/industry risk as being an unduly conservative combination. This logic has been dramatically demonstrated in recent years by the spate of take-overs of mature businesses where the new owners have not changed the business risk but have increased the financial risk of the organization with commensurately increased returns to the shareholders. Therefore it is vital that an appropriate combination of risk profiles is achieved, but this necessitates an understanding of what is meant by financial risk.

Types of financial risk

Perhaps the most obvious example of financial risk is given by the source of funding used by the business. Equity can be regarded as the lowest possible risk type of financing from the user's point of view. Borrowed money (debt) represents much higher financial risk. Thus for an organization to decide to finance the development and launch of a completely new untried

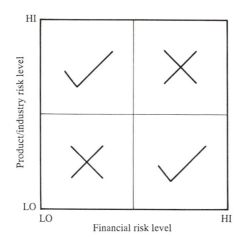

Figure 3.4 Risk combinations – strategic alternatives

product with debt would be a clear illustration of a high business risk unnecessarily compounded by a high financial risk. At the other end of the spectrum there are many businesses which have mature products commanding dominamt market shares in stable well-established industries but which are holding large positive cash balances without any net outstanding debt. These businesses have become obvious acquisition targets because a change in the manner of funding the business so as to introduce a realistic level of debt can dramatically improve the return to shareholders without increasing the total combined risk to unacceptable levels.

The increasingly sophisticated application of this type of combined analysis has led to the development of a completely new range of highly tailored financing products. These should enable organizations to fit their desired level of financial risk into the current and developing state of business risk and the preferred overall risk profile. As mentioned in Chapter 1, this area is the subject of financial strategy and detailed consideration of these tailored one-off financial solutions is outside the scope of this book. However specific examples, such as hedging strategies, etc, will be given in the course of issues examined later in the text.

Another fundamental example of financial risk, which is much more in the area of strategic management accounting, is the cost structure of the business. The breakdown of costs into fixed and variable is a basic part of internal management accounting, but this analysis, if properly applied, has very important strategic relevance. In most organizations there are a wide range of alternative ways of producing the chosen goods or services, and these will involve different balances of internal and externally supplied (ie bought-in) resources. The classic 'make or buy' decision will often alter the nature of the costs incurred from largely fixed (in the case of internal production) to largely variable (in the case of external sourcing), and this will also change the financial risk. Even if the decision is taken to maintain or commence internal sourcing, there may still be options which can avoid the need to incur substantial fixed costs if the corresponding risk is considered unacceptable in relation to the return which will be achieved. The use of break-even charts can illustrate this phenomenon very clearly and this is done in Figures 3.5 and 3.6 which show the cost dynamics for two widely different financial risk strategies in the same industry.

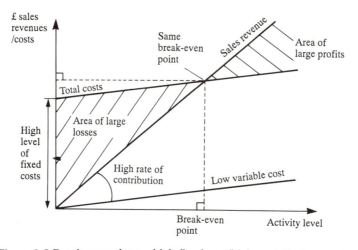

Figure 3.5 Break-even chart – high fixed cost/high contribution strategy

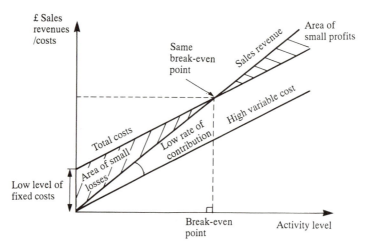

Figure 3.6 Break-even chart – low fixed cost/low contribution strategy

In Figure 3.5 the organization has decided to have a high level of fixed costs which may result from a policy of developing a high level of automation (depreciation and other costs of ownership being regarded normally as a fixed cost). This should enable a high level of contribution to be achieved as the variable costs remaining will form a smaller proportion of sales revenues from any given level of selling prices. (All the normal caveats regarding the use of break-even charts have to be remembered, such as fixed costs being only fixed for their relevant range, with sales revenues and variable costs being assumed to vary proportionately with activity.) Any business which chooses this financial strategy will make high profits when activity levels are above break-even, but will make correspondingly high losses if activity levels fall significantly. In other words, their returns will be very volatile depending upon relatively small movements in sales volumes, and accordingly this should be regarded as a high risk strategy.

Alternatively, as shown in Figure 3.6, the business may have been able to keep its fixed cost base much lower, possibly by using external suppliers or internal variable cost sources to meet its output needs. The diagram has the same break-even point as in Figure 3.5, but shows significantly lower levels of profits *or* losses for the same variations in sales activities. Thus the risk of dramatic losses has been reduced at the cost of also removing the opportunity for very high profits; lower volatility representing a lower risk strategy. In reality what has happened is that some of the risk of variations in demand has been transferred to the suppliers of these variable cost inputs, be they external vendors or internal employees. As risk and return should be positively correlated, these suppliers should demand an increase in their return for bearing this high risk and therefore the total cost structure should increase slightly as a result. Effectively, the organization is paying an insurance premium in the form of this net increase in total costs for the benefit of reducing the overall risk level. Three consequences of this are important.

First, the risk perceptions of the two organizations involved may not be the same, and so the increased return demanded by the supplier may be less than the extra cost which the buyer is willing to pay. This will often be the case where the suppliers are specialists in particular areas, or have several other customer groups to whom they can supply their products. This is the fundamental rationale behind the insurance industry. For example, to many organizations computer analyst and programming skills are important but very specialized and peripheral to their main business objectives. If these skills are bought as a fixed cost by recruiting permanent employees into the organization, the business loses the flexibility to alter this cost level in the short-term in response to changing economic conditions. However, a specialist agency could provide, at a price including a suitable profit margin to compensate for its perceived risks, appropriately skilled technical staff on a contract basis as required; thus making the cost to the user variable rather than fixed. The agency can spread the risk of variations in demand from any particular customer by diversifying its industrial customer base, or even by passing the risk onto the individuals involved, ie by making them self-employed contractors who have no guaranteed job security from the agency. The use of this type of risk analysis has increased dramatically recently and has contributed to temporary employment agencies being one of the fastest growing industries of the last decade. It has also opened up opportunities for large businesses (such as BET plc) to grow by implementing a focused strategy of taking over the supply of a range of peripheral activities to other organizations, thus allowing the customer's managers to concentrate on their organization's key strategic objectives. This is also a good practical development of the use of the value chain concept, because it shows how a company can improve its return, or lower its risk, by concentrating on where it has a competitive advantage.

Second, by changing a fixed cost to a variable cost the organization incurs an increasing penalty whenever sales activity is at the top end of the expected range. Indeed, if sales levels exceed expectations for any extended period of time, the relative performance of the business may be adversely affected to a significant degree. This would be particularly true if a competitor adopted the alternative high fixed cost strategy. Consequently, the success of selecting the high variable cost option depends on the expected variations in output levels actually happening. This requires good information on historical volatilities and forecasts of future key factors which will affect demand levels. For example, in North America the automobile industry was severely affected by the major downturn in demand in 1980–82, with their high fixed cost levels causing all the major companies to record dramatic losses for this period. Although profitability was restored and record profits were recorded when demand recovered, from 1984 onwards most of the companies adopted lower risk financial strategies by changing some of their costs from fixed to variable. Thus the strategy of the 1970s, which had seen increasing levels of automation and consequent increases in fixed costs, was now balanced by a strategic review of what functions needed to be done 'in-house' and what could be transferred to external suppliers. Also, many employees had been made redundant during the recession, and thus the companies had paid a high price to get rid of what was in reality a fixed cost. In order to avoid a repeat of this expensive exercise when demand inevitably declined again, the companies rehired as many people as possible on a temporary basis (ie as a variable cost) either as individual subcontractors or through employment agencies. The financial justification for this action became more debatable as the market demand stayed strong for the longest sustained period ever up to the end of the 1980s, with the consequence that some people had been employed as temporary workers for over seven years! However, the companies have reduced their total risk and have also concentrated on reducing their break-even point when expressed as a percentage of available capacity. Unfortunately for some of these companies, the inevitable downturn which eventually occurred in the 1990s was so severe that they still made significant losses, despite these measures.

The third important consequence of the cost structure strategy example is that it illustrates a transfer of risk from the business to somebody outside. The more valuable form of financial strategy involves the removal of the risk rather than its transfer because there is then no question of competitive negotiation over sharing out the benefit of the risk reduction.

As stated earlier the analysis of costs into their fixed and variable components is included in most organizations' management accounting systems. Unfortunately, the way in which it is done is not normally helpful to strategic decision-making. The question of whether a particular cost is fixed or variable is a matter of the time-scale involved: in the very short term almost all costs are fixed, whereas in the very long term no costs should be regarded as fixed since they can all be changed. Most businesses classify their costs by reference to their operational planning (or budgeting) time periods which may be one year or less, whereas the time-scale for strategic decisions can obviously be much longer. It is therefore critically important that the strategic management accounting system is not restricted by short-term cost classifications and that expenses can be analysed appropriately to the period of the strategic decision under consideration.

More of these analytical techniques and other types of financial risk indicators together with the particular requirements of strategic management accounting are considered in Part Two, but the logic tends to be similar. The accounting techniques used are normally the commonly applied management accounting and financial management concepts, but their method of application has to be tailored to the strategic decision-making environment.

Boston Matrix

The product life cycle has been developed by many organizations into a general strategic planning concept. One of the first and most famous of these was produced by the Boston Consulting Group and is commonly known as the Boston Matrix. This attempts to relate critical strategic issues to the different phases of the product life cycle and to show how successful strategies must be appropriately tailored to the changing needs of the business. The basic matrix is normally drawn as a 2×2 box as shown in Figure 3.7, but more sophisticated versions have been developed by McKinsey, General Electric, A D Little and Shell Chemicals (UK) Ltd. The principle is what is important as, once again, all these techniques require a great deal of managerial judgement to make them practically valuable, and so the Boston Matrix will be used as the example in this chapter.

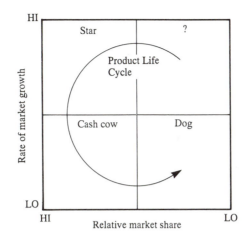

Figure 3.7 BCG Matrix (incorporating the product life cycle)

Figure 3.7 shows the matrix with rate of market growth on the vertical axis and relative market share on the horizontal axis and also incorporates the impact of the product life cycle. The popularity of the Boston Matrix has been aided by the adoption of short emotive titles for each of the four boxes. It is perhaps unfortunate that these titles carry such obvious qualitative connotations, as will be discussed later. Rate of market growth is taken as a prime indicator of the level of attractiveness of the industry because most businesses would prefer to be involved in a rapidly growing market rather than competing in a very mature or declining one. Relative market share can be used as a guide to the competitive strength of the business in the particular market, because a great deal of empirical research has shown that companies with dominant market shares tend to produce higher financial returns. This is particularly so when the market has matured and become more stable. Much of this evidence has been produced from a large data-base (over 3,000 mainly USA based businesses) known as PIMS, which stands for Profit Impact of Market Strategies. PIMS is produced and managed by the Strategic Planning Institute and allows subscribing organizations to compare the performance of their business units with similar organizations and to identify key strategic issues. The data-base is biased in favour of manufacturing businesses which are part of very large organizations and are more likely to be involved in mature industries; this reflects its original base which was General Electric's business units. However the main results that have been obtained are of general interest and can provide some guidance for strategy planning by most businesses.

The analysis of the data-base seems to indicate that three sets of factors are predominantly influential in determining the relative financial performance of an organization. One major element is the relative competitive position of the business, and this can be measured by relative market share, as is shown in the Boston Matrix. However, researchers are increasingly emphasizing relative product quality as the critical determinant of competitive position in many markets. Another set of factors takes into account the relative attractiveness of the market served by the organization and this is, of course, also included in the Boston Matrix as rate of market growth. The third set is not included explicitly, but describes the investment intensity and operational productivity of the industry. This is monitoring the operational or production structure of the business, and can be highlighted by the classical financial ratio analysis showing fixed asset turnover ratios (capital intensity), profit margins as a percentage of sales revenues, etc, as well as incorporating the level of spare capacity available. It is obvious that any such comparative analysis requires very clear and consistent definitions of the market and the industry concerned, as this can dramatically affect the apparent relative market share. One of the key elements in Porter's third generic strategy of focussing on a small segment of a market is that such a tightly defined strategy enables the business to achieve a dominant market share in this chosen focused market. This high share increases the potential financial performance relative to more fragmented but possibly much larger competitors. Another consequence of the PIMS analysis is to highlight again the need to develop and monitor competitive strategies at the business unit level (SBU, ideally) rather than at the overall corporate level because comparisons of market share and industry rates of growth may be completely meaningless in large diversified businesses.

The Boston Matrix can be used as a strategic planning aid for individual business units if the current position of the business can be identified, and the future rate of change forecast with reasonable accuracy. Unfortunately, as already mentioned, it is very difficult to use the product life cycle as an 'ex-ante' forecasting tool, whereas it is relatively easy to establish 'ex-post' where the business was. Even so, identifying the generic strategic thrusts for the different stages of development can be helpful in selecting the most appropriate competitive business strategy and of matching that with a suitable level of financial risk. The development and launch phase requires a concentration on market research and technical innovation in order to identify an unsatisfied need in the market and to produce a solution for that need (ie a product with the right attributes at an acceptable price and quality combination). A predominant management style for this type of business can be characterized as innovative and entrepreneurial and changes in strategy may be quite frequent and fundamental as the business environment may itself be dynamically changing. The system of strategic management accounting must fit this management style and the rapidly changing environment if it is to add value. Critical issues in designing such a system would be flexibility, lack of bureaucracy and formality, and the ability to answer one-off questions rapidly. These issues are explored in much more detail in Parts Three, Four and Five which consider respectively the impact of organizational structures, the stage of development of the business, and the design and implementation of financial control systems. The system should also provide information regarding competitor activities in terms of research and development expenditure, test marketing of new products, etc, and more generally on developing trends and customer tastes in the relevant industries and markets. A key monitoring role is on the time-scale of bringing current and proposed projects to fruition and launch, as well as comparing the actual costs involved in doing so back to those originally forecast, and ensuring the continuing financial viability of the project by producing updated forecasts of future costs.

Another critical factor affecting the launch stage is that the cash flow of the business will be negative because funds will be disbursed on developing, testing and launching the new product while very few sales will be achieved and thus sales revenues will be minimal. Even when sales revenues grow slightly, the profit contribution is likely to be small as the initial operating costs may be high until efficiency levels are improved (the impact and strategic use of experience curves is considered later in the chapter). As the fundamental business risk is invariably high at this stage of development (due to the risk of product failure), and the cash flow is likely to be negative, it would appear sensible to keep the financial risks to the minimum levels possible, eg by funding the business with equity and using variable costs as far as possible. The combination of some of these factors is shown diagrammatically in Figure 3.8.

If the product launch is successful, the business needs to change its strategic thrust so as to respond to its new environment and changed set of critical success factors. As the market rate

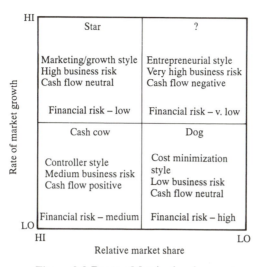

Figure 3.8 Boston Matrix developments

of growth increases rapidly it is vitally important that the business grows its own sales faster than the market, thus increasing its market share. The objective for this phase of development should be to have achieved the maximum possible market share as the market matures, based on the PIMS research of dominant market shares ultimately leading to higher financial returns. A desirable management style would be an emphasis on marketing and a definite orientation towards managing rapid growth. Consequently the strategic management accounting system should be concentrating on analyzing the effectiveness of alternative marketing strategies. It should also provide analysis of competitors' existing marketing strategies and potential responses to changes in the organization's strategy. Thus some sort of modelling and simulation capability might add significant value to the strategic decision-making process.

Sales revenues will have increased significantly from those generated in the launch phase and profit levels should also have improved as normally costs will have decreased faster than selling prices. However, the overall net cash flow may not yet be positive because the investment requirements of the product are very high during this rapid growth phase. If the market is growing rapidly (say 40% pa) but the business is trying to grow still faster (say 50% pa) so as to increase its market share, investors are most unlikely to want the business to do anything except re-invest the available cash flow into the business. Net cash flow, in specific cases therefore, may be slightly positive or negative, but for general purposes it can be regarded as being broadly neutral over the growth phase of the product life cycle. Funds are obviously required to increase production capacities as demand increases, but this investment in tangible assets can be quite small in relation to the expenditure that is needed for intangible assets such as brands, particularly for service industries. Marketing expenditure should be aimed both at developing the market and at increasing market share within this growing market. The goal is to expand the market to its full potential before it matures, and to gain the optimum share of that fully developed market. The word 'optimum' has now deliberately been used in preference to maximum to highlight that the level of market share should be financially justified. As with most economic relationships, it is now widely accepted that a law of diminishing returns applies to marketing expenditure and that to increase market shares

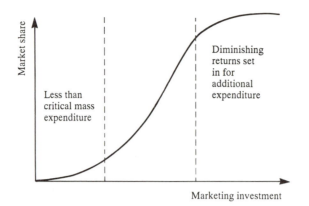

Figure 3.9 Relationship of marketing expenditure and market share

beyond certain levels can be unjustifiably expensive. Unfortunately, there is no generically applicable formula for this relationship and strategic management accounting should be trying to establish the level at which diminishing returns would set in for the particular market. This relationship also indicates that a minimum level of expenditure is required to achieve critical mass and both aspects are shown graphically in Figure 3.9. As discussed in Chapter 4 and later in Part Two, this analysis can be segmented and applied to each of the individual objectives of the particular marketing strategy. One of the greatest challenges facing strategic management accounting is that this demands that marketing expenditure has to be split into development and maintenance activities and the marketing investment has to be treated just as any other long-term investment and financially justified accordingly (this is considered in detail in Chapter 4).

The ultimate size of the market will be influenced by the total marketing activity of all the players. Therefore knowledge of competitive expenditure is important, and the relative shares of total marketing expenditure will affect relative market shares. Indeed strategic options may change dramatically if one or more competitors take dominant positions in marketing expenditure during the growth phase. These alternatives are evaluated in detail in Chapter 16, but again this illustrates the need for strategic management accounting to be capable of identifying, analysing and adapting to changes in strategy due to externally driven factors.

Eventually the market will mature and the rate of growth will slow considerably. Once again the organization should alter its strategy to fits its new external environment. A growth strategy will be much less successful in a stable low growth industry as gains in market share will be harder to achieve and shorter lived due to more fierce competitive responses. The appropriate managerial style can be encapsulated as that of a 'controller' because now the business should be managed for profit. It is important to note that in the first two phases no mention was made of the profit achievements of the business. If too much emphasis is placed on increasing profits during the launch and growth stages of a product, the key strategic objectives will probably not be achieved and the long-term financial viability of the product will be severely impaired. When the product is well-established and its future growth potential is limited, a concentration on profit is valid and, indeed, vitally important.

At last, the cash flows should turn positive and the cumulative cash flow should also rapidly become positive, even after allowing for the time value of money. It is no longer advisable to invest in making the market grow, and marketing expenditure should be directed at maintaining, rather than increasing, market share. This will dramatically reduce the relative proportion of available funds which need to be re-invested in the business on intangible assets. Similarly the proportion required for expenditure on tangible assets will decrease. As sales levels stabilize there is less need to expand productive capacity and there will be much less real growth in funds tied up in working capital. (During the rapid growth phase, this growth in working capital can absorb vast amounts of money for many industries and is, in fact, a major cause of business failure through overtrading.) In many cases most investment will now consist of replacement as existing items of plant and machinery wear out; consequently profit levels will be largely unaffected as depreciation expenses should reflect most of this activity.

However this period of relative stability, if it is forecast to continue for a reasonable period, will reduce the underlying risk particularly for organizations which have achieved a high relative market share. This reducing business risk enables companies to increase their financial risk without creating an unacceptably high total risk. Investment in automation and other ways of increasing fixed costs, but reducing variable costs by a greater amount, can now be considered and financially evaluated. The potential economic life for such investment proposals must be checked against the forecasts for the future duration of the maturity phase of the life cycle, but investment decisions which improve efficiency may become far more important to the business strategy. The emphasis of the strategic management accounting analysis should now be placed on relative cost comparisons with competitors and on considering ways of improving the existing cost position of the organization.

It is important for the financial success of the entire investment in the product that the business spends as long as possible in the more stable cash cow phase, as this phase is the only significant producer of positive cash flows. Unfortunately for many of the more adventurous styles of managers this very stability of the cash cow business and its concentration on increasing short-term returns from the business appear not to generate sufficient excitement and stimulus. Thus diversification strategies are often inaugurated at this time. These result in the positive cash flows from the mature business being re-invested in developing and launching several new products in the hope of creating a few star products in the future (the justification and implications of such diversifications are examined below).

Not only is this exciting and stimulating for managers but, more seriously, it is a logical way of attempting to preserve and even develop their management careers. Once a mature business ceases to be a strong cash generator, its next stage is that of decline and death, which may not be an attractive proposition to the current management team. As in the earlier phases of development, the decline stage requires a particular management style and the most appropriate one is that of cutting costs to the bone and, if necessary, beyond. Hence emotive descriptions such as 'hatchet-man', 'executioner' and 'undertaker' have been used for this style although a more appropriate title might be 'surgeon'. The skilful and timely amputation of a diseased limb can in many cases lead to a long and successful life for the individual concerned, and the analogy can be applied to a business. If costs which are no longer necessary are removed, then the business may continue to function productively for a considerable period. Therefore it is important that the main strategic thrust is altered yet again to focus on removing areas of cost which are no longer adding value to the business. Consequently, investment decisions will be justified against much shorter time periods and against the background of forecasts of declining sales levels. For many businesses, this stage is one of almost no major re-investment in the business as the existing asset base is worked as hard and for as long as possible. Indeed some assets may be realized during this phase as their liquidation value becomes greater than the value which will be generated from their continued use in the business. The cash flow of the business must be at least neutral throughout this period because it is nonsensical to make a net cash investment in a dying business. Thus as soon as the cash flow becomes negative, costs must be further reduced to achieve at worst a balanced position and, if this is no longer possible, the closure of the business becomes the most logical alternative.

In this case, the high financial risk shown in Figure 3.8 should not relate necessarily to a high level of fixed cost because this could increase liquidation costs if this becomes necessary unexpectedly. However the opportunity cost of equity capital for the business will be higher than the cost of borrowed funds. It is always so due to the higher risk associated with equity than debt from the perspective of the investor or supplier of the funds. By unnecessarily leaving equity invested until the ultimate closure of the business, the investor will be worse off. In financial management jargon, the present value of the remaining cash flow can be increased by borrowing against the liquidation values of the residual assets employed in the business, rather than funding them with equity capital during this decline phase. It should also be remembered that the available and distributable cash flows (ie dividends in the case of a company) will be higher than the profits generated by the business during this decline stage. It should be unnecessary to re-invest all the depreciation expense charged in arriving at these profits because it is no longer a fundamental part of the business strategy to maintain the productive capacity and asset base of the organization. All investment decisions, including those previously considered as essential maintenance type expenditures, must be rigorously financially justified during this phase and this includes expenditure on maintaining intangible assets such as brands.

Brands are, for many organizations, transferable among products and so it may be logical to remove the branding image from declining products as the association may be damaging to its future repositioning and application to a more growth-orientated product. If this transfer is well-timed and properly managed it is possible to argue that brands do not have to follow a life-cycle in the same way that an individual product does. This area is also discussed in more detail in Part Two and Part Four.

Tailored financial control measures

The strategic thrusts for the business have been shown to change as the product develops through the stages of its life cycle. As the critical strategic issues alter, the focus of strategic management accounting will need to be tailored to fit the strategy, and the financial control measures should be similarly altered. Unfortunately, most businesses have not yet developed their financial control systems to this stage of sophistication and, as previously mentioned, the overall measure of return on investment is used as the most common financial control yardstick irrespective of the stage of development of the product. This particular measure has the major problems of both being short-term, and relying on measuring accounting profits, which are much more subjective than the more decision-oriented cash flow.

A more logical system is to understand the critical success factors of the main strategic thrusts at each stage and to identify a few key financial measures which can indicate how well these critical success factors are being achieved. This question is tackled in depth in Part Four where detailed examples and illustrations are given but a brief overview can be given here and this is summarized in Figure 3.10.

In the launch phase it is very difficult to establish any meaningful set of full financial *controls* as opposed to financial evaluation of the project. The eventual financial return from the successful launch of a new product is often so far away and so speculative that only spurious

Star	?
CSF: Growth in market share	CSF: Successful development and launch of new products
Control measure:- Discounted cash flow	Control measure:- Research and development milestones
Cash cow	Dog
CSF: Maintain market share at minimum cost	CSF:Minimize cost base
Control measure:- Return on investment	Control measure: Free cash flow

Figure 3.10 Tailored financial control measures

accuracy will be achieved by an over-complex system. The length of time could be coped with quite easily by applying discounted cash flow (DCF) techniques to the future cash flow projections. However, the range of these potential projections is normally so great that no element of real control will be exercised by using such a sophisticated method of monitoring on a regular basis. Obviously the initial financial justification for the expenditure on research and development should have been made against the potential return from the successful launch, weighted for the estimated probability of success. This should have been done using DCF to allow for the delay in receiving the benefit from a successful development programme. If the product is not successful, the actual financial return may be virtually nil and the project would clearly have been a financial disaster. As the risk, ie the probability, of total failure increases, the scale of the potential return from ultimate success must be greater to counterbalance the increased level of risk. However, it is pointless to try to use some expected value of the outcome to *control* the project, which is what many companies try to do. For example, a successful outcome of such an investment may have a value of 100 with an unsuccessful result giving a result of 0. If the probabilities of success and failure are both 50%, the expected value of the return from the investment is clearly 50. This can be used to decide whether or not to undertake the investment but this value cannot be used as a control to monitor the actual performance against. Either success or failure will lead to a dramatic divergence from the expected value and the monitoring process will consequently be worthless. Also the recognition of this ultimate success or failure may only be possible significantly after the expenditure of all the projected research and development funds; whether the project is a failure or a success is therefore not under the control of management during the project if this overall method of financial control is used.

Thus having used the financial expected value of the outcome to justify the expenditure, the problem remains of how the expenditure can be monitored in the early stages of the new product development while the eventual actual outcome is still unknown. The critical success factors of the chosen strategy are likely to revolve around particular stages of the research and development programme, and the accompanying market research activities which will be carried out to ascertain or confirm the likely market demand for the end product. The only logical financial control measure is to monitor the achievement of these significant 'milestones' and to compare the actual costs incurred to arrive at the milestone to those forecast for this stage of development. A further important element of this type of control process is regularly to update the estimates of the eventual outcome and the *future* costs still to be incurred, so as to ensure that the continuation of the project is financially worthwhile.

This area is discussed in more detail in Chapter 15, but it is vitally important to register how significantly this type of strategic financial control process differs from those most frequently in use in organizations. Research and development is normally treated as a cost or expense centre whereby its financial control system consists solely of comparing its actual expenditure levels with its budgeted level. In this environment overspending against budget is taken to represent poor managerial performance while underspending is supposed to be good for the business as a whole. It is not surprising in such a financially irresponsible system, that the research and development expenditure level is often seen as a means of improving short-term financial performance. Possibly, in a good year, the level of expenditure may be increased (often to make up for having reduced it in previous years!). What is needed is a classic example of goal congruence. The role of new products in the business strategy must be identified and an appropriate method for monitoring this long-term activity should be adopted which will highlight the potential damage caused by any short-term tactical modifications to the sub-strategy. If the financial control system is clearly seen as a positive learning process rather than as the method of apportioning blame, it is considerably easier to adopt this more rational procedure.

Once the product has been successfully launched, the strategic thrust changes and so should the financial control system. The critical success factors at this stage of development are growth in market share and overall growth in the market itself, and investments should be made to achieve the objectives set in these areas. Consequently these specific objectives of market growth and growth in market share should be used as management control measures. As in the case of research and development activities, these growth stage investments will not normally produce their financial return until the product has matured and therefore long-term financial evaluation techniques (such as DCF) should also be used to justify the initial investment decision. However, the range of the cash flows which are likely to be generated from the future sales of the product can now be forecast much more clearly than was possible prior to its launch into the market. The key issues now should be the relative scale of success of the product and the length of the product life-cycle rather than the question of whether the product will work or be accepted by the market. Strategic management accounting's role as a financial control system is to model various alternative outcomes for the product given the implementation of the available strategic options, but each of these models will need to evaluate the returns over the longer term. As DCF techniques will be in use in the initial evaluation, but will also be regularly up-dated in order to consider alternative strategies, it is now sensible to use them as a financial control technique to evaluate how successfully the selected strategy is being implemented.

It is still vitally important that the financial control system takes into account the longer term impact of current decisions, and this is a major strength of the DCF process. If financial monitoring is concentrated on short-term results, these could be improved by reducing marketing expenditure on market development or long-term growth in market share. Either of these could prove to be disastrous when the market moves into the mature, cash cow stage. It is surprising that many companies now rely on the sophisticated long-term, cash flow driven DCF technique to justify their initial investment decisions, but then immediately revert to using a short-term, accounting based measure such as Return on Investment (ROI) to monitor the success or failure of these investments, without reference back to the adverse impact which short-term focuses can have on long-term strategies.

As the market matures, the business strategy has to be adapted yet again to focus on the new critical success factors. At last the business can concentrate on making profits and recouping the cash invested in developing, launching and building the product. Thus the shorter term measures such as ROI can now logically be used but the company must still be aware of the desirability of maintaining its competitive position by re-investing at an adequate level. Many products (eg motor cars and washing powders, from previous examples) spend a long time as mature products before sales ultimately decline and the product dies. If the organization tries to maximize, as opposed to optimize, profits in the short term this could be done by damaging the position of the product or brand in the market place, and hence dramatically reducing total profits and cash flow over the full length of the mature stage of the cycle.

This damage can easily be caused by reducing expenditure on research and development, so that new models or range extensions are not available to respond to competitor initiatives, or by not spending adequately on marketing support so that the relative competitive position of the brand is weakened and market share declines while total product sales are still stable. Both of these problems can be exacerbated by the accounting treatment of the expenditures as period expenses which are written off against profits when they are incurred so that a reduction in expenditure now can show as an improvement in this period's profits. This will be particularly true for expenditure which has a long-term impact and benefit, so that the business unit could improve its short-term financial performance by reducing its expenditure on long-term awareness creating advertising. A similar level of reduction in its expenditure on consumer promotion would have a much greater impact on its sales levels in the current period and consequently is less attractive to a business focusing too much on the short term.

It is clearly vital that a good strategic management accounting system ensures that the key elements of long-term business strategy are being implemented, even when the achievement of short-term profit targets becomes of major importance. Another illustration of this problem, which is considered in detail in Chapter 17, is the question of re-investment in tangible assets during the maturity phase. If the market is no longer growing significantly, and the business strategy is to maintain rather than to grow market share, there is no longer such a need to invest in expanding the productive capacity of the tangible fixed asset base. (As mentioned earlier, the organization may invest in cost-saving projects which increase the net fixed asset investment but do not increase overall productive capacity.) However, the business needs to monitor what level of re-investment is required to maintain the 'real' productive capacity of the asset base. In many industries re-investment of the depreciation expense, where this is based on the historic cost of the assets, will be insufficient to achieve this strategic objective and the short-term forecast net cash generation capacity of the business must take account of the need to maintain this real asset base while the business remains in the mature phase of the cycle. Equally, in some industries where the cost of replacement fixed assets is actually decreasing, such as those based on computers, the business does not need to re-invest all its historic depreciation expense to maintain the productive capacity and the net cash generation can be greater than the profits produced in the short term.

Eventually, the product will move out of the mature phase and the demand will decline as the market becomes saturated or a replacement product takes over. At this stage the business strategy ceases to be one of automatically trying to maintain share as this may no longer make sense financially. As stated above, all re-investments into the business should now be rigorously financially justified. This includes expenditures previously regarded as essential maintenance items and which possibly were not seriously evaluated because the alternative was the complete loss of the substantial cash flow from the mature business. As the future cash flow is now likely to decline it is important to minimize re-investments and to maximize short-term cash flows. In this 'dog' phase of the life cycle, profit measurement can be misleading as its accrual basis relies on an assessment of the ongoing value of the 'investment' in the business. Balance sheets are normally prepared using the going concern concept but if the business is dying this could be rendered quite suddenly an invalid assumption. Thus an asset may have a completely different value when considered in the circumstances of a liquidation than in its current use within the business. Also profits are assessed after a number of non-cash provisions have been made and the validity of these provisions may similarly be changed by external factors. A good system of strategic management accounting would emphasize the level of free cash flow which can be generated by the business, and would consequently assist in the vital decisions as to which costs should be reduced and when should the remaining business be sold or closed down.

As previously stated, the strategic management accounting system must adapt to the changing focus of the business strategy as this develops. This can only be achieved for a focused business if management is aware of when the business strategy should be changing and takes positive steps to change the financial control parameters. For a diversified business with different business units at different stages of development and with different rates of development, the complexity of the problem is dramatically compounded.

Diversification strategies

The development of the Boston Matrix and its logical consequences led to a very common business strategy in the 1970s. Using the cash generation form of the matrix shown in Figure 3.11 it becomes clear that two elements of the matrix are broadly neutral in cash flows with one highly positive and the launch phase significantly negative. Thus the potential was identified to use the positive cash flows generated by mature cash cow products to fund the development and launch of new products. As mentioned earlier in the chapter, this strategy also had substantial attractions to senior managers because it meant that the overall business could continue to develop and grow even though the original products and markets had matured.

It is perhaps unfortunate that mature products were christened 'cash cows', although the epithet is obvious because of their high cash yielding nature, because this does not sound exciting and the title 'star product' is much more appealing. Some businesses described their launch businesses as 'wildcats', while others gave a very different impression by using the phrase 'problem child' to describe the same segments of the matrix. In any event, this technique of using positive cash flow businesses to fund new business launches leads inevitably over time to the development of a diversified business as the re-investment opportunities in the original area of business die away with the maturing of the industry.

This inevitable strategy of diversification has been argued as a key potential competitive advantage over a focused non-diversified business with a clear overall corporate strategy. If there is no such overall strategy this diversification caused by the re-investment in other businesses actually reduces the total value of the business from the owner's perspective rather than enhances it. If investors wished to obtain a similar diversified portfolio as is created by any particular company they could do so by buying shares in a suitable array of focused companies. By doing this the investors should obtain separate teams of managers who are concentrating on particular strategies where their skills are relevant and in segments where their business can develop and sustain competitive advantages.

Where a group diversifies into these different businesses, it often argues that it is reducing its risk by spreading the business risk across several different industries. However as stated above, this can be easily achieved by the investor and so this adds no value to the shareholders.

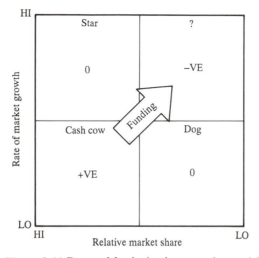

Figure 3.11 Boston Matrix (cash generation cycle)

Also, the lack of focus and the often substantial increase in corporate costs from managing such a diversified portfolio of businesses can, in fact, significantly reduce shareholder value.

Another criticism of a diversification strategy has already been raised when considering the multiple levels of strategic management needed in any complex business. Competitive strategies must be developed at the SBU level and not at the group level in any diversified business. Group strategies may not therefore add value to competitive strategies unless they are carefully thought through.

One major argument for diversification adding value has, not surprisingly, been developed by the Boston Consulting Group and is based on the potential for a well-diversified group to allocate its resources to those areas with the greatest potential for return. In other words the *rate* of cash generation by the mature cash cow can be managed according to the needs of the developing, but cash negative, members of the group. This can be done even if increasing the positive cash flow from the mature business in the short term may adversely affect the longer term prospects for this particular business. As long as the improved return from the developing business has greater value to the shareholders than the reduction caused in the mature business, the overall value of the group has been enhanced by this re-allocation of resources. The argument is based on the assumption that diversification consequently gives broadly based groups opportunities which are not available to more tightly focused groups, as they would not be able to increase their financial or other resources to adjust to a changing environment. If capital markets were truly efficient, the focused new business would be able to raise the increased funds which it requires for the expansion opportunity. The prospects for return from the new total investment would be seen to be improved and investors would make the funds available in exchange for the prospect of improved returns. The diversified business can re-allocate funds without such direct reference to the capital markets. However the concept of agency theory, discussed in Chapter 1, should force the managers to act in a way which does not reduce shareholder value through diversification. Unfortunately, the research work which has been done on the subject all points to diversification as dissipating shareholder value rather than adding to it. However, most of this work has been based on diversification through acquisition rather than by direct investment in new business start-ups, and consequently includes the often considerable bid premiums paid to acquire control of the other businesses.

Another argument in favour of diversification away from the cash cow stage is that of having appropriate managerial skills which are currently under-utilized due to the mature nature of the business. In other words, in order to have developed a successful cash positive business, the company must have had, at some time in the past, the management skills needed to launch and then to grow a business. As previously discussed, the managerial skills required in each segment of the matrix are substantially different and thus these skills may now be under-employed (that is, if they have been retained). Thus the diversified business could argue that it can provide skilled managers for each stage of the matrix and ensure that all the business units implement the most appropriate strategy for their particular stage of development. Conceptually the argument is attractive as it enables a sustainable competitive advantage to be obtained, but this would necessitate the transfer of managers among business units as the critical success factors and business strategies change. Unfortunately, in practice very few large diversified businesses are organized so that key management skills can be accurately deployed to business units depending on their stage of development, even though the consequences of a mismatch between the two are frequently dramatically disastrous.

This strategic concept can be seen in practice in a number of companies where the apparently diverse business units do have a consistent key business strategy and hence require common management skills and financial control systems. Perhaps the best example of this is Hanson plc, which concentrates on running mature businesses which will stay in the cash cow phase for a long time (ie they are not based on high technology or fashion which tend to have shorter product life cycles). Consequently, a common relatively simple financial control system of using ROI can be utilized which enables a very small head office to control a vast empire containing apparently very diverse businesses. A particularly valuable skill for such a business would be an ability to identify a business which had now matured but which was still being run with a growth or star strategy. Post acquisition, a change in strategy could add considerably to the value of such a business. In many cases there is no need to change the business strategy as the added value can be generated by implementing the financial strategy which is more appropriate to the current stage of maturity. If the acquisition target was itself a diversified group with a mix of businesses which were being inappropriately controlled by a single financial measure, the added value can be even greater. By separating the parts of the diversified business and repositioning them, it is possible to sell them to more focused buyers who can value these component elements more accurately according to their proper strategic measure. This strategy can consequently greatly reduce the net cost of the mature cash cow which is retained by the original purchaser.

In this way corporate strategy can be regarded as circular; one strategy argues for building diversified conglomerates, the next argues for taking them apart and turning them once again into focused businesses. Such a circular argument would suggest that businesses learn very little strategy from experience and to counter this argument, this chapter will finish by considering the role of experience curves in the strategic management accounting process. These were used by the Boston Consulting Group to develop the logic of the relative share argument in the Boston Matrix.

Experience curves

Experience curves will be considered again in Chapter 16 but they are being introduced here as an example of how strategic management accounting can be incorporated into the business strategy to add considerable value.

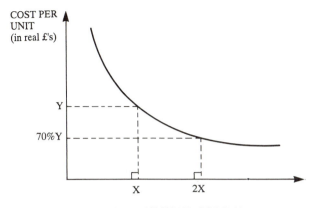

Figure 3.12 Experience curve (includes learning curve)

The simplest concept incorporated into the experience curve is the idea that for many businesses there is a learning process involved which means that as output increases the cost per unit decreases. This can be caused by the work-force carrying out the required tasks more quickly or more accurately and thus reducing wastage levels on subsequent output. Alternatively, managers may learn that there are better, more economic ways of doing things and this enables costs to be reduced as output increases. In some industries, such as aeroplane manufacturing, this learning process has been extensively monitored and for certain complex repetitive tasks it is possible to predict the rate of cost decline through learning as cumulative production mounts up. The relationship is normally expressed in terms of the relative cost reduction achieved for a doubling of cumulative production and hence a 70% learning curve means that the cost has been reduced in real terms to 70% of its previous level as production has doubled in cumulative terms. This is illustrated as a curve in Figure 3.12 but as the curve is used to express constant relative changes in cumulative production, a more normal representation is to use log scales on both axes when the relationship is represented by a straight line rather than a curve as in Figure 3.13. A key impact of such a curve is that an increase in cumulative volume from 5,000 to 10,000 units will create a similar proportionate decrease in real cost levels as an increase from 1 million to 2 million units.

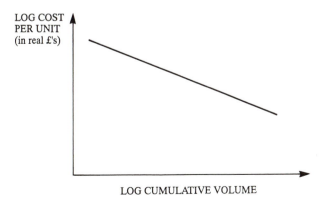

Figure 3.13 Experience curve (using log: log axes)

As a result of the extensive research on this phenomenon in several industries, other effects were identified as well as the original learning process. An obvious potential element was economies of scale caused by the potential for expansion of production facilities as cumulative production increased. In certain industries this could give predictable cost savings, and where automation was involved this could supplement or replace the labour force learning curve impact. However, even without changing the fundamental process there are still often major cost advantages through scale, simply because a machine with twice the output is often not twice the cost. The third element of the experience curve is the changes which can be caused by technological improvements which are only practical when the industry reaches certain volume levels, such as continuous processing replacing batch methods of production.

These three factors combine to give what is now described as the experience curve which enables businesses to forecast where their future costs are likely to be. If this can be done for the organization so that its position relative to competition can be assessed, some clear guide-lines for business strategy can be achieved. In an industry with a high experience curve, such as 70%, there is a clear potential competitive advantage available to the business with the most experience, as it will have a worthwhile cost advantage as long as it maintains its superior cumulative production total. Any aggressive competitors can attempt to overcome this disadvantage in the early stages of the industry before cumulative output levels become so high that the cost penalty is prohibitive. The competitors will need to set selling prices below their existing short-run cost base so that market share is gained and the shortfall in cumulative production can be made up.

Alternatively the first company in the market can attempt to build a sustainable competitive cost advantage by moving the industry rapidly to a very high cumulative output level. This can again most easily be achieved by selling below short-term but above long-run experience curve based costs. Unfortunately for some companies who have erected such barriers to entry, the downside risk of the strategy is that it often totally commits the business to a particular technology in order to obtain the maximum experience curve benefits. If a competitor achieves a technology breakthrough, there is a very real possibility of them starting down a new experience curve at a fast rate from a lower relative start point, and leaving the original company with very few strategic options. This example is considered in Chapter 16 with a numerical illustration.

The role of strategic management accounting should be clear. If experience curves are important in the particular industry, the business needs information on how the cost base has moved in the past and predictions as to how it will be affected in the future. This requires information on competitors in terms of their current costs and cumulative production levels, but it also requires information on customers as it is selling prices which determine long-run profitability as well as cost levels. Thus forecasts of price elasticities are needed to plot the potential rate of growth of demand as real cost levels are reduced, so that the optimum rate of development of the market can be established. These areas of competitor accounting and customer/market accounting are considered in detail in Part Two.

Part Two of the book looks at some key accounting issues which arise from different competitive strategies. As competitive strategies basically concern the answers to the question of which products should be offered to which sets of customers, the accounting issues considered reflect the problems associated with analyzing parts of the business relevant to each real competing sub-unit. In Chapter 2 it was argued that strategic management is neither top-down nor bottom-up but an iterative process. Consequently, this selection of considering competitive strategies before corporate strategies is not meant to indicate seniority but that it is easier to explain some of the strategic management accounting concepts in the more focused area of competitive strategies.

In Part Three, corporate strategies are examined for the varying types of businesses which exist, and how these different overall strategies affect the emphasis of strategic management accounting in each type of organization.

Part Four returns to the question of the impact of the different stages of development on strategic management accounting and the appropriate financial control measures which should be applied. Although the information requirements are considered throughout the book, Part Five draws these issues together and deals with designing and operating strategic management accounting information systems.

Part Two

Accounting for Competitive Strategy

Segment profitability – an overview

Part One has shown that strategic management is required at several levels in any large organization. The highest level, which caters for the overall corporate strategy and the related management accounting issues, is considered in Part Three, where the impact of various organizational structures is discussed. In this part of the book, the more detailed levels of involvement with strategic management are examined: ie competitive strategies. The ultimate level of a competitive strategy relates to a specific product in a specific market against identified competitors. Hence accounting for competitive strategies requires information on products, markets (ie customers) and competition. For any large organization, and also for small multi-product or multi-market businesses, this means breaking the total organization down into segments, and providing the appropriate information to support the particular strategic decision under consideration.

The ideal subdivision structure for the development of these individually tailored competitive strategies is to use strategic business units (SBUs) which are usually defined as having distinct external customers and readily identifiable competitors, as well as producing and selling a specified range of products. However, for some groups this structural breaking-down of their business can present major problems and, if badly done, can create unnecessary and costly internal competition. Individual SBUs will usually have some constraints placed on them by their group parent company so as to avoid such complications and these can be described in terms of a modified version of the Ansoff matrix, which was explained in Chapter 2.

As shown in Figure 4.1, each individual business unit should be allowed to choose its own competitive strategy within its existing area of operations and in any immediately adjoining areas of potentially profitable growth. Thus the SBU may have complete discretion over how it deals with its existing range of products in its existing markets, ie Box 1 on the diagram. Normally the SBU will also be able to launch related products (eg range extensions) to its existing range of customers, but may be restricted from moving into completely new products, if this would either cause conflict with another SBU or divert management attention away from the agreed focused objectives for the SBU (ie Box 2 is OK but Box 3 may not be allowable). Similarly the SBU may be allowed to extend its target market to service related customers (eg those served by the same channels of distribution) with its existing product range, but not to try to break into completely new segments of the market (ie Box 4 is acceptable but Box 7 is not). One area of potential contention is therefore Box 5 which relates to modified products to related customers. Part of the strategic role of the centre of the group is to clarify these areas of planned activity so as to avoid confusion and potential misallocation of resources by individual SBUs.

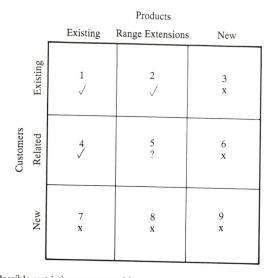

Products

(Possible restrictions on competitive strategies for individual business units)

Figure 4.1 Ansoff Matrix (modified format)

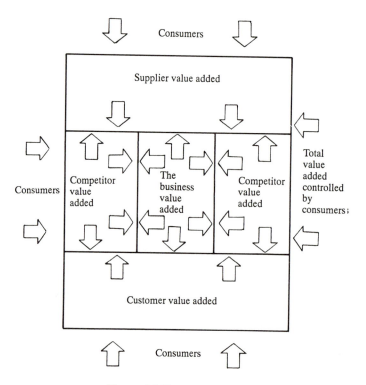

Figure 4.2 Zero sum game

Indeed, many companies see this central directional role as being one of the most important strategic functions performed by group management. If done well it should enable divisional managers to concentrate on a clearly defined competitive arena with well understood, agreed strategic objectives, which cannot be cheated on by suddenly changing the defined product range or target market. However, as discussed in Chapter 3 the external competitive environment can be very dynamic. Any existing definition of an SBU may rapidly become unworkable because of new entrants to the market, new product launches or changes in the customers' buying habits. Consequently, the organization structure may need to be reviewed and the specific areas of involvement of any SBU should be regularly updated. As previously argued in Chapter 2, strategic management is a continual iterative process and not a once-every-five-years planning exercise. It should be noted that some large, successful groups do not see the centre's role as that of refereeing disputes over divisional areas of activity. They regard competition among internal divisions as being very healthy and potentially making it more difficult for external competitors to survive. It certainly makes any such area appear less attractive to any prospective new entrant. In terms of the strategic management accounting requirements, there is little difference between these two extremes at the divisional level, but there will be significant changes in the information needed at the centre of the group; these are considered in Part Three.

Whatever type of direction and control is executed by the group, it is clear that segmented, tailored competitive strategies are critical to the overall success of large, diversified businesses. Not surprisingly, many line managers strongly believe that competitive strategies are the only relevant level of strategic management; this is based on the argument that the ultimate success of any business strategy can only be established in the marketplace.

Profit follows, not leads

In the long-term, any SBU can only succeed financially by implementing a succession of appropriately changing competitive strategies. Therefore it can be very strongly argued that profits follow from achieving a sustainable relative competitive advantage, rather than from any other reason. This is particularly easy to illustrate for a mature industry which is no longer growing, as the total value of the market is effectively independently determined by the end customer of the product or some other external factor. Any individual business can be depicted as engaged in a zero-sum game with its competitors and its suppliers and customers. The financial success of such a business hinges on the share of the total available value added which it can obtain and retain as the competitive environment changes. This is illustrated diagrammatically in Figure 4.2.

A major problem for strategic management accounting is how to take account of changes in these relative competitive advantages. For example, it is very often the case that improving its competitive position will reduce the short-term profitability of a business, and yet this has clearly improved the longer term prospects of enhancing its share of the total available added value. If the business over-emphasizes its short-term profitability, it may be unwilling to invest either in improving its competitive position or in removing or minimizing the impact of any adverse change to its environment. This could have significant long-term consequences. In many businesses, the financial performance measures in use are predominantly indicators of short-term performance and often are heavily biased towards internal comparisons, rather than having an external, longer term relative emphasis. The corporate objectives for the business must take into account the desired time-scale of the forthcoming strategic decisions, so that divisional managers are not encouraged to concentrate on the short-term to the longer term detriment of competitive positioning.

As this relative financial performance against competitors, suppliers and possibly customers is so important, strategic management accounting must reflect this. The historic emphasis of management accounting on internal costs and on the functional analysis which was relevant to external reporting was misguided and of very limited value to strategic decision-making. Indeed, in one of the earliest seminal papers on the subject of strategic management accounting, Professor Kenneth Simmonds[1] defined the area as 'the provision and analysis of management accounting data about a business and its competitors for use in developing and maintaining the business strategy, particularly relative levels and trends in real costs and prices, volume, market share, cash flow and the proportion demanded of a firm's total resources'.

The allocation of total resources to the various elements of the firm is considered as part of the overall corporate strategy in Chapter 8, but the other elements of this definition are discussed in this part of the book. Chapter 5 considers competitor accounting in detail, while the issues of segmented financial analysis regarding customers and products are dealt with in Chapters 6 and 7 respectively.

A key element of this definition, and of the discussion so far, has been on the question of relative, rather than absolute, costs and this is another distinction from the historic emphasis of management accounting. Success in business is fundamentally a relative measure and a sustainable competitive advantage is even more clearly a relative comparison: having a good, cheap product is not an advantage if the competition have better, cheaper products! Despite this, most management accounting information is still produced without any external form of comparison and, in many cases, the internal comparisons are not very helpful.

Presentation of information

There is a need for a dramatic change in the way internal management accounting information is presented to managers if the objectives of strategic management accounting are to be achieved. At present, in most companies, actual accounting information is compared against the previously established budget for the year, and possibly against the actual performance for the same period last year.

The only thing that can be said, with absolute certainty, about any budget is that it will be wrong. This is particularly true if, as is the case for most large businesses, the budget is prepared well in advance of the period to which it relates. The environment can have changed dramatically in the intervening period and the comparison of actual performance back to this now obsolete budget can be distinctly unhelpful. Many sophisticated companies now try to solve this problem by updating the budget to take account of these changes in the external environment; this is normally known as flexing the budget. This flexed budget should, in theory, be more useful as a basis for comparison but unfortunately most methods of flexing the budget introduce more problems than they solve because they are too inwardly focused. For example, if the overall market size is significantly greater than was forecast at the time of the budget, the flexing process would normally increase the expected sales of the business proportionately with the larger total market. However, there are several potential reasons for

[1]Simmonds, Kenneth, *Strategic Management Accounting*, paper presented to CIMA: technical symposium, January 1981

this larger market and the different causes can have dramatically different strategic implications. This unexpected growth could be caused by intense competitive advertising or promotional activity or even substantial price decreases by one or more competitors. In these circumstances the company may have lost market share to these competitors and so its growth in sales would not be expected to be proportionate to the increase in the market. The company should be looking to respond to the threats posed by these new competitive initiatives but, in many companies, the internal management accounts would not even be signalling that there was a problem. Indeed, in a company which did not even have a flexed budget, the monthly accounting reports would probably be indicating an above-budget sales performance, despite the potentially dramatic decline in market share.

A key role for strategic management accounting is to highlight the need for a change in competitive strategy and, preferably, to identify a few key indicators which can give advance warning of the need for such a change in the future. Clearly most of these indicative factors will relate to changes in the company's position against competitors and yet very few businesses regularly incorporate externally based comparisons into their management accounting reporting systems. With such an obvious indicator as relative market share, this could easily be included and is, for many companies, already reported separately through the sales and marketing information system. However, it is the use of such externally based comparisons to explain the relative current changes in sales revenues, profits and cash flows and their future implications which is critical to the strategic decision-making process. If the information has to be compiled by the individual decision-makers, the management accounting system is dramatically failing in its function as a decision support system and is not focusing adequately on the key strategic business issues.

Given our earlier example of possible reasons for unexpected market size increases, an even more useful addition to regular financial management reporting would be relative comparative information on competitor's selling prices, costs, volumes and expenditure on critical success factors. (The stage of development of the market would indicate which areas of expenditure are likely to be critical at any time, as is discussed in Chapter 5 and Part Four.) The key issue is to ensure that financial reports emphasize relative data, rather than the absolute values involved. Holding the increase in internal costs to 5% against a budgeted increase of 8%, and with local inflation running at 10%, may sound like a good performance, and an internally biased set of management reports would probably show it as such. However, if the major competitor is based overseas where there is no local inflation and, due to increasing operating efficiencies, this competitor has experienced net cost *decreases* of 3% over the same period, the relative performance is not looking quite as impressive. The strategic analysis should be concentrated on this competitor and the external environment. Relying on the theoretically sound purchasing power parity model, which argues that exchange rates will adjust to take account of differential inflation rates, to offset such a competitive disadvantage in the short-term is not a satisfactory strategy given current levels of political interference in relation to exchange rates. However, a good strategic management accounting system may have predicted such a potential problem and enabled an appropriate hedging strategy to be implemented as illustrated in Chapter 5, which also considers in much more detail how this relative cost comparison with competitors can be implemented.

This type of comparison highlights a number of complications in strategic decision-making which have very important implications for strategic management accounting systems. First, there is likely to be a need for this type of information at a number of different levels in the organization as strategic decisions, as already discussed, are taken by various managers with complementary but segmented responsibilities. In the above example, the overall group may be competing with several such overseas based companies and could well be, in another division, selling to or even producing other products in the same country and hence be subject to the same nil inflation rate and potentially improving efficiencies within its cost base. Its strategic options, particularly regarding hedging, would be consequently substantially increased, but this potential can only be realized if the information is made available at the right level in the organization so that all these fragmented pieces of data can be drawn together. Another obvious example of this is where the firm sells similar products through different divisions, because they are operating in different markets or through different channels of distribution, eg where electrical products are sold globally through wholesale, retail and direct channels of distribution. The group will inevitably want information on its global sales and profits by product type (eg televisions, etc) rather than merely by division or by channel of distribution. This requires that the accounting system is properly designed to cater for such requirements without a large amount of additional clerical work.

The ideal system for such multi-level needs is a relational data-base in which the data is fully coded when it is first entered into the system, so that it only needs to be recorded once. These associated codes enable the data to be sorted into a wide variety of configurations so that the precise information required for any particular decision can be easily supplied, thus avoiding forcing the decision-maker to process large volumes of data in order to get at the exact information needed. This is discussed in more detail in Chapter 19, but the key element in designing such a system is identifying in advance the potential combinations of data which can be needed so that the coding system is adequate. The good news in this area is that there is a changing cost relationship which should be enabling more businesses to implement good strategic management accounting systems. With improvements in computer technology and declining real costs, the overall cost of processing financial data has been declining significantly over time. However with increasing levels of competition, and more rapid changes in product technology and customer preferences the opportunity cost of bad or non-existent strategic information has been increasing. For many companies the curves, as shown in Figure 4.3, crossed some time ago and their ability to improve their competitive position is now restricted by their lack of access to valid financial analysis on which to base their strategic decisions. Hence managers are making major strategic decisions based on intuition or on what is likely to have the best short-term impact on the perception of them as managers.

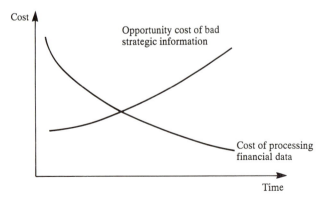

Figure 4.3 Changing cost relationships

Economic versus managerial performance

The second issue which was highlighted by the above example is the essential need to separate two distinct aspects of financial performance. Managers should logically only be judged on their financial performance if they have control over that performance. At all levels of management this means certain aspects which affect the overall economic performance of their business are outside their immediate control (eg the fiscal and tax system of any country, but over time the company could reduce its dependence on this particular economy). The higher up the group one goes the greater the level of managerial control which is possible, while at the divisional level and below there are often a number of areas over which management have little direct control. This is where the level of central involvement in strategic planning is important both in establishing constraints on the division in terms of areas of activity and in setting specific divisional objectives.

If the division receives very tight limitations on its ability to move into new areas, the management can quite justifiably argue that it is incapable of protecting itself against adverse movements in its external business environment. Thus, in our earlier example, if managers were not allowed to consider moving production off-shore and could not themselves move into other international markets or launch new products, they may feel unable to avoid the adverse impact of an overseas competitor with a low rate of local inflation. The managers could argue that the areas that they directly control, ie their cost base, had shown a very good relative performance with a real cost decrease (actual cost increase of 5% against an inflation rate of 10%). This could even be held to be true in comparison to the overseas competitor who had shown a less good cost improvement (actual cost decrease of 3% against a nil inflation rate). However, these costs would need to be carefully analyzed to see whether the improved performance was really due to good managerial control or whether other non-controllable areas were responsible, eg a general reduction in the cost of major raw materials rather than a relative price advantage which was achieved by good negotiation by the company.

However, assuming that the relative exchange rates had not moved to compensate for the higher level inflation rate, our potentially better performing local producer could find that its overseas competitor had reduced its local currency selling prices to pass on its real cost advantages. This delay in adjustment of exchange rates could possibly be caused by the domestic government following a policy of high interest rates which would have the effect both of supporting the exchange rate and of increasing other costs of the domestically based business, exacerbating the competitive disadvantage. The local managers would have to decide how to respond to this new competitive initiative and their decision should be helped by the type of divisional objectives which they have been given. In simplistic terms, the company could decide to match the price decrease of the overseas competitor so as to safeguard its market share but having to accept that, as a consequence, its profit margins would be adversely affected. This may be logical if it believed that the exchange rate would move in the near future so that the competitor would then be forced to increase its selling prices. The obvious alternative would be to hold selling prices or even increase them in line with internal cost increases (which are less than local inflation) and risk losing market share, which could be expensive to regain in the future when exchange rate stability is restored.

The divisional objectives should be set with reference to this division's role within the total group, ie its place in the business portfolio, as this could affect the selected strategic response. If this division is seen as a major growth business of the future, it probably should not allow its market share to be eroded in the short-term; indeed it should be seeking to grow faster than the market, thus increasing its market share. Thus the temporary downturn in profit margins would have to be accepted as part of the necessary investment in the long-term profitability of the business. However if the division has as its main objective short-term profitability and a key financial ratio used in the evaluation of the achievement of this objective is return on sales (ie profit divided by sales revenues), the management team may decide to hold or increase prices because the profit margin on their reduced sales levels will look better. Once again if the market is growing and this growth is further stimulated by the competitor's price reduction, the division may still report actual sales revenues which are above last year's levels or even above the budget for this year although its market share has reduced and its future prospects may be diminished.

In setting divisional objectives the centre of the group should aim for complete goal congruence, which means that what is in the personal interests of the individual managers is in the best interest of their SBU and will also help to achieve the overall group objectives. Not surprisingly managers are motivated to act towards achieving any set of objectives which are set for them, and cannot be blamed for doing so. If these targets and objectives send their area of the business off in the wrong direction, it is the fault of the people setting the targets, not of the divisional managers who are achieving them. For example, if sales managers are set targets which relate exclusively to short-term sales revenue levels, they should not be expected to be overly concerned with the profitability of those sales, or the long-term development of customer relationships or even, necessarily, the collectability of the outstanding customer account balances unless their sales levels are reduced by any bad debts incurred. This also works at the divisional level, where one very sophisticated multinational company paid its senior divisional managers substantial salary increases based on the division's achievement against short-term financial performance targets. These targets were expressed as a Return On Total Assets (ROTA) percentage and this was calculated as profits divided by gross assets, as described in Figure 4.4.

$$\text{Return on total assets (ROTA)} = \frac{\text{Profit before interest and taxes and depreciation}}{\text{Gross fixed assets} + \text{total current assets}}$$

Notes:

(1) Fixed assets were included gross, ie before depreciation, but depreciation was not included as an expense.

(2) The ROTA was calculated four-weekly based on profit for the period and the actual balance sheet figures as at the end of the accounting period.

Figure 4.4 Divisional financial targets

Given large personal incentives to beat these challenging targets, it should have come as no surprise to the group that the management team concentrated on keeping gross assets to a minimum. Initially all fixed assets were changed to a leased basis and so the group had to change the rules to include leased assets as part of the denominator (ie adding in the effective costs of the asset by capitalizing the lease). Next, the outstanding debtors were factored so that they were taken off the balance sheet and, again, the group changed the rules to include factored debtors. As a consequence, the division introduced settlement discounts direct to its customers which encouraged them to pay early; the level of the settlement discount not being set by reference to prevailing interest rates, as one might expect, but by comparison to the divisional targets for ROTA, which were much higher. One division even introduced a scheme whereby it sold its stocks of raw materials and finished goods over its balance sheet date (ie sell at two minutes before midnight and buy-back at two minutes after midnight on every fourth Saturday). Since the division used overdraft financing, the funds notionally received from the sale reduced a current liability on the balance sheet, but the sale of inventories removed a major asset from the key performance section of the balance sheet and hence increased the all-important ROTA percentage.

The important point in this illustration is to highlight how much management time and ingenuity is normally directed at achieving financial objectives. If these objectives are badly established, this effort may not, in reality, be helping to achieve anything worthwhile, eg develop the business, improve the return to the group, etc. Goal congruence is not easy to achieve, but it is impossible unless the group understands the trade-offs between short-term performance and long-term developments and clearly communicates the balance which it wants the division to try to achieve. It should also include some key indicators, possibly non-financial, which ensure that the division and its managers are motivated to head in the right direction.

Thus there are two vitally important aspects to setting divisional financial objectives: First, managers must be set objectives which are in line with the overall group objectives so as to achieve goal congruence for individuals, divisions and the group. Second, managers should only be held responsible for those areas which are under their control and at the divisional level this can be significantly affected by the level of decentralization of strategic decision-making within the group.

This does not mean that the non-controllable elements are unimportant and should not be included in the decision-making process. All the elements must be incorporated into the financial analysis if the correct *economic* decision is to be taken. However, the economically justified decision does not necessarily reflect the relative managerial performance within the particular business. For example, in a recent UK case, British Steel announced the closure of a steel plant at Ravenscraig in Scotland because it would be more economic to consolidate production at its other remaining sites. This consolidation should enhance overall group profitability even though the management and workforce at Ravenscraig appear to have improved their performance significantly over the last few years. It is important that these types of decisions are separated; even though the significance of such a split between managerial and economic performance may be lost on the Ravenscraig workers who will be made redundant as a result of the plant closure.

If an industry is depressed and loss-making, it may be sensible in economic terms to leave the industry or, at least, to minimize any new investment, no matter how good the managers are. In a severe recession, the best managers lose less money than the worst, but even they may find it impossible to make a viable economic return on investment. Equally in a booming economy the worst managers in the world may find it relatively easy to make a good return, but they will always make a lower return than the best management team. Consequently the assessment of managerial performance should be made against a relative standard which shows how well competitors are doing. Economic performance should be assessed against a more overall objective measure of the financial return being achieved as compared to the alternative investment returns which could be earned at a similar level of risk. This raises the important question of how are these alternative investment returns to be calculated, and that depends on the type of strategic decision which is being faced.

Types of strategic decision

In this section, the discussion concentrates on economic decision-making at the divisional level, although a few of the complications of incorporating appropriate managerial performance measures are touched on. Segment profitability analysis is normally a one-, two-, or three-dimensional process as the segments can reflect individually competitors, products or markets, or any combination thereof. The strategic options may affect one entire range of products which is sold in several markets against a diverse set of competitors, or could impact only on one single market where several products are sold, etc. The analytical process has to cope with the complexity of these options and should not distort the decision due to any in-built bias in the way in which the analysis is structured.

This can be a severe problem for many companies which originally developed their segmented financial analysis with only one specific emphasis, but are now trying to apply this segmentation process to one of the other dimensions. For example, many companies have developed some kind of product profitability analysis so as to try to establish which products are more profitable, as is discussed in detail in Chapter 7. In order to do this, sales revenues and costs have to be assigned to the individual produccts and this can require the exercise of a considerable degree of managerial judgement. Gross sales revenues and some cost items can be easily allocated in total to individual products as the product and the item are directly and uniquely associated with each other. Direct product costs, such as specific raw materials and direct variable labour, are good examples. However, there are many other indirect costs which cannot be allocated to a single product and which need to be spread or apportioned among a number of products. These shared costs will include a wide range of general overheads but will also cover many of the customer specific costs incurred by the business (eg sales-force costs, customer promotional activities, sales rebates and settlement discounts, etc, could possibly be directly allocated to individual customers but are not specific to any single product). In order to derive a meaningful product profitability analysis, *some* of these shared costs do need to be apportioned on the most appropriate basis.

Before considering the accounting problems associated with apportionment, the spreading of these customer specific costs to individual products makes it difficult to use any such existing product profitability analysis as the basis for a sound customer account profitability system. In the customer account profitability analysis, all such customer specific costs should be directly allocated to the relevant customer and any previously established method of apportionment from the product perspective must be ignored. Similarly having specifically allocated costs to products is not particularly helpful if the customer dimension is now being developed. These direct product costs will themselves have to be apportioned across the range of customers who buy each particular product. In reality this means that each form of segmented analysis has to be developed separately from scratch. If a massive duplication of analytical effort is to be avoided, the relational data-base mentioned earlier becomes an important decision-making aid.

There is a severe danger that managers become obsessed with excessive accounting neatness when approaching segmented profitability analyses. They often seem to be desperate to produce a completely balanced matrix as shown in Figure 4.5, in which *all* costs are associated both with a single customer and a single product. Moreover the totals of the profits of all the individual customers and all the individual products both equal the total profits for the business. Such an exercise may look very neat and undoubtedly represents a superb example of accounting apportionments, but as a tool on which to base strategic business decisions it is worse than useless because in many cases it can lead to disastrous decisions being implemented based on the false 'information' which is presented.

"Y"

£000's		INDIVIDUAL CUSTOMERS XYZ						Product's total profit
		6						
INDIVIDUAL PRODUCT	ABC	6	4	10	5	15	20	60
		5						
		4						
		16						
		15						
		9						
		11						
"X"	Customer's total profit	70						Business total profit

Note: All costs are spread to a specific product and a specific customer, so that every customer's total profit (Row X) is split across each of the individual products. Similarly each product's total profit (Column Y) is spread to individual customers. This means that the sum of all the customers' individual profits will equal the sum of all the products' individual profits and both will equal the business' total profits.

Comment: Very neat and completely useless!!

Figure 4.5 The 'ultimate neat' segment profitability analysis

Management accounting techniques have been developed to a high level of sophistication over many years in order to cope with a wide range of apportionment problems. Indeed, the whole basis of absorption costing relies on the accountant's ability to apportion indirect costs across a range of products in order to arrive at *the cost* incurred in producing each product. This is a fundamental element of preparing externally published financial statements as the stocks/inventories held by the company at the end of the accounting period have to be valued at the lower of their full costs and their net realizable values. This full cost is calculated using the absorption costing method and hence includes the apportioned share of indirect costs which have partially been incurred in order to produce those particular goods which are still held in stock. The validity of this historic accounting exercise is not in question, but this absorption based cost should not be used as the basis for any subsequent decision regarding:

- selling the stock (when the net realizable value is relevant)
- replacing the stock if sold (when its replacement cost should be considered)
- increasing the level of stock (when the incremental cost incurred is required)
- or decreasing the level of stock in the future (when the severable or avoidable cost has to be calculated).

It is of fundamental importance therefore that a strategic management accounting system can provide the appropriate cost information to support each potential type of strategic decision, and this clearly requires a very different analysis to the historically based absorption costing system. Strategic decisions often involve increasing or decreasing output levels for any particular product in any market, and the financial input must accurately show the true cost and revenue impacts of such a decision.

A good example of such a strategic decision would be the consideration of whether to continue producing a particular product internally or to look for an external supplier from whom the finished product could be purchased. The financial evaluation of such a 'make or buy' decision has to take account of the specific situation which the business is in at the time of the decision and the appropriate costs must be included. Thus the relevant costs would differ from our example above if the decision was considering bringing 'in-house' a component or service which was currently provided by an external supplier. The business might need to invest in new equipment to carry out this function internally, whereas if the product was being transferred outside, existing equipment might become surplus to requirements and could be disposed of. In the case of bringing a function 'in-house' the relevant costs would be affected if the business was already supplying part of the need internally or was carrying out some very closely related function where there could be some sharing of costs. The business must ensure that the right cost estimates are used so that its negotiations with external suppliers are logically based and so that such key strategic decisions have the best available financial justification.

As these impacts are, of necessity, forecasts they cannot be regarded as certainties but good managerial judgement combined with the application of the right financial analytical techniques should give the best information possible to support the decision.

If the output is to be increased, the relevant costs which should be considered are only those additional costs which will be incurred as a result of the increase in output. Not surprisingly, these costs are often described as 'incremental' costs because they are directly caused by the increment in output. This means that any existing fixed costs which will now support the larger total output are ignored in calculating the incremental costs, whereas any new 'incremental' *fixed* costs which have to be incurred have to be included. Thus the level of incremental costs per unit may be considerably different to the previously computed average costs per unit for the existing output, as is illustrated in Figure 4.6. The normal financial decision-making rule can be applied to ignore the existing fixed costs as committed and sunk, when considering future financial decisions.

This logic is equally effective if the strategic decision involves decreasing output or even stopping the sale of a particular product completely. This type of decision should also only take into account those costs which change as a result of the decision. These will be those costs which can be *avoided* if the particular product is cancelled and hence will not include any fixed costs which cannot be saved or any shared costs which will still be incurred to support any other related products which are being retained. 'Avoidable' costs must therefore be distinguished from those costs which have been committed by the division and consequently cannot be avoided even if the segment is completely closed down. [Avoidable costs are often also described as 'severable' costs, and can clearly be seen to be the opposite side of 'incremental' costs in the reversed strategic decision.]

This distinction from committed costs raises one of the key issues for strategic financial decisions, because the time-scale in the decision will often dictate the level of committed costs involved and consequently which costs can really be considered as avoidable. There is a well-known adage in economics that 'in the very long run, all costs are variable while in the

Existing output level	= 20,000 units		
Existing cost:			
Fixed costs	= £50,000		
Variable costs	= £50,000		
Planned increase in output	= 10,000 units		
Additional costs expected:			
Fixed costs	= –		
Variable costs	= £25,000		
Incremental cost of extra 10,000 units	= £25,000		
Average cost per unit calculated:			
	Existing 20,000	New proposed total of 30,000	Incremental 10,000 units
Total costs	£100,000	£125,000	£25,000
Average cost per unit	£5	£4.17	£2.50

Figure 4.6 Example of incremental cost

very short run, all costs are fixed'. Strategic decisions can obviously have very differing time-scales but frequently will have considerably longer time scales than the day-to-day, tactical decisions, which often have their impact over very short periods. This can mean that for strategic decisions the traditional accounting classification of costs into fixed and variable categories may be misleading because, as previously discussed, traditional management accounting techniques have tended to concentrate, almost exclusively, on the shorter term tactical decisions. The strategic management accounting system must avoid any such obvious misclassifications and must ensure that costs are properly classified as committed or not. This is a clearer method of description without the overtones of annual time-scales, which are often associated with the traditional terms fixed and variable costs.

A 'committed cost' should, for the purposes of any strategic decision, be regarded as any cost which cannot be changed at the behest of the particular business during the time-scale of the particular decision without incurring additional costs, and hence can include costs which will be incurred well into the future. For example if a division takes on a 21-year lease for a very specialized building, it now has a 'committed' lease rental cost for the next 21 years, even though the rentals are payable over this period and the amounts payable may vary due to the rent reviews spread through the lease. Should the division consider a decision which makes the building redundant it cannot 'avoid' the lease payments over the remaining period of the lease which may be longer than the impact of the decision. Hence the lease costs do not form part of the cost savings which should be considered in this financial evaluation; if the building, or part of it, can be sub-let or used by the business for some alternative purpose then the specific rental income, or rental saving achieved, could be included. Under this definition of committed cost, the period of commitment is specific to the nature of the contract and must therefore be considered at the time of taking and implementing the strategic decision; ie a committed cost five years ago may now have become avoidable if the circumstances have changed.

Committed costs are often one of the main differences between economic performance measures and managerial performance measures, because divisional managers may not have any discretion concerning certain costs which are committed at the group level so as to achieve overall economies of scale, etc. If so, these committed costs should be excluded from the considerations of managerial performance, as they cannot be regarded as being under the control of the divisional managers. In some cases it is also possible to argue that existing managers do not have control over long-term commitments made by previous management teams, and corresponding adjustments should be made to the managerial performance criteria. This has to be done with great care to ensure that only the genuine impact of the long-term historic commitment is excluded, as a very common excuse for managerial non-performance is to blame the predecessors. Irrespective of their treatment for managerial performance purposes, their treatment for economic decisions must be based on the simple question of whether they will change as a result of the particular decision under consideration and this provides a very clear focus for any segmented financial analysis.

This focus highlights the appropriate method of classifying shared costs in any such segmented analysis. If a decision is being considered to cancel one single product from a range, but to continue to sell the rest of the range through all the current channels of distribution to all the existing customers, then most of the shared product's costs will continue to be incurred and cannot be regarded as avoidable for this decision. However, if the division was to analyse the impact of cancelling the entire product range, many more of these shared costs would be avoidable than could be so regarded for any simple product within the range. If the rest of the range was to be continued but particular channels of distribution were to be closed, the relevant level of costs which became avoidable would be different again. Therefore, the segmented financial analysis must clearly show the hierarchical nature of these avoidable costs for product deletion decisions, and similarly the step-function nature of incremental costs when new products are added to existing ranges, or new customer groups and channels of distribution are taken on.

The key objective of any segmented financial analysis should be to aid strategic decisions and any other outcome of the analysis should be seen as secondary. This role of strategic decision support is not helped by excessive emphasis on accounting neatness or by a simplistic over-generalized approach which provides one level of product or customer profitability analysis as the financial input to all the possible decisions which the business can face. What is required is a flexible system which enables the business to establish the true costs and the sales revenues attributable to any segment and, more particularly, attributable to any specific decision affecting the segment. If this idea of including only attributable costs and revenues does not lead to accounting neatness but forces decisions to be based on the appropriate 'contribution' level rather than on the 'fully accounted profits' of the segment, this can only improve the quality of the strategic decision-making.

A concentration on these concepts of attributable costs and revenues (ie truly incremental and avoidable costs) over the time-scale of each strategic decision makes the issues of apportionment much simpler, as is specifically considered in each of the following chapters of this part of the book. The analysis should try to identify how the various costs will change as a result of each potential decision, and an historic segment analysis is often the best way to identify such causal relationships.

Engineering cost relationships

The easiest cost to forecast is one where there is a well-established relationship between the level of input and the consequent level of output. This is frequently the case in engineering type relationships where for any given level of input, the amount produced can be predicted with relative certainty; indeed the amount which *should* be produced can be calculated exactly. Any difference from this expected level of production can be attributed to the relative efficiency of the production process, rather than the accuracy of the predictive relationship. Conversely for any required level of output, the inputs needed can be calculated using the same mathematical relationship. In many businesses, there are a great range of such engineering style mathematical relationships and they are by no means restricted to the production environment. However, they are normally expressed in terms of physical relationships (eg X tonnes of sheet metal needed to produce 100,000 car bodies, or Y hours of clerical labour to process 100,000 sales orders) whereas financial decisions have to be expressed in money if valid comparisons are to be made. It is very difficult to make any direct evaluation of an investment in new machinery which improves the output of car bodies for a given input of tonnes of metal, or which reduces the labour hours required to produce any given level of output. However, if all these items are converted to their equivalent monetary value it becomes possible to compare all sorts of different types of inputs and outputs.

Unfortunately in most cases, although the physical relationship may be constant and predictable, there is no such certainty in the relationship between the financial value of the inputs and the financial value of the corresponding outputs. Not only can relative cost levels change rapidly and dramatically due to external and/or uncontrollable factors, but there is no reason for these changes necessarily to follow any historical patterns or relationships. It is also essential that economic decisions are based on the costs which will change as a result of the decision under consideration. These are, as previously discussed, the future costs which have still to be incurred or which can be avoided, and again historical levels calculated on an absorption basis will be irrelevant for this comparison. Thus the firm, constant, predictable, physical relationship may need to be combined with a best-guess forecast cost price in order to establish a financially comparable result. The major problem clearly lies in the business' ability to forecast these cost prices accurately and to ensure that the right level of costs is considered for each different possible type of decision as discussed earlier. This would appear to be true for both economic decisions, where including forecasts of future costs is essential, and for considerations of relative managerial performance where a key concern is to include only those elements over which managers can exercise control and hence can be held responsible.

However, if we consider what it is that individual managers really control, it becomes clear that to include wildly fluctuating costs may completely distort our perception of their managerial performance. A silly example can be given by reference to the production of car bodies. If the price of steel increases by 25% how can the manager responsible for body assembly offset such a cost increase – by sending out four-door cars with only three doors fitted? Clearly this manager has no direct control over this substantial element of cost and yet such a significant change in total costs should result in a review of the strategic options available to the business. These may include increasing selling prices to pass on the cost increase to end customers, attempting to reduce the amount of steel incorporated in the car by increasing plastic components, or increasing research into new composite materials to replace steel completely.

The best way of achieving these dual objectives of highlighting the economic problem while still validly evaluating relative managerial performance is through the proper use of standard costing techniques. These techniques have been around for a long time, but unfortunately have fallen into disrepair in many companies as their fundamental objectives seem to have been forgotten. Standard costs consist of two elements: a usage element and a price element. Thus for labour, the usage element is the time taken to perform a particular function and the price element is the wage rate paid to the grade of labour used to carry out the function as is shown in Figure 4.7. By multiplying the two elements, a monetary cost is clearly calculated but

Standard labour cost per unit	=	Standard labour time allowed per unit in hours	×	Standard labour rate per hour for this grade of labour
eg, Standard assembly cost per car door	=	12 minutes (standard time allowance)	×	£20 per hour (standard direct labour rate)
	=	£4		

Figure 4.7 Example of standard cost structure

to be of any strategic value there must be some predictability about this relationship. Therefore the basic key for using standard costs is that there is a valid engineering relationship for the usage element which can be expressed as a link between the physical units of inputs and the expected units of output. For example, the normal number of minutes to carry out the particular repetitive task can be assessed. If such a 'standard' engineering relationship can be developed, the physical efficiency of the operation can be assessed by comparison of the actual units of input relative to the expected or 'standard allowance' of inputs for the actual achieved level of output. Thus returning to the car body example, the assembly shop manager can be held responsible for how efficiently the operation is run by reference to the actual physical material and labour time used compared to the agreed standard levels which should have been used for the actual output produced.

Thus far, no mention has been made of monetary value, as these relationships can and should be controlled in terms of the physical units. Also only the efficiencies of individual elements of the operation are being assessed rather than their overall efficiency or effectiveness in achieving previously established objectives. In many situations, management has a degree of discretion over how functions are carried out in terms of the mix of resources which are employed, eg less labour usage through investment in more automated machinery, or less material wastage through more careful, and hence slower, work practices by labour. One objective of any financial control system should be to ensure that the selected mix of resources helps to achieve the overall objectives of the business; another clear example of goal congruence. This can be most easily achieved by enabling the opportunity costs associated with each such alternative to be easily compared. Accurate relevant cost prices are needed to achieve this. If arbitrary and inaccurate standard prices were used, eg £1 per hour for labour and £100 per tonne for raw materials, managers would not necessarily place the correct emphasis on the most important areas under their control. For example, in a glass manufacturing business an over-usage of 10 tonnes of sand is considerably less important than a similar over-usage of silica due to the substantial differences in their cost prices per tonne.

However, as with all cost forecasts, it is likely that the standard costs will prove to be wrong when they are eventually applied in the business. This is particularly true for very large complex businesses where, for logistical reasons, the standards are set well before the start of the period in which they are to be applied. For the physical aspect of the standard this should present no insurmountable problems. Even if subsequent changes are made to the relationship (eg changes to manufacturing processes, etc), this normally establishes another firm physical relationship. The consequent impact of the change can be quantified, accurately forecast and hence separated in any subsequent analysis. However, for any area with volatile price levels and no logical forecasting relationship to enable firm predictions of future prices to be made, such time lags can be disastrous. Even if all possible care is taken at the time of establishing the standard cost the actual cost relationships may have changed substantially when the standards are to be used.

Indeed in many companies, a major role for the accounting analysis involving standard costing is merely to reconcile the actual costs incurred back to the standard prices established. This is done by calculating out the price or rate variances, as opposed to the operational efficiency measures which are calculated through usage variances. Interestingly, these usage variances are normally valued at standard price levels on the argument that by doing so the engineering style relationship is not distorted by changes in relative cost levels. Mathematically it is clearly important that the same value is applied to both the standard usage allowance and the actual usage level, if a meaningful comparison of efficiency is to be achieved. However, for this purpose as previously stated, any common value (eg £1 per unit for all standards) would indicate if an over-usage or under-usage had taken place. In order to reflect the relative financial importance of the various physical elements, it is necessary to use financial values which accurately reflect their relative current values. Most companies try to achieve this by putting great efforts and hence many resources and much cost into forecasting and calculating very detailed standard costs. Unfortunately, more effort and cost do not normally produce a corresponding improvement in forecasting accuracy if there is no predictable relationship.

More importantly, these companies are producing an unnecessary level of analytical complexity for their managers because the most relevant readily available cost for use in this area is normally the latest actual cost. This latest actual cost may be the best estimate available for future costs, but should be replaced by any such better estimate which exists, and should be used for all discretionary allocation of resource decisions by managers. If these actual costs are used to control managerial performance estimates, the objective of goal congruence is automatically achieved because managers are using the same costs as are relevant to the strategic economic decisions of the business. The use of outdated, incorrect standard costs to assess managerial performance is another aspect of the excessive emphasis on internal comparisons used in traditional management accounting. Standard prices are only relevant as a control mechanism if there is a known engineering style relationship as is required for standard usages and there are very few of these. Without such a relationship, the detailed analysis of price variances is simply indicating the level of forecasting accuracy achieved by the business, whereas what is needed is an aid to strategic decision-making. The problems which can be caused are illustrated in the very simplified example given below.

Example:

Problems of misuse of standard costing

Base data:

Standard cost structure of product X

Standard labour cost	= Standard time ie 4 hours	× Standard rate ie £12.50 per hour	= £50
Standard material cost for Y	= Standard units ie 10	× Standard price ie £10 per unit	= £100
		TOTAL STANDARD COST	= £150

Required output in the period is 1,000 units of X

Actual costs   = Labour rate £10 per hour

                = Price per unit of Y £15

Labour time used = 3,000 hours

Units of Y used   = 11,000

Note: It is possible to reduce raw material usage to 8 units of Y by increasing labour time to
        6 hours per unit of X

Traditional variance analysis techniques

Labour variances

Rate variance:

(Standard rate − actual rate) × actual hours
ie (£12.50 − £10) × 3,000 hours   = FAVOURABLE   £7,500

Usage/efficiency variance:

(Standard usage − actual usage) × standard rate
ie (1,000 × 4 − 3,000) × £12.50   = FAVOURABLE   £12,500

TOTAL FAVOURABLE LABOUR VARIANCE   £20,000

Material Y variances

Price variance:

(Standard price − actual price) × actual units
ie (£10 − £15) × 11,000   = ADVERSE   £55,000

Usage/efficiency variance

(Standard usage − actual usage) × standard price
ie (10,000 − 11,000) × £10   = ADVERSE   £10,000

TOTAL ADVERSE MATERIAL VARIANCE   £65,000

Summary of variances

Adverse material price variance	£55,000
Favourable labour rate variance	£7,500
Net adverse price variance	£47,500
Favourable labour efficiency variance	£12,500
Adverse material usage variance	£10,000
Net favourable usage variance	£2,500

Overall adverse variance	£45,000

ie Standard cost of 1000 units of X	=	£150,000
Actual costs incurred	=	£195,000
	Adverse Variance	£45,000

The variance analysis should be focused to highlight responsibility so that managerial performance can be evaluated as well as helping in the economic decisions which should be taken by the business. The analysis shown above would seem to indicate that the manager is using the available resources reasonably efficiently (ie due to the net favourable efficiency variance) and also that, given the level of standard costs, the business would not be better off by implementing the potential trade-off between labour and raw materials because total costs would increase by £5,000 as shown below.

Standard basis	*Revised basis using trade-offs at standard prices*
per 1000 units of X	per 1000 units of X
Labour costs £50 × 1,000 = £50,000	Labour costs 6 hrs @ £12.50 × 1,000 = £75,000
Material costs £100 × 1,000 = £100,000	Material costs 8 units @ £10 × 1,000 = £80,000
Total Cost £150,000	Total Cost £155,000

However the actual costs faced by the business have changed dramatically from those forecast in the standards and the impact of the potential trade-off is correspondingly affected, viz:

per 1000 units of X at actual prices

Standard basis	*Revised basis*
4 hrs @ £10 × 1,000 = £40,000	Labour costs 6 hrs @ £10 × 1000 = £60,000
10 @ £15 × 1,000 = £150,000	Material costs 8 units @ £15 × 1,000 = £120,000
Total Costs £190,000	Total Costs £180,000

This more realistically based analysis shows that there would be a cost saving of £10,000 to be obtained from implementing the trade-off. This indicates that the manager is not using the resources effectively. If goal congruence is to be achieved the method of assessing managerial performance should make the managers want to implement this trade-off but if they are judged against standard costs, this will not be so. Equally interestingly, this alternative way of calculating the expected base cost shows an expected level of £190,000 against the actual costs incurred of £195,000. This should give rise to an adverse efficiency variance of £5,000, since price variances have already been eliminated, and not the apparently favourable variance of £2,500 identified by the traditional variance analysis. The reason for this should be clear; using standard prices understates the impact of over-using the raw material which has now gone up in value and does not encourage managerial behaviour to be adjusted in the light of real changes in the external environment. Clearly if a competitor has a more rational management accounting process, its managers may be motivated to adjust their relative usage levels to take account of actual costs being incurred rather than the out-of-date standard costs which were forecast some time ago. The analysis is easy to see by contrasting the two formats side by side.

Traditional efficiency variances (using standard prices)		*Current real efficiency variances* (using actual prices)	

Favourable labour efficiency
    1,000 hours @ £12.50
	= £12,500	Favourable labour efficiency
		    1,000 hrs @ £10
			= £10,000

Adverse material usage
    1,000 units @ £10
	= (£10,000)	Adverse material usage
		    1,000 units @ £15
			= (£15,000)

Net	£2,500	Net	(£5,000)

This revised method of analysis is not trying to hold these operating managers responsible for the price changes if they do not control them. However, it *is* trying to force them to take account of the economic realities facing the business which they are running, by including the real economic impact of their actions as opposed to a theoretical analysis of what might have been.

This argues that standard costing can be used as a very powerful strategic analytical tool in terms of assessing detailed competitive strategies in a live, up-to-date way. All that it requires is the combination of sound physically based input–output relationships with the relevant costs which support the potential strategic decisions facing the business. Unfortunately, this type of strategic financial analysis does not necessarily lead to a nice, neat accounting reconciliation of all the actual costs back to the original budget. However, even this can be done if desired. In our example, the differences between the standard cost prices and the actual cost prices were already eliminated. New price variances can be calculated but this time using the standard usage allowances, as this calculation is really highlighting the forecasting error built into the standard cost prices used. Such a calculation is not recommended to be included in management reports because it maintains the emphasis, within the management accounting system, on developing complicated ways of computing standard cost prices. Such practices can still be damaging even if this subsequent analysis is properly undertaken, because many such complex standard cost systems perpetuate the inevitable problems of apportionment.

A recent example from the car industry should highlight the kind of problems which can be encountered. In order to establish a full standard labour cost per hour it is necessary to identify how these costs are incurred and what products they should be charged to. With direct labour which actually produces only a single product this is quite easy and the forecast costs incurred can be allocated to each appropriate product. However, in today's sophisticated manufacturing environment such dedicated direct labour normally forms a relatively minor proportion of the total cost base. Far more important may be the indirect support labour cost which maintains the machinery, provides back-up services, supervises and manages, plans the work allocations, etc. If these costs were excluded from their standard costs build-up, many companies would be worried that they could be selling some products at a loss. Another important cost could be from the machinery used in production with its associated depreciation and maintenance expenses. If the machinery is specifically attributable to one product, these costs can be allocated but even then there can be the problem of calculating a standard cost per unit depending upon the level of output forecast, as is shown in Figure 4.8. Where the machinery is of more general application, its costs also need spreading across the relevant products so as to achieve a 'proper' standard cost.

Base data	Product A:
	Depreciation and fixed maintenance costs = £100,000 pa
	Standard forecast output of 'A' = 10,000 units pa
	Actual output of 'A' = 25,000 units pa
Analysis	Standard depreciation cost = £10 per unit
	If standard cost is applied to actual output:
	Depreciation 'recovered' in standard costs = £10 × 25,000
	= £250,000
Note:	Companies differ considerably in how they show this over-recovery of fixed costs through their standard costing systems, most describing it as 'over-recovery of overheads'. Almost all succeed in confusing both economic and managerial performance indicators with their presentation of this meaningless and unnecessary additional complexity.

Figure 4.8 Incorporating fixed costs into standards

In many areas of the business the total of all these other costs may be more than ten times the level of the direct variable labour costs. Notwithstanding this multiplier factor, many companies, including some leading companies in the car industry, still use direct labour as the method of charging these costs into individual product standard cost formats. Illustrative standard cost pro-formas are shown for a labour intensive and a capital intensive product in Figure 4.9.

	Product B[1]	Product C[2]
Standard costs	£	£
Direct labour costs @ £20 per hour	40	5
Indirect labour and overhead[3] & [4] @ 1,000% of direct labour	400	50
Direct raw materials	200	200
Direct overheads:		
– depreciation[4]	10	250
– other variable	50	100
TOTAL STANDARD COST	£700	£605

Notes:

[1] Product B is labour intensive with a low level of direct capital investment and overhead.

[2] Product C is capital intensive with a correspondingly high direct depreciation charge and low direct labour cost.

[3] Indirect labour and overhead is apportioned to all products on the basis of 1,000% of the standard direct labour charge.

[4] Fixed costs are recovered in standard costs on the assumption that output levels are 70% of plant capacity levels unless more specific forecasts have been made.

Figure 4.9 Apportionments in standard costs

As can be seen from Figure 4.9, the impact of apportioning the indirect labour and overheads into a labour intensive product can be quite dramatic. It is important to understand why indirect labour and overhead levels are so relatively high. In many companies this is due to the increasing level of automation and correspondingly declining level of direct labour. The consequence is an increasing absolute level of indirect support costs, and a reducing direct labour base over which to apportion them; hence an increasing relative rate of recovery. Not only does this make it clearly unrealistic to apportion these costs on the basis of the residual direct labour cost but this can have a cumulatively compounding distortion effect. From the individual product's perspective it appears that a further investment to fully automate Product C would reduce its standard cost not by the direct saving of £5 but by £55, if the indirectly apportioned costs are included. Clearly it is unlikely that many of these indirect costs would, in reality, be avoided by such a decision and indeed incremental indirect costs may be incurred in order to support the additional investment in automated plant and machinery. In most standard costing systems, these continuing indirect costs would simply be re-apportioned across the remaining, but reduced direct labour base. This would increase the recovery rate for all other products and hence make Product B's costs even higher, potentially leading to calls for a price increase, so as to restore profitability levels even though nothing has changed for this product. From the earlier discussion this is clearly nonsensical but a costing system which leads to this type of potential analysis can be extremely dangerous. The relative impact of overhead recoveries can be even more dramatic if direct fixed costs are excluded from the standard costing system as can be seen by re-stating Product C's costs excluding fixed costs; see Figure 4.10.

Unfortunately including these fixed costs re-introduced the potential apportionment problem illustrated in Figure 4.8. This can be very clearly seen if we simply adjust Product C's standard costs to reflect depreciation being spread on altered assumptions of 60% and 80% utilizations, ie by no means dramatic movements in the base assumptions. This is also shown in Figure 4.10.

The marketing strategy implications of such a possible change in the forecast of the standard cost for the product can be quite significant, as it could lead to arguments about pricing strategy and affordable levels of marketing support, etc. What is relevant for the business is to

	PRODUCT C		
	Pessimistic assumption 60% utilization	Base assumption 70% utilization	Optimistic assumption 80% utilization
Standard costs			
Direct labour	5	5	5
Indirect labour (all assumed variable)	50	50	50
Direct raw materials	200	200	200
Direct variable overhead	100	100	100
Standard product cost – excluding fixed costs	355	355	355
Fixed depreciation	292	250	219
TOTAL STANDARD COST	£647	£605	£574

Figure 4.10 Changing base assumptions in standard costs

understand fully how such possible changes in volume affect its product cost structures compared to the impact on its competitors. The management accountants should have a very detailed knowledge of these internal cost-volume-profit relationships. What is unfortunately often missing is the external application of this knowledge, ie to competitors, as is discussed in Chapter 5 and the sensible application of these techniques to enhance strategic decision-making as is discussed in Chapters 6 and 7, rather than confusing senior managers by providing misleading management information. Much current segmented financial information, particularly where standard costing is involved, should only be issued with a warning: 'using this information could seriously injure your business' wealth'. Alternatively, the perceived requirement to provide such a wide range of financial information leads to a plethora of unrelated financial information systems, with a consequent multiplication of costs and confusion among senior managers, who are bombarded with often directly conflicting financial analyses. One such major company is so busy running its five unrelated management accounting information systems that it cannot afford the resources needed to design and implement any form of integrated financial data-base. Such a system could provide the required information to the required manager at the appropriate time without the need for the current level of one-off analytical effort every time any unusual problem or opportunity arises. This area is discussed in more detail in Part Five.

Marketing investment analysis

At the start of the review of the strategic use of standard costing, it was stated that engineering style relationships are not limited to the production areas of the business. They exist in any area where repetitive processes are carried out which clearly includes many clerical and administrative parts of the business, but they can also be utilized as a good method of financial evaluation even if the specific nature of the relationship is not fully understood. This can be particularly true of a critical strategic area which has received very scant financial evaluation in many otherwise sophisticated companies: marketing investment analysis.

Most companies in competitive markets now agree that their overall success is closely linked to the success of their marketing strategy. Consequently, levels of marketing expenditure are often significant and yet these are subjected to far less rigorous financial evaluations than other smaller levels of financial commitments. Very few sophisticated businesses would consider making a major new investment in fixed assets without a full financial analysis, usually including a discounted cash flow appraisal if the investment has a medium to long economic life. However, almost none of these same companies carry out the same degree of financial analysis when similar or even greater sums of money are proposed as marketing expenditures. Even more surprising is that accounting procedures have, for a very long time, differentiated between a capital investment which is treated as an asset with its cost spread over its economic life and maintenance expenditure which is written off in the period in which it is incurred. It can be very strongly argued for many of these businesses that these tangible fixed assets are worth little more than their scrap metal value if the business does not have successful products and customers willing to buy these products. These critically important and highly valuable intangible assets are not considered as such under most management accounting systems, and the potential strategic implications of this are enormous. This issue is not concerned with the largely academic and sterile debate regarding the incorporation of brands as assets on published balance sheets, which is really simply another facet of the creative 'Mickey Mouse' nature of externally focused financial statements.

Much more important is the impact of the management accounting treatment of these intangible assets on the strategic decision-making process of the business. In the case of an investment in any tangible asset, the business will automatically evaluate the return on such an investment over the whole of its economic life. Also the accepted accounting treatment will help avoid the decision being driven by any short-term adverse impact of the expenditure on profitability. For many companies neither of these statements is true in the case of expenditure on marketing, with all such expenditures being regarded as short-term and expensed against this period's profits. Consequently, if there is pressure to improve short-term financial performance, this can be achieved by reducing the marketing programme or cutting back on research and development activity. Both of these decisions could have disastrous longer term consequences, but most businesses have no financial control system which can adequately highlight this future impact.

As previously stated, accounting can apparently distinguish, for tangible assets, between development expenditure, which enhances the value of the fixed assets, and maintenance expenditure, which simply allows the asset to continue to function properly. Moreover, if inadequate maintenance is carried out, management accounts can reflect the impact of this by reducing the remaining value of the fixed asset. This can be done for incredibly complex and unique assets as long as they are tangible, and this process includes tangible assets which are created by the business itself as well as those purchased from outside suppliers. Indeed companies can even assess the portion of the original cost which should be regarded as capital and which elements of this expenditure have no future value to the business (such as excess expenditure incurred on installation or commissioning). Decisions can be made on the potential economic life of the asset, which normally has some reference to the appropriate product or customer asset, and on the suitable method of depreciation which should be applied. It is even possible to forecast the residual value which will be realized at the end of this estimated economic life.

All this is practical and considered sound, prudent accounting for tangible assets, but nothing at all seems possible for the intangible brand or customer assets which fundamentally underlie all these managerial judgements relating to tangible fixed assets. The justification for this complete lack of consistency (which is, of course, one of the four underlying accounting concepts) seems to be that it is difficult and that it would be impossible to get it absolutely right. It has already been stated several times that all management decisions are based on forecasts of the future which are almost inevitably wrong but they are still the best basis available for supporting the strategic decisions which cannot be avoided just because they are difficult. A business which fails to maintain its existing marketing assets or to develop new marketing assets during the growth stage of an industry will never realize the maximum financial return from its activities. In order to evaluate whether this is being done properly the strategic management accounting system must have the correct focus and analytical emphasis.

The first stage is the same as with all elements of strategic management accounting and this is to link the accounting system closely into the strategic objectives of the business. In this case, this means the specific marketing objectives for each of the products and appropriate customer groups or channels of distribution. Nowadays, most marketing-led businesses are quite good at developing qualitative and even quantitative objectives for these areas, eg a product objective may be specified in terms of the sterling weighted level of distribution gained. Companies are also quite good at specifying how these objectives are to be achieved in terms of the marketing activities which will be carried out. Many now produce comprehensive marketing plans which allocate detailed sub-objectives to each specific marketing activity so that its relative success or failure can be assessed. This monitoring process can also be carried out using sophisticated tracking studies which can assess changes not only in customers' awareness of a particular product, but also in their attitudes towards the product relative to competitive offerings.

Thus the strategic marketing objectives can be, and often are, specifically identified but the current gap for most companies is in the linkage to the management accounting system through any form of financial evaluation, monitoring and feedback process. The detailed marketing objectives may show that it is intended to spend £2 million on television advertising in order to create customer awareness of a new product and a target level of unprompted awareness of 25% within the target population for the product is set for the end of the advertising campaign. Despite these specific objectives relatively few companies would attempt financially to justify this level of advertising expenditure. Even fewer would attempt to develop a financial model which would indicate whether £2 million was the optimum level of advertising for this type of launch, even though the company may have done several similar launches in the past few years, and data may be available on many other launches done by other companies, including competitors. Still fewer again would try to evaluate whether an alternative marketing mix would be more productive than using all television advertising.

In some companies, the management accountants do not seem to know where to start this type of evaluation, while in others they seem reluctant to appear to be interfering in the 'black art' of marketing. (Accountants have been happy to get closely involved in almost all aspects of manufacturing and engineering, possibly because they are more tangible and mathematical, but they have always seemed unwilling to get heavily involved in financial evaluations of more intangible areas such as marketing and human resource accounting.) The financial evaluations of marketing expenditures rely on all the normal financial techniques and hinge on the fact that most marketing relationships are intrinsically mathematical! A fundamental tenet of a marketing asset is that, like any asset, unless it is properly maintained it will decline in value. Consequently a good starting point for financial involvement would be to consider what level of expenditure is necessary to maintain the current value of the asset. Since such an evaluation could well lead to an increase in the marketing budget when these relationships are more clearly defined and understood, it should be possible for the financial managers to avoid being perceived as adversaries of the marketing team. This breakdown of resistance is essential if the process is really to add value to the business. As in all areas of strategic management accounting, the financial analytical process is in the role of decision support and its own financial justification is through the improvement of these supported financial strategic decisions, such as investments in marketing. Consequently the development of a team approach to the financial analysis of marketing activities is vitally important and this requires the financial managers to be seen to be making a positive contribution rather than being viewed as ex-post auditors, budget reducers or apportioners of blame.

In order to assess the required maintenance expenditure it is important for marketing management to be able to describe the current attributes of the asset and this must be done in measurable terms, so that changes in these attributes can be monitored. This process stops the inclusion of vague, nebulous conceptual assets and forces the business to consider what really does constitute a marketing asset. It is certainly fair to say that if you can't describe it or measure it, it probably doesn't exist and almost certainly has no value to the business. Hence it is not worth spending money maintaining it! Interestingly, a rigorous application of this process often makes it more difficult to justify existing levels of support for old established products, rather than to support substantial investments in new launches. This is normally because current levels of support are justified on historic levels of support plus an allowance for inflation and a small possible additional allowance to offset any increase in competitive activity. In the past, the marketing support could have been designed to develop the brand and consequently not all of this expenditure should have classified as maintenance expenditure. Thus existing support levels have been falsely justified at too high a level which has tended to absorb a high proportion of what has often been regarded as a fixed overall marketing budget. Very few businesses would argue that they couldn't afford to invest in new plant and machinery because they were already spending too much on maintaining their existing equipment! In fact the argument is frequently reversed, but this is yet another way in which marketing activities are treated as a financial 'poor relation'.

The sort of attributes which are often identified for a marketing asset relate to customer awareness of brand name and product characteristics, propensity to purchase the brand in preference to competitors, regularity of repeat purchasing and availability of the product through the chosen channels of distribution. Each of these attributes can be quantified and a mathematical model of their relative inter-relationships can be formulated. This model can be tested and updated as the various relationships change over time and as a result of specific marketing initiatives by the business or by competition. Thus a standard physical relationship, of sorts, is being postulated which, while not as firm and predictable as for true engineering relationships, is a lot better than arguing for an increased advertising budget because sales should increase by enough to justify it! Once an initial model has been formulated the prospective impact of a change in any of the attributes can be assessed in terms of the impact on sales and hence on incremental profits and cash flows; thus providing the linkages to the management accounting system. Equally the prospective investment required to create or to avoid such a change in the given attribute can also be forecast and subsequently monitored so that additional relationships are developed over time and refined through practical observations.

This type of marketing model works equally with plans to develop new marketing assets and can be used to evaluate the proposed level of investments in marketing during the initial period. As with all business models, it is necessary to make many assumptions, including with regard to competitive responses to these new marketing initiatives. A major benefit of this type of analysis comes from forcing the business explicitly to state the assumptions which are being made. Previously many of these assumptions would have been implicit and consequently could have gone unchallenged, but once clearly stated they can be questioned and the potential impact of different assumptions can be assessed.

Clearly, this area of strategic management accounting represents one of the major challenges for many companies in the future, but some leading edge companies are using these financial techniques in this area to great advantage. It may be more than coincidence that some of the most sophisticated businesses in financially evaluating marketing activities are also the most successful marketing led companies in their respective industries. A very much simplified example of this type of approach by one such company may be a useful way to finish this chapter.

A division of this large group had a large mature brand which had a dominant share in its consumer markets and which was the major cash producer for the division. Sales for the total product category were growing only marginally. In recent periods, this brand's segment (which was the major core part of total product sales) had been declining slowly due to the launch of speciality products by competitors, who included some new entrants to the markets. The business had to decide whether to respond to this new threat which could prove to be short-lived and fashion oriented and, if so, how to do so. The existing brand had very considerable strength in terms of consumer awareness, brand loyalty and retailer distribution. However, its consumer base was in older age groups whereas the new products were primarily aimed at younger consumers, who might become loyal to these competitor brands. The company decided to launch a competing range of products but to do so under the same brand umbrella as its existing dominant brand. The launch would be supported by television advertising and couponing to encourage targeted consumers to try the new products. Because of its existing power in the market, the business was able to achieve considerable economies of scale in its advertising expenditure as much of the expenditure was transferred from the existing budget for the main brand. The justification for this saving was done against the specific objectives of the launch advertising campaign. A primary objective was clearly to create brand awareness, but most consumers already knew the existing brand name and so all that was needed was to communicate the new product range and its attributes. Also by linking the ranges, it was felt that the somewhat staid image of the existing brand could be improved and more of the younger consumers might use the core brand, as well as the new speciality range. This direct linkage was unlikely to increase the sales steal because of the existing dominant share of the core brand and the distinct consumer segmentation of the market. The company also took advantage of the opportunity to use different marketing mixes on a regional basis in terms of weight of activity and relative timing of television advertising and couponing. This enabled the launch to become a learning exercise which was particularly useful as a much more significant major new product launch was planned for nine months later. The financial evaluation process concentrated on establishing the financial impact on the business of achieving various levels of market share for the new product range, given assumed levels of sales steal from the existing products and a forecast required on-going level of marketing support. Having established objectives which appeared achievable, the information system was set up to monitor their relative achievements and to enable the different marketing strategies to be compared. The financial evaluation model also considered alternative ways of achieving the same overall sales levels, such as accepting lower consumer awareness but attaining better levels of effective distribution. The company did not, in fact, attempt to test these alternative strategies during the launch period. It was subsequently agreed that this represented a lost learning opportunity which was to prove expensive when the later, larger scale launch was made with a different and untested marketing mix.

Competitor accounting

One of the major distinguishing features of strategic management accounting is the degree to which the subject concentrates on providing comparative financial information on other businesses. The main area of interest is obviously information on competitors, but this chapter also considers briefly the other elements of the value chain, namely suppliers and direct customers, as a better understanding of their possible alternative competitive strategies can be of great assistance to a business in selecting its own strategy.

Traditionally, management accounting has concentrated on analysing the internal cost structure of the organization and then planning how this cost structure will change in the future so that a long-term plan and a short-term budget can be developed. The actual cost base is then compared against this budget as the year unfolds. For more sophisticated businesses, the original budget is flexed to take account of significant changes in the external environment so that the comparisons with actual results are more meaningful.

Benefits of traditional system

This type of traditional management accounting system provides two main types of benefit to the organization:

First, the analysis and planning process sets out the forecast financial outcome of the proposed business strategies for the planning period. This enables the managers to decide whether this outcome is satisfactory or not. If the outcome is not acceptable, the plan can be modified until the best potential result is obtained. Also, if the critical success factors have been properly highlighted in the analysis process, the sensitivity analysis on these critical success factors can be applied to the financial plan so that managers can identify the key risks and opportunities which may occur. This can again enable the plan to be modified prior to implementation, if this is considered to be appropriate, or the business may try to reduce its exposure to any particular key risk by adopting some appropriate hedging strategy.

Second, once the plan has been implemented the control process provides a method of comparing actual performance against planned performance. This comparison enables changes to be made to the plan as necessary in the light of the actual outcomes of the initial strategic decisions. These subsequent decisions should, as always, be based on the latest information available and this requires that the plan should be updated to take account of material changes since it was formulated; hence many businesses now use a rolling forecast system as the basis against which actual performance is compared.

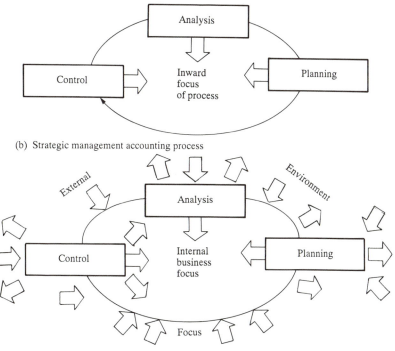

(a) Traditional management accounting process

(b) Strategic management accounting process

(External inputs impacting on process)

Figure 5.1 (a) Traditional management accounting process; (b) strategic management accounting process

The benefits of this type of management accounting system are unquestionable, but such a system does not explicitly address some of the major issues facing organizations when they are trying to develop a competitive strategy. Competitive strategies have already been defined as specific courses of action which are designed to create sustainable competitive advantages in particular products or identified markets in the pursuit of identified objectives. The issues arising from 'particular products' and 'identified markets' are dealt with in the following chapters but in this chapter the question of creating a 'sustainable competitive advantage' will be considered.

A competitive advantage can only, by definition, be created by comparison to competitors and this comparison should be as precise and clearly identified as is practicable. Thus in most good traditional management accounting systems, such competitive comparisons are implicitly included in the essential forecasts of market share gained and pricing levels which can be obtained during the planning period. However, unless these competitive assumptions are made clear and explicit, it can be very difficult during the monitoring and control process to identify the real reasons for any diversion from the forecast results. This change in emphasis is diagrammatically illustrated in Figure 5.1. For example, if forecast price increases cannot be implemented or made to stick because competitors do not increase their prices, the planned profitability of the business can be seriously affected. In such circumstances it is vitally important that the managers of the organization can determine if competitors are holding down their prices as a short-term marketing tactic in order to try to gain market share, even though they may themselves be suffering significant cost increases with a consequent adverse impact on their own profitability. Should this be the case, these competitors will need to increase their selling prices in the short term to restore profits whether the market share growth tactic has proved successful or not. Alternatively, and much more seriously, the competitors could have a relative cost advantage which will enable them to maintain the lower price levels over the much longer term. Clearly the appropriate competitive response to these alternative causes of the same market situation should be dramatically different, but the opportunity to identify the correct response depends on the quality of the financial analysis of competitors.

Relative, not absolute, costs

In any competitor accounting analysis, relative costs and prices become much more important than absolute costs. Changes in cost levels must be assessed against the comparable changes in competitors' costs over the same time period or the proposed competitive strategy may be based on very false assumptions with often disastrous consequences. This has proved to be a major problem for many USA and European based manufacturing companies. In many industries it took these companies a long time to realize that Japanese competitors really did have a sustainable cost advantage which would enable them to continue to sell at apparently very low prices. Previously it had been assumed that Japanese manufacturers were setting selling prices below their true cost levels in order to dominate the market and drive out local competition, and that they would then need to increase selling prices to restore profitability. The European Community definition of 'dumping' is particularly unhelpful in this area as it defines an exporter as dumping if it sells in the export market at prices lower than it sets for the same product in its home market. This raises major problems of measurement of actual selling prices but more importantly can deflect the attention of local producers away from the comparative cost levels achieved by overseas competition. Tariff barriers are now acknowledged generally as being useful only as temporary trade protection for a period of industrial restructuring in any particular area. If used on a long-term or permanent basis, they introduce fundamental inefficiencies into the local markets and increase overall costs and prices to customers to the disadvantage of the overall economy. The most important issue, which is considered in more detail later in the chapter, is whether the competitors are setting prices at levels which are not sustainable in the long term. If they are using their knowledge of where their long-term cost position will be by reference to the experience curve for their industry, they may be happy to incur short-term losses to develop a long-term sustainable competitive advantage.

The position can be made worse if the overseas competitor has already moved further down the cost curve than local producers and so is already setting selling prices above its current cost levels. In these situations there is not such intense profit pressure on the exporters to increase their selling prices, particularly if they are taking a long-term view of their position in this market. It only became clear that this was the case in many such industries when companies started to visit Japan and undertake much more detailed assessment of their competitors' cost bases. Following this revelation many western companies introduced dramatic cost cutting programmes to try to reduce their cost base to the levels of these competitors and so restore a competitive equilibrium. In many of these industries any such relative manufacturing cost equilibrium would have established a significant competitive advantage for the home market producers because of the transportation and importation costs imposed on Japanese companies selling their products in Europe or North America.

However, establishing a competitive strategy in a dynamic environment based on aiming at where the competition 'was' is inherently flawed and many companies have found that, despite their own significant cost cutting drives, they now face an even greater cost disadvantage than they did in the past. This is obviously caused by already more efficient competitors improving their efficiency at even greater rates than have been achieved internally. Alternatively, it has been caused by the original competitors themselves being ousted from their low cost position by new foreign competitors who may have started with lower costs for certain critical factors, eg labour, or who have come into the industry following a technological break-through which has completely transformed the previously existing experience curve, as discussed in Chapter 3. A combination of these two events when an existing fierce competitor relocates its manufacturing base to a much lower cost location is a terrifying but all too real threat.

Thus effective competitor accounting depends upon a range of factors, which will now be considered in sequence. The existing and potential competition must be identified in order to define and focus the comparative analysis. The possible alternative competitive strategies for each of these competitors should be assessed, as should their commitment to the particular product/market arena under consideration. Closely linked to competitor strategies is the comparison of relative costs and investments, and hence sustainable pricing strategies. The key to these cost comparisons is the prediction of future relative levels rather than the measurement of historic relationships. Clearly for many companies it is very difficult even to measure the historic level of competitor costs, particularly when the competitors are part of very large diversified businesses which only publish overall financial results and therefore release almost no meaningful information on the performance of specific operating divisions. Various methods of identifying differences among competitors and the originating business are considered, and the importance of the stage of development of the marketplace is also highlighted as this can dramatically affect the critical area for comparative analysis.

Defining the competition

The first stage in defining who the competitors are should be done as part of establishing the mission statement, or divisional charter, of the particular business unit under consideration. As previously discussed, competitive strategies have to be established at the level where the business sells products in distinct markets and against identifiable competitors. Thus this definition of the individual business units and how their quantified objectives have been extracted from and related to their mission statement and business goals should highlight the existing competition. If it is not possible easily to identify the area from which competitors will come this normally indicates that the business unit has not, itself, been properly defined. This is where the concept of the Strategic Business Unit (SBU) is helpful because each SBU should have a clearly defined purpose of selling defined products to defined markets and this combination of products and markets should distinguish one SBU from any other in the organization. In some cases the actual product (ie goods or service) may not define competitors because the customer may be purchasing a group of attributes or benefits rather than the specific product and the real competitors will be other businesses providing what the customer perceives as a comparable group of benefits even though the product may physically appear very different. For example, cinemas show films to the public and thus compete directly with other cinemas; however video rental shops also enable the public to watch recently released films, as do the even newer satellite based television film channels. Hence these are also competitors which are simply using a different channel of distribution. Cinemas may well decide that these are not their only competition as their customers may choose to spend their leisure time in alternative ways and thus competitors should include 'live' theatre, spectator-based sporting events and other forms of passive entertainment.

Identifying competitors therefore consists of finding other businesses who supply alternative products to the same markets even though they may use different strategies, including very different channels of distribution. For example, in the UK, retail dairies (ie businesses who deliver milk on a daily basis to the end consumers) had established fierce competitive strategies against other retail dairies (the obvious visible competition). This competition was based on service levels but did not include price which was uniform across the industry because of the pricing control exercised by the Milk Marketing Board. Thus some dairies would emphasize the time of delivery, while others extended the range of products delivered by the milkman. Unfortunately the cost of providing the service increased as the market place for other retail services matured rapidly. Consequently a new form of competitor emerged with a completely different method of satisfying the ultimate consumer need, which is clearly for milk to be available in the home for use as needed. The large supermarket chains entered the market using a combination of competitive advantages including their bulk-buying power and technological developments which increased the shelf life of the product. They were also aided by packaging improvements, which enabled larger volume plastic containers to be used without tainting the product, and the increasing car ownership of their customers, which enabled them to travel to larger out-of-town supermarkets and buy more bulky products, which would have been difficult to carry home on public transport (eg the bus). This combination of factors allowed the supermarkets to attack the retail dairies on price alone. Their competitive strategy was not based on any level of service at all, but hinged on their existing customer base who were already driving to their large supermarkets and could be willing to buy yet another product at the same time if the price was attractive. In terms of the Ansoff matrix considered in Chapter 3, the supermarkets are clearly selling more products to existing customers based on price advantages, which is potentially very effective if the original competitive advantage has reduced in perceived value.

For the existing retail dairies this created a new level of competitive pressure which resulted in a variety of strategic responses. One type of response was to try to convince their customer that the value of the service provided was worth the extra cost. An alternative was to reduce the service by cutting out the most expensive elements and thus attempting to become more cost competitive. In this example it was possible to reduce the cost without giving the new competitor a direct opportunity to gain an even greater share of the market. This was achieved in some areas by cutting out Sunday milk deliveries which cannot be directly countered as many of the retailer competitors have still, by law, to be closed on Sundays.

Another very similar example in the UK can be given by examining the competitive response of building societies (the UK equivalent of savings and loan institutions) to the seemingly arrogant attitude of the clearing banks towards their customers over the question of opening hours. It appears that each major bank looked only at the other banks when considering their competitive strategy. Thus as long as they were all open for the same, albeit decreasing, periods they could reduce their costs and maintain their relative competitive position. However, building societies were able to take advantage of this by continuing to open for longer hours during the week as well as on Saturday mornings. Their attitude to the cost problem was to invest heavily in front office (ie teller related) computer systems and they added value to this aspect of their business by expanding their product offerings (eg cheque books, regular direct payments, and even paying interest on current accounts). The clearing banks have had to respond by increasing opening hours, including re-opening some branches on Saturday mornings, and accelerating the development of automated teller machines (the machines in the wall outside the bank branch which are supposed to stay open 24 hours a day, 7 days a week). This can be seen as a classic example of two sets of competitive strategies coming into head-to-head competition as they each try to take an ever larger share of one total market. What starts out as a niche or focus strategy can become eventually industry-wide and brings a whole new group of competitors into play. In other words, banks and building societies both now see themselves as capable of providing all the financial services needed by the individual.

A competitor analysis based on relative efficiencies against direct, obvious and existing competitors can be far too simplistic and may indeed attract new entrants into the market, if they can identify a new method of distribution, etc, where they have a sustainable advantage. The areas of concern for this competitor analysis can be summarized using the Porter model referred to in Chapter 3 and reproduced in a slightly different format as Figure 5.2.

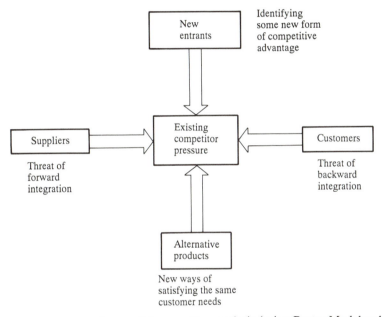

Figure 5.2 Current and potential competitor analysis (using Porter Model as basis)

It is also possible that the significance of competitors may change suddenly as a result of external factors, which may be legislative or environmental. Privatization of businesses is one obvious such factor, but the good news for any competing business is that this is normally heralded well in advance so that the changes in competitor strategy should, at least, not come as a big surprise. Other changes in ownership, such as a management buy-out of a division from a large well-diversified business, can have similarly dramatic effects on competitive strategies and the changes can be implemented much more rapidly. However, much more subtle changes can also have wide-ranging impacts. Staying with the retail services industry as the example, there have been significant changes in some sectors of petrol retailing in the UK over the last few years. Originally motorway service stations had to pay a levy on all the sales revenues they generated including petrol sales, and this levy was generally incorporated into the retail selling price at the petrol pump. Consequently motorway service stations were always uncompetitive in terms of price. They made sales based purely on convenience, ie their location at the side of the motorway. Thus the alternative for the long distance drivers, who needed fuel in order to complete their journey, was to leave the motorway to look for a cheaper source of fuel. The true opportunity cost involved in this search would normally outweigh the savings made on the eventual petrol purchase. During this period the operators of these service stations were also required to offer a broad range of petrol brands and thus they were unable to use their potential bulk buying power effectively with their suppliers. This method of paying rent was suddenly changed as was the requirement to sell more than one brand, and the operators were then able to buy effectively and to recover their operating costs from their total contribution based on the normal volume and price relationship which had always been used by the majority of petrol station operators. Pump prices moved down to become significantly closer to other competitive sources of petrol, thus removing the previously high incentive for motorists to minimize their petrol purchases while on the motorway.

In strategic management accounting terms, the levy on sales had been treated as an incremental variable cost in the past and hence had been fully passed on to customers in higher selling prices. Once this price was converted to a seemingly fixed basis, either by being reflected in a purchase price for the freehold of the site or as part of an overall rental cost, the businesses felt that they had much more flexibility in selecting their competitive strategies. Consequently, they were able to price competitively on items which were already price-sensitive and to advertise these prices much more openly. This left the motorway service station operators with the problem of recovering their total costs either through substantially increased volumes or by increasing contribution levels on product groups which were felt to be less price-sensitive. These types of choices are always available to any business when selecting the most appropriate competitive strategies for its range of products, and the company should, itself, decide on how it wishes to regard critical costs from a strategic viewpoint rather than automatically accepting the traditional internally based management accounting perspective.

Another competitive change in this market has been through the entry of a new player with a very different strategy to the existing competitors. With the growth of large out-of-town shopping centres based around a large supermarket, these sophisticated supermarket retailers rapidly identified a new way of attracting customers to their new retailing locations. Discount priced petrol stations were opened on these sites, using the logic that customers would have to use their cars to drive out to reach these off-centre locations. Also using the reducing brand loyalty among petrol purchasers, the retailers were able to sell their own branded petrol. This strengthened their competitive advantages for such a mature commodity style product which is largely bought on price and convenience in the absence of any other loyalty generating marketing ploy such as trading stamps. However, the critical factor is that their strategy had another aim than simply selling petrol at an inevitably very small profit margin; they wanted to attract more customers to their new stores. Indeed some retailers made the linkage direct and obvious, by giving vouchers away with petrol purchases which could only be redeemed against other purchases in their next-door supermarket.

In this case, the original petrol retailers, with their focused business, are now facing competition which is not exclusively driven by the direct financial return which can be made out of selling their mainstream product. However, it should be remembered that most petrol companies have tried for several years to improve the financial return from their large retail petrol sites by increasing the range of merchandise sold in the shops located on most of these premises. This competitive strategy can once again be described in terms of the Ansoff matrix as expanding the range of products sold to existing customers. Alternatively in financial terms it can be regarded as increasing the total contribution which can be generated from a given high level of fixed costs such as are incurred by having the site and staff selling petrol and oil. In many cases the new strategy can tend to overwhelm the original base business and strategically in the longer term no such costs should automatically be regarded as fixed. Also these seemingly small moves in terms of adding new products or markets can bring the business up against new competitors who may fiercely attack the business on all fronts as their defensive way of seeing off this unwelcome intrusion. It should be remembered that many of the major oil companies only moved into retailing of petrol and oil as a vertical integration out of their original exploration and refining businesses. This is considered further in Chapter 10 but it has undoubtedly brought them into direct competition with companies whose only area of business is direct retailing to customers, and who consequently can have a clearly focused strategy in terms of their customer base.

These new large supermarkets have also used some new competitive strategies to overcome one of their most obvious and seemingly permanent disadvantages in the eyes of some of their potential customers: their out of town location. To many non-car owning or immobile customers, the distance and frequent lack of any convenient means of public transport made the new out-of-town shopping malls completely inaccessible. Also the large supermarkets have a very high level of fixed costs whether they are full of customers or virtually empty. Many working customers have very restricted opportunities to do their shopping and most of the large retail chains have consequently extended their opening hours (8.00 am to 8.00 pm at least) to cope with this segment of their market. This inevitably means that there are some periods of this very long operating week when there are very few customers in the store (eg Tuesday mid-morning) and many of the larger out-of-town supermarkets now provide a free bus service to and from their store during these low activity periods. By doing so, they not only attract new customers, but bring them to the shops at the most convenient time from the retailer's perspective. Indeed where the location is suitable the retailer may set up a rota system of collecting from one area (say south of the store) on Tuesday, etc.

Clearly this has presented the smaller local stores with a completely new competitor and has changed one of the key success factors of retailing: *location*. If your shop is in the wrong place for some of your customers, transporting the customers to your shop seems to be an answer. The financial justification is quite simple: if the contribution generated on these genuinely incremental sales is substantially greater than the incremental costs incurred in the transportation project, the new competitive strategy will increase profits. However if most of these customers would have come to the shop anyway, using their own transport, then the financial justification is less clear cut. It is possible that giving them an incentive to do their shopping during a slack period at the store will increase total sales and thus the overall contribution generated. This could occur in two ways: first, these customers may buy more products because they can shop in a more relaxed and pleasant environment and also because they do not have the problem of transporting these products home themselves. Second, other shoppers with much more restricted shopping opportunities may have been put off using the store because it was so very crowded at peak times (eg Saturday mornings). By reducing some of this overcrowding, these shoppers may also be attracted into increasing their usage and hence the potential profits should increase. This particular result may be achieved more cost effectively and in a more specific way by offering a direct incentive to shoppers to come at specified times. Such promotional ideas as giving double savings stamps and reducing selling prices of specific items during particular periods of the week are also used to achieve this.

Another service industry in England and Wales where the major competitors have been transformed recently is estate agencies. Estate agents are responsible for handling the vast majority of the sales of domestic and commercial properties. The industry originally developed in a very fragmented way, being dominated by small localized firms, many of which still operated as partnerships. Over time, some of these firms had merged or been acquired to form larger regional groupings, with a few developing looser relationships with other firms in other geographic areas so that they could provide some kind of nationwide service. However, the major industry upheaval was caused by completely new organizations entering the sector, with only a peripheral interest in actually selling houses. As the financial services industry rapidly developed in the 1980s some of the companies in it identified that the ability to gain access to customers at the most appropriate time should be a major competitive advantage in the future. For life assurance companies this 'most appropriate time' could be linked to house purchase as many people take out new endowment life assurance policies as the means of repaying their mortgages. Consequently some insurance companies and also banks started to establish, through a massive series of acquisitions, national chains of estate agents which were justified in gaining them access to a steady stream of potential customers. Some building societies, the largest providers of actual mortgage finance, also moved into the industry. Other banks and building societies have developed a different, more direct, strategy by establishing links with the insurance companies. These insurance companies do not want to provide the actual mortgage finance themselves but want to sell the life policy to the new house purchaser.

This acquisition-based strategy proved very expensive in the short-term as activity in the housing market went into dramatic decline with the rapid rise in interest rates during 1989. However any such new competitive strategy is clearly a long-term measure and is principally designed to position the businesses for the maturity phase of the personal financial services industry. It is therefore surprising that several of these newly created national chains of estate agencies are taking very short-term action to reduce their operating losses, by closing substantial numbers of branches and making redundant large numbers of employees. Indeed a few entrepreneurs have been able to re-purchase all or part of their original business at substantial discounts to the prices at which they sold them between two and four years earlier!

All these examples have been designed to illustrate the need for businesses to consider carefully who they regard both as current and potential competitors. Competitive analysis should be done regularly on all current competitors and all potential competitors should be monitored so that no strategic moves they make come as unpleasant surprises to the business. As far as possible, the business wants to adjust its own competitive strategy to keep these potential significant players from entering the marketplace. The estate agency example illustrates the potential danger of trying to respond rapidly to a new competitive strategy without necessarily having thought through the long-term implications for the business.

Current and future competitors

If one of the best competitive strategies is to stop new competitors from emerging, it becomes important for the business to analyse what types of entry barriers can be erected. An entry barrier can be anything which represents a significant economic disincentive to a new business which is considering entering a particular market, or developing and launching a competitive product, and is shown diagrammatically in Figure 5.3. Therefore, it can either increase their perception of the risks involved or it may reduce their anticipated financial return from the investment involved. Consequently some entry barriers are fairly obvious while others are much more subtle but equally effective.

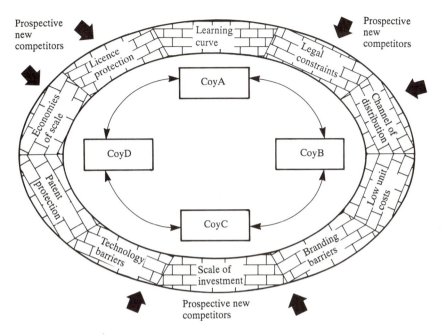

Figure 5.3 Use of entry barriers

The sheer scale of the investment required to set up a viable operation may be a substantial barrier to new entrants and this is frequently the case for high technology industries where the overall length of the product life cycle is also very uncertain. For example, the fixed costs involved in establishing a silicon chip manufacturing business are very high indeed. The risk is obviously that selling prices will fall substantially, as they did, shortly after these very substantial new investments have been committed. This highlights the need for these potential competitors to be kept out because, if they actually invest, this large entry barrier no longer has any value as a disincentive. Also, if the cost structure of the industry is predominantly fixed with a low component element of truly variable cost as it is for the silicon chip industry, once in these new competitors will fight fiercely for more market share as soon as the dramatically increased productive capacity exceeds demand. This will exacerbate the problem of falling selling prices and a serious price war can quickly result. It will prove very difficult to force any of these new entrants to leave the industry in many cases because although their original investment was very high, it will probably have a very low residual value. Consequently the financial opportunity cost of staying in is very low. The specific application and relevance of exit barriers are considered in the next section of this chapter.

One possible way of keeping these potential new competitors out is to maximize early sales demand and so force the industry as far down the experience curve as possible in the shortest practicable time. If the experience curve has a significant impact in this industry, this will change the relative cost levels of the established producer and any new prospective company. The strategy is to increase the cumulative volume produced so as to reduce production costs per unit accordingly for the original entrants into the industry. Consequently any new competitors will now face very large operating cost disadvantages when they start up in business. Thus, in addition to their large initial investment, they will make substantial operating losses in their first years of operation. This is assuming that market selling prices have fallen at least in line with the real cost decreases and that it is these falling real prices which have stimulated the increased levels of demand.

Indeed it is probably true that, for this pre-emptive competitive strategy to be fully successful, the original business will initially have to reduce selling prices below its own current cost levels in order to increase sales volumes sufficiently. Thus as mentioned earlier in this chapter, the business is effectively making a financial investment in its market position by deliberately incurring losses until its cost level has reduced, through increased efficiencies etc, to below these reduced selling prices which it has created in the market. This is normally referred to as implementing a 'penetration' pricing strategy but the principle advantage, which is the decreased profitability of new competitors entering the industry, is often missed. In too many cases the first company in the market looks at the short-term opportunity only, and so takes advantage of this dominant position to set prices at a level which enables it to show a good profit level initially. This 'skimming' type of pricing strategy may seem attractive in the short-term but it will delay the growth of volume sales due to the high selling prices. This lower sales volume reduces the cost advantage which the business can build up over any prospective competitors, because its cumulative volume will be less and it is the cumulative total volume which gives rise to the major benefits of the experience curve. Also the early high profit margins may quickly attract several new competitors. If the cost structure of the industry is one of high fixed costs and low variable costs, a change in pricing strategy once the new capacity has been installed will not prove successful for the reasons mentioned above. These new competitors must be kept out if at all possible.

Some industries can protect themselves through patents or product licences etc, but at most these provide protection for the prescribed period. The business should utilize this protected period to position itself for its optimum competitive strategy in the phase of free markets which will inevitably follow. This area of competitive strategy is of critical importance in the pharmaceutical industry because a company launching a new drug has a limited period of patent protection in which to recover its massive investment in developing, testing and launching the new product. Once the patent has expired the market will be supplied by several 'generic' products which can effectively copy the attributes of the original product. The originating company therefore has either to become the low cost, efficient producer of the now commodity style product, which may be possible due to the cumulative production level it will have as a competitive advantage, or to find a different competitive strategy. One alternative is to heavily brand the new drug during its protected period and try to maintain this position when new products are launched on their 'me-too' platforms. This is discussed below but for pharmaceuticals this can depend on the channel of distribution through which the drug is sold, as the medical professional is more likely than the average member of the public to make their buying decision on the attributes of the product rather than the brand association.

However for many businesses, with and without any initial regulatory protection, the potential use of economies of scale and the other attributes of the experience curve is very limited and insufficient to safeguard their early dominant position in the industry. These businesses need to create alternative entry barriers to deter potential new competitors from coming into the industry.

One commonly erected entry barrier uses heavy marketing investment in brands to try to create customer loyalty to the existing product offerings. If successful this can force any new entrant to invest very heavily in advertising and promotional activity so as to create an alternative brand. This significantly increases their risk of failure but also magnifies their consequent financial losses as they try to gain market share. A new competitor could try a different positioning in the market and reduce their selling prices well below those of the existing branded products. This type of unbranded low price strategy is much more likely to be successful for a more mature product where its attributes are well understood by its users and the ability to differentiate the branded product is more restricted. It may, however, still be important to the original businesses in the market to keep out all new entrants at any pricing level. These new entrants could automatically affect the future profit levels which are achievable in the industry, particularly in a market which is no longer showing strong growth.

Some companies have achieved this by dominating one critical aspect of the industry and hence making it much more difficult for the new business to get established. This can be done in some fast-moving consumer goods (fmcg) industries by developing a plethora of separate brands, even though this multitude of brands do not increase the size of the total market. This argument can reasonably be applied to the washing powder industry which is dominated globally by Procter and Gamble and Lever Bros (part of Unilever). It is difficult to justify the wide range of washing powder brands on the premise that this significantly increases the total market size. People presumably wash their clothes when they are dirty. Also each of the businesses involved tends to have a very similar spread of brands with almost the same set of value propositions for the consumer. The brands are also deliberately supported individually without direct linkage back to the owning business so that no real group identity is created with the consumer. Thus there is little economy of scale involved in the marketing messages being sent to the end consumer. A wide range of brands will however mean that retailers do not want to stock any more new products which may be offered to them by a new entrant, and it is therefore very difficult for this new potential competitor to gain a distribution foothold. Without strong retail distribution, any other marketing expenditure will be wasted as consumers are unable to find the new product even if they are made aware of it by media advertising or direct couponing, etc. However this competitive marketing strategy can still be effective even if the new business does gain some degree of retail distribution. When a consumer market is mature there is much research to support the view that many consumers have developed a strong level of loyalty to one particular brand and are not interested in switching brands. Other consumers are willing to try other products and will select their alternative purchases on almost a random basis from those new products on offer. Hence if the existing market is dominated by two or three brands, any new brand that is launched will have a chance of picking up between one-third and a quarter of the floating consumers. If there are already twenty or thirty existing brands on offer, the newly launched product will find it much more difficult to achieve a viable market share. This is more clearly illustrated numerically in Figure 5.4.

Assuumptions:	50% of consumers are loyal to one brand		
	50% of consumers will switch and try another brand		
Number of existing brands		2	20
Potential switching consumers		50%	50%
Share of switching customers trying new product based on random decision-making		25%	2.5%
[Obviously, new entrants can increase their prospective share by investing more on marketing their new product, but the potential financial return has been greatly reduced and the chances of success are also lower!]			

Figure 5.4 Impact of increased number of brands

Also a larger number of existing brands enables the current businesses to position the brands differently so as to cover all the possible marketing propositions which could be used by incoming new businesses. Thus the same business could supply the market with apparently independent brands which are quite differently positioned in the eyes of the consumer; eg a premium priced high quality brand, a medium position of good value and good quality, and a much lower priced commodity style product. In this case it is much more difficult for the new entrant to identify any unique selling proposition for their proposed product which could be used to lure customers away from existing products. This is particularly true if more than one business is already in the market and each current competitor is also maintaining a similar range of brands, thus offering a wide range of choices to the consumer. Indeed even if the new entrant identifies a technological or marketing breakthrough there is still no guarantee of success in such an established market. In washing powders, such breakthroughs have been achieved in the form of cold-water washing powders and, more recently, environmentally friendly washing powders. However it is relatively easy for the major companies to match these new products technically. If they see a serious competitive threat they can launch their own new brands before the new entrant has a chance to establish its distribution base and gain a substantial share of the market. Consequently, a new entrant into such a well-established market probably needs to concentrate on identifying a new channel of distribution for its product if it wants to increase the chances of success against the already entrenched and fiercely competitive existing businesses.

It should be clear, from the strategic management accounting viewpoint, that each of these pre-emptive style competitive strategies should be financially evaluated before being implemented. This is by no means easy as it involves comparing a sizeable up-front investment with the *potential* saving from deterring a possible new competitor.

This comparison will normally need to be done over a period of several years as it is the cumulative effect of the potential lost market share which justifies the pre-emptive investment strategy. The best financial decision analysis technique over long periods of time is discounted cash flow (DCF), and therefore the alternative impacts should be compared using DCF analysis. A major problem immediately becomes the reconciliation of employing a sophisticated analytical technique on projected cash flows which are based on some very broad brush assumptions.

The most debatable assumptions are regarding the potential future size of the market, the relative shares of the market that would be gained both with and without the new competitor, and the profit margins that could be earned in the different competitive situations. The difference between the present values of the cash flow projections based on each set of assumptions will demonstrate the maximum amount it is worth investing *now* to try to prevent the new competitor entering the industry. As it is the difference in present values which is of interest rather than the absolute values themselves, the problems involved in forecasting are much more likely to be manageable. A sensitivity analysis should be carried out using the most likely ranges for market size and market shares etc, excluding the new competitor. These can then be recomputed with the inclusion of the new competitor and incorporating a range of suitably reduced market shares or profit margins. It may be necessary to increase the expected size of the total market if it is anticipated that another entrant would increase total consumption of the product. This is clearly more likely for a growth market than for a more mature and already fully developed market, where the new entrants will succeed or fail based on stealing market share from the existing market competitors, such as in the washing powder example. By using these alternative forecast outcomes an expected cost to the existing company of the competitive entry can be calculated. The present value of this expected financial loss can be taken as the maximum current investment which can be financially justified. In strategic financial decisions, it is very often helpful to work backwards to try to calculate what it is worth spending either to achieve something or to avoid something happening. Many businesses seem to find this a difficult concept and yet this reverse type of analysis is actually used quite frequently in financial decisions. For example, every business has to decide whether it is worth paying the insurance premium which has been quoted so as to avoid the risk of financial loss if its factory or office block burns down, etc. The insurance company can employ the statistical techniques which are relevant to the large numbers of insurance contracts it will undertake and hence can calculate the premium quite accurately based on its forecasts of the losses which will occur across the whole market. To the individual company this statistical calculation has no practical relevance. It has to decide based on the financial impact on the business of a loss occurring relative to the cost of taking out the insurance contract. Some level of premium, relative to the corresponding risk which is to be covered, will represent an unacceptable cost and the company will self-insure rather than pass the risk onto the insurance experts. Because of the use of this type of financial analysis many companies are now only insuring outside their group for major catastrophe occurrences, which would otherwise place the entire business in jeopardy.

Effectively this type of financial analysis is working backwards; the business is comparing the present value of the forecast financial impact of the potential event, with the cost of the investment or expenditure which is required to prevent the event taking place. Unfortunately, unlike the simpler insurance premium problem, it is not possible to get an accurate quotation from anyone as to how much the business has to spend now to be *certain* of deterring a new competitor. Also the range of these potential cost estimates will differ depending on the type of investment being considered, but this lack of certainty should still not negate the value of carrying out the analysis.

The required pre-emptive investment may be made in various different forms which can all be equally valid as long as they are appropriate for creating the desired type of entry barrier. Thus if the entry barrier is to be created by accelerating the business down the experience curve as fast as possible, expenditure on fixed assets may be increased. The investment required for this particular entry barrier strategy could alternatively be to set selling prices below short-term cost levels so as to boost demand rapidly before competitors enter the industry. In this case the business will show losses which are, as mentioned before, really an investment in a long-term competitive strategy. Alternatively a range of heavily supported brands could be developed so that all the incremental investment is in intangible assets, but lack of material substance to the investment should not concern the company, as discussed in Chapter 4.

The strategic value of the competitive positioning is what matters and a very strong intangible asset may be created by developing an exclusive distribution system. This has been successfully done in the UK by the motor vehicle manufacturers, who have created exclusive sales agencies for their cars through appointed dealerships. These authorized dealers are granted sole rights to sell a particular manufacturer's cars in a designated geographic area. The dealer therefore should concentrate on competing against other dealers in the same area who will, of course, be selling other manufacturers' vehicles. Any potential new entrants to the market have to find a way of accessing the end consumer and this means either developing their own distribution network (ie geographically spread range of exclusive dealers) or finding a new channel of distribution. What is particularly interesting is that many of the larger vehicle dealers have competitive dealer franchises in different areas (eg a company may be a Ford dealer in one area, a General Motors dealer in another area, and a Volkswagen/Audi dealer somewhere else) and the major motor manufacturers do not appear to have a problem with this approach. Thus it is clear that it is not the total dedication of the company to one manufacturer that is critical. However, the maintenance of exclusive geographic dealerships does give them greater control over their consumer marketing and the service level provided, which is seen as being critical to the end consumer's view of their total product offering. There have been some specific attempts to break down this exclusive arrangement, notably by trying to sell a broad range of different cars in one shopping mall so that customers could make instant, direct comparisons, but so far none has been successful.

This type of distribution channel based entry barrier can be particularly effective against international competitors where their competitive disadvantage is in terms of local market knowledge rather than in the areas of product technology or costs of manufacturing.

Alternative strategies for each of these competitors

Once the existing and potential competitors have been identified, the next stage of the competitor analysis is to consider what principal strategies each of these competitors will employ in the marketplace. Most companies would argue that they do this basic part of the competitor analysis but the really important further element of competitive strategy analysis is to identify the alternative strategies that *could* be implemented by different competitors and to plan responses to each serious potential threat.

This requires an understanding of several factors about competitors and these clearly include relative cost structures and levels of existing and planned investments. However, before considering these in detail, there are other important issues which will determine the alternative strategies which will be considered by competitors. The first of these is the opposite end of the entry barriers considered in the previous section and is usually described as an exit barrier.

An exit barrier can be defined as anything which increases the perceived cost to the company of leaving the industry and which may therefore affect the strategic decisions as to whether to exit or stay in the industry. Obviously the greater the exit barrier the more likely it is that the competitor will remain and this should be taken into account when formulating competitive strategies. It is also important to note that it is the competitor's *perception* of the costs associated with leaving and this may be based on false assumptions. An extreme example may make the point much clearer. In the mining industry it is not easy or cheap to exit the industry if the selling price of the extracted mineral (say, coal) is reduced in the short term. If the coal-mine is to be closed down there will be significant costs incurred in redundancy pay to workers, making the mine area safe, re-landscaping the surrounding area, etc, while the funds generated by selling the plant and equipment will be minimal. This use of sale proceeds (ie net realizable value) rather than the original cost of the investment (which would have been considerable) is obviously a key element of any financial decision. It hinges upon the economic logic of ignoring any sunk costs and only including incremental future cash flows in the financial evaluation. Thus the difference between the initial investment cost and the realizable value of the investment, if the exit decision is taken, can be important in creating an exit barrier; the larger the difference, the greater the likelihood that the competitor will stay in the industry. This was the argument put forward in the silicon chip example used earlier in the chapter. However, in most cases, the act of exiting from the industry merely realizes this loss rather than creates it; thus including the total difference between the book value and the realizable value of assets as a cost of exit is a false assumption. The key element is the low value of the opportunity cost associated with staying in the industry.

In the current coal mining example it is quite possible that it may make economic sense for the mine to be kept open even if it is making a loss, as long as the present value of the total losses is less than the costs which would be incurred in closing it down. Clearly, if the loss is expected to continue in the long term, it will probably make financial sense to close down but once closed significant costs would have to be incurred to re-open the production facilities. Consequently even if selling prices rise marginally above direct variable manufacturing costs it may not be financially worthwhile to invest the money needed to open up again, whereas if the mine had been kept open it would now be generating a contribution towards its fixed costs. In these types of industries managers tend to keep production facilities open through what they hope will be temporary downturns in demand or selling prices. It is particularly important that the potential competitive response to any given change in the environment or company strategy is forecast, and also, in this type of case, that whenever possible potential new entrants are strongly dissuaded from making their initial investment: once in the industry, they will be very difficult to get rid of.

There are other aspects of exit barriers and these are shown diagrammatically in Figure 5.5. Several of these are also relevant to the coal mining example, in that the ability to sell existing assets for a high realizable value will often depend on the alternative uses to which the assets can be put. A dedicated high technology factory will have less alternative uses, and hence probably a lower realizable value, than a standard portal steel-framed building which can be easily adapted to a multitude of industrial and commercial uses, or even transformed into indoor tennis courts.

If the assets used in the business have a long economic life before they need to be replaced, another effective exit barrier is created. Companies often stay in their industries until they face a major re-investment decision which forces them to evaluate the financial return being achieved against the replacement cost of the assets employed rather than against the net realizable value of their historic investment. Hence if the assets are replaced on a piecemeal

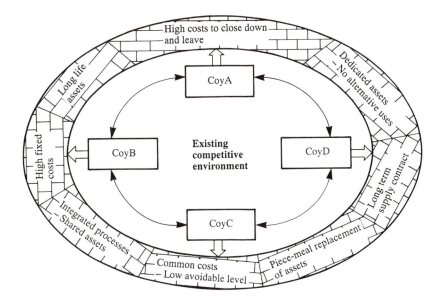

Figure 5.5 Use of exit barriers

basis spread over a long period rather than in one major lump of capital investment, it is quite possible that this re-evaluation of financial return against replacement cost is not made and the company stays in the industry even though this is not strictly economically justified. Remember that it is competitors' perceptions that are relevant.

The cost structure of the industry is also very important as a high level of fixed costs will tend to keep companies in an industry as long as selling prices make a positive contribution over variable costs. In reality, this decision should depend upon the forecast time-scale for the continuation of the depressed selling prices relative to the period over which costs are really fixed: in the *long* term, all costs are variable. Therefore this high fixed cost base becomes even more important when allied to long-term committed costs such as a long-term lease agreement on property or plant and equipment, which would be very expensive for the lessee to buy its way out of, or an agreement to purchase a minimum guaranteed amount of raw materials, etc, over the succeeding years (eg long-term energy supply contracts taken out to gain a discount against the current market price by guaranteeing the volume which would be used annually over the next ten years). Another variation would be a licensing agreement entered into for any particularly relevant technology (such as computer software) where the terms specify minimum royalty payments each year and punitive penalties for early termination. The effect of this type of long-term commitment is not only to change what would often be a variable cost into a relatively fixed cost but dramatically to extend the period for which the cost remains as a fixed commitment of the business. Clearly a large lump sum payment on early termination reduces the attractiveness of leaving the industry, and it is important that a company knows if its competitors are exposed to such long-term contracts.

Another potentially significant exit barrier is created when the competitor is engaged in a number of related businesses so that some of its costs are shared among several industries. This could be due to the level of vertical integration in the business, such as in the oil industry, where the processes involved in the refineries inevitably produce a range of products which are sold to very different markets. In this type of integrated business, it may be practically impossible for the competitor to leave one segment of the industry without giving up all of its interests in the total area. The oil refining process splits crude oil into a range of different graded petroleum products as well as petrol/gasoline and each of these by-products has a significant potential sales value. The oil refining competitor may therefore find it difficult to exit from, say, only the aviation fuel market if its processing automatically produces a certain proportion of this grade of fuel, even if this particular market is showing an unsatisfactory rate of return. The exit decision may, in these cases, have to be taken using the overall return being achieved on the oil refinery and its complete range of outputs. (However the oil company may be able to vary the mix of products produced through the refinery or decide to reduce its commitment to a specifically unattractive market sector, eg by selling its output in bulk rather than marketing it under a branded umbrella, etc.)

Similarly, there could be common costs incurred across several industries and these could be in production, sales and marketing, distribution, or even support areas of the business. This aspect of common costs impacting on potential exit decisions is a classic example of the application of the avoidable cost concept discussed in Chapter 4. If administration and order processing is a significant cost for the company, it may have set up a very sophisticated, automated system to cope efficiently with the complete range of its businesses so as to reap the full benefits of the economies of scale available. On the basis of the apportionment of these total costs to each area of the business, one particular industry may appear to be losing money, and so the company may consider closing down this operation. However, as part of this financial evaluation it should only include the cost which will be saved (ie avoided) by such a decision. If the major costs of the shared system will still be incurred, the avoidable cost saving may be very small; in the extreme case it may almost only be the paper on which the invoices, etc, are printed. Thus the way in which the competition is organized in terms of centralization/decentralization and levels of vertical integration may have a significant impact on their strategic decisions regarding leaving a particular industry.

This can be viewed as increasing their commitment to a particular product, market, or combination thereof, but this question of the level of commitment of a competitor has a much more important role in dictating the alternative strategies which may be considered. It is essential that the analysing company knows for each competitor where this particular business fits within their overall business portfolio as described in Chapter 3. Even if some of these other elements of the total portfolio are not direct competitors a basic review of their position is often very useful. This review should try to reveal what pressures there may be on these other businesses as this can have a dramatic impact on the available competitive strategies in the directly competing businesses. For example, suppose a large competitor has a well-diversified range of other businesses, which are not themselves direct competitors to the analysing company. If the directly competing industry is in a stage of rapid growth, it may require substantial levels of capital investment over the next few years to match this growth and even greater levels of investment if it is planned to increase market share. In this growth phase, it is important to be able to grow substantially faster than the market and hence have achieved a dominant market share when the industry matures. The ability of a competitor to respond to such an initiative may be determined by the relative position of its other businesses. If this competitor has several relatively old, mature and very successful businesses which are all strong net cash producers and this growth industry represents the only serious prospect of growth for the group in the medium term, it will probably be very seriously committed to maintaining its market share. It will also have little trouble in obtaining the funding needed to match or even outspend the increased marketing investment planned by the initiating company. However, an alternative is that the competitor has a portfolio containing several growth businesses, all of which require substantial investments in the short term. If its single main, mature cash-producing business is also facing severe price competition from new overseas entrants, which have dramatically reduced selling prices and rapidly gained significant market shares, the competitor may find it impossible to respond to such an aggressive marketing strategy.

As well as understanding these other business pressures which may affect competitors' responses, the competitor analysis should also rank the particular competing business in terms of its importance to the total portfolio of the competitor. If the competitor is a totally focused business competing in one area only, and has never shown any intention of diversifying, or even worse, has tried diversification in the past with disastrous results, it should be clear that the business is critical to their future. Hence competitive response is likely to be rapid and aggressive. This will also normally be true if the particular business is the largest element of the group's portfolio because any adverse change in the competitive position will have severe implications for the overall group's performance. However, rapid and dramatic competitive response may also be encountered unexpectedly from what appears to be a relatively small, insignificant part of a large group. This is frequently the result if this division is, in fact, the origin of the group or is the part of the business in which the current group chief executive spent the early years of a very successful career. In other words, competitors are not always totally objective and financially rational in their level of commitment to any particular business segment. However, a sound financial analysis can indicate the most likely competitive responses.

Oligopoly modelling

The ideal outcome of this assessment of potential competitor strategies is to identify a limited number of critical competitors, both existing and potential. For each of these, the analysis should highlight the degree of importance of the sector and the relative strength of their other businesses in their group portfolio. In most industries, the market is dominated and led by relatively few companies and this makes it possible to construct a simulation model of the market and these major players. Using computer modelling techniques it is now practical to forecast alternative responses to strategic initiatives (eg reducing selling prices, increasing capacity, raising the level of consumer advertising, etc) and to allow the model to predict the overall outcome for each of the businesses involved.

Using such a model should enable a company to highlight those initiatives which are most difficult for key competitors to respond to, given their current overall business position. It should also indicate certain initiatives which would expose the initiator to severe downside risks if competitors responded in certain ways. This enables the company either to avoid the particular strategy or to institute an appropriate risk reduction strategy at the same time. Clearly, as with all forecasting techniques, the only certainty with such a market model is that it will be wrong in that it will not accurately predict all responses and subsequent outcomes. This makes it vitally important that any attempt at oligopoly modelling is used as a learning process, so that the model is reviewed and updated as each new set of competitive responses is received. It must also be understood that the relationships being modelled are not static and constant, but are subject to very dynamic changes as both the environment alters and the overall business position of each competitor varies. Further, as has already been emphasized in this book, strategic decisions are taken by people and not by companies. Therefore, as decision-makers change, so may the competitive responses of their companies.

One area of modelling which is extremely useful but which can also be very susceptible to changes in decision-makers is the question of risk reduction strategies. A common financial example of this is with respect to hedging strategies, whether in terms of foreign currencies, commodities or interest rates, etc. The basic economic rationale for any risk reduction strategy is to reduce the perceived risk by more than the return is reduced. This justification, as discussed in Chapter 3, depends therefore on the risk/return relationship for the particular business and, more specifically, for the key decision-maker involved. An extreme example is to consider whether the decision-maker would be prepared 'to bet the company', ie place the future of the entire business at risk, on one strategic initiative. If the decision-maker is a third generation family member of the founders of a company which still bears the family name and has had a history of over 100 years of successful and continuous growth, the answer is probably no. However, if the company's key decision-maker is young, aggressive and very ambitious with no history or family connections to the group and no wealth invested in it, but is very keen to establish a position at the top of the industry, the answer may well be yes. If this business fails, the dynamic young executive can always try again in another business!

Thus for individual decision-makers the risk/return graph may have very different profiles, as is shown in Figure 5.6, where there is an acceptable range of risks over which a linearly based increase in return is demanded for an increase in perceived risk. Outside this acceptable range there is no such logically defined relationship between the change in perceived risk and the change in demanded return. Good competitor analysis should establish the risk profile of the key decision-makers in competitors, and should also monitor changes in these key decision-makers or in their apparent risk profiles. These risk profiles may change with age or as the decision-makers accumulate wealth and/or power as they may be less willing to risk losing what they now have.

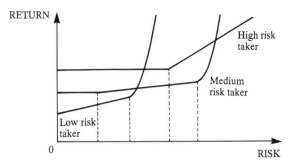

Figure 5.6 Individual risk/return profiles

An illustration of how these hedging strategies can work in practice may be helpful and a very common example is found by reference to any multinational group which automatically acquires exposures to movements in foreign currencies. The automobile industry is a good example of this phenomena and in particular a company such as Jaguar which manufactures cars in the UK but sells a significant proportion of its output in North America. Consequently it has a currency mis-match in that most of its costs are denominated in £s sterling and its revenues are in US dollars. If the dollar increases in value against the £ the company will show increased profits, assuming everything else stays the same, in £s (its base currency as a British-based company). The dollars received will eventually convert into more £s than were originally expected. This is illustrated in Figure 5.7. However if the dollar decreases in value against the £ the profits could decrease dramatically and the company could potentially show a loss even though it has achieved its planned level of sales.

The management may wish to reduce this risk of making an unacceptably low profit, or even a loss, by fixing the future rate of exchange at which the dollars are converted into £s. This can be done by entering into a forward contract for the two currencies involved whereby the company sells US dollars and buys £s for delivery at some specified future date. There will be an agreed rate of exchange for this future transaction (which varies from the current spot rate of exchange by the net difference between the interest rates prevailing in each currency as is illustrated in Figure 5.8) and so the company will now receive a known amount in £s for its US sales. However by reducing the downside risk, the company has also given up the potential profit improvement which would have arisen if the currencies had moved in the opposite direction. [Once again, the only certain thing about future currency rate movements is that nobody knows which direction they will move in. Indeed if any manufacturer, such as Jaguar, believed they could forecast future rates of exchange one has to wonder why they were bothering to manufacture cars as they could make vast amounts of money simply by playing the foreign exchange markets.]

This part of the analysis is illustrated in Figure 5.9 but this illustration shows only the selling forward of known dollar sales proceeds once the cars have been physically sold. The period of collection delay is often relatively short compared to the total risk the company faces due to its exposure to this overseas market. Consequently many companies wish to hedge their future export sales and may go over one year ahead in the forward market. This introduces a very different level of risk as the company is now forecasting its future sales volume and its future selling prices in the foreign currencies. Normally the company does not hedge 100% of its forecast sales revenues, but only sells forward a progressive percentage of future revenues based on the time period involved. However if exchange rates move in this period the

Base information (per car)

Cost of manufacture (sterling based)	£25,000
US selling price	$50,000
Original forecast rate of exchange	$1.50:£1

Potential range over strategic planning period

: strong pound	$2:£1
: strong dollar	$1:£1

Forecast profit per unit:

	£
Selling price in £ ($50,000 ÷ 1.5)	33,333.33
Cost of manufacture	25,000.00
Profit level	8,333.33
Profit margin = 25%	

Possible profit levels at extremes of range:

	Strong £	Strong $
Selling price in £	£25,000	£50,000
Cost of manufacture	£25,000	£25,000
Profit level	–	£25,000
Profit margin	–	50%

Figure 5.7 Impact of rates of exchange movement (simplified example)

company may face a changing external marketplace and it may need to alter its selling prices in local currency terms or find that its market share is seriously affected. In other words, there was an initial assumption which was that everything remained the same, and this may not be so in a competitive market. One essential element of the competitor analysis is to understand how the competition is affected by these changes in exchange rates as their response may be correspondingly differently structured.

If the company is competing in the USA against locally based manufacturers they are not likely to be dramatically affected by any changes in the $:£ rate of exchange, since their costs and revenues are matched in the same currency. It is important therefore that the exporter avoids being forced to raise its selling prices because of foreign currency rate movements. Increasing prices relative to the competition could lose a large amount of market share in a price-sensitive market. However if the exchange rate moves in its favour the exporter has a choice of reducing selling prices and trying to increase market share or of keeping prices stable and making a larger profit margin. Hedging the currency risk in such a competitive environment reduces both upside and downside risk and thus it can be viewed as a risk reduction strategy.

Unfortunately, the problem is further complicated if some competitors are also exporting their products to the particular market but not from the same base country. For instance in the Jaguar example it competes in the USA against Daimler-Benz, BMW and Porsche, all of whom have manufacturing costs denominated principally in Deutsche Marks (DM). Their profitability and pricing strategy is not directly affected by movements in the $:£ rate but will

Spot rate of exchange $1.50:£1

Rates of interest: US dollar   5% pa

UK pounds   25% pa

1 year forward rate of exchange should be $1.26:£1

Reason: Forward rates of exchange will operate to close any arbitrage profit opportunity, thus:

- Arbitragers could borrow $150 million for 1 year at a cost of 5% pa
- They could exchange these funds for £100 million and deposit them for one year at 25% pa

They could sell their £s forward 1 year and so receive a guaranteed amount in US dollars.

Unless this forward rate is $1.26:$1 they can get a guaranteed gain on the transaction as follows:

Initial investment $150.0 million

Cost of borrowing @ 5% $7.5 million

Total costs $157.5 million

Returns:

Deposit repaid   £100.0 million

Interest earned @ 25%   £25.0 million

Total returns   £125.0 million

Total return converted into $ at forward rate of $1.26 :£ = $157.5 million

[Note: this example ignores differential borrowing and deposit rates, tax rates and effectively assumes no transaction costs.]

Figure 5.8 Forward rates of exchange and interest rates

Base information

Company sells 1,000 vehicles this month @ $50,000 each

Cash will be received in 3 months

Spot rate of exchange is $1.50:£1

3 month forward rate of exchange is (say) $1.75:£1

Potential range of rates in 3 months $1.25:£1 to $2:£1

Analysis

Company has generated sales revenues of $50,000,000

This money will be received in 3 months when it could be worth in £s a range of £40 million or £25 million (based on the range of spot rates forecast for 3 months ahead)

Note: today's spot conversion value is £33.3 million

In order to limit this range and hence reduce its volatility the company sells the dollars forward at the market quoted rate of $1.75:£1 and will thus receive, in 3 months, a guaranteed amount of £28.57 million

Figure 5.9 Use of forward contracts to reduce risks (simplified illustrative example only)

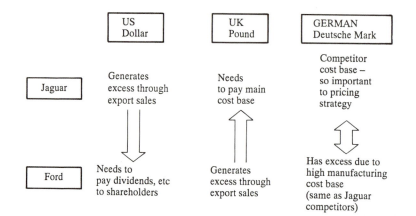

Figure 5.10 Natural hedging strategy opportunities

respond to the DM:$ rate of exchange. Thus Jaguar could hedge its forward sales revenues but find that its German competitors are able to reduce their selling prices in the USA because the dollar has strengthened relative to the Deutsche Mark and they had *not* entered into forward currency contracts.

The key issues are, once again, having the best information possible regarding the strategies of competitors (ie do they hedge forward sales revenues and, if so, how far ahead do they go) and then modelling the potential outcomes of different possible situations. In such a complex environment it is no longer possible to state categorically that hedging is automatically a risk reduction strategy because if one company decides to hedge and all its competitors do not, then it may face a difficult competitive situation if the market goes against it.

Also these areas can lead to even more profound results for the companies involved because in the European automotive industry another major player is the USA-owned Ford Motor Company. Ford's have even more complicated foreign currency management issues in that they produce more cars than they sell in Germany (ie they are a net exporter with an excess of Deutsche Mark costs over revenues), while in the UK they sell more cars than they produce (thus being a net importer, and generating an excess of £ revenues over costs). The USA-based shareholders want to receive dividends and capital gains in US dollars and hence all these overseas transactions are converted back into US dollars for accounting purposes, which gives rise to major opportunities for hedging strategies. Alternatively, as illustrated diagrammatically in Figure 5.10, it makes the acquisition of a controlling interest in Jaguar an attractive proposition as this provides some natural hedges against the major currency exposures involved. (Obviously there would be many other strategic reasons for such an acquisition, but the value of such natural hedging strategies could enable the bidder to increase their offer above that of a rival who had no such natural fit.)

Relative costs and investments

Even when businesses accept that they need to take competitors' strategies, profit levels and costs into account when preparing and implementing their own business plans, the most common reaction is that they cannot get hold of the required information. There seems, in many cases, to be a naive belief that there should be one readily available source of comparative financial and strategic information on all their current and potential competitors. Some managers would seemingly prefer this single source to include information on suppliers and customers, and yet these same managers will normally take great care to ensure that all their plans and critical competitive financial information are kept strictly confidential and internal to their business. There are clearly always going to be problems in obtaining good, reliable, meaningful and useful competitor information but the first key issue is to remember that what is needed is relative financial data, not necessarily the absolute figures.

This means 'relative to one's own business' and, internally, the business should have a number of financial experts who totally understand the interactions of volumes, prices and costs. Management accountants are normally fully acquainted with the internal cost dynamics of their own business, but often have not tried to apply their considerable analytical skills to externally based businesses such as competitors, suppliers and customers. In practice, this skills transfer is not too difficult as certain differences can be readily identified and their financial impact can then be evaluated. For example, a different level of vertical integration in a competitor could force it to buy an intermediate product in the open market and so enable estimates of relative cost differences to be assessed simply by monitoring these open market prices. Alternatively, the existence of an overseas group company which supplies certain products would enable a partial assessment of relative cost movements by reference to any relevant exchange rate changes. The relative physical location of either manufacturing or distribution facilities will give good base data from which to compute their relative distribution costs to particularly important areas of the market.

The overall objective is to build up a comprehensive data-base on each significant competitor, remembering that its competitive responses and initiatives will be primarily driven by future relative cost differences rather than outdated historically based cost differences. Therefore it is essential to keep up-dating this data-base and this is even more important since competitive strategies will evolve as the industry develops. Differences in costs that were considered insignificant last year may now give the competitor a potentially significant and sustainable competitive advantage. Also, although most of the required information is of a financial nature, the competitor analysis should not be regarded as the exclusive responsibility of the management accounting area. The detailed knowledge of these relevant differences will be spread throughout the business and also outside. The role of the management accountants is to apply their financial analytical skills to translating these perceived physical or operational differences into an evaluation of the relative financial position of these key competitors. Thus, as normal, management accounting should act as a co-ordinator and a provider of strategic decision support information expressed in a common currency.

If such a role is undertaken, the potential sources of information are many and varied, as shown in Figure 5.11, without in any way resorting to the unethical or illegal methods of industrial espionage. For example, with regard to the level of investment in fixed assets, the business can use physical observation, information from trade press or trade association announcements, supplier press releases, as well as their externally published financial statements, to build up a clear picture of the relative scale, capacity, age and cost for each competitor. The method of operating these assets can be established by observation, discussions with suppliers and customers, or by asking existing or ex-employees of the particular competitor. Hiring a few key ex-employees of major competitors has been an important element in establishing a really comprehensive competitor data-base for many companies.

This method of operating their productive assets, in terms of hours and shift patterns worked should enable a combination of internal personnel management and industrial

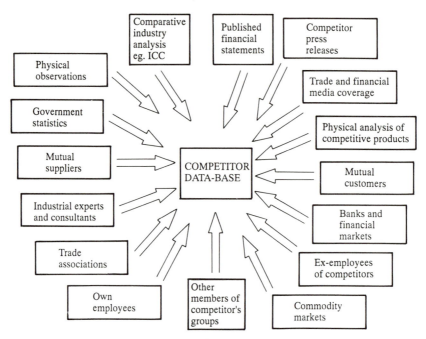

Figure 5.11 Sources of competitor information

engineering managers to work out the likely relative differences in labour costs. In fact, in this case, it should be possible to build a fairly accurate model of their absolute labour costs. The rates of pay and other conditions of employment can be found out relatively easily for most levels in any competitive organization. Reference to nationally negotiated agreements, local and national press advertising for employees, trade and employment associations, and recruitment consultants should give the basic information, but the flow of employees into and out of a business can provide detailed insights into the total packages on offer. When this total employee cost is utilized alongside an intelligent professional assessment of how many employees would be used by the competitor in each area, given their equipment, etc, a very good idea of the competitor's labour costings are obtained. This absolute level can be checked by comparison against internal labour costs to ensure that the relative difference 'feels' right to experienced managers. Similarly, the potential sources of information can be used to build cost models for the other significant areas of competitors' costs, which should highlight the major differences. However, analysing relative cost levels is only part of a really comprehensive competitor financial review, which can indicate strategic opportunities and threats.

One of the chief differences which should be highlighted is the nature of the competitors' costs as well as their relative levels. If a competitor has a lower level of committed, fixed labour costs because it uses a larger proportion of temporary workers, it may be able to respond more quickly to an unexpected downturn in demand by rapidly laying off these people. Equally in a tight labour market and with rising sales demand, it may have to increase its pay levels more quickly and more severely to attract new workers and retain its existing 'temporary' workforce. (The change in employee cost structure in the North American automobile industry which occurred after the 1980 market downturn, which was discussed in Chapter 3, is an example of such a change in the level of committed cost, and shows the ways in which companies can try to alter their strategic cost base.) The method of recruiting and the types of employment contracts offered by the competitor should make it relatively easy to establish the legal nature of its committed costs but there are often other even more important influences which must be considered. If there is strong union representation, the competitor may wish to avoid treating its labour costs as variable in the short term and similar constraints could be felt if the company is a very large local employer or a particularly sensitive, high-profile national business.

However, competitors may be able to increase their effective level of cost flexibility in the short term by only producing a proportion of their total requirements in-house. Clearly information is needed on the regular or intermittent use of external suppliers for components, etc, which are also produced internally. Not only does such action potentially dramatically change the competitor's cost base, but, more importantly, it can increase their strategic options if levels of demand fluctuate significantly and rapidly. If possible some details of any contractual commitments with such third parties should be obtained. Their ownership should also be checked to see if any interlocking shareholdings have been developed as this obviously signals a long-term relationship. It is quite common in Japan to find major companies with a minority shareholding in certain key suppliers. It can be argued that this gives a degree of reassurance to both parties and allows for longer term strategic planning on both sides without the need for formalized long-term contractual commitments. This can give extreme short-term flexibility to the major company and enable a greater range of strategic options to be considered in the face of market fluctuations. Effectively a committed fixed cost may have been changed, once again, into a short-term variable cost by transferring the initial risk of variability in demand to the external, but related supplier. In the much longer term, the competitor may have acquired a responsibility to stand by this supplier and ensure that sufficient purchases are made or capital injected to ensure its survival, but this commitment may be considered differently and be less restricting to the strategic decision process.

The whole area of the relative degree of in-house supply of goods and services is particularly important to this process of competitor analysis as it is here that industries are becoming ever more differentiated. In some industries, most companies may be increasing their proportion of out-sourcing so as to concentrate on their area of greatest added value or to reduce their internal base of committed fixed costs. Other industries seem to be aiming for a completely vertically integrated structure, with almost everything supplied internally. However, in both these scenarios, one or two competitors are normally implementing a completely opposite strategy to the mainstream of the industry. Wherever such an obviously opposite strategy is identified, that competitor should be very closely analysed to try to understand what possible set of planning assumptions or differences in cost structure have led it to the completely reversed decision of the other players in the industry. Another such example is where most companies are investing heavily in new high technology equipment but one competitor insists on sticking with and possibly even expanding its labour intensive processes. In these cases a modelling system is of great value because different external environments can easily be specified and the relative success of the out-of-step competitor can be forecast using the comparative cost data developed from this analysis. If this modelling analysis indicates certain potential situations in which this competitor, because of its singular strategy, gains substantial competitive advantages, the business should try to identify satisfactory hedging strategies to counter or, at least, minimize the damage which can be caused. The basis of these simulation models is always to try to develop alternative strategies to answer any potential move by a competitor, but these potential moves can only be predicted and their impact assessed if a good understanding of the competitor's cost structure is established.

Given the need for this competitor analysis to be comprehensive and up-to-date it should be clear that this relative cost information must be collected on a regular and systematic basis, using all the available sources of information. In some industries, one part of this comparative analysis is surprisingly direct. Each new competitive product is purchased on a regular basis and then systematically taken apart, so that each component can be identified as well as the processes used to put the parts together. The respective specialist areas of the business then assess the costs associated with each element so that a complete product cost is arrived at for the competitive product. Relative differences in cost are highlighted and compared to any perceived differences in customer value.

This leads to the consideration of the other key elements of competitor analysis; relative selling prices and customer values. An excessive concentration on relative cost comparisons in the absence of selling prices and market perceptions can cause very misleading conclusions to be drawn. A premium branded competitor may, on a relative cost comparison, appear to have significant disadvantages but if the cost differences are more than outweighed by its ability to charge higher prices in the market, the apparent disadvantage is in reality a sustainable competitive advantage. Good examples here could be Bang & Olufsen in consumer hi-fi, Rolls Royce motor cars and Rolex watches; none of these businesses *needs* to have a lower cost base than its competitors if it can achieve sufficient compensating price premiums in the marketplace.

Therefore, the relative cost comparison must start from an appreciation of the strategic product positioning that the competitor is currently seeking to achieve. One of its objectives is to highlight whether this positioning is sustainable in the future and to indicate any alternative strategies which could prove successful given its relative cost structure. As the competitor analysis is particularly interested in relative profit or, more precisely, contribution levels, these cost comparisons must be used along with an analysis of relative selling prices. As stated above, these competitive selling prices will be directly linked to the strategic product positioning but even this type of comparative analysis is not necessarily straightforward. The business must ensure that the real effective selling prices are used in the analysis and not take published list prices, etc, if these do not reflect the actual costs incurred by customers.

All trade discounts and rebates should be included and identifying all of these can sometimes be quite difficult. For example in the USA-based stockbroking industry, it has become common practice for bankers to give rebates to major customers in the form of free analytical advice or even computer hardware and software. Comparing the notional commission rates charged in such an industry may not lead to a meaningful and useful conclusion. Another sort of discount may have a distorting effect; settlement discounts are offered in many industries in order to provide an incentive for customers to pay more quickly. This removes the need for the supplier to fund the outstanding receivable balance and therefore the level of the settlement discount should normally be set by reference to the prevailing cost of finance (eg the borrowing cost incurred by the supplier to finance the additional debtor balances). This is outlined in Figure 5.12.

However some businesses set their settlement discount rates at much higher levels and may even allow their major customers to deduct the discount although their payments are not received within the shortened time-scale stated. This discount is not a true settlement incentive but is simply an additional way of reducing the effective selling price below the stated price list. The competitor analysis needs to understand the real reason for all these subtle marketing incentives so that a valid comparison of selling prices is made. One major retailer in the UK has a not very subtle way of passing this responsibility back to its suppliers. If it finds a competitor selling any particular product at a lower selling price than its own, it assumes the

A business, X, wishes to give its customers an incentive to pay for its goods as early as possible. If its standard terms of sale state that 'payment is due 30 days after the invoice date', it could offer a discount if customers pay earlier, say within seven days. If the current borrowing cost is 12% pa after tax it should offer a settlement discount of 0.75% for payment within seven days. It could increase this to 1% to allow for its decreased risk of non-payment because the money is received more quickly.

The calculation is, as follows:

Assume £100,000 is outstanding from a customer.

Without any settlement discount, the payment would be received in 30 days.

The settlement discount should mean the payment is received in seven days.

A saving of 23 days has been achieved

Therefore X has been saved the cost of borrowing £100,000 at 12% pa for 23 days, ie £756.16

This represents a percentage discount of 0.75%

However, the business could argue that, on average, its customers take 45 days to pay for their goods or services and so the time saved by a settlement discount is increased.

Consequently a base settlement discount of 1.25% could be justified.

Figure 5.12 Example of settlement discounts

supplier is selling to the competitor at a lower price and contacts the supplier accordingly. The onus is therefore placed on the supplier to 'prove' that it is not doing this and that the competitor is taking a smaller gross margin on the product than this major retailer: a case of being guilty until you prove yourself innocent. Obviously the punishment for remaining guilty can be very severe, eg the de-listing of all products from their stores.

This shows how this type of analysis can be applied not just directly to competitors but also to key suppliers and major customers. Quite often, a similar but less comprehensive analysis can be applied to these opposite ends of the business value chain. The key objective is to try to obtain a negotiating advantage by understanding their starting position in terms of cost levels and profitability, but more importantly how they will be affected by any forecast changes in the external environment or potential strategic initiative. This requires an assessment of their key strategic objectives and a vital component of these will normally be the level of financial return which they require on their business.

Many businesses take a simplistic approach in this area and assume that their suppliers and customers demand the same level of financial return (eg 25% Return on Investment) as they do themselves. As previously argued, return must be positively correlated to the risk associated with the business, and therefore the financial returns at the various stages of the total industrial value chain can be very different. Indeed, even in the same part of the industry it can be dangerous to assume that all businesses aim for the same levels of financial return. Part of the comprehensive competitor analysis should be to assess the desired returns for each major competitor. Not only may the levels be different but a competitor may place greater emphasis on a different element of financial return, eg cash flow rather than profit, return on sales rather than return on investment, etc. The time-scale for these returns may also differ with some businesses concentrating on short-term results while others are looking for the long-term trend to be improving. Unless the analysis can incorporate such specific competitor objectives, any apparently significant differences in returns which may be highlighted may be taken completely out of context, as the competitor may not regard such a level of return as either unsatisfactory or important.

As stated above, the stage of development of the marketplace will have a big influence on the evolution of competitive strategies and how sustainable competitive advantages can be achieved. Consequently, this level of market development should also indicate where the greatest emphasis should be placed in the competitor analysis. During the launch phase of any industry, competitive advantages are commonly achieved by new product innovation and hence the competitor analysis should concentrate on the relative levels of research and development activity. One obvious measure of relative activity is to compare expenditure levels but this direct information may not be easily obtainable even through trade associations, trade press coverage, published financial statements, government statistics or ex-employees. However, data should be collectable on the number of research scientists and technicians employed, if necessary by identifying the areas occupied by these departments and indirectly assessing the number of people occupying them. With this base information and the internally based knowledge of total expenditure levels per grade of employee (ie not just the personnel costs involved), the relative expenditure levels can be compared. It is also important to try to find out how these research and development departments are financially and managerially controlled in terms of time-scales and budgeting responsibilities. This is discussed in more detail in Chapter 15. The analysis should try to assess what proportions of expenditure are focused on long-term research versus short-term developmental activities. The objective is to predict whether a competitor could achieve a significant technological breakthrough and then to identify how such a threat can be countermanded.

When the industry has moved into the rapid growth phase, a critical success factor is growth in market share. This is often achieved by increasing the level of marketing support. Hence the competitor analysis should concentrate on the relative expenditures on marketing, and on the consequent changes in market shares which are achieved as a result of particular marketing initiatives. This information is often available publicly as far as media expenditures are concerned; again not directly in terms of monetary value but in equivalent units such as TV rating points on which a comparative analysis can be based. It is also possible to identify other marketing support programmes, such as consumer or trade promotions, and to cost such activities using the expertise of the internal marketing managers. This built-up expenditure level can be validated against trade press and other externally published commentaries on the competitor's marketing expenditure ratios, which are frequently referred to in terms of percentages of sales revenues. If possible this marketing expenditure should be split, not only into development and maintenance activities as discussed at the end of Chapter 4, but also between market share development for the product and overall market development. During the rapid growth phase of an industry it is in the interests of all participants that the market should grow to as large a mature size as possible. Consequently it is rational for companies to invest in more general marketing which develops the overall size of the market, eg by discussing general attributes of the generic product, rather than exclusively pushing a single brand. This type of general development marketing should not necessarily be considered as building a competitive advantage for the competitor and thus should be highlighted separately in the analysis. As always, strategic management accounting analysis has to be implemented judgementally not mechanistically.

Even during this growth phase it is quite possible for at least one competitor to choose an alternative strategy and to go for the low-cost production route rather than trying to build a brand through intensive marketing activity. Such an out-of-step competitor needs careful analysis, as mentioned earlier, so that the business is fully aware of the competitor's real cost position and its ability to steal share both now and, more importantly, as the industry matures. Other existing, new or potential competitors who require particular attention at this stage are any late-comers to the industry who may be consequently uncompetitive in terms of cost because they are too far up the experience curve. One possible competitive strategy for such a business is to invest heavily in new technology research and development, as opposed to the earlier new product research and development, so as to get round the adverse impact of this already established experience curve. If the competitor can achieve a technology breakthrough, it can move on to a completely new experience curve possibly at a much lower relative cost base to all the other earlier entrants, who are locked into the now obsolete technology. This strategy is illustrated numerically in Chapter 16. In all these cases, where competitors appear to be implementing alternative strategies, part of the role of the analytical process must be to indicate their likelihood of success by identifying the presence or absence of the key success factors within their businesses. It should always be remembered that the competitor may have chosen a completely different strategy because they believe that the product is at a different stage of development. Assessing the stage of the life-cycle for a product is relatively easy with the benefit of hindsight, but historical analysis has very limited value in strategic management accounting. Competitor analysis always has to concentrate on the future if it is to add any value to strategic decision-making. A detailed cost comparison against last year's competitors' cost structures is a waste of time, unless the analysis indicates how these relative cost differences are likely to have changed since last year and how they will change again in the future given predicted changes in the external and competitive environment.

Once the industry has matured the basis of competition is frequently principally based on selling prices, since the products often have now become more of a well-understood commodity. Consequently, the key success factor is to achieve a comparative cost advantage and this is where competitor analysis should now be concentrated. The analysis should highlight relative costs and in a fiercely price competitive market very small relative differences can be very important. It is quite possible for businesses to use cost-led strategies to gain sustainable competitive advantages, as is argued by Porter, but this requires emphasis on reducing relative cost levels through the whole of the business and not just in one area or at one level of management. In order to create this company-wide emphasis on achieving, and then maintaining, a relative cost advantage, a wide range of managers have to become involved and be kept involved. Far too often, a company carries out a comparative competitor cost analysis as a one-off exercise. This may highlight a relative cost disadvantage which leads to a concentrated effort on cost-cutting, often as a short-term desperation measure, but this type of cost-cutting exercise may be restricted to the direct operational areas. Also the massive intensity of such an effort cannot be maintained and the short-term cost savings frequently turn out to have been 'cost deferrals' because cost levels gradually rise back towards, or even above, their previously unacceptable levels.

A more rational way of using comparative competitor accounting is to carry out the analysis on a regular basis so that the trends in relative competitive advantage are emphasized, rather than the position at a single point in time. This is particularly important given the unavoidable level of approximation and judgement which has to be used in assessing the competitor's position. As long as the regular analyses are carried out consistently, the resulting trend information should provide a very useful guide to changes in relative competitive positioning.

However, throughout this chapter, the need to involve a wide range of managers in this type of exercise has been emphasized, and this is true for companies at all stages of development. As a very positive stimulus to achieving this on a regular basis, the relative competitor data should be incorporated into the regular management accounting reports. These, of course, are circulated through the company and are used as decision support inputs by senior managers. Not only does this inclusion therefore highlight the importance of the relative competitor analyses, which should ensure the continued participation of the appropriate managers, but it also helps to concentrate all managers' attention on these vitally important external aspects of competitive strategy. Thus the all too common over-emphasis in management accounts on internal financial comparisons can be counter-balanced by including these, strategically more important, external comparisons of relative performance against competitors.

These regular internal reports should obviously concentrate on the comparisons which are critical to the current competitive positioning of the company. Thus they will change depending on the stage of development of the product and the type of strategy being implemented for this product. This should help to focus attention on the performance of the appropriate areas of the business, and may reduce the excessive emphasis on only comparing the direct operating areas of the businesses. As discussed in detail in Chapter 11, this can create severe complications in the financial control systems which need to be used in conglomerate-style companies, where the wide range of products are at very different stages of development. The resulting complexity of controlling these businesses can lead to an excessive level of centralized costs, or to a very simplified system of financial measures being applied across the whole of the group. This simplified system may mean inappropriate measures are applied to various businesses, which can put pressure on divisional managers to implement inappropriate competitive strategies, thus decreasing the long-term success of their division.

Summary

It should be clear from the discussion in this chapter that competitor accounting requires the in-put of considerable resources if it is to be done properly but that, even if done as well as possible, the resulting comparative analysis will be approximate and require careful managerial evaluation. However, the potential added value of carrying out such analysis on a regular basis is immense, as it can highlight major opportunities for, and threats to, the competitive strategy of the business.

The key requirements for obtaining these benefits from competitor accounting are the close involvement of both senior managers and a broad range of managers from across the business. Senior managerial involvement can assist in describing the existing and future competitive strategies, which is essential to define the key competitors who should be included in the analysis, as well as highlighting the importance of the analysis. Non-financial managers can provide a vast amount of information on these key competitors (in terms of their strategies, costs and investments), which can be turned into comparative financial analysis by the finance team. Thus it is vitally important that competitor accounting is not seen exclusively as a relative cost comparison exercise, to be carried out, at most, once a year by the management accountants. A more regular cost comparison is obviously part of competitor accounting, but the comparison and financial evaluation of actual and potential competitor strategies, once the basic comparative analysis has been done, is of much greater potential value.

6

Customer account profitability

Overview

An immediate impact of introducing any level of strategic management accounting into virtually every organization is to destroy totally any illusion that the same level of profit is derived from all customers. Obvious distinguishing features among groups of customers or channels of distribution can be differences in effective selling prices and variations in the mix of products purchased, but these may be much less important than the varying levels of customer service that are supplied to each category of customer or market segment.

Indeed, it may well be that the lower selling prices charged to one segment of the market are more than justified by cost savings which are generated by the way in which these customers are serviced. Hence these customers may, in reality, be more profitable than those in areas where the higher selling prices achieved are more than offset by the increased costs incurred in achieving the sales. If the business is to be able to allocate its limited resources most effectively in the future so as to achieve its corporate profit objectives, it must have reliable information on which of the potential customer groupings are its most profitable, and whether there are any existing areas in which the business actually makes a loss.

It is, therefore, not surprising that in a recent research survey[1], companies highlighted customer account profitability analysis as one of the main areas where improvements in management accounting could make a dramatically positive contribution to the future results of their businesses. An illustration of this can be taken from one of the companies taking part in the survey. Like many companies, this company manufactures and sells its products in bulk both to other industrial organizations and to smaller merchants for onward sale to the end user, as well as in smaller amounts directly to end users. The senior managers needed tailored financial information which would help them to assess the effectiveness of their existing activities in these different market segments and would enable sound decisions to be taken with regard to the future allocation of both sales and marketing resources and new product development priorities. Clearly this financial analysis needed to go beyond a simplistic comparison of the relative gross margins achieved in each market segment but, equally, neatly splitting the existing net profit of the total business exactly across these different areas would have provided a very bad basis for future strategic decisions. The subsequent establishment of an appropriately tailored analysis and reporting system in this business was found to assist greatly in the strategic decision-making and planning process.

[1]Marketing Accounting Research Centre, Cranfield School of Management 1987/88

What may be viewed as rather more surprising is that academic interest in this area of segment profitability has been high for over 25 years[2], but it is only in the relatively recent past that many companies have started to match and now even exceed this level of interest. Perhaps this is caused by the enhanced strategic emphasis now placed on customers by these businesses due to their increasingly competitive environments. Many companies now refer explicitly to their customers as 'the most important assets which the business has', even if they do not feature as assets in the externally published balance sheets of the company. Phrases relating to 'customer focus' now proliferate not only in business strategy textbooks but also in corporate mission statements and the related business plans. Another related critical reason is undoubtedly the greater level of segmentation which is being forced on companies as more and more customers have different demands in terms of pricing, distribution, sales support, specialized packaging, etc. Without the implementation of sophisticated financial analysis techniques, the company is usually unable to decide on the relative costs associated with doing business with what are rapidly becoming unique customers. Thus for the purposes of this chapter all the different elements of customer-orientated segment profitability analysis are grouped under the single description of customer account profitability, which is itself abbreviated to CAP.

Definition of CAP

CAP can be defined as 'the total sales revenue generated from a customer or customer group, less all the costs that are incurred in servicing that customer or customer group' and this whole area of the segmented analysis of customers is examined in detail in this chapter. However the fundamental nature of CAP can be illustrated by the philosophy of one major marketing-led company which argues that it does not have profitable products, only profitable customers. This logic can be disputed, as noted in Chapter 4, but is based on the rationale that producing a *product* only incurs cost whereas profit is made by selling the product and in order to achieve a sale the company must have a *customer*. In the increasingly competitive markets facing most companies today, the need to retain and develop customers is accepted as a critical success factor. Indeed even a cursory analysis of many business strategies indicates that the main strategic thrust is to expand the range of products sold to the existing base of loyal customers, as is diagrammatically shown in Figure 6.1. This is presumably justified as a more cost effective utilization of resources than a strategy of trying to expand the customer-base for the existing range of products; the stage of development of the industry and the competitive strengths of the business should be key factors in determining which strategy is likely to be more cost-effective, as are discussed in more detail later in this chapter. However this customer-focused strategy is still based on the premise that increasing sales to these existing customers will enhance the long-term profitability of the business. What if the incremental costs incurred due to the high servicing costs required by certain customer groups outweighed the increased sales revenues achieved?

The essence of CAP is that it focuses on profits generated by customers and does not automatically equate increases in sales revenues with increases in profitability. This emphasis raises the major problem associated with CAP. Since not all costs incurred are directly associated with individual customers or customer groupings, how can customer profitability be

---

[2]Mellman, M., 'Marketing Cost Analysis', *Accounting Review*, January 1963 and Sevin, C. H., *Marketing Productivity Analysis*, McGraw Hill, 1965

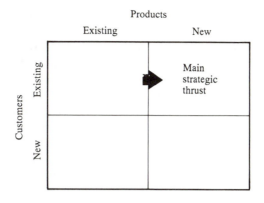

Figure 6.1 Maximizing value of existing customers

analysed except by using a complicated cost apportionment system? Further, if *all* the costs incurred are not included how can a real measure of the *absolute* profitability of a customer be obtained, as per our definition of CAP stated above. In Chapter 4, some of the problems of cost apportionment were discussed and the more relevant types of financial analysis were identified depending on the reason for the analysis being carried out, and whether an absolute measure or a relative comparison of profitability is most relevant. Therefore the obvious starting point for a detailed review of CAP is to examine the benefits which accrue from doing it, and hence to understand the reasons why companies are now so interested in this area of management accounting.

Benefits of CAP

The major benefits which can be and are obtained from CAP are in the area of strategic planning and decision-making. This is because knowledge of the *relative* profitability of different customer groups can enable a company to focus its resources either on those areas which can generate the most profitable growth for the business or on rationalizing areas which are making an unsatisfactory return. It should enable companies to identify unexpected differences in profitability among customer groups and to investigate the reasons for these differences. Also, in the face of aggressive negotiating by specific customers, the company should be able to quantify the financial impact of any proposed changes and hence argue from a position of relative strength: at least in terms of knowing how much any such changes will cost it.

These benefits show clearly that the emphasis of the analysis should once again be on relative differences in profitability, and on the changes in profitability which will result from any strategic or tactical decision. Thus it is not essential to try to reconcile the overall corporate profitability to the total of the individual customer account profits by using excessively complicated cost apportionment systems; the point made in Chapter 4 about avoiding excessive accounting neatness is very important if the information is to be useful to the decision-makers who require it.

The other important factor that these principal benefits highlight is that CAP is not primarily useful as a financial control measure of the efficiency of the sales and marketing function. Setting targets for the profitability of separate customer groups, and then monitoring managerial performance simply against the achievement of these targets is not a logical or productive use of the technique. As discussed in Chapter 4, the competitive environment may have altered adversely so that it would be impossible for any management team to have achieved these previously established targets. It is important that the business does not try to hold managers responsible for things over which they have no control, and the area of customer account profitability is a good example of this problem. Although it is clear that a satisfactory level of profit contribution from all major customer groupings is critical to the economic success of the business, it is not necessarily obvious which individuals could be held managerially responsible for achieving such satisfactory customer returns. In some businesses, customers are seen as the direct line responsibility of the sales areas, with products and brands being placed under the supervision of marketing or brand managers. However in reality the interaction of these two areas is immense. Marketing strategies and objectives should obviously not be restricted to single products or even product groups, but should also be defined in terms of markets, channels of distribution and customer groups. It may be more realistic to define the responsibilities of the two areas much more pragmatically as is done in some businesses. Marketing is used quite normally to mean the identification of customer needs and wants and finding ways of satisfying them, while the role of sales is to get rid of what you already have in stock or in the pipeline! At least this seemingly unattractive definition of the sales function emphasizes primarily its difference in time-scale from marketing and highlights that if customers *are* viewed as key assets of the business they should not be the sole responsibility of an area with a relatively short-term focus. Force-feeding major customers with existing but outdated products will not be a successful strategy in the long term. A more helpful definition is often achieved by incorporating the sales function as part of the marketing area, which is still defined by reference to satisfying customer needs.

Retention of customers

Indeed a key element within the overall marketing strategy should be to set objectives for the level of customer retentions which should be aimed at, as well as the more common objectives for targeted increases in customers. It should be remembered that an increase in market share, which is normally achieved by acquiring new customers as well as increasing sales to existing customers, is much easier to achieve during a period of market growth. The expansion in share can, at least partially, be obtained out of this market growth rather than by directly stealing sales from competitors.

Consequently, in a static or declining market, particularly where competitors are very aggressive, it is especially important to retain customers if profitability is to be maintained or enhanced. For most businesses, obtaining new customers is an expensive process in sales and marketing and support costs. This substantial investment needs to be recovered over time from the sales revenues subsequently achieved and obviously, the longer the customer is retained, the greater is the opportunity to more than recover this up-front acquisition cost. However, the benefits of customer retention may be even greater, particularly if the key strategic thrust is to increase the range of products sold to existing customers, as illustrated in Figure 6.1. Over time, an existing satisfied customer will gain increased confidence in this supplier and will be more likely to buy such a wider range of products, thus potentially increasing its overall profitability to the business. For example, a newly founded focused retailer, with a floating transient customer-base, would probably find it very difficult to launch successfully a completely new unrelated range of products, even if aimed at its existing customers. However, for Marks and Spencer plc, its very well-established quality image and loyal customer-base has been a key success factor in the recent launches of products well away from its traditional ranges of food and clothing. Maintaining its previously proven strategy of selling everything under its own label, St Michael, it has diversified into home furnishings, furniture, and even financial services through the launch of its own credit card, which now offers personal loans and unit trust investment products. As mentioned earlier, the financial justification for such a strategic move hinges on the relative cost effectiveness of the alternative strategies for generating growth. If the costs involved in accessing completely new segments of the market are likely to be substantial whereas the existing investment in this market segment will support an increased product range, the improvement in overall profitability from such an expansion in the range of products sold to existing customers can be dramatic. This can be particularly true where the existing investment has included a strong commitment to developing loyalty among existing customers through maintaining a consistent level of product quality and service, and hence customer expectations, together with a high degree of fixed and long-term committed costs; all of which are true for a retailer such as Marks and Spencer.

In other words, if the existing committed investment in the market segment is considerable and the high fixed cost base has additional business generating and processing capability, any additional contribution from adding new product sales to these existing customers can have a dramatic impact on the overall profitability of the business. The intangible assets represented by the existing, loyal, trusting customers are being more fully utilized (ie their asset turnover ratio is being increased) and other operational costs are also being more efficiently employed (ie net profit margins are increasing). It is clearly important that for such a strategy to be successful, the new products must be attractive to these existing, loyal, trusting intangible assets. This can be reasonably assured if the strategic review carried out by the company not only highlighted that this customer group's loyalty represented a key competitive advantage for the business, but also indicated what were the particular attributes of the existing product range and the overall corporate offering which had created this strategic advantage. In the case of Marks and Spencer, such a review would probably reveal that customers regarded the consistent product quality at a reasonable price together with the famous 'no quibble, money back guarantee' as critical elements in their loyalty to the company. Thus any expansion to the range of products should fit into this set of customer expectations, if it is to be readily accepted by existing customers.

This should make it less surprising that these new products proved far more successful than an alternative recent strategic move which was based on introducing a more up-market, expensive range of existing products, ie clothes. These related products, which were also sold under the existing brand name, did not match with the expectations of existing customers but neither did the existing positioning of the single brand and the overall business image attract a more appropriate new market segment into the stores to buy these new products.

It is clear, that for Marks and Spencer, its loyal customers are now seen as key assets of its business. This current strategy, therefore, is trying to maximize its share of their purchasing power using their trust and faith in the strong brand image, rather than developing alternative brands which could appeal to a different segment of its original markets, eg food or clothing. (It is interesting to contrast this strategy selected by the largest UK clothes retailer with that of the second largest, Burton Group plc. Burton's has ten different brand images in the retail market place, which quite deliberately enable it to appeal to almost every age range and volume sector of the community, but the company has not developed anything like the same strength of overall corporate image. Indeed, very many of the customers would probably not know that their chosen clothing retailer was part of the Burton Group and most would be unable to name all of the other brand franchises operated by the group. However, in contrast to Marks and Spencer's move into other product areas, Burton's have recently publicly stated their intention to concentrate exclusively on clothes retailing, by announcing the sale of their financial services and property development divisions.)

For many retailers and other service businesses, this strategic issue of expanding their sales to existing customers can be of critical importance to their overall profitability. Unfortunately, for many high street retailers, this can be difficult to implement as they do not know who their customers are because they simply walk into their shops, make a purchase and then disappear. Thus, before regarding customers as a loyal asset, a considerable amount of market research has to be done to establish the degree of regular purchasing and also what factors create the loyalty. In many cases, these key factors may have very little to do with the existing product range and if this is so, it becomes much more likely that a strategic move to sell other similarly positioned products to these existing customers will succeed.

However, this strategic thrust to leverage up on the existing customer asset base should not be seen as risk-free. At any time where the product range sold to the same customer grouping is increased, the risk of annoying or completely losing some of these customers is also increased. This is particularly true where the reasons for existing customer loyalty are most clearly defined (which is also normally where the value of the customer assets is greatest) because the customer will evaluate the new product against the well-established set of expectations created by previous products bought from this company. If the new product proves unacceptable, there is a risk that the customer will be put off buying the existing product range. Thus a group such as Mars, which sells a wide range of confectionery products (eg Mars, Milky Way, Twix, Bounty, Snickers, etc) to the same end consumers, did not for many years use any linked marketing of these separately branded products. Even less does it associate its petfood business (Pedigree Petfoods is part of the same group) or its human convenience food business and their respective brands with the other powerful confectionery brand images. Yet all their major brands are positioned as good value for money, with similar other brand values as well. It could be argued that if the Marks and Spencer unit trusts actually went down in value to below their issue price, the investors might want to exercise the 'no quibble, money back guarantee' that applies to the other previous products sold by the company. Failure to be able to do this could create a reduction in the strong customer loyalty felt by these people towards the company, as well as generating adverse publicity. These types of risks should be considered in selecting new product areas and this appears to have been done by Marks and Spencer because the initial unit trusts were positioned as low risk investments, which should not result in sizeable capital losses for new investors.

An essential element in this strategy of increasing the range of products sold to existing customers is the need to retain these existing customers. Indeed wherever possible the new products should be designed to increase their level of loyalty to the particular company. This area has been examined by a number of companies and consulting organizations. Their conclusions are hardly surprising, simply reinforcing the points made earlier. Acquiring new customers is an expensive process and thus retaining these customers enables these initial costs to be recovered over a longer period. Also customers tend to increase their purchase levels over time as their confidence in the supplier increases. However, a very important issue is that regular customers should also be more profitable as they cost less to service. This can be because they create less queries as they begin to understand the supplier's order processing system, but it is also because the set up costs associated with entering a new customer into many modern computer systems can be substantial, including taking credit references, etc. It is repeat business which therefore increases customer account profitability. In many cases it is also true that increasing the frequency of purchase also increases customer loyalty. Therefore if these two ideas can be combined by adding appropriate new products to the existing range, there is the potential of dramatic improvements in CAP.

This type of analysis has led to many strategic initiatives over time and the 1980s saw an upsurge of these strategies in the services sector. Thus several financial institutions tried to become the supplier of all their customers' needs for financial services, with very limited success. Advertising agencies, most notably Saatchi & Saatchi, attempted to provide 'one-stop shopping' for clients in terms of 'creative consultative' services, again without lasting success. In some cases the costs associated with acquiring the new additional product offerings were too high, with a consequent adverse impact on CAP rather than the expected enhancement. In other cases, these new products did not fit with the existing customer expectations and hence the strategy reduced rather than increased customer loyalty. In another group of cases, it can strongly be argued that there was limited transferable customer loyalty available for the launch of new products. As mentioned above, the key factors creating customers as assets of any business should be analysed prior to considering this type of strategic thrust. If the major customers are sophisticated buyers who purchase part only of the existing range of products because they perceive it as the most appropriate for their specific needs, they are unlikely to extend the range bought from this particular company unless the new products also meet this exacting specification. A good example can be taken from the financial services industry. It may be possible to cross-sell investment products to individual customers, for whom current account transaction banking is being done; this strategy is being simultaneously implemented by banks and building societies in the UK. However in investment, or merchant, banking this process is much less likely as the buyer is normally much more sophisticated. Thus trying to sell cash management services to a major corporate customer, for whom the investment bank currently provides advice on mergers and acquisitions, is unlikely to succeed unless the supplier can offer the customer an extremely attractive cash management service. However even in this area of very sophisticated customers, most long-term successful investment banks use a very expensive system of relationship management, which is designed to build loyalty and improve the long-term profitability of retained clients. This is discussed further at the end of the chapter.

Another important issue which arises out of this customer-based strategic thrust is that it can, over time, change the main competitors facing the business. This is particularly true if other companies, with the same basic customer groupings, are also attempting to expand their range of products so as to improve their profitability from their existing customers. By looking forward it is possible to hypothesize as to how this could affect a company like Marks and Spencer over the next 5 to 10 years. As previously discussed, Marks and Spencer has been increasing its range of products outside its traditional areas. However, it has also expanded the products within its traditional areas of food, household goods and clothing. Indeed, it has recently opened its first few 'food only' stores.

It is possible to see that a continuation of this strategy could result in the company becoming a competitor to the more up-market supermarket chains; in fact, this is already happening in the higher margin convenience food sectors. At the same time Sainsbury's, arguably the largest food retailer in the UK, has been following a similar strategy of expanding the range of products which it sells to its similarly loyal group of customers. Until recently, Sainsbury's had avoided moving into clothing, but it has now bought out its joint venture partner, BhS (part of Storehouse), from Sava Centre. As a result, it would not be unexpected for Sainsbury's to move into clothing retailing over the next 5 years. [Sava Centre runs very large stores which are divided between supermarket goods, supplied by Sainsbury's, and clothing, etc, supplied by BhS. Under the purchase agreement, Sainsbury's can continue to source the clothing range from BhS for 5 years.] These strategic moves by the two leading UK retailers could place them in direct competition with each other as they both continue to try to increase their share of the same group of customers.

Understanding the profitability of different groups of customers both at present and as a result of proposed strategic moves is obviously critical to long-term decision-making. CAP analysis must be designed to assist in this process, and it should highlight potential changes in competitors, as discussed in Chapter 5, as well as providing relevant financial analysis for forthcoming decisions.

Appropriate customer groupings

If CAP is to be of assistance in allocating resources to these areas of greatest opportunity, the question of how to group together customers must be carefully considered. As mentioned earlier, in some industries it is possible to argue that each customer is unique and therefore should be analysed individually. This may indeed be necessary for a few major customers, but is impractical for a large number, and some level of aggregation is essential to make the task cost-effective. Also as the groupings become smaller in composition and hence more individually specific, the problems of cost apportionment become greater and these can make the final analysis almost meaningless unless sensible managerial judgement is exercised.

Even at the extreme, where it is recognized that the very large individual customer is the ultimate profit centre, it is still important to group together all of these large customers which display similar characteristics. At the other extreme, where there are a vast number of very small customers, such as in the case of a retailer, the benefits of CAP have already been discussed. In particular the matching of complementary products to satisfy additional needs of existing customers can be achieved by sophisticated CAP analysis. Most organizations, however, have a number of large customers and a significantly greater number of smaller ones. It is here that most benefit is derived from strategic segmentation which combines groups of customers into meaningful sets where marketing efforts can be differentiated to increase the profitability of the company. Unfortunately, this is not necessarily the way in which customers are segmented within the company.

Since the major objective of the analysis is strategic decision support, the customer classifications should be chosen to fit the business strategies which are being implemented and considered. This may require a completely different emphasis from the historical way of grouping customers, as the strategy is likely to be driven by the external environment rather than being based on the normal internal focus of traditional management accounting. Thus in many companies, customers have been classified and coded into geographic areas and regions, as illustrated in Figure 6.2, because that is how the sales-force is organized, and sales information is consequently needed internally by individual salesperson, area sales manager, regional manger, etc, in order to exercise financial control. In many cases, this segmentation was originally limited to collecting sales revenue information, but subsequently many companies realized that allocating sales-force resources solely on the basis of increasing sales revenues was unsatisfactory. As a result the same customer groupings were frequently used to prepare some sort of geographically based CAP, from which conclusions were drawn as to the appropriateness of sales-force resource allocations. In many cases this was bad enough but,

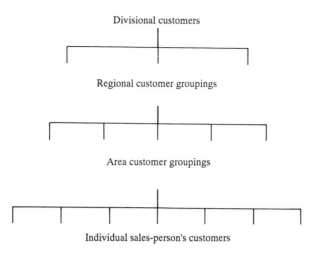

Figure 6.2 Geographical customer classifications

unfortunately, many businesses used exactly the same analytical information to make comparisons about the relative performances of sales personnel, even though the individual sales peoples may have had little or no control over a number of factors included in the analysis.

Some companies have now incorporated more layers of segmented analysis which may separate out customers of a particular type, irrespective of their geographic location. These often include separation by channels of distribution (eg wholesale, retail and industrial), or by size (eg classifying accounts in terms of sales revenue bands), or by number of sales points (eg multiple retailers, broken into national and regional, etc), or by sales method (eg direct sales force, third party sales force, telephone sales, mail order, etc) and may use a matrix form of presentation as shown in Figure 6.3.

None of these analyses is necessarily wrong, provided that they only include relevant costs, as each analysis may relate to a specifically relevant question of resource allocation but equally

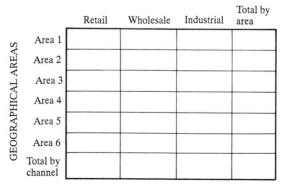

Figure 6.3 Matrix form of customer groupings

none may focus directly on the essential strategic thrust of the business. In many cases, these groupings of customers are based more on ease and convenience than usefulness in application. If a key strategic aim is to differentiate among customers in more qualitative terms, the CAP analysis should not ignore this type of customer grouping merely because it creates a more difficult analytical problem. Many business strategies now emphasize the need to find and retain 'quality' customers, but this strategy has not been translated into a meaningful set of factors which would enable a relevant segment profitability analysis to be carried out. What is required in this instance is for the identification of the relevant features which would characterize various potential types of quality customers.

Defining a 'quality' customer can be quite difficult for some companies but this probably indicates that it has not yet developed a clear-cut customer focused strategy. It may simply mean a customer who appreciates the particular competitive advantage offered by this supplier, and who is consequently likely to remain loyal as long as this competitive advantage is maintained. Thus, this can range from the extremely cost-conscious buyer who could be a 'quality' customer for a company who is emphasizing their low-cost production capabilities. Alternatively a manufacturer, which is producing a very high quality product, would find this type of buyer unsuitable and should be focusing its attention on customers who are willing to pay extra to receive such a high quality product. This does not mean that these 'quality' conscious customers necessarily want a high quality, high cost *sales support* function, and this is another way of differentiating customers who are attractive to any particular business.

In one real-life example, these different classifications of quality customers included non-price sensitive customers, loyal customers, low service cost customers and customers requiring a high level of service but who were willing to pay a premium for such a high level of service. In this particular example, the company was trying to reposition itself in the market so that it protected itself from the cyclical price wars which regularly ravaged its industry. Its initial strategic plan was to focus on 'quality' customers who would be loyal to a consistent service level rather than switch suppliers for a short-term price advantage, and this meant a considerable restructuring of its customer base. Unfortunately there was no initial financial information available on these different types of customers as no such classifications had been made in the past. The important financial implications of such a change in strategy were consequently impossible to forecast until some base data could be provided which indicated the possible number of such 'quality' customers and the cost implications of maintaining the required consistent level of service.

Once these relevant sets of 'quality' characteristics are agreed, customers can be appropriately characterized and a suitable coding system devised which enables aggregation into these strategically significant groupings. The aggregation of individual customers with similar characteristics enables the business to carry out two differently important types of analysis. It is possible to compare the relative profitability of one such aggregated group with another, such as in the case of different channels of distribution where the profitability of, say, wholesale customers as a group can be compared with the retail customer group. Also any individual customer or sub-group of customers within any particular aggregated grouping can be compared to the average profitability of the group, with less worries about the validity of the comparison as the same cost allocations will have been applied in both cases. This once again reflects the importance of relative profitability comparisons, as a way of reducing the impact of the problems caused by cost apportionment.

As long as the methods of cost apportionment have been consistently applied to each of the customer groupings, the relative profitability comparisons within each grouping should be valid, even though this CAP analysis may not give a complete picture of the absolute profitability of any market segment. The appropriate method of cost allocations for these more absolute decisions was initially discussed in Chapter 4 and is covered in more detail in the next section of this chapter.

From the above discussion it should be clear that any single business may require a number of different bases for CAP analysis, but with modern computer processing power this should not be too much of a problem. The critical element is in the design of the initial customer coding references, as if these can be used as the basis for each different segmented analysis it will be possible to avoid additional time-consuming, expensive clerical analysis or re-sorting of the initial sales data. In order to achieve this, it is essential that the probable strategic decisions are identified before designing the management accounting system as is discussed in more detail in Chapters 19 and 20. If properly conceived and implemented, the business should be able to analyse the profitability of its customers in the wide variety of different groupings which are relevant to the different decisions it has to make, such as whether to increase or decrease levels of marketing activity in any specific segment.

Profitability analysis issues

The ability to segment customers into a variety of different groupings which are not mutually exclusive may be relatively easily achieved by a suitable coding system. However such variety adds considerable complexity to the analysis of sales revenues and costs if a meaningful measure of profitability is to be achieved. At the highest level all the divisional costs can be, by default, directly associated with customers whereas at the micro level of the individual customer relatively few costs can be so directly associated. Direct allocation would have to be combined with a very comprehensive method of cost apportionment, as graphically shown in Figure 6.4, if individual customer net profits are to be calculated. Equally, if only direct allocated costs are to be included, the CAP analysis will not go beyond a superficial gross margin comparison, which is the level at which many companies still end their customer profitability reviews.

However a deeper analysis is possible without excessively increasing the dependence on apportioned costs if CAP is being properly used to support strategic financial decisions, which should be based only on the attributable costs associated with the changes caused by any such

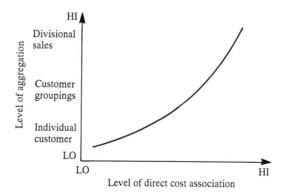

Figure 6.4 Cost directly associated with different levels of aggregation

decision. This concept of attributable cost was defined by Shillinglaw[3] back in 1963 as 'the cost per unit that could be avoided, on the average, if a product or function (ie service to a customer) was discontinued entirely without changing the organization structure'. The fundamental logic remains valid even if its application has been developed to cover partial rather than total cessation and it is now used both in terms of cost savings, as the avoidable cost, and as an expression of the increased costs incurred through a decision, ie as the incremental cost. As discussed in Chapter 4, a key element is the inclusion as part of these attributable costs of both variable and fixed costs for the segment, if they would change as the activity levels altered. Thus avoidable and incremental costs are separated from committed costs rather than being divided into fixed or variable categories, and as such it also becomes clear that the level of such attributable costs still increases as the level of aggregation increases. Costs which are common to all the customers in any division, such as the sales and marketing director's salary, would not be avoided unless all the customers were discontinued. Consequently this cost should not be included in any segmental CAP analysis. Likewise another layer of costs will only be avoided if an entire channel of distribution is closed, such as retail sales when the whole retail sales-force could be saved, whereas if one particular retail customer is being considered only relatively small savings in sales personnel may be possible even if the individual account is itself very large.

The coding system used by the business is critical to achieving the most relevant financial analysis. In this type of environment, costs should be coded to the lowest level of aggregation of customers which makes them change, eg at which the cost is avoidable. If particular costs are not attributable at the specific customer level, they should be excluded from consideration at this level of CAP, and only included at the appropriately higher level of aggregation. Thus the whole CAP analysis becomes oriented around the decision support concept rather than attempting to spread all the costs of the division across the existing customer base. Some of the costs, such as new customer development, may not be attributable at all to existing customers and many will only change if major directional changes in strategy are implemented. Including these costs in the CAP analysis could distort the decisions taken based on the financial information supplied to the relevant management. As previously mentioned, businesses should not be surprised if managers actually use financial information with which they are provided! This may become clearer if a more detailed example is given. A common area of focus on CAP is within businesses which sell a high a proportion of their products through major retailer channels of distribution. Large retailers have, in recent years, become even more sophisticated negotiators and, as customers, now have very specific demands in terms of the supporting service levels provided as well as the actual selling prices of the goods or services being supplied.

The very large retail chains, such as Sainsbury's and Tesco's in the UK supermarket industry, should be separately identified as individual customers in a CAP analysis, but should also be appropriately grouped so that relative profitability comparisons can be made. Sales revenues are easily and automatically allocated to individual customers through the normal sales accounting procedures but this is not the case for many of the cost items. Retail customers normally buy a mix of individual products and hence the relevant direct product costs can be allocated according to the specific mix of sales which has been made or is forecast. (Remember that as CAP's main benefit is as a tool of planning and decision-making, historical profitability analyses are only of value if they provide a relevant guide to the future.) However, as argued in Chapter 4, great care must be taken in selecting the appropriate level of

[3]Shillinglaw, G., 'The concept of Attributable Cost', *Journal of Accounting Research*, Vol 1, 1963.

product cost which should be used. If the total product costs include a high level of apportioned costs which may have been spread in an entirely appropriate way to the individual products, it is perfectly possible to distort subsequent profitability analysis by customers. For example, distribution costs may be significant but would not be directly allocatable to individual products if deliveries are made on a mixed product basis. For product profitability purposes, these total distribution costs may be shared across all products according to their relative freight weights, which may seem completely appropriate if that is how the distribution costs are actually incurred.

This would take account of the different sales mixes of individual customers, but would not allow for the completely different methods of distribution which may be demanded by these same individual retailers. One group of retailers may require goods to be delivered on a weekly, or more frequent, basis to all their separate stores spread all over the country without any differential selling prices being charged to the more outlying locations. Another group may specify delivery to their centralized or regional warehouses, from where they will deliver on to their individual shops. Clearly this represents a significantly reduced distribution cost to their suppliers and an additional on-cost to themselves: normally these retailers will wish to negotiate an appropriate discount in their selling prices or some other form of rebate in compensation. The problem for the supplier is how big should the discount be? A simple solution is to give the retailers whatever amount they ask for, but this may not maximize long-term profitability!

There may be yet a third category, perhaps comprising only one retailer, who requests delivery to a centralized warehouse conveniently located near to the particular supplier's production plant. This retailer is also prepared to place orders which are load efficient and will comprise only full pallets of individual products and only full lorry loads of such full pallets. Clearly further savings are possible not only in terms of freight costs but also in the warehousing area, where a major cost normally consists of breaking down pallets for delivery purposes. Once again, the question is how much is the cost saving and how much of this saving should be passed on to the specific retailer. If a sensible solution to this analytical problem can be found, the supplier can become pro-active by offering a mutually attractive discount to other retail customers to encourage them to switch to this more cost-effective way of ordering. If a supplier does not have an adequate system for CAP analysis, the negotiating power is very firmly with the retailers, who have themselves invested very heavily in direct product profitability analysis systems as is discussed in the next chapter. Although the distribution cost needs to be spread across the range of products, it is much more of a direct cost to each of these various categories of customers and should be allocated accordingly so as to reflect as accurately as possible the relative cost differences caused by their alternative service demands. This means that the appropriate level of product cost should exclude any cost apportionment areas which can be more appropriately treated from the customer profitability perspective. This could include specific customer packaging and size requirements, and even variations in the product's formulation, which are direct to either a small group of customers or a particular individual customer.

It is quite possible that the cost may only be directly allocatable to a group of customers, and sensible managerial judgement has to be exercized as to how the cost should be treated at the individual customer level. For example, many smaller retailers have grouped together to form voluntary buying groups so as to increase their total buying power and gain better buying prices from suppliers. Some of these groups also specify their own private label goods, which can only be sold to the buying group's members. Any incremental costs associated with this additional product are only direct at the buying group level, even though the extra sales discounts granted can be allocated to individual customers, because if any single customer ceases to trade the private label costs will still be incurred. Realistically it may serve no purpose to analyse the profit contributions of individual members of such a buying group if the effective negotiating body is the group and it is therefore at this level that strategic decisions will be made. The main objective of the CAP analysis in such a case would be to highlight and compare the relative profitability of the various voluntary buying groups with each other and with the other major retail customers. Consequently all the significant differences in the methods of doing business should be brought out in the costings.

As well as differences in distribution requirements, retailers may make varying demands in terms of sales support activities. Some retailers may require regular, frequent calls at all stores by field sales-force personnel and expect them not only to recommend an order level to the store manager but to carry out a number of other administrative and operational functions as well. These might include physically merchandizing the in-store displays of the company's products, checking the physical stock levels held, resolving any outstanding queries relating to deliveries or damages by issuing credit notes, and directly negotiating in-store promotions or special offers with the store personnel. Alternatively, the retailer may control all of its stores more centrally and not even want the sales-force to call at the individual stores, requiring only a single group-wide negotiation of all selling prices, stocking levels, promotional activity, etc. Once again there are significant cost differences between these two extremes and there may be several middle-ranking variations requested by other customers which may require increased or decreased sales-force call frequencies.

CAP analysis must reflect these cost differences so that the alternatives can be compared, which means including either the avoidable or incremental costs as appropriate. Thus if a customer currently does utilize the field sales-force but is negotiating the level of discounts which would be granted if it ceased doing so, the relevant cost is the avoidable cost which would be saved. Alternatively, if a customer currently takes deliveries into its centralized warehouse but is negotiating for direct distribution to individual stores, the incremental cost which would be incurred should be calculated and used as a basis for a minimum price adjustment. It must be remembered that obtaining such a price adjustment or only giving away the avoidable cost discount cannot be guaranteed no matter how good the CAP system is, as this end result depends on the relative negotiating power of the two parties. However, in negotiations, information is a very strong source of power.

This need to include the appropriate form of attributable cost, eg avoidable or incremental cost, indicates a further significant complexity to the provision of CAP information. In most cases, the cost saving arising from a particular event not happening is not equal to the incremental cost incurred from an additional similar event occurring. In the earlier examples, the avoidable cost generated by one customer no longer utilizing the field sales-force may not equal the incremental cost incurred by another customer starting to use the field sales-force; unless the two events can be engineered to happen at the same time and the sales-force resources can be directly reallocated from one customer to the other. Similarly the incremental cost of moving to direct store delivery for one customer does not necessarily equal the cost saving generated by making the reverse move for another customer. The specific impact of each decision on the overall costs incurred by the business will lead to significant differences in these cost levels. This variability can make it very difficult to provide regular CAP analyses which are meaningful to managers.

However, this should not be seen as an insurmountable problem if the fundamental reasons for carrying out CAP analysis are remembered. The main benefits are achieved through its use as a decision support system, and clearly the analysis has to be tailored appropriately to the type of decision which is being considered. Thus, if senior managers are considering ceasing doing business with specific customers, it is important that the CAP information is based on avoidable costs. Alternatively, if the strategic thrust is to enter new market segments, the CAP forecasts should include the incremental costs which would have to be incurred if the strategy was to be implemented. However the CAP system should, in any case, enable the relative differences between different customer strategies to be highlighted and compared as required by any strategic decision.

Information collection problems

The above examples should have clearly highlighted the sort of problems which are likely to be encountered in collecting the information required for a comprehensive system of CAP. Costs must be allocated at varying levels of customer groupings depending on how the cost changes, but more importantly, it may not be relevant to include the actual historic level of cost at all. The costs required may be hypothetical as in the above illustrations of the customers negotiating to stop using the field sales-force and to take deliveries into stores rather than to a centralized warehouse. However, the key here is to use the strength of a good CAP system, which will enable a comparison of relative costs and profitabilities. Consequently if some customers do not use the field sales-force while other similar ones do, it should be possible to extract the differences in their relative cost levels in respect of the sales-force and hence estimate an approximate avoidable cost involved in ceasing to use it. Similarly, if some customers already receive individual store deliveries the incremental cost involved can be estimated. For this comparison of relative cost levels to generate accurate answers, it is important that each customer analysis is computed on a consistent basis and that there is no attempt to spread the total costs incurred in any area across the customers. If this apportionment is done, the differences will cease to represent the appropriate form of attributable cost which is required.

Some businesses may wish to include some elements of such apportioned costs, particularly if they are likely to have a material impact on the relative levels of customer profit contributions. However it is clear that an *even* apportionment of such costs will not have any such material impact on relative levels of CAP. Consequently, these shared costs need only be incorporated in the CAP analysis if significantly different levels of cost can genuinely be apportioned to different categories of customers. For example, senior management costs (eg the group chief executive, etc) are often excluded from any segment analysis and treated as a general overhead. These general overheads should not be forgotten and must be paid for out of the total contributions generated by all the customers. However, spreading these types of general overheads to specific customers using a single overall basis of apportionment merely serves to introduce a spurious level of accuracy into the segment profitabilities, and does nothing to alter the relative performance of one sector against another. Thus, apportioning total senior management costs across the customer groupings in proportion to their relative sales revenue levels, as is done by many businesses, achieves nothing positive and may lead to damaging decisions being based on this false financial analysis. A common argument used to justify this practice is that the business needs to highlight those areas which are not fully contributing to divisional or corporate overheads, so that changes can be made where necessary. This last statement is what makes these over-simplistic apportionments dangerous; if changes are made to cut out these apparently 'loss making' customers, what is then done with their previous share of these general overheads? In such 'logical systems', they are normally re-spread over the remaining customers which may, of course, make a few more customers appear to be non-performing and ready to be dropped. Quite quickly all the customers can, one by one, be classified as unprofitable and the whole division can be closed down, at which stage it may, but only may, be possible to save the actual cost which is being apportioned. The illustrations of this abuse of cost apportionment could be hilarious if they were not so tragic for the businesses concerned[4].

If senior management actually spends a disproportionate amount of time on one or more particular customer groups, the extra cost involved in servicing these groups should be included in the CAP analysis. A favourable change in the method of doing business with these customers could result in a cost saving to the business. However, even if such a change is unlikely, the consequent adverse impact shown on this group's relative profitability should act as a reminder of the real costs incurred by an excessive involvement of senior management and serve as a disincentive to moving any other customers into this method of operation unless, of course, other factors generated more than compensating advantages, which should be shown up in the CAP analysis. At the other end of the business, there may be significant differences in the costs of order processing between two customer groups. One type of customer could send in large regular bulk orders which contain the supplier's product reference numbers and precise delivery instructions which result in a minimum of queries, returns and complaints. The other type all raise very small, irregular orders seemingly whenever they run out of stock which means demands for immediate delivery, but frequently the corresponding delivery instructions are ambiguous, impossible or simply wrong. This results in a mass of queries, returns, complaints and a very demoralized order processing staff in the supplier's offices. Once again these real differences in the costs of servicing the different categories of customers should be incorporated into the CAP analysis, so that a fairer comparison of relative profitabilities can be made. Any simplistic general apportionment of the total order processing costs across the customer groups will be worse than useless.

The management accountants should analyse the nature of the costs incurred in the order processing department so as to understand how they change with the different aspects of the functions performed in the area. In most businesses there is a fixed level of cost incurred in any order, no matter what size, and then an incremental cost if there are more products and extra unusual delivery instructions to process. (After all the extra time required to key in 100,000 units ordered rather than 100 is minimal!) Much of the cost incurred is normally spent on resolving queries and handling customer complaints, rather than on the routine processing of documentation. A sound analysis of these specific costs should therefore enable a good estimate to be made of the incremental costs incurred by the poorly organized customer group relative to the efficient one. It is very unfair, as well as being a very unsound long-term strategy, not to attempt to reflect the financial benefit achieved by dealing with efficient customers. This is true where the customer operates in a particular way so as to enhance the overall profitability of the mutual business interface, but is especially vital if the customer also incurs additional costs as a result of the specific method of operating.

An increasingly important example of this issue is the relative payment record of particular customer groupings. Late payments by customers require the company to incur additional financing costs. Even more importantly, in the UK, they have been cited in several recent business reports as a major contributory factor in the financial collapse of many small and medium-sized businesses. Thus the financing costs associated with these outstanding receivable balances should be built into the CAP system wherever they are significant.

[4]See Ward, K. *Financial Aspects of Marketing*, Butterworth-Heinemann, 1989, pp. 258–263.

However, this is another case where a general level of apportionment is of no real benefit, because the impact of different payment records should be highlighted. This is particularly important because there is a *reciprocal* cost or benefit to the customer resulting from the timing of their payments. Sophisticated customers will expect some financial compensation in the form of a settlement discount, etc, if their payment records are to be improved. Unfortunately even in companies which have CAP systems, the level of financial analysis would often include the discount granted for prompt payment but would omit the corresponding element of costs incurred in financing the debtor balances of those customers who do not take advantage of any prompt payment discounts. Thus the relative profitability comparisons are once again distorted.

This absence of appropriate financial analysis and subsequent relative comparison may help to explain the poor strategic use of settlement discounts in most companies. The principal objective of a settlement discount is to avoid the need for the company to finance the outstanding debtor balance. In other words, the company is paying its customers to settle their outstanding accounts more quickly and the level of discount offered should therefore be established by reference to the company's cost of funding, which would be used to finance the increased level of receivables (using opportunity cost logic). Consequently, the discount percentage offered should, on an annualized basis, fluctuate with movements in interest rates; but most companies never vary their settlement discount percentages. More significantly, in the UK particularly, the situation is even more bizarre. If a company has a higher opportunity cost of capital than its customers, it is completely illogical and uneconomic for that company to be paying the financing costs associated with outstanding debtor balances. Thus large, financially strong customers should negotiate a settlement discount which is above their opportunity cost of funds but below that of their smaller, less financially strong suppliers, and both parties become financially better off. According to the reports mentioned above, it is the late payments by such very large companies which are the major contributors to the liquidity problems of smaller suppliers. This phenomenon is by no means as common in other countries, notably Germany where direct debit payments to suppliers on the due date are far more common. However some very successful companies in the UK, eg Marks and Spencer, and Mars, have deliberately avoided this dubious and inefficiency creating practice.

Settlement discounts can be regarded as achieving other aims, which would enable companies to offer levels of discount above those justified in the financing saving alone. Most obviously, if customers pay more quickly the risk of incurring bad debts is reduced and some companies may see this as significant. However, in most cases this saving is rather nebulous because if a customer is in financial trouble it has normally ceased taking advantage of early payment settlement discounts some time before the company actually ceases trading. The most important factor is therefore the change in payment strategy which is indicated by a previously fast paying customer which becomes a significantly slower payer; such a change requires rapid and thorough investigation. A more substantial potential cost benefit caused by implementing some early payment incentive scheme is through the reduction in clerical and management time wasted in chasing outstanding balances. This unnecessary cost is incurred by both supplier and customer, and therefore a mutually beneficial improvement should be possible. Suppliers can devise improved ways of dealing with customers which increase the profitability of both businesses, but the incentive and base information to achieve this rely on an appropriately designed system of CAP.

Another area of working capital management has also become very significant in its impact on relative customer profitability levels. Many companies have implemented strategies which are based on holding minimum inventories; just-in-time (JIT) inventories are the normal description of these strategies. The financial justification is obviously based primarily on the saving generated by the lack of financing required but there are many other claims of improved operating efficiencies which can be achieved under such a strict regime. This JIT philosophy was started in Japan where it operated successfully because of a close working relationship between the customer and the supplier. Thus a fundamental element in achieving the maximum economic benefits of JIT is that the customer evaluates its requirements from these suppliers based upon its forthcoming production schedules. The suppliers then produce the required components, sub-assemblies, etc, in line with the predicted usage by the customer. As a result, neither company holds unnecessary stocks! This can only be achieved by the use of sophisticated materials requirement planning software, which is capable of exploding finished goods production schedules into their component elements, with required delivery times. This sophisticated computer technology is in use in many western companies but, in many cases, the benefits achieved are much lower.

The actual result of the implementation of a JIT strategy by many western companies has been to transfer the ownership of the excessive levels of raw material inventories onto their suppliers. The customers refuse to hold stocks and demand very fast response times from their suppliers. In order to meet these response times, suppliers have to hold buffer stocks of goods from which they actually deliver to customers and they re-fill the buffer stocks from actual production. The end result is that, in several industries, JIT has not led to an overall reduction in stockholding levels but merely to a change in ownership. In several specific instances, the location of the inventory has not even changed, although its ownership has, because the change in strategy by the customer meant that it no longer needed large raw material warehouses next door to its factories and these are now used by suppliers to store buffer storage to meet the new, very short delivery demands of the 'more efficient' customer. [It is very difficult to meet a 4-hour delivery response time by any other means if the supplier's factory is located 6 hours away from the customer.]

For this and a number of other strategic reasons, many suppliers are finding that they now have to hold an increasing level of stocks which are specifically attributable to individual customers. The costs associated with holding such stocks should be incorporated into their CAP analyses as it is another way in which the relative profitability of different customers can be affected.

Relevant level of analysis

These examples highlight the relevant level of analysis for CAP. A good system of CAP should help to enhance the overall profitability of the business and a major way of achieving this is by indicating the financial impact of actual and potential strategic moves by customers. Not only should this forewarn the company of the dangers and costs associated with certain moves which might otherwise appear beneficial but, more positively, it should also point out good strategic options which should be pursued pro-actively by the company in order to improve the profitability of *all* customers.

Therefore, CAP analysis should go as far down the costs of the company as are relevant to the particular decisions which are being faced by the company. This will normally only involve those costs which differ by customer groupings as many decisions will be initially based upon relative indications of profitability. However for the evaluation of major closure decisions, the analysis will need to highlight the absolute levels of avoidable costs which are affected by the decision. Unfortunately this means that several different forms and levels of the CAP analysis the CAP analysis will need to be produced to support the various strategic decisions which need to be taken by the business. Consequently, the single regular historical CAP analysis which is produced by many companies is clearly inadequate for this role as a vital decision support system. Indeed it may, on many occasions, indicate a significantly incorrect decision as it contains the wrong information, analysed inappropriately. Figure 6.5 indicates a potential customer account profitability analysis statement for a business which has many of the issues discussed in this and the preceding sections of this chapter. However, it should by now be clear that all such CAP statements should be tailored to the specific needs of the company and the strategic decisions which it is facing.

			£000s
	Sales revenues of actual product mix		428
less	Direct product cost		278
		(35%)	150
less	Specific variable costs		
	– distribution	30	
	– customer rebates	12	
	– customer based advertising and promotions	13	55
			95
less	Share of other costs		
	– field sales-force	15	
	– customer service	10	
	– senior management	3	28
			67
less	Financing costs		
	– outstanding receivables	10	
	– specifically attributable stock levels	6	16
	CUSTOMER CONTRIBUTION (11.9%)		51

Note: Costs are charged to customers only on an attributable basis and not in order to recover fully the total costs incurred by the division.
Hence customer specific costs which are included have been charged on an avoidable basis only.

Figure 6.5 Illustrative customer account profitability analysis statement (based on previous month)

One substantial benefit of this need for tailoring of CAP reports, is that it can be a great advantage to the previously mentioned problem of defining 'quality' customers. The initial CAP analysis should highlight the major areas of relative cost differences among the various categories of customers, and of variations within each category. These differences can be further analysed to ensure that the initially indicated profitability improvement opportunities are genuine and are not offset by other cost elements which have not been included in the CAP analysis. Once the analysis has been validated, the strategic options available to the company can be evaluated and this should include the identification of customers which represent a good strategic fit with the relative competitive advantages of the company. This correlation or 'customer compatibility' measure is the best method of identifying 'quality customers', which should form the main focus for the sales and marketing efforts of the company.

This can be achieved by the use of a marketing planning technique, known as the directional policy matrix, and this is illustrated in the next section. However, this type of detailed comparative analysis is also vitally important if a meaningful comparison of the financial contributions of two very different strategies are to be evaluated. This can be illustrated by a large company in the drinks industry, which was trying to evaluate the relative values of its alternative selling methods. A major part of its sales efforts went into direct selling to retailers, wholesalers and to end customers such as restaurants, hotels, etc. However this company, unlike most of its major competitors, did not have its own chain of public houses through which it could gain distribution for its wines, spirits and mixers. Further, its agreements with its major wholesaler customers meant that pubs were supposed to buy the range of drinks from the wholesalers rather than direct from the company. There was a major concern that, if the publicans were left alone, they would not bother to buy the products as they could, in most cases, get an alternative brand direct from their main supplier. Consequently, the drinks company employed a sizeable sales-force, whose job was to encourage the pub trade to purchase from their local wholesaler.

Initially, this indirect sales-force was seen as a good idea but, during a period of pressure on costs, the senior managers wanted a more formal financial evaluation of the costs and benefits involved. Interestingly, in this example of CAP, identifying the costs associated with the indirect sales-force was easier than identifying any related profit contributions. If the evaluation had been carried out at the time of launch of the new sales-force, it may have been possible to monitor the contribution derived from any increased sales levels achieved after the launch. However, this had not been done and the company did not want to conduct an experiment of withdrawing the sales-force for a period of time, even on a regional basis and evaluating the impact of any resulting drop in sales levels.

It is still possible to conduct a meaningful financial analysis which not only evaluates the existing level of activity, but also assists in the assessment of the optimum level of resources which should be dedicated to this area of activity. The critical basis of the analysis is for the company to develop a model of how the indirect sales-force can influence the decision of the publicans as to which products they should buy and stock in their pubs. Thus a first-stage successful outcome for this sales process would be the trial of the product by this indirect customer. The continued purchase of the product will primarily be influenced by how well it sells to consumers and how relatively profitable those sales are to the publican. Again, the company needs to consider where and how the role of the indirect sales-force fits into this process of continuing sales to these indirect customers. The overall performance in this sector can be evaluated by analyzing relative market shares for different products in the differing market segments and comparing these indirect segments with those directly controlled by the company. However, any under- or over-performance should not necessarily be attributed solely to the indirect sales-force because the motivation and effectiveness of the wholesalers, from whom the pubs actually obtain their stocks, will have a significant impact on the overall business performance.

This is why, for any such segmented analysis, the objectives of the activity should be clearly identified, so that the actual outcome can be compared against these specific objectives. In this example, it was found possible to identify several key objectives for the indirect sales-force and these were used to evaluate their financial performance. Indeed, it was also found possible to compare the financial impact of different levels of resource by evaluating the relative differences in success for these critical objectives, all of which were under the control of the indirect sales-force.

Further developments

CAP analysis can be applied in almost all the segmented areas of a business where major financial decisions have to be taken. Far too often however, the process is treated as a routine regular piece of financial analysis which is always looked at in the same way. This greatly restricts the benefits which accrue from the application of CAP analysis. With the advent of ever cheaper, more powerful computers to carry out the greater variety of analyses required, more and more companies will begin to realize the much greater benefits which can result from a more forward-looking use of CAP methods.

Thus, as argued throughout this chapter, CAP analysis can, and should, be a major element in the strategic planning process. It can highlight the potential for new strategic thrusts for the business or of new channels of distribution which could be developed. A good way of highlighting this potential as a strategic planning tool is by using a variant of the directional policy matrix, illustrated in Figure 6.6. The horizontal axis represents the relative customer compatibility factor for different customer groups. This should be evaluated from the customer's perspective by considering what are the factors which are taken into account by the customer when considering the purchase of a particular product (both goods and services).

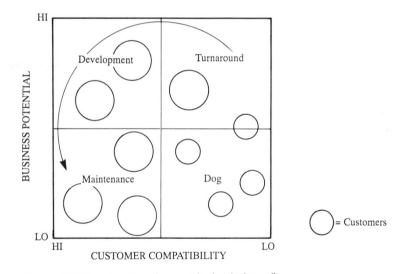

Figure 6.6 Directional policy matrix (variation of)

These factors are then made the subject of an objective comparison of the company against its competitors. The key question is whether the relative strengths of the company (ie its main competitive advantages) are relevant to this particular group of customers. Thus, if a company has built up a strong branded image, with a reputation for quality and a high level of service, potential customers who are looking for a low cost, adequate product would have to be considered incompatible.

The vertical axis normally shows the business potential of the customer. This relates to the share of their total business which the company, at present, does *not* have, because this is the potential which the company has to go for. The overall size of the customer is indicated by the size of the circle used to represent individual customers. By classifying both existing and target customers in this way, a business can allocate its resources in line with its strategic planning objectives. Also it makes it possible to ensure that the right type of resources are dedicated to each category of customer and that the performance of the customer is evaluated appropriately.

This can most easily be illustrated by following the life-cycle of a customer, as shown in Figure 6.6. A new customer should have high business potential but may initially be low on perceived customer compatibility (ie top right hand box). The initial strategy for such a customer should be to change this perception of compatibility, by placing great emphasis on the weakest areas as seen by the customer. This explains why it is vital that the compatibility assessment is done, as far as possible, from the perspective of the customer and that it is done objectively. The results will otherwise be useless, and the customer strategy may focus on completely the wrong areas. The objective is a 'turnaround' in the way the customer feels about the company as a potential supplier. However, as in the much earlier discussion about the product life cycles in Chapter 3, this initial phase of development for a customer should be seen as a period of investment. Consequently, the business should not control this classification of customer by comparing its relative profit contribution to customers which are in a much more mature stage of development. The decision to make this initial development should be made by evaluating the total returns which can be expected to be achieved from this customer over its life cycle. In many cases, this can be more accurately evaluated in advance for customers than for products because the company may already have similar customers, with which it has been dealing for a number of years. The most relevant financial control technique is clearly discounted cash flow analysis but, as previously discussed, this technique cannot meaningfully be used unless it is possible to construct realistic cash flow forecasts for the customer as the potential trading relationship develops.

Therefore, for potential new customer segments where the company has had no previous experience, it may be impossible to build any such meaningful cash flow forecasts. The evaluation consequently becomes more judgemental but the business should also remember that this increases the risks associated with this segment. The required financial return must be increased accordingly.

The next stage of the customer life cycle is where compatibility is high (ie the customer believes that the company is an attractive supplier) but the business potential is still high. High business potential indicates that the company's share of this customer's total demand is not very large, despite the high level of compatibility. The customer strategy at this stage is clearly therefore to improve this relative share of the total business and, in so doing, to reduce the remaining business potential to a low level. In other words, the longer term customer strategy for all customers is to get them into the highly compatible, low business potential box, where the company should maximize the customer profitability. While the customer still has development and growth potential, the financial objective should not be to maximize short-term profitability, as this may damage the longer term profitability of the customer. Thus, the appropriate financial control measures should still be discounted cash flow, although now the improved compatibility may mean that it is no longer necessary to invest net new funds in the customer and some level of CAP return may be achieved. Another good performance measure at this stage is also the same as for the products analysis, ie increases in share (in this case of the customer's total business).

As stated, the main customer strategies are to make targeted customers as compatible as can be financially justified (since this should build a competitive advantage), and then to increase the share of their total potential business. Once this has been achieved, the remaining strategy is to maintain the existing dominant position while making substantial profits. At this stage, it is obviously valid to use customer account profitability as a major objective but even now it should not be seen as the only criterion for judging the successful management of a customer account. The key profit issue is still the maximization of the long-term profitability of the customer relationship. The question has to be considered of for how long will the customer remain in this maintenance box, as this element of the life cycle can dramatically affect the overall financial return which is achieved.

Although it is inevitable that demand for any product will eventually decline, the same is not necessarily true for any individual customer or group of customers. Customer needs may change over time but the company can adapt its product offerings to meet these altered requirements and so maintain its dominant customer position. Indeed this flexibility and adaptiveness may be a critical customer consideration in the compatibility rankings for some rapidly changing industries. Thus it is not inevitable that the customer moves into the 'dog' box due to a reduction in customer compatibility, but the competitive situation may lead to a dramatic change on the other axis. For any customer placed in the 'maintenance' box, the company should consider very carefully how its competitors will be planning their customer strategies. Some of these competitors will almost certainly see this customer as a 'development' account; ie the customer is regarded as highly compatible but the competitor has a low share of the total business due to our company's dominant position. Their strategies should therefore be to try to increase their share and they may do this without regard to the short-term profit implications. If our company is trying to increase this customer's profitability at the same time, the whole customer account may be placed at risk. Thus, even where customer demands do not change and affect the customer life cycle, the dynamics of the competitive environment are very likely to create such changes.

These changes can be particularly dramatic when there is a regulatory change in the environment, such as is faced by an industry undergoing privatization. Normally the government wishes to introduce an element of competition into all privatized industries so as to protect customers from the potential abuse of a monopoly position. In the case of the electricity industry, the UK government split power generation into two companies and separated these from the regionally based distribution companies. However, even more important elements of competition were introduced by changing the legislation to allow other companies to construct power stations (thereby ending the supply monopoly) and by enabling large customers to negotiate direct supply agreements with producers (rather than being forced to buy from their local regional distribution company). In order to compete effectively in this new environment, all the supply companies need very good financial analyses of the profitability of their major existing and potential customers, as an error on a long-term supply contract could prove very costly indeed.

A similar example from privatizations is the problem faced by British Telecom (BT) since being placed into a more competitive environment. BT still has an effective monopoly over the supply of telephone services to domestic consumers but it faces increasing competition in the business area and in the overall supply of international and trunk calls. Under the rules established when it was privatized BT was only allowed to increase its average selling prices by 3% less than inflation. The problem here refers to the 'average' because BT is trying to demonstrate, using customer account profitability analysis, that its selling prices to its various customers for its different services are irrational, so that some prices need to come down while others need to go up substantially. Not surprisingly, its analysis indicates that selling prices in areas where it faces competition need to be reduced while the costs incurred in its monopoly areas require that selling prices be increased dramatically. Thus business charges have tended to be reduced with consumer rates rising faster than inflation as a result. Now, within the consumer sector, BT is arguing for an increase in line rental costs with a corresponding reduction in call charges (particularly trunk and international calls). This is a clear and powerful example of the application of segment profitability analysis being used strategically, even if the reports regarding the total *apportionment* of all *existing* costs to a particular segment indicate some fundamental flaws in the way the process is being implemented.

CAP in action?

Having just considered the impact of CAP on very large monopoly type companies, it may be useful to finish this chapter by considering CAP in the context of a very much smaller, faster growing company. D & M Confectionery Ltd was a Nottingham based, privately owned company which specialized in marketing and distributing cakes. Its initial success was based on focusing on the smaller retailers (ie individual shops and small chains, which tended to be owner managed) where its product expertise added significant value to the customer. It added further value through developing its own regional brand (Country Style was the brand), which helped to create consumer loyalty for the product range which was actually sourced from a number of locally based bakeries. The owner and managing director, Mike Ato, had considerable skill in identifying and specifying successful new products and this expanding product range was a key element in the profitable growth of the business. At this stage, the company had cash on deposit at the bank as it collected the cash due from its customers before it had to pay its suppliers and its needs for capital investment were relatively low. This meant that the financial risk of the business was low but the business risk was relatively high. All the products were branded by D & M as Country Style and hence any problems in product quality in any individual product could reflect adversely across the whole range. The major risk was associated with the relationship with the customers, who relied heavily on the product expertise of D & M and its van salespeople for the range and quantity which they bought. This was particularly true in view of the seasonal nature of the product range and its limited shelf life. Given the branded nature of the product which meant that the risk of stale product was really borne by D & M, in effect D & M was renting space in the retailer's shop and paying a variable rental based on sales achieved.

This was true because D & M effectively controlled the stock held by the retailer and the efficiency of D & M's distribution system determined the amount of shelf life remaining when the product was delivered to the retailer. Further, D & M's brand support and pricing strategy influenced the rate of sale but, if the product remained unsold at the sell-by date, it was in D & M's best interest to uplift the stock so as to avoid potential damage to its brand image. Thus D & M was really dealing with its customers on a sale or return basis whereby it bore all of the product risk and yet it did not have full control of the manufacturing process since it had a range of suppliers. Due to its small size and lack of financial muscle it did not have the negotiating power of Marks and Spencer, who are able to transfer much more of this business risk back to the supplier.

However, its early growth was rapid and successful as its profit margins more than adequately compensated for the high level of business risk, which was partially offset by the low financial risk (high variable costs and no debt financing). Mike was ambitious and wanted to grow. He identified a demand for a new range of high quality cakes which were already available from Danish bakeries, and he rapidly set up supply lines to import these cakes (modified to his exact specification) into the UK. The success was astonishing and this new product range brought D & M to the attention of the major supermarket chains. In negotiating for distribution access to this new market segment, it rapidly became very clear that these national retailers were not interested in the regionally based brand developed and supported by D & M. What they wanted was the product which could be sold under their own private label, thus removing the added value generated by D & M's branding. They also wanted D & M's ability to distribute it efficiently to either their retail outlets in some cases or their own regionally based warehouses. Another change in the customer relationship was caused by the much greater sophistication of the buyers for these new customers, who did not need to rely on the product and marketing expertise of D & M. Indeed they regarded D & M's sales-team as simply delivery drivers because they believed they had the expertise centrally to cope with the seasonal fluctuations in demand for the various products.

D & M acknowledged that this new channel of distribution would require significant changes in its business strategy and it responded positively to the challenge. The vastly increased throughput volumes required much bigger warehousing space and much more sophisticated inventory control procedures. Delivering to the much larger superstores of these new customers was also not practical from its existing fleet of small vans, which had been designed for a daily succession of smaller deliveries. Thus new vans had to be acquired and, because delivery timings were much more specific for the new customers, a sophisticated logistics system was introduced as well as on-site garage facilities to improve the vehicle availability. The administration system also had to change because new deliveries were being made to stores in accordance with orders received from regional or national head office. This meant that delivery notes had to be supplied to the store, with a matching invoice sent to head office. However, the customer required an overall monthly statement which included all the invoices for all the deliveries made to all the stores in that month and, once reconciled and agreed, this statement would be used as the basis for payment. In the past, the van salesperson had produced the invoice at the time of delivering the goods (since they controlled what was actually delivered, there was no point in a pre-ordering system) and, in many cases, had been paid in cash immediately.

Not surprisingly, this new system required a significant investment in computer technology, which was also needed for the stock control system and for logistics planning. Despite this sophisticated accounting system, the inevitable in-built time delays and added complexity dramatically affected the relative cash flows from customers. Continual reconciliation problems further delayed cash receipts while the increased volumes led to demands for more prompt settlements from the suppliers. As a consequence the company became significantly dependent on bank financing at the same time as its fixed cost base increased. This increased financial risk and the associated costs could have been reflected in a segment profitability analysis, if one had been prepared. Such an analysis would also have highlighted that the increased negotiating power of these larger customers had reduced the operating margins achieved as they had negotiated volume buying discounts. Theoretically these reductions were compensated for by the removal of many of the marketing costs and reductions in the distribution costs incurred in the original market segments serviced by the branded products. However, the increased costs in technology and higher stock levels needed to achieve the rapid delivery responses expected by these new customers should also have been taken into account.

Unfortunately, D & M relied on overall financial data and even this was very superficial during the critical period of rapid growth and change in business profile. Increases in sales revenues were equated to increases in profitability and the decline in the cash position of the business was not regarded as exceptional in view of the dramatic growth. Management accounting information was produced retrospectively but because of the major problems involved in managing these monumental changes in the company's operations, these periodic financial reports were not produced for several months until the new business settled down and the new sophisticated computerized accounting system came on stream.

The company did consider the overall risks associated with this changed business strategy, but came to the conclusion that the business risk was reducing to compensate for the increasing financial risk. This was based on the fact that the product risk was significantly reduced under the new method of operation because the company no longer dealt with its customers on a sale or return basis. The new sophisticated customers did not rely to the same extent on D & M's recommended stocking levels and the product was being sold under their logo not D & M's. Thus the main product risk had apparently been transferred to the retailer and consequently D & M could either be satisfied with a lower profit level or try to maintain its profitability by increasing the financial risk. As the CAP analysis eventually showed D & M had a substantially reduced profit level despite the significantly higher financial risk; indeed some of these new major accounts were being operated at a loss.

What was very important for the manager to realize was that the key competitive advantages which had made D & M successful so far were largely irrelevant to the new segment into which it was now moving so rapidly. D & M's original strengths had been in its ability to identify and source new cake products, and to add value to its customers by branding these products plus using its sales-force's expertise to reduce the overall risk to the small retailers of selling these specialized products to their customers. This strategy was based on high added value and was clearly differentiated in its focused segment of the market. D & M was not, and did not need to be, the most efficient, low cost distribution company in the market as distribution was a means to an end in itself. However in the new competitive environment into which it moved, all D & M was contributing to the new customers was to identify the product range and to distribute it to their stores. Consequently, an efficient distribution system was essential to the success of the new strategy and D & M spent considerable sums of money to become an efficient distributor.

In the short term this almost certainly would lead to depressed profitability because of excess distribution and other operating costs as the new systems were being developed, installed and brought up to speed. This created a major problem due to the increased financing risk taken on by the company in the form of increased reliance on external bank financing, all of which was of a relatively short-term nature (eg bank overdraft, invoice discounting, vehicle and computer leasing) and capable of being immediately called in by the bank should it feel it necessary to do so. D & M needed to safeguard its other remaining competitive advantage which was the identification and sourcing of the products. Disastrously, the company concentrated the Danish imported product with one supplier as this minimized the administrative and operational problems during this period of major upheaval in the other areas of the business.

The growth with the new customers was all in the area of these imported products and the Danish supplier saw its business with and dependence on D & M increase dramatically. The supplier became understandably very concerned when D & M's bank started making worrying moves regarding supplier payments. This happened when D & M disclosed to the bank its lack of profitability on the dramatically increased sales revenues. This loss was revealed by the retrospective management accounts and largely resulted from the combined problems of such rapid growth and change in a small company. Unfortunately, the company was not able immediately to produce a financial analysis which showed that the majority of the loss was due to one-off non-recurring items and that the new business would very quickly move into a sustainably profitable position.

The result was that the bank insisted on some improved security before continuing to support the company; the Danish supplier agreed to extend its credit period as it did not want the company to collapse. However, as a consequence its owners asked to be given a greater level of involvement with D & M's activities in the UK, to which Mike quite readily agreed. This involvement included visits to the new major UK customers and within three months the Danish supplier had agreed with the major retailers to deliver direct, bypassing D & M completely. Inevitably D & M Confectionery Ltd went into liquidation as its remaining business could, in no way, support the massively increased fixed cost base taken on for the new market segment.

Obviously there are many reasons contributing to the collapse of this company and it would be far too simplistic to say that a good system of CAP would have prevented this happening. However a major contributor was the lack of up-to-date relevant financial information and the dramatic strategic moves were made without a valid financial evaluation of the potential consequences and risks. Certainly where the strategic thrusts involve a move into a new segment it is very important that the decision-makers are provided with a forecast of the financial impact of the new segment. The simplest way to highlight these implications is through an appropriate form of segmented profitability analysis. This indicates that, as discussed in Chapter 4, much of the material related to CAP in this chapter is also applicable to the topic of the next chapter, ie product profitability analysis. It is not considered helpful to repeat these issues with a different heading and therefore the next chapter will refer back, where appropriate, to the issues discussed in the context of customers.

7

Product profitability analysis

Introduction

As already discussed in the earlier chapters of this part of the book dealing with competitive strategies, business managers' interest in segment profitability has been increasing significantly in recent years. This can most easily be seen in the area of product profitability analysis. 'Product costing' has been a mainstay of cost and management accounting for many years, and many companies have developed very sophisticated cost apportionment systems. However, even for many of these financially sophisticated businesses, the concept of applying a decision-based analysis to relative product profitabilities is still new and is proving difficult for many managers to come to terms with.

The financial analytical techniques used in such a decision-based analysis of relative product profitabilities are not new, and hence it is strange that its development and implementation should be a recent introduction for so many businesses. One possible reason for this could be that in the 'not so competitive' past, contribution margins were high enough on each of the products sold to cover all the other costs of the business and leave an acceptable profit margin. However this is unlikely! Inevitably therefore this lack of adequate financial analysis would have led to some highly profitable products subsidizing the less successful, or more cost intensive items in the total product range. As discussed later in the chapter, this cross-subsidization may be a very successful long-term strategy, but it should be the result of a conscious management decision and not occur by default.

However, in many marketing led companies it is still true that managers concentrate on the profit/volume relationship as a key determinant of the financial success of their main product lines. This simple relationship, which is shown graphically in Figure 7.1, highlights the direct relationship between sales volumes and profits. It is, of course, based on a whole series of restrictive assumptions, which include the need for constant selling prices per unit and a stable product mix. The most important assumption is that fixed costs remain fixed and that variable costs move directly in line with changes in output, throughout the volume range covered by the graph. Thus all costs have to be divided into either fixed or variable, which is by no means impossible but requires yet another restriction on the use of the technique. The nature of most costs changes depending upon the time-scale involved, with more costs becoming variable as the time-scale increases. This means that all costs have to be classified by reference to the appropriate time-scale for the particular decision being considered. As mentioned several times in the book already, financial information must be tailored to the particular needs of the specific decision which it is being used to support. Once again, this means that the business

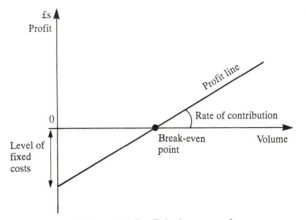

Figure 7.1 Profit/volume graph

should not produce one such profit/volume graph, but the relationship should be specifically represented for different categories of decision over differing time-scales.

Another issue raised by the absence of detailed product profitability analysis is the assessment of the financial impact of particular marketing strategy decisions. Is it reasonable to assume that managers did not need detailed information on the financial impact of their proposed marketing decisions, which might involve repositioning brands, changing the marketing mix and even launching a new product or cancelling an existing one? Basing these types of decisions on an assumed linear relationship of sales volumes and profits could lead to disastrous results for any business.

Thus, for this type of marketing led company, the traditional assumption that as long as sales volumes were maintained at an adequate level, the contribution generated would automatically cover the fixed costs and produce a satisfactory level of profit, is no longer regarded as an acceptable basis for a sound, long-term marketing strategy. Financial information is needed both on the impact of changes in the product mix, and on how total costs are likely to alter if new products are introduced or existing products withdrawn. Also an alternative traditional use of product costing has also been demonstrated to need considerable modification in today's competitive environment. Some companies were, and still are, more technology and product oriented than driven by marketing strategies. In this type of company, selling prices were often set by reference to a cost plus calculation. This normally entailed establishing the direct costs of the product by using a product costing system and then adding on an allowance for overheads, sales and marketing, distribution etc and profit.

Historically, many long-term contracts tended to be negotiated on such a cost plus basis, but clearly this was not in the best interests of the customer. Not only was the customer bearing the whole risk associated with any cost overruns on the project but, if the profit element was included as a percentage of direct costs or total costs, the supplier made a larger profit if the project costs did overrun. Hardly a large incentive to keep project costs to a minimum, and this problem was exacerbated in certain cases where all overheads, as well as profit, were charged as a percentage of direct costs. Not surprisingly customers have, in most industries, woken up to these associated problems and have adjusted the bases on which such contracts are agreed.

In many industries cost plus pricing has largely, if not completely, been replaced by fixed price contracting which, of course, completely transfers the cost overrun risk back to the contractor. This has been the case in the computer industry, where many turnkey projects are now placed with suppliers on a fixed price basis, even though the contract specifies very stringent performance parameters for a computer system which has not yet been developed. This clearly changes the business environment for software and hardware companies tendering for such contracts. Instead of simply charging the clients for the number of consultant days spent on the project at an agreed daily rate and billing for hardware separately, the contractor now needs a very sophisticated project forecasting system which assists in building up the bid price. This system must allow for sensitivity analysis on the critical items and must also incorporate a risk weighted profit level, which should be specific to each individual project depending on the assessed level of associated risk. The financial control system during the implementation of successful tender bids is also a critical issue for the profitability of the company. In this fixed price contracting environment, lack of financial control can have a disastrous impact on the long-term survival of the business as has been learned the hard way by a number of previously successful software companies. This is yet another example of the need for the management accounting systems to adjust and respond to significant changes in the business environment, whether caused by a change in competitive strategy of the company, a competitor, supplier or customer or by some other external influence.

Another area where this type of change has been dramatic has been in defence contracting, particularly for the UK government. Historically much of this work was done on a cost plus basis, but this was reviewed in the 1980s when a new head of defence procurement was brought in. Many defence contracts were moved to a fixed price basis and the majority of those that had to be kept on a variable price were subjected to many more stringent conditions. These included controls on acceptable levels of overheads which could be charged to projects and even extended to specifying acceptable rates of pay for labour used on the contract. As a result, the commercial relationship between customer and supplier became much more like that in most other industries. However, the change created major upheavals for some large defence contractors over the following years during which they had to introduce the newly required management accounting forecasting and control systems and develop the management skills to apply these systems properly.

At present therefore, there are relatively few areas where a true cost plus pricing system can be applied without the risk of rapid and severe sanctions from customers or from competitors. Indeed it can be argued that only a genuine monopoly supplier could contemplate such a pricing strategy today.

Even for a monopoly supplier, such an insensitive pricing strategy could be disastrous as these cost plus selling prices could dramatically affect the volumes sold of different products and hence have an impact on overall profitability. The product or technology led strategy is not, of itself, the problem but this type of strategy still needs careful implementation in the market place. Returning briefly to the Ansoff matrix, this type of strategy would be characterized as a market development led strategy, as shown in Figure 7.2. For this to be successful, the company should have its main competitive strengths in its mastery of a particular technology or in the control of particular defendable product attributes, such as could be encompassed in a brand. This makes it more cost effective for the business to expand its sales of these existing and new, but related products to new customers, rather than trying to develop completely different product concepts for its existing customers. Such a strategy is clearly the converse of the customer led strategy discussed in the previous chapter. This indicates the principal basis for deciding whether the segmentation analysis focuses primarily on customers or products. Even where the strategic thrust of the business is based around products, CAP analysis can still be of great value in planning resource allocations for the

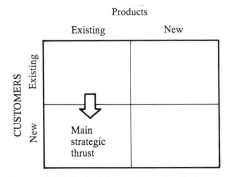

Figure 7.2 Maximizing value of existing products

different market segments in which these products are sold; but the main area of strategic planning interest will be on the future development of these key products and their associated competitive advantages. It should be remembered that decisions affecting these alternative segmentations (customers and products) cannot be based on the same financial analysis, as what is direct to a customer group may not be direct to any particular product sold to that customer, and vice versa.

Direct product profitability (DPP)

The original main thrust behind the development of sophisticated product profitability analyses was therefore, not surprisingly, from such product orientated companies, which wanted to use the analysis as a major marketing tool in order to expand their customer base. Procter and Gamble (P & G), a USA-based fast-moving consumer goods (fmcg) company with a wide range of well-known branded products, is normally credited as the first company to turn product profitability analysis from an internal, historical review to an externally focused, forward-looking strategic marketing tool. The basis of this strategy was a clear understanding of its marketplace and how the external business environment was changing. P & G's products are principally sold through retailers and, at this time, retailing in the USA was going through a process of concentration giving the major retailers much greater negotiating power. Also the rapid growth in the variety and range of consumer goods, both branded and private label, was placing great pressure on retail space, ie access to the channel of distribution.

Clearly, as a producer of fmcg branded products, there is no point in spending vast sums of money on advertising to create awareness of and demand for the products, if the consumers cannot find them when they go shopping. Effective distribution in the major retailers is a critical success factor for such a company, but the larger retailers are becoming increasingly powerful and sophisticated. P & G used this increasing sophistication to present the retailer with a financially based argument for buying, stocking and displaying its products in preference to those of other suppliers. A good example of how this worked can be given by using washing powders, which is a market dominated globally by P & G and Unilever, through its subsidiary Lever Bros.

To a retailer, washing powders might be seen as a necessary evil. They have to be stocked as they are an essential product for the consumer but they take up a lot of space and generate a relatively low return per unit due to their low selling price. (This is particularly true if washing powders are compared to razor blades, which have a much higher apparent selling price for their size.) The danger to a company like P & G is that, as a result, retailers may try to minimize the shelf space and warehouse storage space dedicated to washing powders. This could lead to fewer brands being stocked or to fewer facings of product on the shelves, or both. To a marketing led company this would be disastrous as a reduction in effective retail distribution could reduce the value created by the rest of its marketing efforts. P & G's response was to carry out a sophisticated relative product profitability analysis for its own and competitive products. However, this was done, not from its own perspective, but from that of the retailer. The objective was to stop retailers regarding certain products as unattractive by showing them as major profit contributors to their business.

In order to achieve this, the analysis had to relate the profitability to a critical success factor for the retailer and this was clearly going to be the limited shelf space available in the retail outlets. Therefore the sales and attributable costs for each product needed to be calculated and presented as a contribution per square metre of shelf space occupied by the product. [The analysis has now become still more sophisticated in that the contribution is now related to the cubic capacity occupied by the product; this is because the retailer can increase the number of shelves on a display fixture if the products are shorter.] For this analysis the sales revenues by product would be readily available, as would the direct buying-in costs of the product.

Even if the comparative analysis was restricted to this gross contribution by the product comparison, it could still be of value. Relating total contribution levels to the shelf space occupied by each product would highlight differences in the rates of sale among various products. Thus a product, like washing powders, which had a low contribution per unit could have a compensatingly high relative rate of sale. The net result could be a good relative level of contribution per square metre of shelf space occupied. However, there are other attributable costs which need to be included if validly comparative results are to be achieved across widely differing product areas.

It is important, yet again, to remember that this type of segmented analysis concentrates on the relative profitabilities of a range of products. Consequently the analysis can focus on those cost areas which vary among the various products. This should include differences in the way the products are ordered, delivered, stored, put on display in the store and paid for by the retailer, as well as the more obvious marketing promotional offers made by the manufacturers.

Such a relative comparison, as is illustrated in Figure 7.3, could well show an apparent low margin item in a better light if its rate of sale and ease of handling indicated that its total net contribution generated per unit of space occupied was greater than a higher value but slower moving or more difficult rival product. When it was first introduced, the product profitability analysis had a significant impact. Not surprisingly, it was rapidly picked up by the retailers themselves and applied to all their product ranges using their more detailed inside knowledge of these costs differences. It was also adopted by a range of consulting organizations for application to other manufacturers selling into retail. It was also used more generally as a valid marketing tool for any business selling products through an intermediary channel of distribution, which is vitally interested in its own overall profitability. Highlighting the relative profit contribution advantages of one's own products is a good way of drawing attention to an attractive competitive advantage to such an intermediate customer. This technique is now very well-developed and can be applied through tailoring software packages which are available from the consultants in the area. It has become known, for obvious reasons, as Direct Product Profitability or DPP for short.

Many companies now use DPP in conjunction with their CAP analysis in an attempt to show how advantageous it is for a customer to buy their whole range of products, rather than

Retailer analysis	Product A	Product B
Net selling price per unit	200p	100p
Buying-in cost of goods	160p	90p
Gross contribution	40p (20%)	10p (10%)
Shelf area occupied per unit	20 sq cm	100 sq cm
∴ Simple Contribution per unit of limiting factor	2p/sq.cm	0.1p/sq.cm
HOWEVER incorporating other relevant factors into the relative profitability comparison may change the picture eg Other direct costs incurred by the retailer		
Per unit of product	10p	1p
Giving revised contributions per unit	30p	9p
Total shelf space per product line	1000 sq cm	2500 sq cm
Total sales volumes per week	50	500
∴ Revised contribution per unit of limiting factor per week	$\dfrac{30p \times 50}{1000}$	$\dfrac{9p \times 500}{2500}$
	= 1.5p	1.8p

Figure 7.3 Relative product profitability comparison

selecting only the top few brand leaders. This strategy can be enhanced, where financially justifiable, by giving the customer an additional discount if the whole range of products, including any new products which may be launched, is stocked. This is a variation on the logic of giving discounts based on the sales revenue generated over a specified period (commonly the financial year of the supplier, when it is normally described as an over-riding discount) and should also be carefully evaluated. The problem is that the discount is normally given on *all* the business done with this customer, rather than on only the incremental business. Consequently, the product mix may be significant if the net contributions vary considerably across the range. The extra discount for full stocking is normally beneficial to innovative companies, which are regularly launching new products or additions to existing products. Such a discount can be used to guarantee a critical mass of distribution immediately upon launch, so that the launch advertising is not wasted due to an absence of effective distribution. This can be particularly cost effective if the discounts are only given to leading customers, which are likely to influence the buying decisions of the majority of remaining potential customers. Gaining immediate distribution for new products in these opinion-formers may almost guarantee a large level of initial orders from the rest; obviously, if the new product subsequently does not sell through this launch channel, there are unlikely to be many repeat orders!

This external use of product profitability analysis, and particularly DPP, is a powerful example of its strategic value, but the technique also has substantial value when it is applied internally within the business. However, its internal application can lead to some interesting questions about the nature of products and particularly the difference between a product and a brand.

Products versus brands

There is a well-known marketing adage that 'products have life cycles whereas brands do not'. This is meant to illustrate that the properties of a well-developed brand can be transferred away from declining products across to new products so as to extend the brand's life cycle far beyond that of the originally linked product. Whether this separate brand life cycle can be infinitely extended by this process will be considered in Chapter 14, but this adage still raises an important issue for all companies which is the need to distinguish between products and brands in their strategic planning and decision-making. In any company where the strategic thrust is concentrated on market development using existing products or technologies, it can make a significant difference to the implementation of that strategy whether the principal competitive advantage derives from a specific product and its functional attributes or from the brand which has been created around the product. These implications for the strategic thrust of the business, not surprisingly, have a significant impact on the design and implementation of the appropriate strategic management accounting systems, which must focus on the key driving force of the company whether that is the product or the surrounding brand.

A clear illustration of this difference is when the brand name is also the corporate name, so that the customer automatically associates the two together. In some cases this idea of corporate branding has been used to extend significantly the product range which is sold by the company under a single brand positioning (such as was discussed in the previous chapter in the case of Marks and Spencer). As a consequence, individual products become less important to the overall strategy, as long as they comply with the attributes of the dominant brand. However in most of these cases, the main competitive strategy is, in fact, to leverage off the well-developed customer base so as to extend the range of products sold.

In the initial stages of such strategies, the new products are frequently closely related to the existing product range so that the brand and product association are kept clearly identified in the mind of the customer. As the branding image becomes better established, and hence more dominant, it is often possible to extend the product range well outside the previously identified groupings, and to use the power and consistency of the brand identity to maintain the loyalty of the customer. This has most clearly been achieved by the major retailers, which now spend massive amounts on advertising their own brand image as opposed to any particular product. As a consequence, customers are prepared to buy a vast range of products many of which are sold under the retailers' 'own brand' name, as the brand image creates a consistent expectation of quality, value, etc in the mind of the customer. As in all the competitive strategies, a sound financial evaluation is essential. These high levels of corporate brand advertising should be financially evaluated by assessing the added value created by the increased level of customer loyalty established or by the enhanced rates of contribution which can be achieved both from the existing range of products and from the more easily extended range. Profit margins can often be enhanced, as discussed in Chapters 5 and 6, because of the increased negotiating power which the retailers create as a result of this branding strategy, having reduced their suppliers to the role of producing commodity products. Such a corporate brand positioning could clearly be of immense value in fashion or high technology product sectors, where the short life cycles of any individual product make it very difficult to justify financially the high initial marketing investment required to achieve customer awareness and to gain effective distribution for the new product.

Such customer led strategies are particularly common where corporate branding is used and could be applied to the electronics sector with companies such as Sony, which now sells a wide range of consumer electronics products based on a single brand positioning. It can even be applied to some companies in the automotive sector where the brand association of the company name, eg BMW and Ford, is designed to surpass the individual products which have their own brand identities. As customers mature and become better off, they are supposed to trade up from a Ford Fiesta, through Escort and Sierra, to an executive positioned Ford Scorpio. Unfortunately this overall brand positioning can also be self-limiting as it restricts the ability of the company to launch products which do not fit with the well-established brand image. This can explain certain strategic acquisitions, such as Ford's purchase of the more up-market Jaguar, as the quickest (although not necessarily the cheapest) way to change the brand positioning of new product offerings. The financial evaluation of such strategic acquisitions is clearly of vital importance. This is particularly true where the main asset which is being purchased is something as nebulous as a brand. The realizable value of such an intangible asset, if the acquisition has subsequently been seen to fail, may be much lower than the original purchase price. It is also important to remember that an acquisition is only economically justified if the business purchased is worth more to the buyer than it paid for it. In the case of most brand acquisitions, this added value is supposed to be generated by either the extension of the product range sold under the acquired brand, or by the expansion of the markets in which this brand is sold. Clearly the buyer needs existing competitive advantages in either these products or markets if it is likely to be able to realize this potential added value. Applying this logic to the Ford acquisition of Jaguar, the added value is potentially through both routes, as the extension of the Jaguar product range by launching a smaller model becomes possible utilizing Ford's engineering and volume manufacturing expertise. Also its global marketing power and financial strength may make it possible to expand the sales of Jaguar's existing models. However, each of these moves could also be argued as being a high risk strategy as it involves changing the existing positioning of the Jaguar brand name, for which Ford had just paid a vast amount of money. High risk demands a correspondingly high level of return, and this should be incorporated into the financial evaluation process.

It is therefore important that companies consider the risks associated with such a strategic move outside their existing brand positioning, particularly where the brand is very strong and very clearly identified. Thus if Jaguar's prospective customers were now to perceive the cars as 'really a Ford', they may be unwilling to continue to pay the premium pricing currently obtainable for the existing marque. This type of financial impact could be even more dramatic if Ferrari customers perceived themselves as actually buying a very expensive Fiat. In reverse, this argument can be applied to Mercedes-Benz, as it would have been concerned that the launch of the 190 series, as a smaller sized luxury car, could have had an adverse impact on the image of its much larger and much more expensive, existing branded range.

This type of essential financial analysis is a clear example of the strategic use of segment profitability but it hinges on the ability of the company to evaluate the financial impact of such a strategic move on the value of its existing brands. This is very difficult, if not impossible, for many companies because they do not have adequate information on the current value of their existing brands. Consequently it can become more difficult to assess the financial impact of these strategic initiatives. The proper financial evaluation of brands is vitally important for many marketing led companies where the value of these intangible brand assets can be much greater than the other more tangible assets of the business. This question of brand assets and their valuation has recently been the subject of a heated debate within the UK accounting profession or, more precisely, a debate between the professional accountancy firms and the financial managers working for large marketing led companies. Unfortunately the debate, which has centred on whether brand assets should be included in the externally published balance sheets of these companies, has completely missed the key strategic management accounting issue. Whether or not brand assets are included in external financial statements, it is essential that the financial impact of decisions concerning these vital business assets is considered *internally* by managers. Thus the valuation of marketing assets should not be regarded as an exercise exclusively for external consumption but must be an integral part of the internal strategic planning process. This valuation can be carried out by using the normal financial techniques such as discounting the future cash flows which are expected to be generated by the brand or by applying an appropriate price/earnings multiple to the current earnings of the brand. These techniques have been fully discussed by the author in a book dealing exclusively with brand valuations[1].

Many accountants have expressed concern regarding the ability of a business to separate out the cash flows or profits which are specifically attributable to the brand. In other words, the 'brand' value is only created by earning excess returns by having a branded product rather than selling an unbranded product, produced on the same physical assets using the same process. Clearly this evaluation is complex and requires the exercise of considerable managerial judgement, because the brand could increase the return to the business in a variety of ways. Thus a premium price may be achievable without losing market share, or higher sales volumes at the same price can be generated than would be the case without the creation of brand loyalty. However, many other strategic management accounting issues are complex and all decisions affecting the future require the exercise of considerable managerial judgement; so there is no automatic reason for not tackling this critical issue.

Indeed the process of trying to assess the financial impact of strategic decisions on brands can be very useful in clarifying the positioning and real value added of the brands concerned.

The brand creates enhanced value because it builds up over time a set of specific attributes, which result from the advertising and promotional support, etc which has been used to develop the brand. The concept of separating development marketing from the maintenance level of support needed merely to hold the brand attributes at their current level was discussed in Chapter 4, but these varying brand characteristics have been developed much further both by academics and by leading marketing companies. Thus, in many companies, the marketing strategy will set out specifically to improve certain characteristics of the brand, such as customer awareness or effective distribution levels. Unfortunately, in most cases the financial evaluation of these very specific and easily monitored marketing objectives is non-existent; the effectiveness of the required marketing expenditure simply being measured by the short-term overall change in profits or cash flows, which may, of course, be totally unrelated to these specific longer term marketing activities.

Leslie de Chernatony[2] has analysed the varying types of brand assets in great detail and has identified five key factors which should be used in planning the marketing strategies for the brands. These key factors could similarly be used in assessing the financial impact of marketing decisions. If a company cannot identify what attributes of the brand contribute to its ability to create 'added value', it is more than likely that the brand does not, in reality, create any such added value. It is also virtually certain that within a short period it will definitely not add value because the company cannot know what marketing support is needed to maintain or develop these existing brand attributes. In an earlier piece of research, conducted with Gil McWilliam, Leslie de Chernatony divided brand characteristics into two main groupings. Thus brands could be regarded as being mainly functional or representational; a purely functional brand is

---

[1]Ward, K., *Brand Valuation – Establishing a True and Fair View*, Hutchinson, 1989, Chapter 7.

[2]de Chernatony, L., The varying types of brand asset: the control issue in brand strategy development? IBC Conference, London, June 1990

dominated by the physical attributes and the actual useful performance of the product, whereas a totally representational brand can be regarded as being bought so as to express something about the lifestyle or self-image of the purchaser of the brand rather than for any particular enhanced value in use. The brand characteristics can be neatly depicted diagrammatically, as is shown in Figure 7.4.

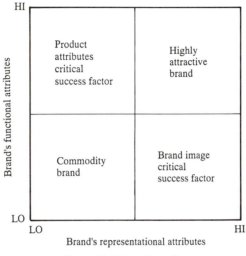

Figure 7.4 Brand attributes

This matrix shows that some highly attractive brands can be both highly functional and highly representational (Rolls Royce cars would probably fit into this category). The logical marketing strategy for these brands is to build or maintain the brand by ensuring both superior product quality and an up-market exclusive image. The premium pricing, which the strength of the brand should allow, should more than adequately compensate for the extra costs incurred in producing and positioning the product. For many successful brands in certain market sectors, the representational characteristics of the brand can be regarded as much more important than the actual functionality of the product (which may not be superior to many other products available in the market). This type of analysis can be applied to many luxury branded goods such as perfumes, alcoholic and other drinks, personal accessories, etc. The marketing strategy for these products is clearly to maintain or strengthen these representational characteristics by carefully positioning the image of the brand. It may be necessary to restrict access to the product if this helps in strengthening the representational qualities of the brand. However it can be possible to develop a branding strategy which is fundamentally based on representational characteristics but which also allows for massive volumes to be achieved. A good example might be sports-wear such as based on the team strip of a famous club or the national side or the endorsement of a leading player; the brand sells high volumes at premium prices, not because of its functional attributes but because of its representational identification of the wearer with their particular team or heroes.

Such mass market representational brands can often generate increased value by regularly changing the appearance of the product, albeit in a relatively superficial way; such as when a leading football team changes the design of its kit at least every three years and, as a consequence, causes a large demand for the new representational image from its loyal supporters. The functional attributes of the product become much less important and, in many cases with sporting and leisure wear, the product may not even be used in its originally designed context (eg wearing designer track-suits and training shoes for normal occasions, as opposed to active sporting pursuits).

Financially these strongly representational brands often require a high initial investment in building the image of the brand (as, for example, in the case of a large, guaranteed, up-front fee to the sporting superstar who is going to endorse the product). This initial investment is recovered through the enhanced contributions made on subsequent sales achieved at premium prices. Consequently if the image is unsuccessful, the high initial expenditure is lost and these representational brands should, at the time of launch, be regarded as high risk strategies. Also, because the major investment is in the brand's representational associations, it may be advisable to change the product very regularly so there is always a new version for the leading opinion-forming group of devotees to buy. This happens, at present, with sports shoes from the leading branded companies (Reebok, Nike, Adidas, etc) but the combined costs of marketing these products and changing them so rapidly has severely adversely affected the profitability of many companies in this market. This is despite high and increasing selling prices. A key financial evaluation technique for this short product life cycle problem would be the pay-back period for the incremental investment (including launch marketing expenditure) associated with each new product innovation; in many cases, it is clear that the pay-back period exceeds the life of the last few products introduced into the market.

Another strategy for these strongly representational brands is to try spread the very high initial marketing support costs by extending the product range more widely. This, as mentioned earlier, seems logical as the specific product attributes are now less important to the continued success of the brand. However, each time the brand image is used to support a new product or even a replacement product (when the original product has come to the end of its life cycle), there is a risk of damaging the image of the brand and thus reducing its value. This issue is discussed again in Chapter 14 but the risks associated with spreading a strong representational brand across other product areas are normally lower than for a correspondingly strong functionally based brand. All the added products in the case of a functional brand should fit closely with the existing product attributes of the original product group (eg good value for money). This can restrict the extent to which the brand can be extended but there are examples of representational brands which are now very successful and the original product is largely irrelevant or even no longer in existence (the luxury products brand, Dunhill fits this category, as it started out as an up-market tobacco brand). Not surprisingly, strongly representational brands tend to be associated with consumer goods.

The problem box on the matrix is the brand with low representational attributes and no relative strength in functional attributes either. This is really a commodity style product and it is difficult to see how any significant marketing expenditure on such a brand can be financially justified. There is little likelihood of achieving an adequate future return to repay such an investment. It is important that companies regularly review their brands from this type of attribute perspective, as it highlights both the type of marketing strategy and the level of marketing expenditure required, given the specific marketing objectives which have been established for the brand.

So far the brands with high functional characteristics but low representational attributes have not been discussed in detail. These brands depend for their success on the 'value in use' generated by the products marketed using the brand image, and hence any umbrella branding of a broad range of products will only work if all the products so grouped together share a similar set of functional characteristics. This makes it possible to consider the strategic management accounting issues for these types of brands along with the products themselves.

Product attributes

When trying to design a segmented profitability analysis for the various products sold by a business, an obvious initial problem is in defining what constitutes an individual product. For example, in many companies, the same basic product may be packed in different sizes and sold under different brands, each of which offers a specific value proposition to its respective customers. The managers have to decide whether the product profitability analysis classifies all these elements as one product or are they separately analysed as independent products.

In most cases, this apparent dilemma is easily resolved if the managers go back to the original reasons for carrying out the product profitability analysis. These should be to aid strategic planning and resource allocation decisions. These fundamental reasons indicate that the definition of a product is driven by the product-based decisions which are currently being considered by the business and those that may need to be considered in the future. This normally results in products being classified into a hierarchical structure, with differing degrees of financial information being required at each level. A detailed specific example can illustrate this point most clearly.

A division of a very large fmcg company produced a wide range of food products which were sold through various distribution channels, eg retail, wholesale, catering and industrial. One large element within this product range was dehydrated instant mashed potato (IMP). This was primarily sold through retailers as two separately positioned brands, but was also supplied to certain major retailers packaged as the retailer's own brand. To a large extent the initial manufacturing process was the same for all the varying final product derivatives. This process consisted of sorting and grading the raw potatoes, passing them through a steam peeler and then a continuous cooker and masher, followed by a drying and dehydration process, which left a low moisture content potato powder. At this stage the processing diverged somewhat depending upon the final form which the product was to take, so that different additives were mixed into certain products and there was a quality grading process as well. The premium priced brand was also passed through a re-agglomeration spray process, so as to form the powder into small pieces of dried potato, which were felt to be more attractive to the consumer. Obviously, once differently processed, the products had to be separately stored, although there was also common bulk storage of the basic product before any separate processing took place. This bulk silo storage was relatively expensive as the powder had to be kept under nitrogen; not surprisingly, dehydrated potato absorbs moisture from the air.

The packaging operation was also segmented but not by type of additive or form of product. The size of packaging and channel of distribution dictated the appropriate form of packaging machinery and process used. Consequently, as illustrated in Figure 7.5, the differently processed bulk products went through a range of packaging processes, all of which were shared with at least one other final product category. The end result of this manufacturing process was a range of products, all containing IMP which had been produced through the same basic process. However, these products then went through another series of business areas where the specific inputs varied (eg the marketing and distribution function), but this time the different processes were dictated by the channel of distribution, through which the product passed, or by the positioning of the particular product. Some product groups, eg retailers' own brands, only passed through one channel of distribution and, even then, possibly only through a small specialized element of that channel (such as one retailer's stores). Other specific product elements, such as the economy sized value brand, were sold very widely through two distinct channels of distribution. In some cases the same product in terms of size was packaged differently to cater for the specific needs of the different channels of distribution.

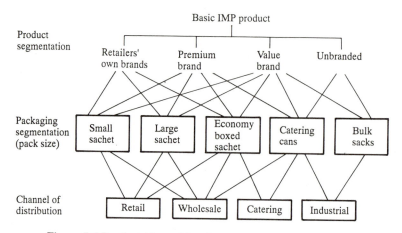

Figure 7.5 Product hierarchies (instant mashed potato example)

This very common problem of complex shared resources makes it very important that the product profitability analysis is carefully designed and structured. If this is not done, the resulting product contribution statements can lead to some disastrously wrong decisions being taken regarding either ceasing the production of particular products or increasing the resources allocated to other lines. Certain business decisions will be taken which only affect the resources allocated to individual brands, or even specific pack sizes of that individual brand. For instance, is it still economic to continue producing the premium branded product in three pack sizes, or should the smallest size be dropped? Other decisions will affect the different segments of the product mix, eg is it worthwhile to maintain two separate brand positionings in the market and what would be the financial consequences of merging them? Still broader decisions may concern the overall capacity for either producing IMP or storing the various forms of final and intermediate products. In order to provide the required financial support to all of these decisions, the segment profitability analysis must be carried out at each relevant level. However, as the levels become increasingly specific, less and less of the costs are specifically attributable to individual products. For example, at the overall IMP product level, most of the manufacturing costs were specifically attributable to this product group; but most of these manufacturing costs were clearly shared at the level of the individual pack sizes of each branded product. Unless the relevant portion of these manufacturing costs was included in the product profitability analysis, a very misleadingly high apparent contribution would be included from the sales of individual products. Some form of cost apportionment system was clearly needed to spread the raw material and other indirect but variable manufacturing costs to these final products. The first stage was to break the manufacturing costs into the differently based processes, so that products were only charged for costs they have caused to be incurred. In this example, this meant that the basic manufacturing process was separated from the more product specific, later manufacturing and packaging areas of the business. It should be clear that even this stage of such an analysis requires the use of a considerable degree of managerial judgement, as the costs of any business do not all fit neatly into these segmented boxes.

These overall costs must now be spread to the relevant products and this requires the selection of the most appropriate basis of apportionment for each of the costs involved. This is where the objectives of the exercise must be remembered, rather than the normal obsessive concentration on accounting neatness. The objective is to assist in the allocation of scarce resources among the various alternative possible uses available to the business, ie a classic case for the application of the opportunity cost concept. This means that the basis of apportionment should reflect the proportionate usage of these scarce resources and this requires the identity of the limiting factor which applies to each critical resource. The limiting factor is, of course, what makes the resource scarce in the first place. Thus, applying this logic to the IMP example, the basic manufacturing process is limited in terms of the tonnage of dehydrated potato which it can produce. If this is the critical constraint, the basic production costs should be spread across the total tonnage produced so as to arrive at a common cost per tonne for the basic IMP product. This basic cost is then increased by the specifically apportioned costs of the subsequent specialized production processes, with these costs again being spread according to the limiting factor concept.

In this example, the production process costs can initially be spread by weight as this is the critical limiting factor on the output produced and is also the relevant unit in which the final product is sold. However, if the production process for different final products resulted in different total output weights depending on the mix of products produced, then tonnage is no longer an appropriate basis of apportionment as it is a moveable basis of measurement. This could happen if the different IMP end products had differing moisture levels, since the drying process time is controlled by the desired level of moisture left in the powder. In the tissue industry this is very definitely the case, as producing either facial tissues or kitchen towels (at opposite ends of the weight spectrum) on any given tissue machine will result in significantly different total weights of tissue produced. This is discussed in more detail in Chapter 10 in the context of transfer pricing. It is important that a different method of cost apportionment is found, as otherwise the heaviest weight product will be unfairly charged the highest proportion of indirect costs. As explained in Chapter 10, the normal answer for such variable output machines which run continuously is to apportion indirect costs by reference to the machine hours needed to produce the particular output of each different product.

Returning to the IMP example, the apportionment of costs based on the limiting factor principle still does not provide a valid financial input for *all* the potential strategic decisions which the company may face. Apportioning total manufacturing costs on the basis of the total tonnage produced inevitably produces an average cost per tonne, whether the calculation uses actual historic data or forecast planning information. Thus this average cost may not, of itself, be the relevant cost which should be incorporated in the decision analysis. For example if, as happens from time to time, the local market supply of potatoes suitable for processing becomes scarce, due (say) to a drought, prices of the basic raw material will rise considerably. Consequently, the company needs specific financial information on how it should respond to this significant and potentially previously unexpected future cost pressure.

One response could be to import finished bulk product (IMP) from other countries and this possibility needs to be financially evaluated by comparing the delivered cost of imported product against the increased cost of local production. However, if a large volume of IMP is imported, the local factory may be shut down temporarily or put on short-time working. The cost implications of this must be taken into account and only genuine cost savings from such reduced local manufacturing should be included in the comparison. Thus if the labour force have an agreement whereby they are paid a guaranteed work week even if they are laid off, this amount of the total wage cost should be treated as a fixed cost for this decision. As mentioned previously, the classification between fixed and variable costs must be done by reference to the specific timescale of the issues being considered.

Alternatively the company may want to consider the relative impact of these increasing costs on the different final products. This can easily be demonstrated by re-calculating the product contributions using the latest forecast costs for raw materials. The impact could well be to show some of the lower added value products (eg industrial sales) making a negative contribution at current selling prices, while the higher priced branded products may be showing a lower but still positive margin over the higher forecast costs. This financial evaluation may indicate the short-term logic of re-allocating available output to the higher selling price products during the shortage, but the strategic decision must always take account of the longer term implications of such short-term actions. The company may have long-term contractual obligations on some of its industrial contracts and therefore it may not be able simply to stop supplying. Also the customers in this sector will be more directly aware of the cost increase of their alternative purchases (eg raw potatoes, which they cook themselves) and therefore it may be easier to renegotiate selling prices in this sector so as to pass on the raw material cost increases. The brand managers will also be very concerned at maintaining, or even increasing, the supply of their branded products during such a period of potato shortage. If alternative prices are high, there is a strong possibility of an increased level of trial by new consumers and higher levels of usage by existing consumers. This could improve the positioning of the brands and lead to a higher level of continuing sales and consumer penetration when the shortage has ended. Thus the business should evaluate the longer term benefit of such a developmental marketing strategy against the short-term costs of not increasing selling prices of these branded products during the shortage and even buying in extra supplies of expensive raw materials which may be sold at a relatively low profit margin.

Once again, the product profitability analysis must be designed to enable such decisions to be supported by sound financial information which has been tailored to the needs of the specific decision. There is another very good example from this company which demonstrates how this type of process needs to be applied in the distribution area of a business. Distribution costs (ie freight and warehousing) are, in most companies, partly fixed and partly variable in the short and medium term. The balance between the two depends on the level of internal versus external provision of these essential business support functions. If the business owns and operates its own fleet of delivery vehicles, as well as owning and operating its warehousing facilities, a larger proportion of its distribution costs are likely to be fixed than if it buys in these services from external suppliers on a variable basis (ie without giving the contractor a guaranteed contract for a fixed period). However, because the total cost incurred by the business is dependent upon the volume or weight of product despatched, distribution costs should be incorporated into the product profitability analysis for the company. This is particularly true where the cost of distribution differs considerably among the various products sold by the company.

In the IMP business, this was particularly true because the retail packaging was flushed with nitrogen to improve the shelf life of the product. This made the product relatively bulky and inefficient to transport in terms of freight weight ratio to volume. The industrial sacks of product were much more freight efficient as 40 of the 25 kilo sacks were stacked on each pallet, giving good delivery vehicle utilization. This was also true for the catering packs, which were packed in cases containing 6 cans, each of which held 5 kilos of IMP. Forty of these cases were stacked on a pallet for distribution purposes.

These substantial differences in freight weight to volume ratios meant that it was not satisfactory to apportion the freight budget across the product on a tonnage basis. Such a process would adversely impact on the heavier weight but more efficiently packed products. Also, it was not possible to spread the warehousing costs to the products simply by using a combination of pallets and time stored, even though this was how much of the warehousing cost was incurred. For operational reasons, the company would sometimes pack product into catering cans so as to relieve pressure on the bulk storage facilities irrespective of the specific inventory or outstanding order position of this particular product. This was because this product had a very long shelf life when sealed into a can which was flushed with nitrogen, and the pallets of product were also easy to store in the warehouse. These pallets could be stacked on top of each other, whereas most of the other IMP products had to be stored in pallet racking and had much shorter product lives. Consequently the inventory of catering product would often be disproportionately high relative to its sales volumes, and under a simple cost apportionment system, its profitability would have been unfairly reduced. In fact the nature of the product reduced the need to increase the investment in bulk storage of the other products. It was important that the product profitability analysis system helped senior management to focus on these key elements of the different products. In order to do this a very flexible and responsive type of accounting system was implemented, which enabled each different level and type of decision to be supported by the required tailored financial information.

Problems of cross-subsidizing products

The importance of designing the management accounting system to fit the specific needs of the organization cannot be overemphasized and this is considered in detail in Part Five. However, this issue is also important when dealing with products which are linked more by common customers than by the internally shared resources discussed above. Given the common emphasis of management accounting on the internal aspects of the business, it is not surprising that companies are often better at dealing with the problems caused by internally shared resources than with externally based conflicts of product profitability.

As mentioned earlier, it is a quite common competitive strategy for a business to use one product as a 'loss leader' in order to sell other more profitable products to the same or related customers. This process, quite clearly, creates severe complications for any product profitability analysis and yet it is vitally important that this kind of competitive strategy is carefully financially evaluated and monitored. Obviously if the majority of customers only purchased the subsidized loss leader product, the overall profitability of the business would disappear even though growth in sales revenues might be substantial. It is also important that the external environment, including competitive responses, is carefully monitored as any change in, say, relative competitive pricing could make the existing cross-subsidizing strategy unacceptable in the future. An example of the way this kind of cross-subsidizing strategy has been developed in the computer industry should make this point more clearly.

Initially, most computer manufacturers saw themselves as producing and selling hardware boxes, which provided large volume processing power to their customers. The size of the box was determined by the volume of data processing required by the customer. Almost coincidentally the customer needed software to operate the hardware and technical support functions in order to maintain the complex kit now installed at its premises. In some cases, these extras were included in one overall price for the system. As processing volumes increased, due to the inclusion of more software programmes on the computer, the customer needed ever more hardware. Thus add-on memory and extra central processing units were bought by the company to plug into the existing hardware. This phase raised the first issue of relative pricing strategy for the early computer suppliers. If one company supplies all of a customer's computer needs (hardware, software and maintenance), the customer is likely to focus exclusively on the overall price for the complete package. Thus as long as all competitors follow the same strategy the only realistic profitability analysis is for the complete installations sold to the customers.

However, as soon as new competitors enter the industry with different, more focused strategies, the relative pricing of the component elements of the total package becomes much more important. If the prices of the hardware are set relatively high, and the software and maintenance are provided at cost, the potential for new hardware manufacturers to enter the industry becomes clear. This is particularly true if they specialize in one particular peripheral device (such as printers, disk drives, etc) so that they quickly acquire optimum economies of scale and good product quality. These new competitors can severely affect the overall profitability of the main computer companies if they reduce the original companies' share of the highly profitable add-on markets. One consequent strategic response by the original computer companies could be to alter the relative pricing strategy of the component elements by, for example, reducing the selling prices of their peripherals and increasing software and maintenance prices. This reduces the attractiveness of the industry to focused hardware manufacturers, but increases it to independent software houses and third party maintenance companies. As illustrated in Figure 7.6, the cross-subsidization almost inevitably makes it attractive for a competitor to concentrate on the product which is showing the excessively high profit margin and to ignore the product which is being heavily subsidized. It is therefore vitally important that the relative pricing strategies for related products are established after careful examination of the potential competitive response which any particular set of inter-relationships could create.

A key part of this analysis is the evaluation of the different entry barriers which exist for the different products involved. Obviously it will be easier for a company to maintain its overall market share *and* increase its total profitability if it maximizes the selling price of any product areas where it currently has a monopoly position and the entry barriers are very high to any new prospective competitor. Eventually these high profit margins are likely to attract new

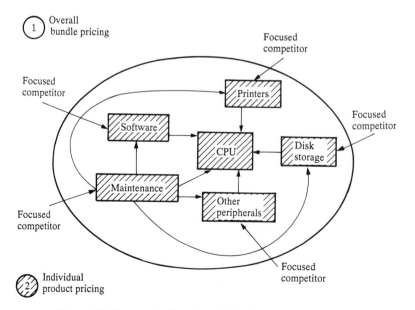

Figure 7.6 Cross-subsidization within the computer industry

companies who will try to break down the monopoly position and, consequently, erode the value of the initial competitive strategy. A good externally focused competitor accounting system, as discussed in Chapter 5, should provide an early warning system which may enable the company to minimize the impact by altering its relative product pricing and product profitabilities. In the computer industry these differences have results in a plethora of companies focusing on very limited elements of any computer user's total needs and a declining number of very large companies which try to provide the complete range of customers' requirements.

Creating a competitive advantage

The key reason for such a complicated relative product pricing strategy is to create a sustainable competitive advantage against existing and potential competitors. Thus the pricing policy should either discourage new entrants or be difficult to follow by existing competitors. This requires, once again, externally based information on the competitors' cost structures so that strategic moves can be made which would be very expensive for them to follow.

A simple example is where one company has a number of manufacturing or service outlets well dispersed across its sales area, while its main competitors have single sources of supply. For many customers it would be logical for the company to offer a delivery inclusive selling price or, for service work, to quote a collect and return inclusive price, as this would be more expensive for its competitors to match and may offer a perceived benefit to these customers.

A more complex version has been used by Japanese car manufacturers, and other consumer durable companies, as a way of communicating their product quality to the consumer. The logic is that good product quality will lead to less operating costs over the product's lifetime due to less breakdowns and consequent repairs. However, the danger is that customers do not necessarily take this fully into account when making the buying decision, although they will be aware of the risk of incurring substantial repair costs in the future. Therefore if the quality manufacturer offers a much longer warranty period (ie free repair period) on its product than is normal in the industry, this should be perceived as reducing the risk and total cost of ownership as well as clearly demonstrating its faith in its quality. Thus these car companies now offer three-year, unlimited mileage warranties, and some television producers include a free five-year guarantee covering all repair costs, ie both parts **and** labour.

The important aspect of this strategy is that the cost to the innovator is relatively low, because it produces a good quality product anyway but may not be able to achieve an adequate premium price in the market due to its brand image, etc. However the cost to its competitors of matching such a marketing strategy would be much higher, unless they can rapidly improve their product quality to the leader's levels. Such an improvement in quality is likely to be expensive and time-consuming and may even then not be adequate. In the car industry this type of product quality is measured in terms of 'things gone wrong' (TGW) in any particular period of ownership (normally the first 12 months). As many European-based producers have invested heavily in improving their quality and hence reducing their TGW, they have found that the gap between themselves and their leading competitor has been maintained or got even wider. In other words, the leader is improving its quality at an even faster rate and is also extending the period of the comparison as well!

Clearly such an important element in any competitive strategy puts very great demands on the management accounting system in terms of the requirements for internal product based information and the external comparisons which are vitally important. If the comparative financial analyses can highlight substantial competitive advantages in any particular area, it may be possible to develop a competitive strategy which builds on them and maximizes their value to the business.

Even in the case of a completely integrated product, these issues of product profitability analysis can be important. A new product company, which did not in the end survive to develop its concept, was set up to launch an innovative form of trading stamps. The idea of Holiday Stamps was that the company sold savings stamps on an exclusive basis to retailers, which then gave them away to their customers as a way of building customer loyalty. The customers saved the stamps by sticking them into savings books and then redeemed the full books by using them as part payment for any holiday they wanted to take. Although the concept was clearly for a single product, the new company had four sources of income. First it received payment for the stamps from the retailer but there was obviously going to be a delay before the stamps would be redeemed, and thus these funds could be deposited in a bank account and earn interest income for the company as a second flow of income. The third source was from the travel industry which would receive a boost of cash flow from these redeemed savings books, and hence a fee could be charged as the bookings were made. The final source was by selling advertising in the savings books, as such space was of great interest to the retailers involved in the scheme and to travel companies against whose products the stamps would be redeemed.

However, in order to sell such advertising space the design of the savings books had to be substantially improved so that appropriately glossy advertising would not seem out of place. This necessitated a financial comparison of the additional cost to be incurred in improving the quality of the savings books with the extra income which could be generated from the sales of the consequently created advertising space. Such a system also needs regular monitoring as the relative balances between the specific costs and revenues can alter over time, and the initial financial justification may no longer be valid.

Product attractiveness matrix

This issue of continuing to monitor the financial justification of any separable element of a product's competitive strategy is clearly important to all products as strategies need to be developed and changed as both internal and external environments alter. However, most products can be analysed into their key attributes and the competitive strategy designed accordingly. This analysis can have significant implications for the level and type of investment which should be made in the product in the future. Consequently, it should form part of the product analysis within the strategic management accounting system.

A simple way of illustrating this type of attribute analysis is shown in the product attractiveness matrix in Figure 7.7. As can be seen from the diagram, the product is analysed as to its relative strengths against its competing products in terms of its level of cost advantage and degree of differentiation. The appropriate competitive strategy and level of attractiveness can be easily obtained from the resultant position of the product in the matrix. However, if this strategic type of analysis is then allied with the product profitability analysis, the appropriateness of the current competitive strategy for the product can be assessed. For example, a product which is classified as having a strong relative cost advantage from the attractiveness matrix should have this positioning confirmed in its product profitability analysis. In other words, its perceived competitiveness cost advantage in terms of the customer should not be achieved at the total expense of its level of internal profitability. It should have

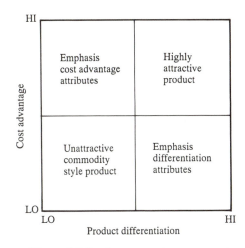

Figure 7.7 Product attractiveness matrix

specific internal cost advantages which are enabling the lower relative selling prices to be achieved. Similarly a highly differentiated product should be achieving a good internal gross profit margin in order to sustain the higher marketing support which its competitive positioning normally demands.

It is also important that the strategic planning process identifies the desired direction for each product within the matrix as the strategic management accounting system can ensure that adequate investment funds are made available where necessary and that conflicting objectives are not established for any particular product. For example, if the strategic plan indicates that a product should increase its level of differentiation in the market, while the financial plan indicates a short-term improvement in its level of product profitability, the appropriate financial analysis should ensure that the most important business priority is highlighted and one set of objectives is amended appropriately.

This raises another common but important accounting issue which must be considered in the context of product profitability analysis. The overall business is interested in the net contribution made by each of its products and whether that level of contribution is acceptable given the strategic positioning of the particular product. This does not mean, as has been argued throughout this part of the book, that the total net profit of the business has to be attributed to the specific individual products which make up the overall business. However, these economically valid net contributions will inevitably include a range of costs which have been correctly charged against the product in order to arrive at the contribution measure but which are not directly controllable by the managers who are held responsible for the product. Managerial performance must only be judged on elements over which the manager can exercise control. Consequently, managerial performance should be evaluated at the level of controllable contribution even though additional shared costs may be charged below this level in order to arrive at the economic contribution of the product.

Exercise of managerial control

Where different levels of management are involved in the control of the products, through the product hierarchies discussed earlier, the product profitability analysis system needs to be able to generate financial information on the appropriate level of managerially controllable product contribution for each level of manager. Once again the accounting analysis has to be developed to cope with the complexity of the way in which the business is managed rather than acting as a constraint on the business.

The financial support to managers in the product area is often vital, and yet it is an area which is very under-developed in many companies. Partly this may be caused by the way in which the area is managed in that many marketing departments have 'brand' managers who are the key decision-makers. Thus the emphasis is on brands whereas, in many of these companies, most of the financial information is produced for products not brands. The brand managers are often regarded as the managing directors of the brands and are held responsible for the overall performance of the brands under their control. Unfortunately, this is often an extreme example of responsibility without authority or even, in some cases, access to the necessary information on which sound decisions can be based. Similar issues exist in this area as were discussed in the previous chapter for sales managers in terms of the frequent lack of access to the detailed financial analyses on products, brands and customers which are essential to effective product management.

Organizational structure issues

Clearly the way in which the management of the organization is structured can have a significant impact on the effectiveness of the organization in all the areas of its business, but this is also true in its ability to produce meaningful financial information. This part of the book has been concerned with examining the appropriate methods of accounting for competitive strategies but, as stated in Part One of the book, these competitive strategies have to be integrated within the overall strategy of the organization. If the overall structure of the organization is no longer appropriate to the majority of these competitive strategies, perhaps because they have changed in response to a changing external environment, it can be difficult for the accounting system to produce relevant financial information at all the appropriate decision-making levels of the organization.

This is frequently the reason for individual managers and areas of the business declaring UDI, and starting their own accounting systems in order to obtain at least some usable financial support for their decisions. In Part Three, the book considers the accounting issues raised by different types of overall corporate strategies, while in Part Four the two areas of competitive and corporate strategies are brought together by considering businesses at different stages of development.

Corporate Strategies – The Role of Strategic Management Accounting

8

The relevance of organization structure

Overview

Most financial investments should today be viewed as two stage processes. Investors (ie primarily shareholders but including other providers of funding, such as banks) put money into a business in the expectation of receiving an acceptable return in the future in relation to the perceived risk associated with the particular business. As shown diagrammatically in Figure 8.1, the business attempts to produce at least this required financial return by, in turn, investing the available funds in a range of business projects. These projects may involve a

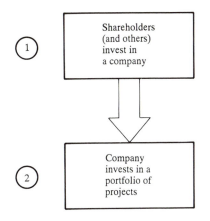

Figure 8.1 Investment as a 2-stage process

number of unrelated products being sold in varying markets. Indeed the complexity and scale of most modern large organizations have effectively removed the investors from any possible direct involvement in, or even evaluation of, the detailed competitive strategies which are selected and implemented for each of these product/market related investment projects.

As a result, the investors have to base their investment decisions on a broader evaluation of the probable overall success of the corporate strategy for the whole organization in which they can invest. However, the introduction of this intermediary organization inevitably increases the costs of the investment process. Consequently, in order to justify this higher level of cost, there should be an even greater improvement in the resulting return to the investors.

It must be remembered that shareholder value is only created by delivering a greater return to the shareholder than is demanded for the associated risk. Also in a perfectly efficient capital market this is impossible to achieve on a sustainable basis; this is demonstrated in the numerical example given in Chapter 16. Therefore, the creation of shareholder value requires imperfections and inefficiencies in the market. These can clearly occur at either stage in this two stage investment process. As has been discussed at length in Part Two, there are major opportunities for creating shareholder value through implementing competitive strategies which create and sustain a competitive advantage by exploiting these 'imperfections and inefficiencies' at the product/market stage of the investment process.

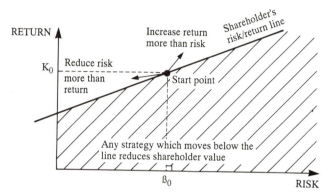

Figure 8.2 Value creating alternatives

However, it may be less obvious how an overall corporate strategy can 'add value' to shareholders at the first investment stage; but this must be achieved if the continued existence of these large, diverse, modern organizations is to be financially justified. Added value can be generated in two ways; either by increasing the return achieved without commensurately increasing the perceived risk, or by reducing the associated risk more than the return is reduced. These alternatives are illustrated in Figure 8.2 and it may be possible for a large organization to develop a portfolio of investment projects which have such a reduced risk when combined together, eg the individual business risks are partially offset by being counter-cyclical. The return achieved is automatically reduced in this case, due to the cost involved in designing, implementing and subsequently managing such a portfolio of projects, but the demanded return may be even further reduced due to the lower perception of risk. [There is a very strong argument that sophisticated investors can design and monitor their own balanced investment portfolios at much lower costs than companies can, as was discussed in Chapter 3.]

This reduced overall risk profile may also assist the large business in another way. Other providers of funding, most notably banks, are also interested in the risk/return relationship. Thus, if the risk of this portfolio of projects is reduced from the lenders' perspective, a greater level of lower cost debt funding may be available to the broadly based company than would be available to more focused businesses. Any such reduction in the cost of funding will reflect in an increased return to the shareholders of the business; the way in which combining counter-cyclical cash flows can achieve this is illustrated in Figure 8.3.

The detailed issues relating to the raising of finance for large organizations have already been stated as being beyond the scope of this book, as they are covered within financial strategy. However, in this part of the book, the ways in which overall corporate strategies can

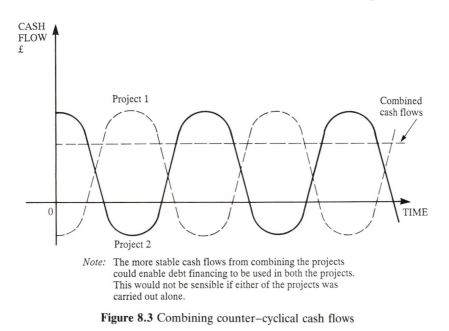

Note: The more stable cash flows from combining the projects
could enable debt financing to be used in both the projects.
This would not be sensible if either of the projects was
carried out alone.

Figure 8.3 Combining counter–cyclical cash flows

be used to enhance shareholder value are considered. This highlights several strategic accounting issues, and these are discussed and illustrated in the context of different types of organizational structure.

Introduction

Part Two was concerned with the management accounting needs of the particular competitive strategies adopted by any specific business unit. This section considers the accounting implications of the different types of corporate strategies which may be selected and implemented by a company as a whole. It is therefore logical to start this part of the book by considering why there may be a gap between the overall corporate strategy of the company and the individual competitive strategies of the business units which comprise the company. Clearly, if there is no significant difference between the corporate and competitive strategies, there is no obvious reason for different financial information to be needed either.

[For the sake of simplicity in this discussion, it is assumed that each separate operating unit of the group (eg each Strategic Business Unit) has a dominant or single competitive strategy. Removing this simplifying assumption does not, in any way, affect the arguments discussed in this part of the book; in practice, as discussed in Chapter 2, strategic management is a multi-layered process with interactions of competitive and corporate strategies taking place at each of these layers.]

The fundamental reasons for the existence of the organization should be encapsulated in its vision and mission statement and be more specifically defined in the corporate goals and objectives, which were discussed in Chapter 2. These statements are drawn up for the total organization and should take into account the interests of all the various shareholders, ie they must not focus exclusively on the wishes of either shareholders or managers. For many small, tightly focused and owner controlled businesses these overall goals and objectives can be directly translated into specific competitive strategies, which indicate not only which products the business should produce and which markets the business should enter but also *how* this should be done. However, in larger organizations, such direct linkage is not practical.

This may be due to the wide range of products made or markets served by the total organization, but can also be caused simply by the scale of the company's operations, which require that intermediate functional and segmented competitive strategies are developed for the various areas of the business. It has often been said that very large, diversified businesses do not themselves compete directly with other businesses. Hence they do not need, and indeed cannot have, meaningful *overall* competitive strategies. The operating divisions, or Strategic Business Units, of such large businesses all have direct competitors and thus they require specific competitive strategies. If this is true, it has major implications for the type of financial information which is needed at the centre of these large, complex organizations. Should the detailed financial competitive, customer and product analyses, which were considered in the previous part of the book, be provided to the centre, or should the available information be restricted to a more overall review of the actual and projected financial performance of these operating divisions?

As usual, the answer is that the financial information needs of the centre of any large organization are driven by the particular role fulfilled by the managers located there. What is clear for most large, complex businesses is that managers with group-wide responsibilities cannot function effectively if they receive exactly the same financial information as is prepared for and provided to the managers at the divisional level. At the very least, the information must be summarized so as to make the volume received manageable, but these summaries must not remove or reduce the value of the information which is provided. There are a wide variety of ways in which large groups are controlled, and the accounting implications of these are considered in detail in the following chapters. However, there are some fundamental alternative organizational structures which must be examined, before going on to consider some common issues of control which should be borne in mind when designing an accounting information system for the centre of a large group.

Functional, divisional and matrix structures

Historically, large organizations were normally organized on either a functional or divisional structure. A functional structure groups together all the particular functional skills within the business into one area, under the supervision of ultimately one line manager (eg the marketing director, who has direct control over *all* the product and brand managers). This type of organization is illustrated in Figure 8.4. The justification for such a structure is primarily that, by concentrating similar resources in one area of the business, the greatest possible level of economies of scale can be realized. Thus such functionally based management structures are felt to be of most value when large scale investments are needed in certain areas of the business, and such a scale of investment can only be justified on a group-wide basis. The areas of both product and process research and development, information technology, and many aspects of finance and accounting are good examples where the potential benefits from economies of scale can be significant.

However, there is a substantial downside risk from having a completely functionally organized group. Economies of scale may be generated in certain areas of the business and better technically based managers can be recruited and retained to control these larger

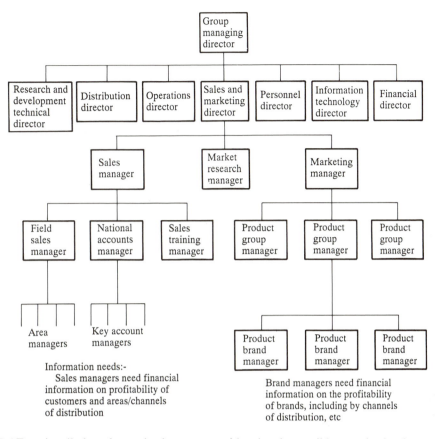

Figure 8.4 Functionally-based organization structure (showing the possible organization for one element only ie the sales and marketing function)

functional areas; but the group may lack a close market focus, particularly if it is trading with a wide range of products in a diverse group of markets.

As previously discussed, the best way of focusing managerial attention on specific markets and products is to break the business down into appropriately defined operating divisions (eg SBUs), as shown in Figure 8.5. The divisional managers are made directly responsible for their unit's operations in a specified market with a specified range of products. The key benefit of such a structure is to focus managerial attention on a small part of the overall group's business. This should ensure that a clearly defined competitive strategy is developed and implemented in each of the divisions. If this is done, a series of appropriately different sustainable competitive advantages can be developed.

Such a level of managerial market focus is difficult to achieve in a purely functionally organized group, but the completely divisionalized structure cannot achieve the same degree of economies of scale, particularly if each division is made effectively a stand-alone, self-sufficient business. Not surprisingly, therefore, mixed organizational structures have been developed which try to obtain the benefits of both the traditional formats. A common form of such a mixed structure is illustrated in Figure 8.6, where the separate operating divisions concentrate on their existing products and markets. However, the centralized group organization provides those overall support functions which can greatly benefit from the

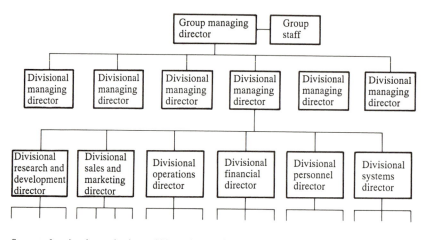

Separate functional organizations within each operating division
(replicated across all divisions)

Figure 8.5 Divisionally based organization structure

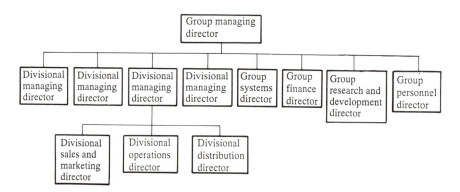

Figure 8.6 Mixed organizational structure

economies of scale which can only be achieved by carrying out these operations for the group as a whole.

Unfortunately, this combined type of organization creates almost as many problems as it solves. Although the group-wide functionally organized areas can achieve good economies of scale, there is now a risk that they will lose the market focus which is achieved by locating smaller, less efficient units within the operating divisions. Thus the group may gain efficiency but lose effectiveness if the functional support areas do not concentrate on areas of most interest to the divisions, which they are supposed to be supporting.

Several different methods of attacking this problem have been tried, including setting up a system of transfer pricing, under which the centralized support area (such as information technology) sells its services to the operating units using an internal set of prices. This is designed to make sure that the operating divisions get the new computer systems, etc which they want as they will be asked to pay for them. Yet again, internal transfer pricing systems create new sets of control problems which are considered in Chapters 10 and 11. Another

Functional Organizational Structure

Division No.	Sales and marketing	Operations	Research and development	Finance	Systems	TOTAL (by division)
1						
2			●			
3						
4						
5						
TOTAL (by function)						

Divisional Organizational Structure

● This Research and development unit is part of Division 2, but is functionally also considered as part of the overall research and development activity of the group.

Figure 8.7 Matrix based organization structure

increasingly popular way of trying to solve the problem of achieving these potential economies of scale is by creating a matrix type of organization structure. In its simplest form, this consists of most areas of the business reporting in to two different managers, who have different types of responsibilities for the area. Thus an area will have a functional boss and a divisional line manager as well. Clearly this type of structure, which is illustrated in Figure 8.7, creates a number of complications in management reporting, which require that the differing managerial roles are clearly defined and understood by all those involved and affected by the matrix.

The major role for the overall functionally based managers is to ensure the efficient utilization of existing resources and the development of adequate future skills to serve the overall strategic needs of the group. Conversely, the divisionally based managers should concentrate on the effective use of the resources under their control, or available to their divisions, so that the selected competitive strategies can be successfully implemented. If these overriding objectives are remembered, it becomes much easier to define, individually for each large group, the specific ways in which all the matrix cross-over points are to be managed. This degree of specific clarity is essential if confusion and the consequent costly mistakes or demotivation of staff are to be avoided.

One way in which this matrix structure has been still further developed is to allow at least part of the group to be managed as a series of projects, which are resourced and staffed as required. This method is frequently used by people based businesses such as large firms of accountants, investment banks, advertising agencies and other service organizations, which regularly need to put together multi-disciplinary teams for special projects. Thus, the various types of skills may be permanently organized on a functional basis, with managers who are responsible for people development and overall resourcing levels. When a particular project team is required, the appointed project manager specifies the people skills and career background needed for the project, together with all the other resources, and these are supplied to the project by the resource controlling functional managers. Once the need within the project is satisfied, the particular individual or other resource is re-allocated to the next assignment by their appropriate resource manager. Thus the projects are really a series of temporary subdivisions of the group. This enables the project manager to concentrate on the specific needs of the project; creating a clear focus of managerial attention. However, the longer term people development and resourcing needs of the group are also considered by the functionally organized resource controlling managers. This sophisticated type of management structure has been particularly well-developed by many software companies; as their businesses really are a series of major projects, with skilled people as their critical resource, such a structure is very important to their long-term success.

As a consequence of these developments in organization structures, most large groups now consist of some form of tailored combination of functional and divisional structures. These make the design of strategic management accounting systems for the centre of such groups even more complicated, but there are still some common issues involved.

Common issues of group control

The day-to-day control of the operating businesses must be delegated to some degree to the responsible divisional managers; if not, there is no point in dividing the organization into separate operating units. The differing ways of decentralizing this responsibility are discussed later in this chapter, but the clear implication is that the major role of the centre of a large group should be strategic rather than tactical or operational. In order to justify incurring the inevitable central costs involved in running a large group of businesses, the organization should be able to demonstrate that there is synergy created by the group as a whole. This means that the value of the group as an integrated whole is greater than the sum of the values of the individual business units. The large number of corporate raids and demerger (or 'unbundling') proposals aimed at very large, publicly quoted groups of companies in the 1980s clearly challenged this precept for many such companies. This has led the senior managers of many groups to question both the overall corporate strategies of their organizations, and whether they are really adding value by continuing to develop the group. Several surveys in the early 1990s have indicated a greater tendency for large groups to concentrate on their 'core' businesses rather than to continue to diversify into other areas, which was a common trend in the early 1980s.

This desirable emphasis on strategic issues at the centre of a group has significant implications for the financial information required by the managers involved. They require financial information which enables them to direct, evaluate and control the various competitive strategies of their SBUs in a way which adds value to the combined businesses forming the group. This means that, although the different operating units do not all have to be implementing the same type of competitive strategy, their strategies should be complementary and not in conflict. It also means that the financial information required at the centre from each business unit should be tailored both to the particular competitive strategy being implemented by the business unit, and to the strategic role within the group which is being fulfilled by that particular area of operations.

In many groups, it is therefore of concern that most of the financial information which is actually provided to the centre deals with the detailed operational performance of these business units. Thus, it does not provide the centre with valid financial support to its strategic management role, which should be the main emphasis of central group personnel. There is another clear need for financial information at the centre of a group and that is to support the monitoring and up-dating of the overall corporate strategy. For many groups, this will involve identifying new areas of business for the group to move into where its existing skills could enable it to gain a sustainable competitive advantage. As discussed in Chapter 4, by their very nature SBUs tend to be limited in their area of operations and consequently no individual business unit may be evaluating these more general business opportunities for the overall group. If this gap in strategic planning is to be effectively filled by the central management team, it will need good external analysis of areas of potential interest and good internal knowledge, not only of existing internal skills and competencies, but also of the planned future developments of all the operating units of the group.

Thus there are several potential gaps which can arise between the centrally driven corporate strategy and even a well co-ordinated set of divisional competitive strategies. Closing these gaps requires the provision of good financial information at the centre, but the detailed form of this supporting information and its source depends on the particular organizational structure in use within any group.

Different strategic types of organizational structure

There are many different strategic types of organizational structures which have been used over the years with varying degrees of success. This demonstrates that there is no 'right' or 'wrong' way for an organization to be structured, and success has far more to do with how well the chosen organizational structure is implemented and subsequently managed, than with what structure was selected in the first place. However, it is also clear that certain types of organizational structure are more appropriate for particular types of business and at different stages of development. As businesses are themselves dynamic and subject to significant change over time, this implies that the organizational structure may itself need to change in line with these varying business needs. Clearly, this has severe implications for the strategic management accounting system which is supplying the financial information needs of the centre of the organization.

Organizational structures can themselves, of course, be categorized in different ways. For the purposes of this current discussion, organizations are being considered in terms of their strategic business structures, which are then discussed in more detail in each of the following chapters. The more traditional organizational alternatives of functional, divisional and matrix structures have already been outlined. The appropriateness of each of these to the different strategic business structures is considered in this discussion and in the relevant following chapter.

The simplest type of strategic group organization can be described as a single business, which has merely grown too large for it to be controlled effectively as one unit. These single focus groups are dealt with in detail in Chapter 9, but their organization structures can develop in many different ways depending upon the nature of the common 'single focus' of the group. The main strategic thrust of many such focused businesses is a single product or very restricted range of products. This type of organization can continue to be controlled as a single business unit (ie using a functional organization) implementing only one clearly defined competitive strategy, as long as the market in which the product is sold is also relatively restricted. As the success of the product in its initial market grows, the group often decides to expand by moving the product into new markets. Not only does this product-led strategy introduce the need for a more complex managerial structure within the organization, but it often also requires different competitive strategies to be implemented in these differing markets.

In its initial home market, the company may well have established itself as the market leader, in what may now be a maturing market. Indeed, it is frequently the lack of future growth opportunites in this original market which leads to the proposed expansion into other markets. It would be most logical for the company to try to identify potential new markets which are less well developed and not already dominated by products which are equivalent in their attributes to the current source of its domestic success. Given the clearly defined focus of the existing business units in their current markets, part of the corporate strategic role is normally to identify these attractive new market opportunities. This would provide the company with the opportunity for the future growth which is missing in its existing areas of operation, while the financial investment required to launch and develop the product in these expanding markets could be funded from the current successful operations. Thus although the business still consists of a limited product range, the corporate strategy has now developed into needing to manage a portfolio of markets so as to add value to the overall business, with each element of the portfolio being given specific objectives and individually tailored competitive strategies depending on their positions within the total portfolio.

Alternatively, the main strategic thrust for growth within such a basic single product, single market business, could come from its perceived strength with its existing customer base. If there is such a perceived opportunity to expand the range of products which are sold to these customers, this type of market-led strategy also requires the overlay of a portfolio management structure. This is necessary to ensure that only appropriate new products, with complementary value propositions to the existing range, are launched into this market, as otherwise the original competitive advantage of the business (ie its loyal customer base) can be damaged or destroyed by this expansion into other products. The organization structure may also need to be carefully designed in order to ensure that the desirable close co-ordination and integration of all contacts with the all-important customer base is achieved. In many such cases, this is achieved by having a single business unit responsible for all such customer contacts, while the products may be actually produced by a range of other separately controlled operating divisions. Separating the external sales and marketing functions from these operational and production roles clearly raises important issues regarding the type of financial information which is needed across these separated areas. For example, there may be a need for an internal transfer pricing system if the production units are going to 'sell' their output to the sales and marketing division.

These different types of strategic thrusts are both good examples of how goal congruence should work in terms of the overall corporate strategy giving a sense of direction and focus to the individual divisional competitive strategies. As discussed in more detail in the context of conglomerates, the corporate strategy may demand that a particular business unit follows a competitive strategy which appears to produce a sub-optimal result for that business unit. However, if it enhances the financial performance of the organization as a whole, it may be a valid justification for the combination of these individual business units into a single group.

Another apparent type of single business which may require a group structure, with the concomitant complexity of both corporate and competitive strategies, is where the overall business is highly vertically integrated. Thus companies in the oil and the tissue industries, which are considered in more detail in Chapter 10, may have a focused and relatively limited range of final products, but the key strategic issues facing managers in these industries differ considerably at various stages in their production, distribution and marketing functions. Consequently, the financial information requirements should also differ tremendously between, for example, the managers responsible for oil exploration in a major new offshore oilfield and the managers in charge of the retailing operations (ie petrol sales through garage forecourts to final consumers) in a clearly defined market. The group management should play a key strategic role in balancing the allocation of resources within the group, and in directing the separate competitive strategies of the business units at the various levels in the value chain. Once again, much of the information needed for these overall strategic decisions will not necessarily be automatically produced by the existing operating units, as they do not face the same corporate decisions. For example, in the light of recent major interruptions to supplies, a large 'global' oil company may want to review the degree to which it should be self-sufficient as a group in terms of refining capacity or the supply of certain types of crude oil. The group may add a further constraint which relates to minimizing its geographic dependence on a single region of the world (eg the Middle East) for such a critical resource. These overall group issues should always be tackled at the group level so that the vested interests of any regional or divisional managers are not allowed to bias the decisions, even though all the financial information required to support the decision may be supplied from existing, internal, divisionally based management accounting systems.

Perhaps the most common type of organization structure where corporate strategy has an important role is the conglomerate group, which brings together an apparently disparate group of operating businesses. Such groups are normally run as divisional structures, but even such an obvious choice can create problems. As mentioned before, the initial role of corporate strategy in this type of group is to justify why the group should be kept together, ie where is the added value, or synergy, of 'the group'. What is often forgotten is that the benefit of a conglomerate structure can come from a variety of possible strengths, which can be gained from such a diversity of business operations. As a result, the strategic management accounting system at the centre should concentrate on the appropriate cause of any overall group advantage, so that it can be maintained and built upon.

The classical view of the conglomerate as operating a balanced portfolio of businesses may still be valid, but the definition of 'balanced' can differ among a variety of such groups. The portfolio may be balanced in terms of the cash flows of the businesses, so that development units are funded from the cash flows generated by the more mature businesses within the group. In this case the key financial role for the centre is in co-ordinating the cash flow planning for the group and controlling the overall rate of growth of all the cash negative business units by reference to the available internal and external sources of funding. If the businesses are completely unrelated there may be few other synergistic benefits which can be obtained. Of course, in anything approaching an efficient capital market, the added value generated by the continued existence of such a group is negligible.

An alternative view of the balanced portfolio looks for an inverse correlation among the diverse business units forming the group, in that the overall risk of the group is reduced by combining business units with counter-cyclical business cycles. The concept of the positive correlation between risk and the return demanded by investors has already been discussed at length, and this concept is critical to the added value of such a conglomerate strategy. The risk associated with the competitive strategy of any individual business unit may be high, with a consequently high demanded return. However, if a collection of such high risk businesses can be compiled, where the individual businesses have offsetting risk profiles, the combined risk of the overall organization may be reduced, as was illustrated in Figure 8.3. (Obviously, if the wrong businesses are combined, the overall risk may be substantially increased by putting these businesses together.) As the risk reduces, so does the return expected by the investors and consequently the combined group may have greater value than the sum of the values of the individual businesses. However, as discussed in Chapter 3 and developed in more detail in Chapter 11, this potential increase in value by the creation of such a balanced portfolio can be obtained directly by a sensible investor, by simply selecting a balanced set of companies in which to buy shares. Consequently, the investor does not need the organization to diversify in order to obtain this risk reduction, and there may be no added value created as a result. Indeed, implementing such a strategy and managing a large diversified conglomerate inevitably adds costs to the organization and hence can reduce value for the investor, rather than enhancing it.

There is a strong argument that one of the main driving forces behind the development of many conglomerates during the 1970s and early 1980s was the desire of senior managers, rather than shareholders, to reduce the overall risk of the business. Obviously, it is impossible for senior executives to construct a comparably well-balanced portfolio, ie of jobs, as it is for the well-diversified shareholder; this is illustrated in Figure 8.8. This argument hinges on a breakdown in the operation of agency theory, which was discussed in Chapter 1, as the capital markets should not allow managers to act against the interests of shareholders. However, any such breakdown can be argued as being temporary, because the more recent tendency to take apart, or 'demerge', many such conglomerates can be argued as the shareholders' response to the decrease in total value caused by inappropriate corporate strategies.

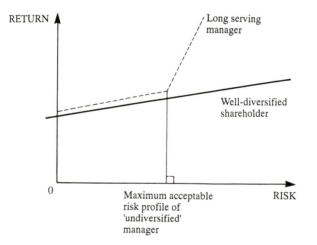

Figure 8.8 Relative perceptions of risk and return

A much more rational reason for the creation of conglomerates is that they enhance value for the shareholders, and other stakeholders, by methods other than simply diversifying risk. The businesses which are grouped together may come from many different industries but there may be some common elements, which create added value when the businesses are combined into one overall organization. A clear example of this is given by the economies of scale which can be achieved in the common support areas of these businesses; these economies may be more difficult to realize if a strict divisional structure is implemented. Thus research and development resources may be combined where the businesses utilize common technologies or processes, such as a combination of electronics businesses which serve completely different markets through diverse ranges of end products. The impact of these economies of scale is considered in more detail in Chapter 11, but there is also another aspect of this type of benefit which can be of far greater value but is less frequently identified from the outside of large conglomerates. The different managerial skills which are required at the different stages of company development have already been discussed and these are considered in detail in Part Four. One potential strength of a conglomerate is that it concentrates on one particular phase or type of business where it has specific management strengths. As a consequence, the individual competitive strategies of the operating business units should be very appropriately tailored and should also be well executed. The potential advantage of the larger group has often been misleadingly referred to simply as a benefit of size; ie a larger group provides more career opportunities and is therefore able to retain better managers. A more relevant approach is that a focused group can both attract and retain the appropriate calibre of managers because it has a good supply of *suitable* career opportunities for these people.

One particular group could concentrate on businesses where a key element is 'branded marketing', while 'process engineering' could be the common attribute for another successful group. It is possible to combine the two and make the group even more focused; it could be argued that a group such as Mars Inc is very successful because it has concentrated on consumer branded products which are produced in high volumes by a continuous production process. Consequently the managers, both at the centre and in the operating divisions, can share in a clear understanding of the corporate mission and objectives, and there is less risk of confusion arising in the translation of the overall corporate strategy into the detailed divisional competitive strategies. The financial information needs at the centre of such a group are also relatively straightforward, because this information will concentrate on the key element of the group's strategy and how well this is being achieved. For example, if the group is focused on branded marketing, the financial information would need to include details of relative market share and other key issues for the future performance of major brands, such as brand awareness and information on relative levels of competitive marketing activity.

An alternative form of this type of focus within a conglomerate is that the group concentrates on a particular phase of development, because that is where its managerial skills are likely to give it the maximum competitive advantage. This type of concentration is often driven by the specific financial control system which has been developed in the original core business of the emerging conglomerate. If managers have developed over a long period in a particular environment, they become used both to receiving and to responding to the signals issued from a specific set of financial indicators. It is not surprising, therefore, that such behavioural conditioning makes them look for similar signals if they are placed in a new situation. Where the new situation is completely different, these financial signals may be irrelevant or even may require a reversed response, which removes a considerable degree of value from these managers' previous experiences. There are many examples of managers, even in apparently sophisticated groups, moving into a new set of circumstances and trying to apply their previously successful formulae, with unfortunately disastrous consequences.

A very simple example of this is a group which has a successful, mature core business and decides to acquire or invest in a more exciting growth industry. The mature core business may be appropriately financially controlled using some form of Return on Investment (ROI) criteria, and central management expect the ROI percentage to increase from year to year. Capital investment proposals in the group may be evaluated using either discounted pay-back calculations or by examining the projected ROI on the new investment in its third year of operation. As most such investments, at present, tend to be for replacement equipment or to improve operational efficiency, these measures may prove both simple and relatively effective. However, if these financial control procedures are simply carried across into a high growth environment, the consequences could be horrendous in the medium term. A significant lack of adequate longer term investment is an almost certain result of the application of such an inappropriate set of financial controls.

If the group believes its particular set of financial controls is very good for its existing businesses, it would be much better advised to invest in new businesses for which these controls are equally appropriate; unless the centre of the group is prepared to cope with the added complexity of using several different sets of financial controls for its various operating divisions. Thus the successful group in the example may find it advisable to concentrate on mature businesses, where its simple set of financial controls may also be ideal. Indeed if these new businesses had previously been using a more sophisticated, but no longer appropriate set of financial controls, there may be considerable added value in their acquisitions by the more focused conglomerate.

This frequent representation (ie acquisitions) of the key strategic role for management accounting at the centre of large groups raises another important aspect of control within such groups; what is the impact of differing levels and forms of central control in large groups?

Levels of decentralization

In some large groups, the strategic decision-making process is very decentralized, with the centre of the group acting almost exclusively in the role of shareholder and banker to the operating divisions. Even among these groups there are still significant differences in the level of central group involvement. The extreme level of decentralization can be described as where the operating division sets out its proposed strategy for the next 3, 5 or even 7 years; if approved by the group's central management, the division is then left to implement the agreed competitive strategy with periodic progress reports being provided back to the centre. Clearly, the financial information required at the centre of such a group on each operating division is relatively limited and should be supplied quite easily from the more detailed financial reports which are needed by the divisional managers, for their own use. It is also clear that there is the risk that very little added value is being generated by the group structure, if the operating divisions are left as largely autonomous businesses. There are, however, two ways in which considerable additional benefits may be obtained by combining these independent operating units.

The first has already been discussed in terms of creating an optimum portfolio of businesses which add value to each other. If this is the key group strategy, it is quite logical for group management to leave the operating divisions alone, once their positions within the portfolio have been agreed. In many such groups the key strategic emphasis at the centre is on managing the portfolio itself and making sure that the balance is still correct. This may entail acquisitions and divestitures (as mentioned above); the actual performance and development of existing businesses inevitably alters their positions in the portfolio and potentially creates an unbalanced mix. As previously mentioned therefore, the main emphasis of the financial information required at the centre would be on the interaction of the existing businesses and the identification of suitable new additions to the portfolio.

The second way in which a very decentralized group can add synergistic value to the component businesses is where the centre acts as the banker or fund raiser to these operating divisions. There are often economies of scale which can be achieved in fund raising and a large group may have access to capital markets which are not practically available to the smaller operating units. This can be true for the long-term funding needs of the group, particularly if the business units are counter-cyclical in terms of business volatilities. This group involvement can have even greater efficiency gains for short-term financial management, but it can have dramatic consequences for the real level of central involvement in the divisional decision-making process. Before considering the implications of this more operational involvement, there is still the question of how the 'central banker' of the group should allocate resources to the operating divisions.

A good starting point is to ensure that strategic (ie developmental) funding decisions are separated from operational (ie maintenance) funding decisions, as the implications of the centre withholding maintenance funds from its operating units will normally be both immediate and severe. The development level of funding allocated to each division should be by reference to the needs identified in the division's approved strategic plan, but this does not mean that the total amount should be immediately available without any further vetting or approval process. Ideally the strategic plan should indicate a phased requirement, with corresponding early indicators of success as the plan is implemented and prior to the release of the next funding tranche. These funding phases should be geared both to the risk level of the competitive strategy, and the previous level of success in achieving strategic objectives of this divisional management team.

In some groups this funding allocation process is done for each SBU in total, whereas in others each major project within the SBU is funded individually from the centre, thus giving the centre a much greater and continuing degree of involvement in the divisional planning and decision-making process. The implications for the level and mix of resources which are needed at the centre of the group are clear, as is the impact on the need to provide financial information to the centre. However, the impact of any operational involvement of central financial management in managing fluctuations in working capital and foreign currency flows is even greater.

Surplus short-term cash in one operating unit can be re-allocated by the centre to another business within the group which has a need for additional working capital funding; this avoids the costs of using external financial markets for both transactions. Quite frequently, large international groups can use similar 'netting' procedures to manage their foreign currency transactions, where the savings to the group can be even greater. Thus, if one business unit is exporting goods from the UK to the USA while another unit is importing goods into the UK from the USA, the central 'banking' operation of the group can 'net off' most of these offsetting foreign currency balances, leaving the group with a need to buy or sell only the residual amount of US dollars.

Such an operational financial role for the centre requires detailed forecast cash flows (including specific foreign currency flows where appropriate) from all the operating units so that these activities can be actively managed and properly co-ordinated. In many groups where such a central treasury has been developed, a major area of difficulty has arisen in the way in which the real economic benefits which arise to the group are shared out among the operating units involved. Some groups have even set up the central treasury function as a profit centre (the issue of responsibility centres is considered at the end of this chapter). This can introduce more problems than it solves if the treasury department start to see their main role as one of making money for the group rather than providing cost-effective financial support to the operating divisions. There have been some disastrous examples of large groups (such as Allied-Lyons) losing very large sums of money (eg over £150 million) because their treasury departments started taking large bets on either interest rate movements or foreign currency fluctuations, particularly where these financial transactions were not directly carried out to hedge the physical trading activities of the underlying businesses. Clearly, in these cases, there had been a complete failure of, or breakdown in, coordination and control between the overall corporate strategy and the specific competitive strategy of the group's central financial managers.

In other groups, the central management team take a much more active participative role in the operations of the divisions rather than acting mainly in the guise of shareholder and banker. This pro-active involvement in decision-making must be supported by adequate financial information. This is why the degree of involvement by the centre must be clearly understood by all relevant parties and why it should be consistently applied. If centrally based group managers flit in and out of the divisional decision-making process, it is likely to result in chaos. First, the divisional managers will never know what their levels of responsibility and authority are; this is frequently demonstrated by divisional managers abdicating any decision-making role for themselves and waiting for group management to tell them what to do. This often results from these line managers being 'second-guessed' by central managers on a number of occasions and, not wanting to have their decisions reversed yet again, they prefer not to make any decision at all. Clearly, in this position, the added cost of the sophisticated group organization structure is adding very little value to the business.

A very common example of this type of central management role is where the group have a number of centrally based senior 'staff' managers. These staff managers do not have direct line authority over the divisional line managers, and they travel regularly around their part of the group offering advice based on their experience and deep knowledge of the business. However, in reality, because of their seniority and ready access to *the* group management team which does have clear line authority over the divisions (eg the group chief executive officer), the advice of these staff managers is often taken as if it was a direct instruction. Unfortunately, this can give these staff managers the authority, but the responsibility remains with the divisional managers who *appear* to have taken the decision, particularly when it goes wrong. Once again, the financial justification for incurring the significant additional cost from such group 'staffs' should be carefully evaluated, in terms of the improved overall financial performance of the group.

The key requirement is for the desired role of the centre to be clearly defined, and then for centrally based managers to stick to it. One almost universal role is to conduct the high level corporate planning function, to identify the key driving forces for the group which were discussed in Chapter 2, and to define any company wide strategic thrusts. In other words, the centre must consider all the group based issues which are not directly relevant to the more focused concerns of the divisional managers. Part of this role therefore normally includes clarifying the areas of planned activity for each division; thus increasing the sharpness of the focus. This can include avoiding gaps and eliminating overlaps for the group as a whole and, by doing this, avoiding internal competition among the divisions of the group; the centre effectively allocates exclusive product and market interfaces to particular divisions.

However, in other groups, the central management refuse to restrict divisional freedom in this way; implicitly, and even explicitly in some successful companies, encouraging internal competition. This is done in the belief that all competition, even if internal to the group, encourages efficiency and that, in the long term, such improved efficiency can only lead to improved financial results for the group as a whole. As in the other alternative methods of financial control for large groups, there are not clearly right or wrong ways to manage a complex, dynamic business but the selected method has significant implications for the type of financial information which is going to be needed at the centre of the group, particularly if group managers are regularly going to need to play referee over which division has the ability to do what! It is therefore vitally important that any system of financial control does not increase the level of 'game playing' at the divisions, whereby divisional managers seek to improve their own perceived level of performance even at the expense of the total group's performance. Equally, the information which is required at the centre should not represent an undue burden on the operating divisions, as any unnecessary increased costs reduce the overall group financial performance. A simple test is often very useful; does any of the information demanded by the centre have to be specially produced by the divisions? If so, this indicates that the divisional managers do not need this information to run their division. Therefore, the question should then be asked, why is it needed to run the group? It is possible that there is a valid reason, but in many cases there will not be a good answer to this simple set of questions.

Before going on to consider particular types of group organizations in the remaining chapters of this part of the book, a brief review of the different types of responsibility centres used by large organizations is given. This brings together and develops various issues which have been mentioned already in the book and which will be referred to in the succeeding chapters.

Responsibility centres

A responsibility centre can be defined as an area of a business which has inputs and outputs (ie controls resources), and where management responsibility can be associated with a particular individual or group of managers. Thus, as discussed in this chapter, responsibility centres can be broken up in two main ways:

1 functionally by type of management responsibility
2 divisionally by products, market segments etc

A division is therefore a responsibility centre of the group for which it is easy to measure output, whereas in a functional organization it is often very difficult to establish a measurable output (eg for the research and development function). Every responsibility centre will have non-financial objectives, as well as financial ones, and this must always be remembered when designing financial control systems. Indeed, these non-financial objectives (eg physical milestones for a new business unit which is developing and launching a new product) become even more important when it is more difficult to define appropriate financial measures of assessing performance. As mentioned earlier in the book, managerial performance can only be assessed on elements over which managers exercise control and this means that responsibility centres need to be classified according to the level of control which can be exercised over financial matters.

Cost centres (or expense centres)

If a responsibility centre does not generate any financially measurable output (eg sales revenue), the only realistic level of financial control is by reference to the level of expenditure incurred. If a meaningful plan has been developed, and circumstances have not changed significantly, the actual expenditure can be compared with the planned level, but this is a tenuous exercise of financial control. Research and development into new products is often run as an expense centre due to the absence of financially measurable outputs. The planned level of expenditure should reflect the strategic importance of developing new, or improving existing, products. Consequently, underspending against plan but not developing the required new products may create a significant problem in the future, and the financial control system should highlight this. This can be achieved by closely linking physical, or other non-financial, objectives into the monitoring process, so that failure to achieve these objectives is not overshadowed by an apparently *good* financial performance. As discussed in Chapter 4 when considering standard costs and variance analysis, part of this problem is caused by the predominant psychological view of managers that underspending (ie showing a favourable expenditure variance) represents a *good* managerial performance, irrespective of the underlying issues which caused it.

In no cost centre are managers expected simply to spend the budget. They are required to spend the resources wisely so as to achieve the range of previously agreed objectives. This requires the use of performance control measures which monitor the effectiveness of their expenditure, as well as the efficiency.

Revenue centres

Some areas of the group can be regarded as controlling the levels of sales revenues achieved, but not controlling all of the costs which go to make a profit or loss on their activities. Sales departments are consequently often financially controlled by reference to sales revenue targets, while their internal costs are controlled separately as a cost centre. Once again this type of interim financial control system creates more problems than it solves, because it can send confusing signals to the responsible managers.

The key objective from the group's perspective may be for the sales department to generate profitable sales rather than to grow the sales revenue without regard to the sales and marketing costs incurred. Of course, this group objective will, itself, depend on the stage of development of the particular division and its place within the group's portfolio. Thus, rather than simply using overall financially specified revenue targets, these areas of the business also need appropriately specified non-financial targets, which concentrate on market share, sales mix, etc.

Profit and contribution centres

If the sub-division of the business controls both sales revenue and the relevant costs, it can obviously be regarded as controlling its profit level and this can then be used as a means of financial control. Where the division does not control all of the relevant costs, such as central head office costs, it can be regarded as a contribution centre, with its financial performance being judged by the level of controllable contribution.

The use of profit centres is very widespread because, as a major group objective is to earn a satisfactory profit, it is seen as a relatively easy way to achieve goal congruence between the group and its operating divisions. Indeed, many large groups have instituted complex internal transfer pricing mechanisms for service and support areas, so that these functional sections of the business can also be financially controlled as profit centres. As previously mentioned, transfer pricing systems can create complications if they are used for managerial control purposes, because their primary aim should be to ensure the efficient allocation of resources within the group.

This concentration on the use of profit centres can itself be dangerous unless the divisional targets, against which performance is compared, are carefully established in the context of the group's total portfolio of businesses. Thus, by no means all divisions should be attempting to maximize their profit levels in the short term and this can also be true for many of the artificially created, internal support functional profit centres (such as the central treasury departments mentioned earlier). If managers are given inappropriate methods of performance evaluation, the group should not be surprised if they manage their areas of the business so as to achieve their personal targets (even though this may not be in the best long term interests of the group).

Investment centres

The most common method of measuring business performance is to use some form of profit in the context of the investment needed to generate that profit; ie a return on investment (ROI) measure. In order to use this concept at the divisional level, the division must exercise control, not only over sales revenues and the relevant associated costs, but also over the level of investment made in this area of the business. Investment centres are therefore only appropriate for relatively self-contained, independent units within a large group (eg the operating divisions of a diversified conglomerate) but, even then, their application needs to be mindful of the problems of portfolio management mentioned in the context of profit centres.

By definition, no division of a large group is completely independent and the main central control is frequently over access to funding. The group wishes to allocate its available funds to those divisions which will generate the best risk adjusted return over time. This can, to some extent, be measured by the relative ROI forecast on the competing investment opportunities, although there are several problems involved in using this measurement which have already been referred to and which are illustrated in Chapter 17. One particular problem is that ROI is a percentage measure and managers may try to manage the ratio by reducing the level of investment rather than increasing the profit; after all, a £1 profit on a zero investment represents an infinite return when expressed as a percentage. It is also more difficult to allow for the relative risks associated with the different divisions within the group when percentage returns are being compared.

Consequently, many groups now use a related concept known as Residual Income (RI), in which the group makes a notional interest charge to the divisions for any funds used. The level of the interest charge can be varied according to the perceived risk associated with the division and its related assets but, in any case, this interest cost reduces the profit of the division in proportion to its net investment. The remaining divisional profit, ie its residual income, is therefore a measure of its net contribution to the wealth created by the group (ie the economic profit after paying the cost of capital) and the financial performance is now measured by an absolute number rather than a percentage.

Although using RI does remove some of the measurement and managerial 'game playing' problems associated with the traditional ROI measure, many of the main issues relating to financial performance evaluation remain. Thus, it is vitally important that large groups concentrate on achieving goal congruence among the group's overall objectives and the individual targets which are set for the divisions and functional areas and, equally importantly, the ways in which the relative achievement of these targets is monitored. In most cases, this can only be achieved by the sensible combination of financial and appropriate non-financial measures of performance.

The following chapters in this part of the book illustrate the applications of these issues in the context of various different types of large groups.

9

Single focus businesses

Overview

In its simplest form, the single product and single market focused business should have no problem in achieving goal congruence between its competitive strategy and the overall corporate strategy, as the same type of competitive strategy is being implemented in all parts of the business. The business may, however, be so large that a functional organization structure is needed to ensure effective managerial control of all the resources involved. The role of central management is primarily to co-ordinate the strategies of these functional areas to achieve the common corporate and competitive objectives. However, it must be remembered that this overriding objective will change with external competitive circumstances and with the stages of development of the product. Consequently, the co-ordination function must be managed carefully, or the separate functional strategies may become inappropriate.

Over time, most tightly focused businesses become more complex as either new markets are attacked with existing products or new products are aimed at existing customers. Once this happens, the business is effectively managing a portfolio of different competitive strategies; each competitive strategy being appropriately tailored to the business environment in which it is to be implemented. This introduces additional complexity to the role of central group management. It also means that the centrally based managers will now require different financial information on these different business units (despite the common feature across them of either product or customer) in order properly to manage the developing group portfolio. Indeed these managers would have needed appropriate financial information to identify and financially evaluate the most attractive opportunities for the group to enter in terms of new markets and/or new products.

A key issue for almost all single focus businesses is that, although the appropriate management styles and corresponding financial control methods change as the businesses develop and mature, the managers in control do not necessarily either change or develop with the business. This can lead to the wrong set of corporate objectives being applied to the business (eg a growth stategy being implemented in a mature or even declining market) or to the wrong financial control mechanisms being used (eg DCF analysis being used to monitor capital investments for a dying product). Either of these can be disastrous for the financial success of the business, and can completely destroy the main benefits of remaining a single focused business, which is the concentration of managers on a clearly defined set of objectives.

Introduction

Many businesses start out as tightly focused, owner managed organizations with a very restricted range of products serving an incredibly well-defined market. At this stage there should be little, if any, conflict between the corporate objectives, which have been prepared from the overall mission statement, and the detailed competitive strategy, which is actually being implemented. Except of course that, at this stage, very few businesses have clearly defined mission statements, corporate objectives or competitive strategies. Even so, the combination of majority investors and senior managers as the same people means that there is not yet any potential gap between the aims of owners and the key internally based strategic decision-makers. Also, the restricted product/market interface of the organization normally means that the competitive positioning of the initial operation is quite easily decided. It is during the ensuing growth phase and beyond, for successful start-ups, that the complexity of larger group organizational structures appear and frequently threaten the continued success of the enterprise, unless the business develops and adapts to its new environment.

A recent phenomenal UK-based success story has been the dynamic growth of Body Shop. The business was started by the Roddicks in 1976 with one shop selling a new style of cosmetics and toiletries. By the end of 1990 there were 580 Body Shops in 37 countries and the stock market value of the group was £470 million. What is particularly interesting from the strategic management accounting perspective is that, despite the public flotation in 1984, the original owner/managers (Anita and Gordon Roddick) are still very substantial shareholders in the expanded group and, respectively, managing director and chairman. Also the business is still focused on its mainstream product range of environmentally friendly, own-branded, natural cosmetics and toiletries; however this should not be taken to mean that the business is still managed and controlled in exactly the same way as when it had only one shop.

Indeed many of its 173 UK-based shops are franchised and this proportion was recently increased by the sale to managers and staff of a number of previously owned stores. Obviously this method of controlling the retail operations of the group changes the financial information required at the centre, and Body Shop International (the publicly quoted group) is now really a manufacturing, wholesaling and marketing organization, rather than a retailer. The group role is in identifying, designing, and either manufacturing or buying-in the stream of new products which maintain consumers' interest in the retail outlets. The centre has also always kept tight control over the marketing strategies of all the outlets and, particularly important for this group, its high profile public image as an environmentally concerned business.

Body Shop has also, as its name implies, expanded internationally and this strategic move clearly adds complexity to the financial control problems at the centre of the group. Although it is still increasing its number of stores in the UK, it clearly ranks as the leader in its segment of this market (it is arguably the creator of the 'environmentally friendly retailer' segment) and the UK business is now highly profitable and cash generating. The initial moves into major overseas markets (such as the USA and Japan) were, not surprisingly, loss-making and would normally have required high levels of investment. However, the use of franchising enables the group to expand rapidly without tying up vast funds in new stores and additional working capital. Thus it can concentrate its own investment programme on new production and warehousing facilities, which will rapidly improve the already impressive operating margin and return on shareholders' funds achieved by this rapidly growing group. What is important for the success of the international growth strategy is that the central group management balance the increasing portfolio in terms of the demands for funds of these newer, higher growth potential markets and the internal cash generation capabilities of the rest of the operations together with the external fund raising capacity of the total group. An inability to adjust to this added financial control complexity has led to the collapse of several similarly focused and initially high growth concept retailers of the 1980s. Thus it appears clear that, despite Anita Roddick's regular public protestations to the converse, appropriate and responsive financial controls at the centre of Body Shop are a major contributor to its existing and continued success.

The inevitably developing business

Even if the originally tightly focused business can avoid the usually insurmountable temptations to develop into new products or new markets, the business and its associated financial control system are still a dynamic, continually evolving entity. The external business and competitive environment are constantly changing and the product itself is progressing through its life cycle, which means that the most appropriate form of financial control mechanism must also develop to keep pace with these changes. Thus, although the single focus business can be effectively managed using a straightforward functional organization structure, the separate objectives for each functional area must be defined in the context of the particular current stage of development.

This inevitable progression of the business, which has already been outlined and which is considered in detail in Part Four, also changes the relative importance of the various functional areas of the business. These changes should be reflected in the resources invested in each area, and in the relative attention focused on each area by central management. In the initial stages of product development and launch, the emphasis is logically on market research (to assess the potential demand for the new product), and research and development departments. A high level of expenditure in these areas should be matched by a flexible, relatively informal and rapidly adaptable system of management accounting information, because there is likely to be a need for quick strategic decisions as the project unfolds.

During the growth stage, the functional area of critical importance is marketing, and the required investment levels should be reflected in a similar emphasis within the management accounting area. The business should also be financially evaluating the alternative ways in which barriers to entry can be created at this time and whether concentrating on economies of scale, or other aspects of the experience curve, represent the most financially attractive route to follow. It may be that an alternative marketing strategy of segmenting the market by launching a wide range of slightly different products may create a better barrier to entry. This type of strategic decision should be financially analysed rather than being taken based only on the 'gut-feel' of the senior managers.

Two issues are raised as a result of this first change in strategic thrust of the business. First, the re-allocation of resources within the management accounting area needs to be properly managed. The additional resources required to focus on the significant marketing expenditures and increasing investment in tangible assets which are normally sought at this time must not lead to either an explosion in the costs of the management accounting department or to a loss of control in the other areas of the business. This requires the design of automated accounting systems, which can provide the bulk of the routine, regularly required financial reports, so that the skilled accounting resources are free to concentrate their efforts on the critical analysis of the one-off strategic issues as they develop. It is, of course, impossible to automate to any large degree the financial analysis of a completely new strategic decision, because there is no solid historic data for even an 'expert' computer system to learn from. This area is considered in more detail in Part Five.

Second, the business itself has to change its focus of attention as the critical strategic functional area moves from research and development to marketing, and so on. This is easy to say and very difficult to achieve in practice, particularly if the company has spent a relatively long time in any specific strategic mode. The critical functional managers will have grown used to the emphasis given to their functional expertise, to the high profile they receive at group management level and to the substantial proportionate share of resources dedicated to their area of responsibility. Over time, these managers will have acquired a substantial power base and may well have been promoted to senior management roles at the group level. Consequently, they will be reluctant to see things change and by fighting an effective rearguard action they can probably delay the required change in strategic emphasis for some time. This delay can prove disastrous, particularly if competitors respond quickly to the desirable change in competitive strategy. Some large companies have never fully recovered from these effects, while many others have been taken over by other groups while still suffering the consequences of such an over-extended competitive strategy. One of the key roles for a really effective strategic management accounting system is therefore to indicate in advance a forthcoming need for a change in competitive strategy.

Returning to the impact of the developing life cycle on the functional emphasis of the business, the growth phase comes to an end as the market moves into maturity. The business should now be concentrating on achieving a financial return to justify the earlier periods of net investment and re-investment. Consequently, the relative efficiency of the operational areas of the business compared to major competitors becomes a key strategic issue, with a corresponding increasing focus on the functional areas of production, distribution and selling and administrative support. The strategic management accounting system should be delivering comparative competitive cost analyses, as these can indicate areas of concern and need for improvement together with opportunities for developing a competitive cost advantage.

Still further through the cycle, the single product focused business is in decline and on the way to ultimate extinction. The management accounting system should be evaluating the alternative options of leaving the industry before it actually dies (the exit option or 'voluntary euthanasia' choice), or of staying in for a further period. The staying-in choice normally consists of a series of alternatives depending on the relative levels of periodic re-investments made in the business, and it is important that the best economic choice is exercised by the business. This next stage is clearly not attractive to senior managers within the business. For the originators and current investors in the business, the position does not have to be disastrous, if the overall financial return has been satisfactory and the original business mission has either been achieved or been made irrelevant due to subsequent development. It appears to be a commonly held view that no business needs to end up in this decline or dog phase as long as the original mission statement is either drafted sufficiently generally or is regularly updated to take account of future changes in the competitive environment. Thus, Professor Theodore Levitt is credited as stating that the American railroad industry would not have been in such serious decline if it had defined itself as being in the 'transportation' industry rather than the railroad industry. This presumes that a restated 'mission statement' would suddenly have made senior managers aware of the strategic threat to their existing business of new developments in transportation, which they were otherwise unaware of. It also assumes that managers with long-term experience of running a mature, steady state railroad had the necessary skills not only to move into the rapidly developing competitive areas based on different technologies and with completely new market dynamics, but also to achieve a sustainable competitive advantage against focused new companies, without any preconceived ideas of how to run their new businesses.

These are large assumptions.

Moving into new products or new markets

It is very common during the cash generating maturity stage for group managers, seeing the inevitable stage of decline and death staring them in the future, to use the considerable positive cash flow of the business to move into new, higher growth areas. In our single focus businesses this cannot involve true diversification but normally consists of finding new markets in which to sell the existing product range or of finding new products which can be sold to existing customers. Thus the company builds on its main strategic advantage, whether that is product based or customer related. In order to fulfil the desired managerial objective, these new areas of activity should be less developed than the existing business so that new growth opportunities are opened up.

However, by moving into businesses which are at different levels of development, the complexity of managing this originally focused group is significantly increased. The group is now running a restricted portolio of businesses, and it is quite easy for a conflict to develop between the desired competitive strategy of one business unit within the portfolio and the overall corporate strategy of the group. This can be illustrated by considering the strategic management of one of the major global car companies and the different positions on the product life cycle of the car industry around the world. This is shown in Figure 9.1, with the relative positions of some of the major car markets indicated at their appropriate stages of development. Clearly the appropriate strategies for the same company must be tailored to the

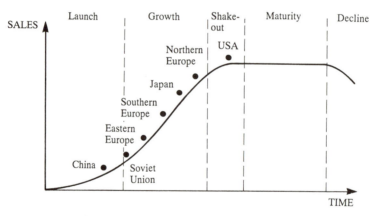

Figure 9.1 Car industry product life cycle (global view of markets)

stage of market development and the related competitive environment. The expectations of financial return should be conditioned by these same issues, with the methods of financial justification of investment opportunities, and financial control of actual operations being different at each significantly different stage of development. Interestingly, this degree of financial management sophistication does not seem to be consistently applied by many of these incredibly large, technically sophisticated, 'global' companies.

The justification for moving into these new areas is more generally one of obtaining critical size in order to be able to compete effectively against other 'global' companies. Critical mass is only a valid argument if there are genuine large economies of scale to be gained from such movements outside the existing proven area of operations. This has been a common claim of the recently privatized UK utility companies (eg British Telecom, British Gas and the water companies), which have used the high profits and cash flows from their monopolistic but relatively mature local markets to finance their investments into new and more exciting growth areas, both overseas and in 'related' products. The significant increase in the complexity of managing these new areas, when allied to the lack of relevant experience of several of their senior managers and the absence of well-developed, proven internal management accounting systems for either their original or new business ventures leads to a high degree of risk for the successful integration of several of these new business ventures. Such strategic moves should not be made either because senior managers want to run a bigger business or because the core business is generating a lot of cash at present which they don't know what to do with, even if they realize that this cash generation rate cannot continue for ever. The cash flow can be repaid to the shareholders and other stakeholders if it will not be needed in future in the business, and any move into new areas should be properly financially justified. This is true even for strategic moves into apparently related products and markets, where it may be possible to show that a sustainable competitive advantage can be created. For less related moves, the financial justification is likely to be more problematic.

10

Vertically integrated businesses

Personal view

The main economic justification used by vertically integrated businesses for their existence is that they add more value than if they were not vertically integrated. In the author's opinion, this is one of the all-time great myths of the business world. Most vertically integrated businesses started life concentrating on one stage of their value chain. In most cases they were very successful during this stage of their development and used this base to expand their range of interests into other areas of activity; either up or down the value chain, as illustrated in Figure 10.1. Economically, the rationale was presumably that a greater financial return could be generated from this type of move than by further horizontal expansion. The only way in which additional value is created by such a strategic move is, as has been discussed before, if a sustainable competitive advantage has been developed. However in most cases, vertical integration strategies take the business away from their previous areas of competitive strength and involve managers in new products with new technologies and new processes. It is therefore difficult to see how shareholder wealth can be created by such a strategy, particularly when competition is joined against existing, well-entrenched businesses in this sector.

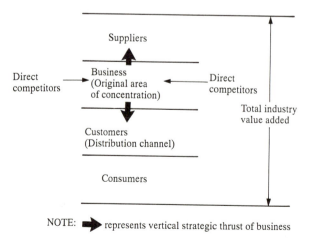

NOTE: ➡ represents vertical strategic thrust of business

Figure 10.1 Vertical integration strategies

Unfortunately there is one almost guaranteed impact on investors of such a vertical integration strategy. This is an increase in the total risk of the organization due to its concentration of investment in, and hence exposure to, a single industry.

It should by now be obvious that any increase in risk, without a corresponding increase in return leads to a decrease in the total value to the investor.

Overview

Vertically integrated businesses are created by a conscious decision on the part of managers to move up or down the value chain. In other words, the business takes over a function which could alternatively have been carried out by a supplier or customer; the exercise of choice is vitally important in this definition. If there is no alternative, the business should not be regarded as being vertically integrated as the whole segment of the industry covered by the organization represents a single, non-separable business. Once there is a valid option of obtaining supplies from an external vendor or of selling to an external customer, the business makes a strategic investment decision to integrate vertically if it decides to carry out this function itself.

As with all strategic investment decisions, there should be a financial evaluation before implementation, and an ongoing financial monitoring process to ensure that the expected benefits have been obtained. This monitoring process should include a regular review of whether the current degree of vertical integration should be maintained or increased. All such financial evaluations must use the opportunity cost concept and, in the case of the internal transfers caused by vertical integration, this necessitates the establishment of a transfer pricing system. It is important that this primary reason, ie the validation of the overall economic decisions made by the group, for developing transfer pricing is remembered, as many transfer pricing systems actually in use do not lead to the best economic decision for the group.

It may appear that a vertically integrated focused group can be organized on a functional basis, as the competitive and corporate strategies of the single, overall business should be the same. However, as with the originally single focused businesses considered in the previous chapter, the normal development of the business over time leads to the need for a more complex organization structure. In any case, the nature of the key strategic decisions facing the manager responsible for the differing vertical segments of the group are likely to vary dramatically. Accordingly, the financial information which is needed to support and monitor these different types of decision should be appropriately tailored. It should also be remembered that most decisions to carry out functions internally which *could* be provided by external suppliers (eg the provision of many business services) should be evaluated using the opportunity cost technique as these decisions represent a form of vertical integration.

Development of vertically integrated businesses

At the inception stage of many new industries, the innovative, early pioneering companies may have little choice but to be highly vertically integrated. It may be impossible to obtain the necessary supplies and required services from outside suppliers, or the desired new channel of distribution may not exist. Thus, the business has to carry out these functions itself, at least until the infrastructure within the industry has developed sufficiently to offer a viable alternative. At this time, the organization should decide whether it wishes to continue at its existing degree of vertical integration or to out-source non-critical elements where suppliers or customers may have a significant competitive advantage.

The car industry can be used as a good example of how this strategy of decreasing vertical integration can be applied. In the early days of the industry there was no network of sophisticated engineering suppliers of the multitude of sub-components required to produce such a complex final product. Therefore, the early construction by Ford of an incredibly highly vertically integrated manufacturing plant at Baton Rouge in the USA was potentially the only way of achieving meaningful economies of scale and, at the same time, guaranteeing the timely supply of good quality components. Thus iron ore and other basic raw materials were delivered to the site and finished cars were despatched, although there were still certain areas which the business did not enter (eg tyre production).

As the industry volume increased and the number of different models also multiplied, it became more difficult for any car manufacturer to remain totally self-sufficient. It became more economic to buy in certain general semi-processed components, where the supplier was able to generate greater economies of scale by also supplying other companies, both in and out of the car industry. Gradually a new industry of finished component suppliers developed because these companies could supply their products not only direct to the manufacturers but also to car owners through the 'after market' for replacement products (such as oil filters, spark plugs, batteries, etc). Once again these volumes generated greater economies of scale than could be matched by the car companies, and so it made sense for these new companies to succeed, in partnership with the car manufacturers. Also their focus on a limited area meant that they developed technological advances and product improvements which could be incorporated into the new car models. The problem for the car manufacturers was that these new products were also available to their competitors, because they had been developed by outside companies.

This highlights one of the key elements of vertical integration decisions; the business must incorporate into the financial analysis the value of restricting access by competitors to any new technological or product development. If it is probable that competitors will be able to copy the idea anyway (ie it cannot be kept secret or patented, etc), there may be no significant value in owning the idea itself, although there may still be value in 'owning' the creator of the idea. This is true for many service industries (eg investment banking), where individual products have competitive advantage life cycles measured in weeks or days, because competitors can immediately analyse the newly launched product and rapidly develop their own version. As mentioned in Chapter 5, this has become very sophisticated in several industries, such as the car industry with all the major companies literally taking apart each new competitive product to analyse and cost any changes incorporated.

If the car industry is analysed today, it becomes clear that many companies are now much more reliant on outside suppliers, including other car companies, for large elements of the final product. Some companies can almost be regarded as designers, assemblers and marketers of cars, rather than vertically integrated manufacturers. Indeed, in some of these major players, a higher discount rate is used in evaluating the projected cash flows from projects which require in-house production compared to a proposal to move to an external source of supply. This financial criterion reflects the perception of the increased risk associated with in-house investment, due not least to creating a higher level of fixed costs, compared with the greater flexibility which can be obtained by using outside suppliers. Of course, this transfer of risk to the outsider should be reflected in the higher buying-in price demanded by this supplier, but the buying power of the large company may partially offset this premium.

This trend towards a reducing level of vertical integration is quite logical as the industry matures and the technology becomes more complex. Any company should concentrate its limited resources on those areas where they can add greatest value, and this often means buying-in a range of goods and services from other, differently focused companies. If there is an alternative method of doing something, including out-sourcing, this alternative should be properly financially evaluated by the company.

It is interesting to consider the strategic developments at the other end of the value chain for the motor industry because the car companies have continued to have a high degree of involvement in the exclusive dealerships which sell the cars, despite pressure from governments regarding the restrictive trading practices involved. A car is a classic example of a highly branded product and, consequently, car manufacturers want to have control over the marketing strategy of their products. However, the actual sales process and, particularly, the very important after-sales service function require very different skills from those of designing and manufacturing highly complex products in large volumes on a global basis. It is not necessarily sensible for the car companies to become directly involved in locally focused dealerships, which are selling single cars to individuals for whom it is a very significant capital investment. The tie-up with exclusive, long-term dealers, which specialize in selling and maintaining cars, is therefore a logical development as it ensures continuity in access to the market for the car manufacturers, while allowing them to retain control over the national and, indeed, global marketing strategy for the individual products and the overall brand.

This strategic logic can be applied to a completely different type of company, Benetton. When the family company started designing and manufacturing knitwear (initially using outworkers rather than investing heavily in capital equipment), it had to decide how it was going to access the end consumer. If it sold its products through the normal retail channel of distribution it ran the risk, as a small fashion goods supplier, of losing control over the future development of its brand and indeed its overall strategy. Also the company had identified that it was critical for its success as a high fashion knitwear manufacturer that it obtained very fast feedback on actual sales to consumers. Thus the company wanted daily information on what had been sold *by* the retailer, rather than on what had been supplied *to* the retailer but which could still be sitting on the shelves in the shop or even still be in transit. In order to ensure this information flow and to make the delivery pipeline as short as possible (thereby reducing the risk of goods going out of fashion before reaching the shops), the company set up its own chain of retail outlets, selling only its branded products. However, the risk associated with this vertical integration move was substantially reduced by franchising out these retail outlets to locally based owner managers, etc. This gave the group the advantage of immediate information via direct computer communication between head office and retail outlet, while retaining control of the overall branding and marketing strategy but reducing the investment in both retail assets and local market based retail management skills. The group has rapidly expanded into an almost global network of shops, without losing financial control over its business.

Staying vertically integrated

If the logic of gradually decreasing any initially essential vertical integration, or at least of challenging the financial justification for its continuation, is so strong, it should be illuminating to examine the arguments put forward by major companies for staying highly vertically integrated. The oil industry is an example where most of the major companies have maintained the strategy of being vertically integrated.

Most oil companies started out as exploration-based businesses and subsequently have vertically integrated in stages by developing their own oil-fields. This process continued through operating tanker fleets, owning refineries and wholesale distribution businesses, and ultimately in having businesses concerned in end product branding, marketing and consumer distribution. Several of the largest groups owning and even managing chains of retail petrol stations. Quite clearly this adds immense complexity to the role of group management as the critical success factors, stages of development and relative competitive positionings of each of these businesses will differ. It is perfectly practical for oil companies to concentrate on a single level of the industry and this has been successfully done by a number of participants in the industry. Therefore, as there are alternative strategies available, the decision to continue as a vertically integrated company should be financially justified in terms of either the enhanced return which can be generated or the reduction in the overall risk of the integrated group.

Both forms of this financial justification have been used by managers within such vertically integrated companies. The most common argument is based on the fluctuating level of oil prices in world commodity markets. If the crude oil price is high then the short-term profits of the exploration and production sides of the business are dramatically improved, because this increase in sales revenues is not matched by any corresponding increase in operating costs. However, these higher raw material prices are normally rapidly reflected in increased selling prices for the final products. These higher prices will reduce the potential profitability of the downstream operations of the group (ie marketing, distribution and retailing of refined products). Conversely when oil prices are low, these downstream operations can improve their profit margins because of the lower input costs for their most significant bought-in item, but the profits of the raw material production end of the business are adversely affected. Thus it is argued that, by being vertically integrated, the oil companies reduce the volatility of their overall group profits and hence reduce the risk of the combined business when compared to an oil company which is focused on either end of the industry.

An alternative way of viewing this argument is that this type of integrated company never makes exceptionally high profits even when its industrial environment is particularly favourable, because one element of its business is always, to some extent, cross-subsidizing another. However, by remaining within the oil industry, the company still bears the high business risks (eg political, environmental, economic volatility) associated with this type of industry. If it genuinely wishes to reduce its business risk, it should surely diversify it by making other investments which are outside the industry; yet most senior managers within the industry argue against such a strategy because of their lack of relevant managerial expertise and consequent inability to develop and sustain a competitive advantage.

It is difficult to see the common managerial skills involved in managing a several billion dollar oil field project with a development life of many years and in running a retail chain of petrol stations. In fact, a very different integrated strategy can be used to illustrate an alternative route to success in the downstream segment of the industry. Petrol in its more mature markets is now a commodity product with relatively low levels of brand loyalty; hence the critical petrol retailing success factors are selling price and location of outlets. Selling prices depend upon having a critical mass of operations to achieve the best buying terms from suppliers but, given that refined petroleum products are globally traded commodities, a flexible and rapidly responsive buying operation can often create greater short term competitive advantages.

Therefore an oil company which focuses on petrol retailing and buys in its required supplies from the cheapest international source can create a niche in the market. If it is to be successful as a retailer of a commodity product, then it must be efficient and keep its operating costs to a minimum. Petrol stations occupy, in retail terms, large areas and are often inefficient in terms of their customer throughput. A sensible strategy for our focused oil company is therefore to operate large filling stations (which spreads the predominantly fixed costs over a larger volume of sales) and to encourage sales volumes by discounting selling prices (based on its competitive buying advantage). The group does not need to spend large sums of money on advertising in order to try to build a strong brand image because it is targeting car owners who buy petrol when their car is nearly running out from the most convenient, cheapest petrol station available.

The added integration element to the strategy is to regard the petrol stations as property investments as well as access points through which to sell a commodity product. These large attractive filling station sites are, by definition, located on or by major roads and near to large residential or business communities. If the sites are bought and used initially as filling stations, there is an opportunity to realize a significant capital gain by re-developing the site when the relevant nearby community has expanded to reach it. Such a strategic option may appear much less attractive to a fully integrated oil company, which may view such re-development as losing part of its share of the downstream retail market.

The profit streams of such a focused oil company will be more volatile as, when oil prices are low and supplies are plentiful, it will buy effectively and make high profits. When supplies of refined product are scarce and spot market prices are high, it may be more difficult for this type of company to obtain supplies and it will have to pass on its increased costs immediately in the form of higher selling prices to the end consumer. Unless it is able to maintain its sales volumes and profit margins, or increase its margins to offset any decline in volumes, its profits will be reduced; it will, of course, not have any compensating increased profits from its non-existent upstream operations. However, it will have developed a position in the local market as a 'cheap' retailer of petrol. When selling prices are rising rapidly, as they do in this market, consumers are likely to become more cost conscious and try to buy from the source which they perceive as the cheapest!

This makes it even more difficult to understand the strategic responses made to changes in spot oil prices by the large, integrated oil companies. These integrated businesses immediately change the selling prices of their finished products (eg petrol) when the quoted crude oil commodity price changes. This is in spite of the facts that their internal production costs have not altered at all and that the investments in both the oil field developments and downstream operations were originally justified on a long-term basis, while most of these commodity price fluctuations are short term. Also by responding so quickly and predictably, they weaken considerably the major potential competitive disadvantage of the non-integrated oil companies, which is their exposure to short-term price fluctuations in international oil prices. If these large companies really are implementing a long-term risk reduction strategy by being vertically integrated, it would seem more sensible to smooth out some of this volatility in end product prices and, consequently, in demand for their products. Their counter argument is that delaying a petrol price increase, when crude oil prices have risen, costs them a lot of money; in other words there is an opportunity cost involved. This concept is rigorously used by these companies as the price increase is applied even to existing stocks of finished products; the supporting argument being that the cost of the replacement stocks has risen due to the increased price of crude oil. Since selling prices are raised immediately, public outcries and government pressures seek to ensure that selling prices are also reduced equally quickly in response to reductions in quoted crude oil prices; such action clearly increasing, rather than smoothing out, the volatility for the industry as a whole. [It is difficult to imagine almost any other industry behaving in this way, even where the major companies are not vertically integrated. For example, a major element in the cost of a chocolate-based confectionery product is the price of the commodity cocoa, which fluctuates almost daily in the world markets. Mars and Cadbury do not alter the selling prices of their confectionery products in response to short-term raw material price movements, even though neither is exactly self-sufficient in raw material supplies due to vertical integration. Indeed they use financial hedging strategies which involve taking trading positions in the commodities futures markets in order to reduce the volatility in raw material costs and hence reduce the need for them continually to change their selling prices of the finished products.]

The reason that the oil companies feel that they need to respond so quickly is partly driven by these opportunity cost arguments, but this pressure is also increased by the tendency to separate the different operational levels within the industry. Although the group is vertically integrated, the upstream and downstream operations are normally run as independent business units, and these will also be broken down into many more discrete units. For reasons of size, it may well be necessary to break the business down into geographic and functional sub-units, but this is taken a stage further by introducing a divisional structure as well. This should focus divisional managers' attention on a smaller vertical section of the industry, which is clearly helpful, but leaves group management with the role of co-ordinating and integrating the competitive strategies of these divisions. This is particularly important in a vertically integrated group because of the inter-relationships among the various divisions. Most of the oil groups use profits or ROI as financial control measures at the divisional levels, so as to try to focus even more intensively the managers' attention. However, where the divisions are largely trading with each other, this requires the establishment of a transfer pricing system between any two divisions. In order to ensure objectivity, the transfer prices are normally set at the externally established and quoted spot market prices, eg for crude oil or refined products.

This means that changes in the external market price are immediately reflected in divisional financial performance. Pressure is consequently increased on divisional managers to respond to these changes as quickly as possible and as fully as possible, ie in order to maintain or improve their own divisional performance. The changes in divisional profitability due to altering the internal transfer price are obviously completely offsetting and have a neutral effect on the group; the group is affected by the external action taken by the divisions as a consequence of the changes in their perceived financial performance. Interestingly, it is normally based on these internally generated divisional financial measures that managers in these companies claim the counter-cyclicality of their divisional profit streams; since the internal group accounting system makes it happen, the result is hardly surprising!

For any vertically integrated business which wishes to use divisional financial performance measures, a sound internal transfer pricing system is essential but, in many cases, the basic essentials for such a system are forgotten.

Transfer pricing

Transfer prices should be primarily used to enable economic decisions to be taken regarding such issues as the allocation of resources within a group, and whether a particular function should be carried out internally or not. Thus these internal prices must use the appropriate level of relevant costs, which may be incremental or avoidable, rather than being based on an apportionment of actual costs. This is particularly important where a major use of such transfer prices is likely to be in selecting which of a range of products is the most financially attractive. The business should want to concentrate its resources on those opportunities which generate the greatest level of contribution to overall profits. This clearly excludes fixed costs which will not be affected by the decision, but does not necessarily highlight how the relative contribution rates should be calculated to make them appropriately comparable.

All businesses suffer from constraints which restrict their ability to expand infinitely. The key to this type of financial decision is to identify the key limiting factor which is currently restricting the development of the business. If the company then concentrates its resources on those products which generate the highest contributions per unit of this limiting factor, the overall profits of the business will be maximized. An example may make this concept much clearer.

It is very common for companies in the paper products industry to be vertically integrated; indeed there has been a recent trend for several Scandinavian forestry products companies to move very heavily into vertical integration by acquiring paper, packaging and nappy producing companies due to their high usage of wood pulp as a raw material. This integration is found in the tissue products industry and our example is based on such a vertically integrated tissue producer, which has a large mill producing bulk tissue from wood pulp and recycled waste paper. It also has converting plants to which much of the bulk tissue is transferred, where it is transformed into finished products such as toilet rolls, facial tissues and kitchen towels. These products are then sold to large retailers, generating external sales revenues for the converting division. If this part of the group is to be run as a profit or investment centre, it must be charged for its internal transfers of bulk tissue. The transfer pricing issue is further complicated because there is an intermediate global market in bulk tissue and consequently the tissue mill can sell some of its output onto the external market. Similarly the converting division can buy in some tonnage of bulk tissue from other suppliers, when the price and quality make this attractive.

Obviously from the group perspective it is very important that this level of external buying and selling is only done if it improves overall group profitability. This must be achieved through the design of the transfer pricing mechanism, as each subdivision of the group must be expected to maximize its own profitability. The existing transfer pricing system starts with the variable cost per tonne of the particular product to which is added a contribution per tonne to cover the fixed costs of the tissue mill and the required level of profit; this is illustrated in Figure 10.2 for a small sample of products.

Fixed costs of tissue mill	=	£12m
Budgeted divisional profit for year	=	£4m
		£16m
Budgeted output in tonnes	=	80,000
$\therefore$ Required Contribution per tonne	=	£200

Thus transfer prices were

Type of tissue	Variable cost/tonne	Required cont^n/tonne	Transfer price per tonne
White facial	250	200	450
Coloured facial	230	200	430
White toilet	225	200	425
Coloured toilet	205	200	405
White kitchen towel	210	200	410
Coloured kitchen towel	195	200	395

Figure 10.2 Existing tissue transfer pricing system

	Budgeted output tonnes	% age	Actual proportion
Facial	25,000	31.25	50%
Toilet	35,000	43.75	37.5%
Kitchen towel	20,000	25.00	12.5%
	80,000	100.00%	100%

Figure 10.3 Tissue mill production tonnages

However, with this transfer pricing system in operation the tissue mill managers find themselves being asked for a higher and higher proportion of facial tissues and less and less kitchen towel by the converting plant, as is shown in Figure 10.3. This increases when potential outside sales and purchases are taken into account; some of these deals are shown in Figure 10.4.

	Buy-in opportunities		Sell-out opportunities		Decision
	Tonnage	Price/tonne	Tonnage	Price/tonne	
White facial	100	£500	750	£460	Sell-out
Coloured facial	300	£480	–	–	No deal
White toilet	–	–	200	£400	No deal
Coloured toilet	330	£400	–	–	Buy in
White kitchen towel	–	–	275	£375	No deal
Coloured kitchen towel	550	£380	–	–	Buy in

Figure 10.4 Latest market prices

Comparing these available market prices with the required transfer prices for the same product illustrates the trend towards production of facial tissues. The group has an opportunity to buy in white facial at £500 per tonne and coloured facial at £480 per tonne; but its own transfer prices are, respectively, £450 and £430, thus these deals are unattractive. However, there is also the chance to sell 750 tonnes of white facial at £460 per tonne, which is £10 higher than the internal transfer price. Thus the tissue mill wants to take up this deal, but this requires it to free up capacity to do so. This can be achieved by buying in the coloured toilet tissue at £400 per tonne (against a transfer price of £405) and the coloured kitchen towel at £380 per tonne (against a transfer price of £395).

However, this strategy is not leading to increasing divisional profits at the tissue mill, in fact they are well below budget even though the mill is operating 24 hours a day, 7 days a week. Preventive maintenance is carried out during the 2 factory shutdowns during the year and consequently the maximum machine availability is 47.62 weeks per year. This gives 8,000 maximum available hours and, since the mill has 5 similar tissue machines, the total production time is 40,000 hours. This is important because the switch in production time between facial tissues and kitchen towels represents different tonnage outputs due to their different processing characteristics. Kitchen towel is a heavier product than facial tissue (this is measured by the basis weight, which is the weight in grammes per square metre of the tissue) and with heavier products the tissue machine can be run faster, without holes appearing in the tissue. The combination of these factors means that different tonnage outputs are achieved from the machines depending on the type of tissue which is being produced; these are illustrated in Figure 10.5.

	Basis weight (gms per sq. metre)	Output in tonnes per machine hour*
White facial	16	1.5
Coloured facial	16	1.5
White toilet	19	2.2
Coloured toilet	19	2.2
White kitchen towel	24	2.75
Coloured kitchen towel	24	2.75

*Assumes economic runs for each product

Figure 10.5 Product weights

These differences indicate why the change in production mix is altering the profit performance of the tissue mill, because as the proportion of facial tissue increases it becomes impossible for the mill to achieve its budgeted output of 80,000 tonnes. What this really signifies is that the tissue mill is not constrained by its total tonnage output as this changes according to the product mix, as is indicated in Figure 10.6.

	Tonnes per hour	Total hours	Maximum output (tonnes)
100% Facial tissue	1.5	40,000	60,000
100% Toilet tissue	2.2	40,000	88,000
100% Kitchen towel	2.75	40,000	110,000

Figure 10.6 Tissue mill potential tonnage outputs

The real limiting factor for the tissue mill is the available machine production hours, as these cannot be increased from the 40,000 hours which are already being utilized. If the group wants to ensure that its resources are being allocated most efficiently, it should concentrate on the usage of these available machine hours. This can best be achieved by using this critical constraint as the basis for setting the transfer prices which are used for internal and external resource allocation decisions. In this example, this means basing the transfer prices on the contribution per hour required to achieve the budgeted profit for the tissue mill; this is shown in Figure 10.7.

The impact of this change in transfer pricing is quite significant as can be seen by reviewing the latest market prices shown in Figure 10.4, as is done in Figure 10.8. This revised set of transfer prices reverses the previous decisions on which products to buy-in or sell-out, and it will also reverse the recent trend of the increasing proportion of production resources dedicated to facial tissues. Given the longer time needed to produce a tonne of facial tissue and the limiting nature of the production time available, it is important that the facial tissue is charged for its relative critical resource intensity.

This example illustrates the key issues in designing a transfer pricing system, which is to use the limiting factor of the business as the driving force of the transfer prices. If this is done, any decisions involving allocating this critical limiting resource will be soundly based. Managers will logically concentrate their resources on those products which generate the maximum contributions per unit of the limiting factor. It is important to realize that the optimum position for the company is to equalize the product contributions per unit of limiting factor.

Product	Output per hour in tonnes	Cont^n per hour*	Cont^n per tonne	Variable cost/tonne	Transfer price/tonne
White facial	1.5	£400	266.67	250	516.67
Coloured facial	1.5	£400	266.67	230	496.67
White toilet	2.2	£400	181.82	225	406.82
Coloured toilet	2.2	£400	181.82	205	386.82
White kitchen	2.75	£400	145.45	210	355.45
Coloured kitchen	2.75	£400	145.45	195	340.45

* Contribution per hour is given by:–

Fixed costs   = £12m

Budgeted profit =   £4m

£16m

Maximum available hours 40,000

∴ Required Cont^n per hour = $\frac{£16m}{40,000}$ = £400

Figure 10.7 Transfer prices using contributions per hour

Product	New transfer price	Buy-in price	Sell-out price	Decision
White facial	516.67	500	460	Buy-in
Coloured facial	496.67	480	–	Buy-in
White toilet	406.82	–	400	No deal
Coloured toilet	386.82	400	–	No deal
White kitchen	355.45	–	375	Sell-out
Coloured kitchen	340.45	380	–	No deal

Figure 10.8 Impact of new transfer prices

This will maximize the overall profit of the business as no reallocation of the critical resource among products can increase the total profit.

Using this system for designing transfer prices is of equal importance where internal services are involved, as otherwise very poor allocation of resources decisions can result; these areas are considered in the following chapters.

11

Conglomerates

Overview

Conglomerates are the clearest example of the need for an overall corporate strategy which may be different to the individual competitive strategies of the various business units. By definition, a conglomerate consists of several different businesses, each of which will be selling its own products in its own markets. Hence, each of these businesses must develop its own appropriate competitive strategy, which will take into account the particular business environment, degree of competition and stage of development of the market.

Thus, if the conglomerate consists of a group of unrelated, almost autonomous businesses, the logical organization structure is to control each business as a separate division. In order to justify the continued existence of the group, it must be possible to show that keeping these separate divisions together adds value to the stakeholders in the group.

This added value can be generated from the central group management of a balanced portfolio of operating businesses. Such a portfolio can itself be 'balanced' in several different ways. If divisions are grouped together so that their combined risk is lower than their individual risks as stand-alone businesses, the value to the shareholders of the slightly reduced combined profits of the group should be increased. However, it is relatively easy for sophisticated investors to construct their own, similarly balanced diversified portfolio, and this can normally be done far more cheaply than by developing a large conglomerate. Conglomerates can also have balanced portfolios in terms of the cash flows generated by the operating businesses within the group. This means that the investment funds needed by the newer, growing business units are produced by the more mature, cash positive businesses. Once again, large sophisticated investors can construct their own cash neutral investment portfolios if they want to.

A better way for conglomerates to add value to shareholders is by generating and using economies of scale, which are not available to the individual component business units. This can also be achieved in a number of ways, which include generating economies of scale in managerial skills as discussed in Chapter 8. The most common economies of scale in conglomerates are gained through shared resources at the group level. Due to the diverse, unrelated business operations of most conglomerates, these shared resources are normally in the business support areas, where similar skills are required across the group. Thus centralized research and development, information technology, market research, and finance departments are quite common, even in groups which are very diversified.

Although such centralization can generate quite significant economies of scale in many cases, it also creates control problems and complicates the organizational structure. As mentioned, it is quite practical to have a simple divisional structure, with almost no head office staff, in a diversified conglomerate, where the business units are almost completely autonomous. Once certain functions are centralized so as to provide services to a number of operating divisions, such a simple structure is no longer adequate. These centralized support areas need to be controlled on a functional basis, but their expenditures and focus should be controlled by the operating businesses. This is normally achieved by using some form of transfer pricing, which means that the most appropriate system of setting these transfer prices must be implemented. It is also possible that the lack of market and product focus in these functional areas may cause greater diseconomies of scale than the value of the original benefits created by centralizing the functions.

Introduction

The dictionary definition of a conglomerate, which was not originally meant to be applied to a type of business structure, is a 'mixture of various elements, clustered together without assimilation'. This does appear, at first sight, to paint a fairly accurate picture of most existing large conglomerates as they do contain a variety of virtually unrelated businesses. However, if this is true, there is no immediately apparent economic justification for the creation or maintenance of a conglomerate structure. Using the previously discussed logic of agency theory, there should be a common objective between the owners of the group and its senior managers. Managers should not therefore adopt a corporate strategy which diminishes shareholder value. As has already been argued most of the obvious breakdowns in agency theory have been of a temporary nature; such as where a conglomerate is created primarily to diversify the risk of the senior managers. If no added value for the shareholders is created there is a strong possibility of a corporate raider acquiring the group and dis-aggregating the constituent businesses. It is perfectly possible for large institutional shareholders to construct their own investment portfolios which diversify their perceived risk and provide any required balance between capital growth and current dividend yield. Thus there is no obvious economic value added by the managers of any single company trying to do this for them. Indeed constructing and managing such a direct investment portfolio incurs a significant cost within the conglomerate group, with a consequent decrease in shareholder value if no additional value has been created.

However, there is one class of shareholder where the creation and maintenance of a conglomerate may be quite logical. Family-based shareholder groups may want to diversify their overall risk but still to maintain direct involvement in, and control over, the businesses in which they invest. This can be achieved by constructing a conglomerate structure, where the 'family' control the centre of the group. Outsiders to the family can be brought in to manage, and possibly even can have a minority ownership stake in, the individual divisions comprising the conglomerate. In this form, the conglomerate fulfils the role of the overall investment portfolio for the family and the logic of diversifying risk or balancing cash flows may add value to the 'family's' investment strategy. This type of conglomerate group is by no means uncommon, as many large publicly quoted groups are still dominated by family-held shareholdings (in some cases due to the differential voting rights of different classes of share). The overall corporate strategy for such groups is clearly dictated by the interests and concerns of this key stakeholder group. Initially, this does not normally create any problems, because family representation within senior management is either dominant or very strong. Over time, frequently two or three generations, senior management of the expanded group tends to pass into the hands of professional managers, who are not family members. At this stage, it becomes more difficult for the family shareholders to ensure that their desired corporate strategy is maintained by these new managers. Obviously, if they still control the group, they have the ultimate sanction of voting out these group directors but, by this time, the family shareholding is often diluted and is also spread across a number of individuals (cousins, nephews and nieces, etc). Consequently, exercising this voting control can be more difficult than in the past, and the corporate strategy can be diverted away from its original path. The conglomerate group appears to acquire a life of its own, although the main economic justification for its continued existence has now virtually disappeared.

Apart from this reason for developing a portfolio approach to structuring a conglomerate, there are the other reasons which have already been mentioned. These are now reconsidered and the management accounting implications of such a corporate strategy are discussed.

The balanced portfolio approach

As was mentioned in Chapter 8, the benefits of a conglomerate having a portfolio of apparently unrelated businesses can take several different forms. The group could try to reduce its overall risk by deliberately investing in businesses with counter-cyclical risks. Thus even though the risk of an individual business is high, the total risk associated with these combined businesses is lower. This is, of course, based on the logic that risk is determined by the level of volatility in returns and so, reducing the overall volatility by combining these counter-cyclical businesses reduces the risk of the group. A silly example might be to combine a business making beach balls and deck chairs with a business producing umbrellas. No matter what the prevailing summer weather, one of the group's divisions should be doing well and the other relatively less well. This argument has been used, to a degree, by the chairman of Cadbury Schweppes as a benefit of the merger between the two previously independent companies. If the summer is very hot, consumers apparently buy less chocolate but more soft drinks, and vice versa in a cold, wet summer; thus the cyclicality of the combined businesses is reduced.

A different form of this argument includes part of the economies of scale justification as well. One of Unilever's subsidiaries, Wall's, developed two different business streams, namely ice cream and meat products. Sales of these product ranges are counter-cyclical which generates savings, when they are combined, in terms of better utilization of cold storage and distribution facilities.

This type of rationale for developing a conglomerate creates a specialized demand for information at the centre of such a group. Financial information is needed initially to evaluate the potential benefit from reducing the volatility of profits and cash flow generation by combining the businesses.

Subsequently, the managers at the centre need financial information which enables them to monitor the level of achievement of the predicted net benefits, so as to ensure that the continuation of the corporate strategy is economically justified. This type of financial analysis can only be done at the group level as divisional managers should be concentrating on their competitive strategy for their particular product/market interfaces. Such a centrally based group financial evaluation should also include the incremental costs which will be incurred in controlling these businesses as part of a group, so as only to use the *net* benefit. Unfortunately, it is these central costs which normally invalidate this type of conglomerate strategy if viewed purely from the shareholder's perspective. As already stated, the sophisticated investor can achieve a similarly diversified portfolio at much lower cost than is incurred by most large groups. Consequently, there is no net benefit to this type of shareholder from investing in a conglomerate, which only tries to diversify investor risk.

A further way of considering this issue is to reconsider the arguments previously used, initially in Chapter 2, with regard to diversification in the context of the Ansoff matrix. Using the Ansoff classifications, diversification consists of selling new products, which the company has no experience of, to new customers, who the company has never traded with before. This is illustrated in Figure 11.1 and raises the question of whether diversifying into unrelated areas really does reduce the risk of the group. If group management have no expertise at all in these new divisions, there is little likelihood of any added value being generated either through the corporate strategy or by the exercise of financial controls at the centre of such a conglomerate. Consequently, the types of counter-cyclical investments which are most likely to create added value for the group are ones not only where the individual business cycles are suitably offset, but also where the nature of the products or the markets have common factors which enable group managers to add value. The earlier examples of Cadbury Schweppes and Wall's meet this additional criterion, but this type of risk reducing portfolio has implications for the financial information required at the centre.

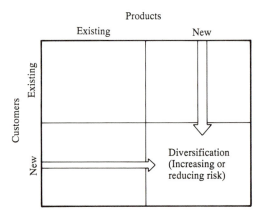

Figure 11.1 Diversification using the Ansoff Matrix

If unrelated businesses are combined, so as to reduce overall risk, the role of group managers is to manage the portfolio of businesses from this risk reducing perspective. Very little involvement is required in the competitive strategies of the largely autonomous divisions and consequently little detailed financial information is needed from divisions at the centre. Comparisons of financial performance against plan can be used to decide whether the portfolio is still balanced, but a key indicator will be forecasts of future volatility in profits or cash flows. By definition, the 'balanced' portfolio should show one division's forecast decrease being offset by a forecast improvement in a compensating division. When this is not true, group managers may need to intervene to rebalance the group. However, due to the lack of detailed operational expertise in the differing businesses, such rebalancing is normally done through acquisitions and divestitures of complete business units, rather than by modifying the competitive strategy of any particular division. This highlights that central managements should regularly be considering what available options there are for buying-in suitable businesses or selling-out ones which are no longer appropriate for the portfolio. Clearly this places a heavy emphasis on externally focused financial information at the centre; it is not logical to expect divisional managers to volunteer that their operation should be sold or, even worse, closed down because it no longer fits in with the overall corporate strategy!

However, where the counter-cyclical businesses are related in some way, it becomes logical to have a much greater degree of interchange of information among the divisions and between each division and the centre of the group. Thus, some of the financial information produced by the operating divisions may have important implications for other parts of the group. A key role for the centre is to collect this information and to pass it to the relevant areas in an appropriate form. If this function is not carried out effectively at group level, the only alternative is for the divisions to communicate directly; this massively increases the volume of irrelevant or incomprehensible financial data which is transmitted around the group. The problem of having a central group involvement is that the added value depends on the level of knowledge and understanding on the part of group managers about the detailed operations of the various business units. Thus, if one division has faced and solved a problem of negotiating a new type of discount structure with a major group of customers due to a change in its product mix or method of distribution, the group managers need to know which other divisions may face a similar problem in their own markets. This changes the type of managers needed at the centre of the group and dramatically increases the level of financial information required to support their greater level of operational involvement.

This type of result can also occur from the other major type of balanced portfolio strategy used by conglomerates, which balances out the overall cash generating capability of the group. As previously discussed in Chapters 2 and 3, the concept of the divisional portfolio grew out of the Boston Consulting Group development which was based on using the positive cash flow from mature businesses to invest in cash negative development businesses. The alternative to this corporate strategy is to return the positive cash flow to the owners of the business, eg in the form of increased dividends. If the re-investment strategy is to be economically justifiable, it is again important to demonstrate that there is added value from keeping cash within the group rather than returning it to the shareholders. As before, sophisticated investors could use their increased dividend streams to make their own investments in developing businesses, if they wanted to, and thus build up their own cash neutral portfolio. This can normally be done more cheaply than can be achieved by creating and maintaining a large conglomerate, although the different taxation treatments of dividends and capital gains can create distortions for certain classes of investors.

A more general justification for this kind of conglomerate strategy is through a more positive input by the central group management. The cash flow from a mature business which is made available to a passive shareholder is the dividend stream paid out by the management. These dividends will be paid after re-investing what these managers believe is advisable, and setting aside whatever contingency fund they feel is necessary to shelter the business from economic cycles and unexpected downturns in trading activity. In other words, there may be some slackness in the flow of funds which can then be re-invested by the shareholder into the identified growth opportunities. If this type of business operates as a division of a conglomerate, the expected level of cash generation can be much more positively planned, monitored and 'encouraged', so that the re-investment opportunities are maximized.

Indeed, it is quite common to go even one stage further, and this is where the main added value is created. If more very attractive investment opportunities are identified for the group than can be funded from available internal and external sources, it may be possible for central management to extract more cash flow from one of its major, mature, cash producing divisions. Generating this extra short-term cash flow may force the division to implement a sub-optimal competitive strategy in its own markets (eg by a more aggressive pricing strategy which may damage its market share). The group must ensure that the decrease in this division's future prospects is more than compensated for by the benefits gained from the enhanced level of new investments. By this type of juggling with the component elements of the overall group cash flow, central management can add value to the shareholders, which they could not obtain from a similar portfolio of independent shareholdings. However, this role of managing the portfolio can, yet again, be enhanced by increasing the level of interaction among the divisions within the conglomerate. Central management can become actively involved in managing the cash flow of the group, smoothing out seasonal peaks and troughs for operating divisions by providing cash management and funding services. By such a route the group may decide to increase its overall borrowing level rather than force one division to make sub-optimal decisions, if it is confident that the divisional cash flow forecasts are sufficiently accurate and robust. This requires that group treasury management have a much closer involvement with the divisional operating managerial decisions, than is needed if the group only has the role of providing long-term funding in accordance with the divisional strategic plan. It is clearly an example of a potential economy of scale which can be achieved by performing certain functions on a group-wide basis, but also highlights that the management accounting system must provide adequate information to support the new role which is being fulfilled by the centre.

Economies of scale

In many conglomerates, there are opportunities to generate substantial economies of scale by sharing resources across the group, but this sharing process complicates the autonomous divisional structure of the simple, diversified conglomerate. If central management still want to use financial performance measures by controlling divisions as investment or profit centres, they have to devize a method of charging each division for its usage of such shared services. As conglomerates are, by definition, producing and selling a wide range of products, the potential for sharing resources across the group tends to be in the areas of support services. This can be in the research and development area, where common process technologies may be applicable in several divisions of the group. Divisions may well be attacking similar markets, or markets with similar characteristics, but with different products (eg consumer goods markets) so that basic market research information on these common customers would be of widespread interest.

Before a large group can achieve this type of economy of scale, it is essential that someone is aware of such common interests. This can only realistically be done at the centre of the group, by creating a functionally focused manager with responsibilities for identifying and then efficiently supplying such shared needs. If this group initiative is to be successful it must be seen to be cost effective by the divisions, as well as by group managers. If divisional managers do not believe that these central group support functions are efficiently and effectively focusing on their particular concerns, they will ignore the group effort and continue to function in a completely stand-alone mode. This can result in very costly duplication and demotivation within the group management team. Unfortunately, in many groups such a result has been caused by a lack of effective co-ordination of the central support area's objectives with the needs and desires of the operating businesses. For example, centralized research and development areas are often accused of becoming far too academic and long term in their focus, and of not concentrating on product areas and markets which are of more immediate interest to the operating divisions.

This type of criticism can often be resolved by the use of the most appropriate form of management accounting system. In this particular research and development example, the group senior managers may want to invest some funds in more long-term 'blue skies' research in an attempt to open up long-term growth opportunities for the group. However, if the current operating divisions are clearly focused on their existing products and markets, the divisional managers will quite reasonably complain if they are asked to pay for such generic research and development. Therefore, this expenditure should be funded by the centre of the group, and the divisions should only be charged for activities which they have agreed should be carried out.

It is still important that where this charging process is operated, the fundamental principles of transfer pricing are incorporated. As discussed in Chapter 10, transfer pricing should be mainly designed to ensure that resources are efficiently and effectively allocated within the business. This is clearly of relevance in the case of any shared service, but many commonly used methods of charging out these services do not achieve this end. A detailed example should make this clearer.

The transfer pricing of information technology (IT)

In most organizations, some aspects of information systems (IS) and technology are managed as a central resource, even if much of the technology is now physically decentralized. The financial management of expenditure on IS and IT involves two major elements: evaluating prospective and actual investments to ensure that funds are optimally deployed, and ensuring that the consumption of these resources is properly justified.

The first stage is achieved by the normal economic evaluations of capital expenditure proposals using discounted cash flow techniques, etc and then monitoring the actual returns from projects both as a learning process and to ensure that the investment should not be curtailed. However, part of the problem in the IS/IT area is that many of the benefits are difficult to measure and are also obtained in a different area of the business from where the expenditure takes place. In order to try to value these benefits and also to make sure that users do not make unjustified use of these expensive resources, some form of pricing mechanism must be used. The process should be seen as a pricing exercise and not as an arbitrary cost recovery mechanism, under which the systems department automatically cross-charges the operational areas whatever costs it incurs. Such a cost apportionment system achieves nothing in the way of efficient resource allocation nor in terms of improving the accountability of either user managers or IS/IT managers for the resources they consume.

One of the key objectives of any such service based transfer pricing system should be to ensure that the *real* cost of IS/IT resources to the organization is reflected in the price paid by users for the specific services involved. If this can be achieved, these prices can be compared by the users against the benefits which *they* will achieve from this use of resources. As long as their managerial performance is judged on some measure of adding value, they will then be motivated to use IS/IT resources only when they are economically justified from the group perspective.

Transfer prices cannot be based on historic costs if these costs do not represent the real cost of the resource to the group. Where the business is constrained by a shortage of IS/IT resources, the opportunity cost of what benefits are being foregone should be used. Alternatively, if the investment has already been made and the resources are underutilized, the avoidable cost which can be saved by getting rid of these spare resources becomes relevant. Neither of these methods is likely to charge out, neatly and exactly, the actual costs of the IS/IT department, but this should not be seen as the major objective of the process.

The primary element in any pricing decision, whether external or internal, relates to improving the overall economic performance of the business as a whole and this can only be evaluated by reference to the relevant time periods and costs, ie opportunity and avoidable costs. If managerial performance indicators are superimposed on this economic resource allocation decision, it is clearly vital that there is no conflict between the two criteria. This idea of goal congruence was discussed in Chapter 4 but it is often overlooked in the area of charging for internal services.

Where a group is trying to evaluate managerial performance, eg of the computer department, through a 'market' pricing mechanism, the logical charging system is to use the competitive alternative prices available in the 'markets'. If such alternatives are genuinely available, this can serve as a measure of both the managerial performance and the relative economic success of the department. In such a system, the IS/IT department is no longer trying to recover its costs; it is, itself, functioning as a profit centre or investment centre. The conglomerate can now evaluate requests for additional investments in IT against the projected returns (albeit internal) from that investment; what is important is that the user departments, paying these internal returns, are also carrying out economic evaluations.

The corollary to this idea is that there should be a free market (eg by allowing user departments to out-source new systems applications from external software houses) so that these transfer prices are not artificially constrained. A one-sided constraint would be unfair on the IS/IT department and thus, in such an environment, they should be allowed to sell any surplus resources externally. Several large groups have implemented this type of free market system in IS/IT so that all user departments can buy computer services from anyone, including their in-house supplier, and this in-house department is free to sell to anybody. These decisions should be based on optimizing the individual department's economic performance. However, this is a potentially significant change in the group's overall business strategy, as it effectively represents a diversification into IT as a business unit in its own right. This diversification for some groups has created a new large division, which is now doing almost nothing to support the internal needs of the other business units.

If the group wishes to avoid this type of change in business strategy, it should not use a completely free market transfer pricing strategy. The charging system should be attempting to allocate the available limited resources based on the real costs incurred by the company. The objective of user department accountability is critical and can be achieved by focusing on the resources committed by them, or at their behest, to a particular application. Their management performance is more effectively monitored by reference to their achievement of the proposed economic benefits flowing from the expenditure on computing resources.

Management performance of the computer department can also be controlled by monitoring the delivery of services (including new systems developments) in line with pre-set agreed targets and budgets. This is in keeping with the concept of only judging managers against items over which they exercise control.

Comparing alternative investment proposals, for systems developments or hardware upgrades, in an economic sense can be done, as already mentioned, by using the normal financial decision-making rules. The most common problem is in identifying the opportunity cost involved in any project, but, as in the previous example, identification of the relevant limiting factor makes this quite straightforward. In the case of IS/IT the pace of change is so rapid and the technological advances are so fundamental that the limiting factor can change quite quickly.

This has been particularly true due to the changing cost relationships, as costs of hardware and its processing capability have dramatically reduced over the last ten years. In many companies, a key limiting factor in developing new systems applications is the skilled personnel base available either to do or to manage the project. This no longer means computer programming skills or even systems analysts, as these skills can be bought in from third party contractors, but represents computer skilled managers who also have a good understanding of the business needs of the new system. The opportunity cost for the project must be related to the time involved for these key people, and the economic benefits can be expressed as contribution rates per person per year so that alternative projects can be compared.

Where hardware availability is the constraint, the opportunity cost must be expressed in terms of the appropriate constraint (eg contribution per unit of processing time), but alternative ways of removing the constraint should be considered. For example, increasing storage capacity in the computer may enable processing intensive systems to be run in a different manner, so that some of the limited processing capacity can be freed up. Also certain applications may be capable of being processed on stand-alone systems which could also increase available capacity on the main-frame computer.

As in all transfer pricing issues, it is particularly important to distinguish clearly among the economic assessment of alternatives, the subsequent monitoring of the implementation of selected projects and the use of financial control measures of managerial performance. If this is not successfully achieved, the desired economies of scale can not only disappear but can turn into diseconomies of scale.

Diseconomies of scale

Complete centralization of support services in some very large conglomerates creates such massive functional areas, that they are impossible to control as a single unit. Consequently, these functional areas are broken down into sub-units, which require their own organizational structures and financial reporting systems. It is not difficult to see that the initial justification for centralizing such common functions because of the potential economies may no longer be valid. Indeed the additional costs involved may outweigh the benefits of bringing these functional areas together. Even more important in many cases is the removal of the divisional focus which is achieved by leaving these support areas in the separate business units.

It is therefore only logical to centralize these support functions when the individual divisions cannot justify a critical mass in this area and where there are significant potential economies of scale to be obtained. The group must also avoid the risk of creating off-setting diseconomies of scale by making any functional area too large. This can often be avoided by only centralizing those specific shared areas of activity, rather than the whole functional department. Diseconomies of scale are a frequent problem for multinationals and these issues are considered in the following chapter.

12

Multinationals and global companies

Overview

There are several global products and some global markets, but, as yet, no truly global companies. However, several large multinational groups have altered their mission statements to incorporate global aspirations. Consequently, this chapter includes the particular problems of multinationals and, for the future, global companies.

A key element of financial decision-making in multinationals is the impact of foreign exchange movements. This has to be separated into its long-term aspects and its short-term effects, both on the performance of the locally focused operating divisions, and on the group as a whole. Over the long term, the impact is mainly on strategic investment decisions, which should be evaluated using the normal discounted cash flow techniques. The exchange rate between two currencies will, if left to market forces, adjust to reflect differences in the relative rates of inflation between the two countries. In the short term, these market forces can be distorted by government interventions but, in the long term, this concept known as purchasing power parity, does hold. Consequently, when considering a long-term strategic decision the multinational can validly assume that exchange rates will adjust to offset differential rates of inflation.

This makes long-term financial decisions easier to evaluate but the volatility in short-term exchange rates must be taken into account. The multinational can attempt to reduce the impact of these potentially disastrous short-term movements by implementing an appropriate hedging strategy. Such a hedging strategy must be linked to the overall business strategy and must take account of the more restricted interests of the single country focused divisional managers.

The sheer range of options and alternatives which are available to multinationals must not be allowed to create diseconomies of scale in either the organizational structure or the way in which the group is financially controlled.

Introduction

There are an increasing number of companies which have expanded their mission statements and corporate objectives to include the word 'global', thus giving the impression that they intend to extend their presence and influence to all parts of the world. To date, it is difficult to accept that any of these companies has succeeded in changing itself from a multinational business, which operates in a number of countries, to a truly global enterprise. To be truly global a company should not really have a home-base which is significantly more important to it than any other area. Thus its spread of business should be spread around the world in proportion to the relative shares of relevant purchasing capability but, more importantly, its ownership and management team should also be drawn from, and be representative of, this global base. Most companies, however multinational their operations, still have a dominant home investor base and a restricted source for their senior managers.

Thus, although there are an increasing number of global markets (particularly financial markets), which do not worry about international borders or time zones, and several global products (such as Coca Cola and Marlboro cigarettes), which are marketed in a consistent way around the world, these global markets and products are still, respectively, serviced and produced by multinational companies. The title of the chapter has been chosen to allow for the first of these globally aspiring companies to succeed, but the bulk of the chapter will refer only to multinational companies and their specific management accounting issues.

Multinationals take various forms in that they may be focused on a relatively narrow range of products but sell these products in a wide range of countries. They can be vertically integrated and this can mean that they manufacture in one country and sell the products in another, or that they are fully vertically integrated in several distinct regions of the world. The major oil companies are a good example of this first form of vertical integration on an international scale, because they extract oil from a limited number of countries, refine it in other countries, then distribute and market the finished product all over the world, with sales depending upon demand rather than upon that country's supply of the raw material. Alternatively, the multinational may be a conglomerate which uses its geographic spread of operations as a way of reducing its overall risk or as a way of achieving economies of scale in each area of its operations. Thus multinationals can face the full range of corporate control problems which have already been discussed in the preceding chapters of this part of the book. Consequently, this chapter concentrates on the specific and largely common problems caused by being a multinational, irrespective of the nature of the underlying organizational structure.

These common issues obviously include the problems of managing cross-border financial exposures but, in many cases, being multinational also gives the group many more strategic options and alternatives in terms of the location of various component elements of its operations. In some cases there are very limited alternatives and the choices are relatively clear cut. In the example of the oil companies mentioned earlier, the multinational cannot choose where it finds its crude oil. However, it can decide whether it wants to develop this particular oil field itself, as it can sell it to another company or possibly swap the field for another set of oil reserves in a more favourable geographic location for the group. Also this multinational oil company can decide where it locates its oil refineries, relative to its oil production fields and its final product markets. These decisions need to be taken at the group level, so that the vested interests of the locally based managers are not allowed to bias the decision. The decision must be based on the economic impact of each alternative on the overall group; any resulting internal issues affecting perceptions of divisional and managerial performance must be resolved by implementing an appropriate transfer pricing system. These issues can be illustrated by considering some detailed examples for a particular multinational, which has a much greater degree of freedom over its choice of location.

Multinational sourcing decisions

A large, USA-based, multinational car manufacturer produces cars, or components of cars, in 5 countries around Europe but sells its final products in 15 West European countries. The first financial control issue is how it should regard its long-term investments in these differently

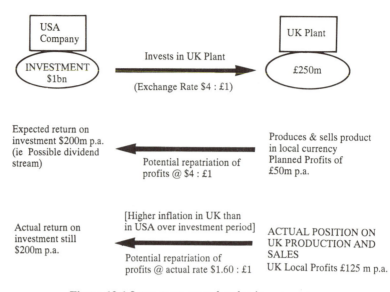

Figure 12.1 Long-term cross border investments

located manufacturing plants in terms of the exchange risk involved. Assuming that its initial investment in the UK cost £250 million when the exchange rate was $4:£1, this represented a cost to the shareholders of $1 billion (being a USA-based group, its shareholders will look for an economic return in US dollars on this investment). However, with the subsequent devaluation of the £ sterling against the US dollar, this original investment would now have a converted value of only $400 million (£250 million at a spot rate of exchange of £1:$1.60). This does not necessarily indicate a substantial real economic loss to the USA multinational, because it did not make its initial investment in order to sell the factory at some time in the future and repatriate the proceeds. Obviously, the value of this investment in £ sterling has actually decreased over time due to the depreciation of the plant and equipment anyway. The investment was made in order to produce cars which would be sold at a profit around Europe, and the present values of the net cash flows generated by these sales were the economic justification for the initial investment. This is illustrated in Figure 12.1 and, as long as the profit margins on these sales can be maintained in real terms and the sales volumes do not decline, it becomes clear that the long-term devaluation has not, in fact, adversely affected the economic return from the investment. This actual devaluation resulted from a higher level of inflation in the UK than in the USA over this period.

Higher inflation means that UK incomes rise in terms of their £ sterling values relative to incomes in the USA. If the rate of exchange between the US dollar and the £ sterling stays the same, people with incomes denominated in £s will be able to travel to the United States and buy goods more cheaply than they can at home. When the gap becomes large enough, arbitrageurs will start exporting these goods from the USA to the UK and will make a profit by converting their £s to US dollars, buying goods in the USA with these dollars, shipping the goods to the UK and selling them at the higher £s denominated selling prices, as is shown in Figure 12.2. As more people start doing this, there is an increasing demand for US dollars in the foreign exchange market and a correspondingly increased supply of £ sterling. In any free market, such a shift in relative supply and demand leads to a compensating change in price, until supply and demand are once again in equilibrium.

	Price of goods		Rate of exchange	
1 INITIAL SITUATION	USA	UK	US$	: £
	$10,000	CAR £5,000	2	: 1

The equivalent price of the product in the 2 markets is the same: thus no gain can be achieved by a transfer.

	Price of goods		Rate of exchange	
2 INFLATION IN UK 20% HIGHER THAN IN	USA	UK	US$	: £
USA – NO CHANGE IN EXCHANGE RATE	$10,000	CAR £6,000	2	: 1

Arbitrageur can now buy the car in the USA for the equivalent of £5,000, take it to the UK and sell it at the new UK price of £6,000.

	Price of goods		Rate of exchange	
3 INFLATION HIGHER IN UK – EXCHANGE	USA	UK	US$	: £
RATE ADJUSTS	$10,000	CAR £6,000	1.6667	: 1

Buying the car in the USA for $10,000 now costs the equivalent of £6,000, which is its UK selling price.

Figure 12.2 Purchasing power parity

Clearly this position can remain out of balance in the short term due to government indirect interference through monetary or fiscal policy, or straightforward regulatory direct impact on the ability to import or export. Over time, the market pressures will force governments to move into line with the underlying economic reality. Consequently, it is valid to argue that in the long term, all relative purchasing powers in local currencies are equal; this economic concept is known as the purchasing power parity theory. It means that any relatively high inflation country will see its currency depreciate over time to restore its relative purchasing power against other currencies. In our example, the devaluation of sterling against the US dollar has been caused by the higher inflation experienced in the UK.

This higher inflation means that selling prices for cars in £ sterling will have also increased. The critical issue for the economic return on the investment is whether the UK business was able to maintain its profit margin during this inflationary period. If so, its £ sterling profits would be increased and should convert back into an equivalent US dollar return on the original investment, as was shown in Figure 12.1.

For this group, this analysis was also valid for several other long-term investments. Many multinationals decided to build manufacturing plants in Spain in the early 1970s based on the post-Franco era of industrialization and prospective entry into the European Community. The financial evaluations were dominated by the much lower employment costs for Spanish labour compared to either British or German workers (after allowing for their relative productivities). During the following fifteen years relative inflation in Spain was very much higher than had been forecast in the early 1970s and, consequently, local labour costs increased dramatically in pesetas. However, this local currency increase was almost exactly offset by the depreciation in the relative value of the peseta, so that the predicted relative labour cost advantage for the Spanish production units was maintained. Thus, in the long term, the purchasing power parity theory can be demonstrated as working and this means that long-term strategic investment decisions can be based on the underlying economic fundamentals. However, in the shorter term the performance of a multinational can be dramatically affected by movements in exchange rates; yet financial decisions should still be based on economically sound logic.

	UK		US dollar equivalents		Germany
Budgeted rates of exchange	£1	:	$2	:	4DM
UK selling price	£7,500	@ $2:£1	$15,000		
UK production cost	£6,000		$12,000		
Profit	£1,500		$3,000		
			$12,000	German selling price	DM 24,000
			$10,000	German production cost	DM 20,000
UK selling price	£7,500		$2,000	Profit	DM 4,000
German production	£5,000	@ 4DM:£1 ⇐		Export production	DM 20,000
New profit	£2,500	@ $2:£1 ⇒	$5,000	← (Improved group profits)	

Figure 12.3 Sourcing decision – exchange rate impact

Returning to the US-based, multinational car manufacturer, it had another significant sourcing issue during much of the 1980s. Its production capacity in Germany exceeds its sales levels in Germany, but it has an efficient, productive work-force which it wishes to utilize fully. This can be achieved by exporting cars from Germany to other markets in Europe, but if there is a locally based manufacturing plant the economic justification must be carefully evaluated. For several years, this group was manufacturing cars in Germany and exporting them to the UK even though its UK plants were not working at maximum capacity. There are some simple financial comparisons which can be done to ensure that this is in the best overall interests of the group, but this evaluation will be done at the planned or budgeted exchange rates. If the actual rates differ, the business needs to monitor the effect and be prepared to change, while trying to reduce the risk of exchange rate volatility invalidating the original decision. In Figure 12.3, the basic logic of the initial decision is set out, using the illustration of the same car produced and sold in the UK and Germany, with the equivalent impacts being shown in US dollars (which is how the group will view the outcome).

The important thing about the logic of this decision is that there are *two* key prerequisites before it makes economic sense to manufacture cars in Germany and ship them to the UK, while leaving capacity idle in the UK. The first obvious point is that the German production costs must be relatively lower than the British equivalent; this is satisfied in the example with, in US dollars, the German cost at $10,000 and the British cost at $12,000. This cost differential must be large enough to cover both the physical costs involved in shipping the car from Germany to the UK and the increased manufacturing costs in Germany (ie of producing a British specification, right-hand drive car).

If this more efficiently produced car could be sold in Germany at the same equivalent price as in the UK, the group would be substantially better off doing this. First, the on-costs of shipping and manufacturing complexity would be avoided and second, the UK demand could be profitably satisfied by producing the car in the UK, using the available spare capacity. Thus for this decision to be logical, the group must be forced to sell its cars in Germany at lower equivalent selling prices than it achieves in the UK. In Figure 12.3 this is true with the German selling price being only $12,000 compared to the UK equivalent of $15,000. Indeed this lower selling price means that, despite its superior manufacturing efficiency, the group makes a lower profit in producing *and* selling a car in Germany ($2,000) than by producing and selling the same car in the UK. However, by combining the lower production base with the higher priced markets, the group profit is substantially increased. The rationale for this situation is that the UK selling price is dictated by the dominant, domestically based producers, which all face the higher UK production costs, while the German selling price is driven down by the more efficient, domestically based, and even more market dominant, producers. The selling prices in each market for the group's cars were also affected by the relative market shares in each country and this also enabled higher prices, relative to the market, to be achieved in the UK.

Thus, at the budgeted rates of exchange, the decision to produce cars in Germany and export them to the UK markets makes sound economic sense, but it introduces an additional foreign currency exposure for the group. If the rates of exchange deviate from the budget, as they almost certainly will, the decision may no longer be valid, and the group may end up worse off financially. If we take the actual rates of exchange as being as shown in Figure 12.4, the decision can be reworked. Initially, assume that the changes in exchange rates are caused by differences in relative rates of inflation; ie in the USA 0% inflation, while the UK had general price rises of 20%. During this period, the strengthening of the Deutsche Mark is explained by productivity gains in excess of price rises, ie real cost *deflation* in the manufacturing sector.

If the German division was able to maintain its selling prices in local currency, it would show a small increase in its US dollar equivalent profits ($2,307 versus $2,000), but if it had to pass on the reduced production costs to its customers it would merely maintain its equivalent profitability. As long as the UK division is able to increase its selling prices in line with inflation, thus maintaining its real margins, it will generate the same US dollar equivalent profit. This is true for both locally produced and for imported sales; therefore there is the same economic logic for importing cars as there was originally. Also the US dollar comparable profit on selling a German manufactured car in the UK is still considerably higher than the profit generated by selling the same car in Germany.

However, in the short term exchange rates do not move directly in line with relative rates of inflation. There is a consequent risk that the exchange rates may move to the actual levels indicated without any compensating differences in inflation. A further review of Figures 12.4

	UK		US dollar equivalents		Germany
Actual rates of exchange	£1	:	$1.667	:	DM 3.25
Increased UK selling price	£9,000			Unchanged German selling price	DM 24,000
Increased UK production cost	£7,200 (Converted @ £1:$1.667)				
Profit	£1,800 Same US$ profit		$3,000		
	Increased profit on German production and sale		$2,307	Reduced German production cost	DM 19,500
				⇐ Profit	DM 4,500
Imported product Increased UK selling price	£9,000		⇐	Reduced German production cost	DM 19,500
Imported cost	£6,000 ⇐ @ £1:DM 3.25				
Profit	£3,000 Same US$ profit		$5,000		

Figure 12.4 Sourcing decision – Continued – actual rates of exchange

and 12.3, together with a consideration of the implications of the initial decision will clarify the significance of this analysis. If the group decides, on the basis of the financial evaluation in Figure 12.3 using budgeted rates of exchange, to export cars from Germany for sale in the UK, there are a number of significant operational implications. Production capacity in the UK will be made idle, while additional resources may be committed in Germany to meet this increased anticipated demand. There is a physical planning period during which it may be impossible, and certainly would be very expensive, to reverse the decision, once implemented. It would be disastrous if, during this physically committed timescale, the exchange rates moved so violently that the economic logic was destroyed. For example, if the rate suddenly changed to £1:3DM, the group could find itself committed to importing cars from Germany which were now more expensive than those it could produce locally (ie 20,000DM @ 3DM:£1 gives an imported cost of £6,666.57p against a local cost of £6,000). In fact, Figure 12.4 shows that a rate of 3.25DM:£1 makes the even *more* efficient German production cost translate into the base level UK cost of £6,000 per car. It would be sensible for the group to consider hedging against the possibility that a previously sensible decision becomes economically disastrous due to a change in external circumstances, as long as the hedging cost itself does not affect the logic of the initial decision.

In this example this could be done by fixing the rate of exchange for the cars to be imported from Germany; this can be achieved by taking out a sterling denominated forward purchase contract for the amount of Deutsche Marks needed to pay for them. If the rate on the forward contract was better than 3.33 DM:£1, the company has effectively guaranteed that the imported cars will be cheaper than the equivalent locally produced car. An alternative hedging strategy is to try to safeguard the downside risk associated with the exchange rate movement but to retain the potential benefit if the exchange rate moves favourably. Thus if the £ sterling actually strengthened against the Deutsche Mark in the short term, to say 4.25 DM:£1, then the imported cars become even more attractive when sold at UK prices. This up-side potential can be retained if an option to buy the required Deutsche Marks is purchased in the financial markets; if the actual rate declines, the option is exercised but, if not, the currency is bought directly in the market at the spot rate and the insurance type option contract is not used. (Forward exchange rates are driven by interest rate differentials as was explained in Chapter 5.)

This specific illustration shows how a multinational can use sound financial analysis to gain the maximum benefit from the increased number of available alternatives, which are created by its organizational structure. However, unless the group is to have a very large head office staff carrying out these overall evaluations, it is important that these economic justifications can be linked into the divisional managerial performance measures.

Managerial performance measures in a multinational

The key objective is to achieve goal congruence between the divisional manager's objectives and those of the group. At the group level, the objective of this example is to use the international sourcing alternatives to improve total profitability. This must not conflict with the separate objectives established for the individual divisions located in each country. At the same time these divisional managers should not be judged on areas which they do not control.

For the German divisional manager, the key objectives are to produce the cars in the most efficient manner and to be willing to make available the increased production level for export to the UK. Running the division as a profit centre and allowing the two countries to negotiate a transfer price should achieve this, except for the issue of exchange rate risk. The German division has almost all of its costs denominated in Deutsche Marks, as are its local revenues. It is simple to fix the export transfer price in Deutsche Marks as well, and use this local currency to judge managerial performance. If the rate against the US dollar moves favourably, as in Figure 12.4, have the divisional managers performed any better? However, in the importing division the position is slightly different as the managers are willing to take on the added exchange rate risk of importing cars in order to improve their division's financial performance. The transfer price can be fixed in Deutsche Marks, but their performance can be judged in £ sterling. This encourages them to manage the currency risk and to ensure that their decision to import cars is originally, and remains, economically sound. Thus the group objectives are closely linked with the separate divisions.

The group may want to go one stage further and encourage the divisions to focus on their US dollar denominated profits, since this is what is used to judge the overall group's performance. This can be done by using divisional profits expressed in US dollars as the measure of divisional performance, but this can now confuse economic and managerial measures with detrimental impacts on management motivation.

For such a USA-based group, its perceived overall economic financial performance may be adversely affected by unfavourable exchange rate movements in countries where it has significant operations. (As mentioned earlier, a truly global company should not face the same degree of problem from changes in exchange rates.) Thus, in our example of exporting German produced cars to the UK, the combination of an appreciation of the Deutsche Mark against the US dollar and a devaluation in the £ sterling against the US dollar could affect the financial performance of the total group quite significantly; due to the excess of German based costs and the surplus of UK generated revenues. However, trying to hold local country managers totally responsible for such exchange rate movements is not the answer.

It is a common complaint of divisional managers in multinationals that they are personally penalized (through managerial incentive schemes, etc) for adverse exchange rate movements over which they have no control. Not surprisingly very few managers complain about being credited with the similarly uncontrollable benefits of favourable exchange rate movements. If the multinational decides what degree of financial risk it wants to encourage at the divisional level, it is perfectly practical to design and implement an appropriate system of evaluating both economic and managerial financial performance.

A key part of this type of system is based on ensuring that the local currency evaluation is logical and fair. Any financial plan, against which actual performance is compared, depends on a number of assumptions and forecasts, which will be wrong. In order to have meaningful analyses between the actual outcomes and those planned, the plan or budget may need flexing to reflect the impact of these false assumptions. For example, the forecast inflation rate may prove to be significantly lower than the actual level; this difference could make the comparison of actual and budgeted sales revenues meaningless unless the plan is adjusted. If the pricing objectives were established in real terms, eg increasing selling prices by 2% more than inflation, rather than absolute values, it becomes relatively straightforward to revise the financial plan so as to include the desired objective. The actual achievement can then be validly compared against this revised plan, with the forecasting error between the two plans being shown separately (this is often called a revision variance).

This type of analysis is even more relevant when exchange rate forecasts are involved. It has already been argued that, in the long term, purchasing power parity theory works, so that exchange rates adjust to offset relative differences in inflation rates between countries. However, in the short term it is quite easy to see how the UK-based car business could, in a

UK company plans to sell 10,000 imported cars at £7,500	−£75 million
German cost of those cars @ 4DM:£1–£5,000 each	−£50 million
Expected local currency profit	£25 million

Forward exchange rate at time of plan $2:£1

Planned US dollar profit on these sales – $50 million

[Spot rate of exchange at time of doing plan was $2.095:£1]
UK company can 'guarantee' this US dollar profit by selling forward its net £ sterling profit, ie buying the US dollars in the forward exchange market at $2:£1.

However: This increases risk in several ways:–
1 the company may not actually sell 10,000 imported cars in the UK, due to a recession, etc
2 the profit in £ sterling may differ from the planned £25 million and the group may find itself with excess US dollar purchases
3 other parts of the group may have the reverse need for foreign currencies and so may be selling US dollars and buying £ sterling in the forward exchange markets
4 the actual spot rate of exchange may not depreciate as forecast in the forward rate (due to interest rate differentials), so that the group would have been better off by not taking the forward exchange contract.

Figure 12.5 Forward and spot exchange rates – impact on performance

period of higher relative UK inflation, outperform against its plan in terms of both £ sterling profits and US dollar profits, if the rate of exchange did not immediately reflect the higher UK inflation. If the multinational wishes to reduce its risk exposure to such exchange rate movements, it can judge divisional performance in terms of US dollars. However, it should set the exchange rates at those levels which can be achieved in the forward market and not at the spot rates. This would encourage locally based managers to hedge their profit back into US dollars by taking forward currency deals, so as to guarantee achieving the targeted rate of exchange. If they met their local currency profit objective, they would consequently automatically achieve their US dollar profit plan as well. The impact of this is shown in Figure 12.5, which also shows the potential problems caused because forward exchange rates are not good indicators of where the spot rate of exchange will actually be on that future date.

As illustrated, the UK division does not need to cover exchange risks on its sales revenues, as these can largely be offset against operating costs. This is true even though many of these operating costs originate outside the UK. As discussed earlier the UK based managers should have guaranteed, if possible, the economic logic of their decision to import by hedging this element of foreign currency exposure; thus either fixing, or providing a maximum for, the £ sterling imported cost. The US dollar exposure is on the expected profit from these sales. This can be covered by buying the US dollars forward at the planned exchange rate; assuming that the planned rate of exchange represents the average forward rate for the ensuing year. However, as discussed in Figure 12.5, this forward exchange cover does not really guarantee that the USA-based parent will receive the desired dollar denominated profits and also increases the risk in other ways.

In particular, if the actual spot rate of exchange stays steady at $2.095:£1, the group could have increased its US dollar profits by $2.375 million by 'doing nothing', ie converting its actual UK profits at the prevailing spot rate of exchange. This is why it is important for any multinational to specify what type of risk profile it wants its overseas businesses to take with regard to foreign currency. Their behaviour will largely be conditioned by the way in which their performances are judged, and yet very few multinationals have clear policies on foreign exchange management at all levels in the group. In this example it would be relatively easy to divide responsibilities yet again so as to focus managers' attention on the areas where they can exercise most control. Thus operating managers in all countries could be judged on their US dollar profits, but these would be assessed using forward rates of exchange, set at the time of doing the financial plan. This would mean that these managers should only consider buying in the forward foreign currency market when they were confident of generating the local currency profits. However, once they were sure of producing the £25 million profit shown in Figure 12.5, they should remove their exchange risk of not achieving $50 million by fixing the forward exchange rate.

This does not mean that the group should automatically go into the market and immediately buy $50 million for future delivery. The treasury managers may decide that it would be better to wait and take the spot rate of exchange when the profits have been made, or to arrange a different form of hedging contract, such as an option to safeguard the downside risk on the exchange rate. They are employed to use this type of expertise and their performance should accordingly be judged on how well they manage the foreign exchange exposure of the group. This can be done by comparing the actual rates achieved against the forward rates of exchange used in the plan, but this gives far too much importance to these arbitrarily calculated forward rates which may not be achievable during the year. A far better way is to monitor their performance against the 'do nothing' alternative, which uses the actual spot rates of exchange during the year to compare against the rates achieved by the active treasury management role.

In summary, therefore, this multinational now has a multi-tiered approach to managing its foreign currency exposures. The German based exporting company has an export transfer price set in its local currency, but will manage its profit in terms of the parent company currency by using the forward rate of exchange. The UK-based importing business has to manage its foreign currency exposure on its import costs so as to ensure that it is still sensible to source from Germany. It has also to manage the translation of its local currency profits into US dollars by using forward rates, but the active management of these profit transactions is done by the treasury managers who are separately judged. They can be judged against the spot market rates which would be achieved without any active currency management.

Diseconomies of scale

Such a sophisticated system is important to a large multinational, but must be individually tailored to the needs of the particular group. It must take account of the business strategies in use within the overall group and in each locally based business unit. The centre must also clearly signal, through this financial control system, how it wants its operating units to behave in terms both of taking risks and in working together as a group. Thus the group (eg an oil company as mentioned in Chapter 8) may restrict divisional operations by insisting on a balanced source of supply geographically. It should go further and ensure that marketing divisions, in regions which are consequently short of raw material supplies, can gain access to supplies from other regions at sensible market prices. If they cannot, are they allowed to go into the open market to buy in supplies from outside the group?

Once the centre of a multinational becomes involved in this type of problem, it is easy to question whether the group has become too complex and has ceased to add value. Diseconomies of scale are a serious problem for many multinationals and senior managers of such large groups frequently speak, at length, about the complexity of their businesses. What they seem to forget is that, to a very large extent, they are responsible for creating that complexity. The scale and spread of the multinational should have been justified because it

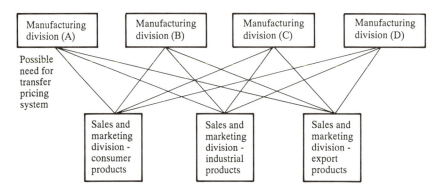

Figure 12.6 Transfer pricing: sales between divisions of a large multinational

added value to the shareholders in the group through increased economies of scale, etc. If the problems of financial control and managerial motivation have become so great that they outweigh the advantages of size and geographic spread, the multinational should simplify its structure or its span of business.

The complexity involved in many multinationals can be easily illustrated by considering the transfer pricing problems involved in a group with four manufacturing locations and three sales and marketing divisions. As shown in Figure 12.6, this introduces twelve possible internal sets of transfers, requiring transfer prices which must be soundly economically based while still correctly motivating managers. Most multinationals involve many more sourcing options than twelve and one such large business 'proudly' illustrates the complexity of its business by stating that it has over 2 million internal cost classifications. One may wonder as to how such massive complexity adds value to the key stakeholders in this multinational. Unfortunately, as is discussed in Part Five, the sheer scale of these types of complexity problems makes it more difficult for these vast multinationals to take advantage of the new information technology solutions, which can make it practical to cope with such large data handling and processing issues. The group with over 2 million cost classifications needs a new costing system which would give it meaningful financial decision support information, but cannot see how it can afford to develop such a large computer system.

Two better arguments are first, that it cannot afford not to develop the new decision support system as its competitors already have such information and second, that if it was broken up into smaller bits it would not need such a complex costing system at all!

13

Non-profit organizations

Overview

The title of this chapter, non-profit organizations, covers a very wide range of 'businesses' which have a correspondingly wide range of differing objectives. The only unifying feature being the absence of the normal overriding objective of commercially oriented companies, which is to generate a satisfactory profit return for their shareholders. In fact for many of these organizations even this distinction is no longer completely valid as they do use a 'profit' measure as a key financial indicator of their performance.

However profit in this context can only really measure their efficiency in generating revenue and controlling costs, whereas the main performance criterion should be to assess the effectiveness with which they fulfil their principle strategic objectives.

For most of these non-profit organizations, the strategic goals and mission statements are quite clearly defined (eg in the case of charities). However, for some of the more recently created entities there is a danger of some confusion being created in terms of their main goals (eg hospital trusts; is the logic to create greater efficiency, more customer focus, more freedom of choice, more competition or all of these?). It is vitally important that these non-financial goals are clearly understood by all the parties involved and are compatible with the financial objectives which are established. Even more critical however is that both these sets of objectives are either fully compatible with the goals of the senior managers of the organization, or are sufficiently clearly defined so as to restrict the freedom of action of senior managers.

Many non-profit organizations are now very large businesses with large revenues and sizeable cost bases, but they do not normally have to face the ultimate sanction of the financial markets in the same way as commercial companies do. So far in the book, the arguments of agency theory have been used as a means of ensuring, albeit in the long term, that managers must act in the interests of the shareholders and other key stakeholders. If they do not the 'market' will eventually remove them. However if there are no 'shareholders', or if they are most unlikely to act as a unified body, and there is no prospect of any 'takeover' by outsiders, there is a danger that the senior managers can implement their own strategy in order to achieve more clearly focused personal goals.

Overall size is not necessarily a good measure of success for a non-profit organization, any more than it is for a commercially run business. Consequently, there should be a financial control on the proportion of revenue spent on the marketing activities which are designed to raise the revenue. This is most clearly seen in terms of charities where it is possible 'to grow the business' by spending an ever increasing proportion of existing donations in attracting new donations, particularly by using external professional, profit-oriented fund raisers.

There should also be financial controls on the proportion of other expenditure which is not spent directly on the main objectives of the organization. Administration expenses are not the main objectives of a charity, a university or a hospital. They are a necessary evil which should be kept to a minimum and the efficiency of the organization's operations can be partially monitored through this type of financial ratio.

The real difference between non-profit organizations and commercial enterprises is that non-profit businesses do not have to distribute their surpluses. Normally they are allowed to re-invest any excess funds back into their organization. While this sounds wonderful and should help to achieve their overriding goals and objectives, in reality it tends to cause a growth strategy to be implemented even though this may not be appropriate for the current stage of development of the organization.

Introduction

Non-profit organizations come in all sorts of shapes and sizes. They include truly international charities, which are engaged in massive projects in many countries at any one time, very large building societies and large nationalized utilities, which control a very high proportion of most nations' gross domestic product.

Indeed the UK government has, through its recent policy of privatization, given an ideal opportunity to consider the main differences between non-profit organizations and those businesses for which a profit measure is vitally important. The best examples to consider are the 'privatized monopolies', ie the utility businesses previously owned by the government but now, partially at least, sold to external, profit-motivated investors. This change in ownership has led to significant changes in the way these organizations are structured and financially controlled with correspondingly substantial, if not even more dramatic, alterations to their management accounting systems. In most of these cases many of the changes subsequent to the decision to privatize the organization can be viewed as serious criticisms of the previous systems of management control; ie without the incentive of the profit measure, senior managers apparently did not need financial information on their different business segments, or on specific group-wide cost levels.

However, other aspects of financial control changes have been driven by the different environment which the business is facing. For example British Telecom (BT) was the first utility monopoly to be privatized; due to the effective monopoly of the domestic telephone system, combined with its dominance of the business market, the government set up a scheme to regulate its pricing policy. In order to stimulate efficiency and to keep price rises down, the regulatory body (known as OFTEL) can insist that BT raises its prices by less than general price inflation. Unfortunately, this pricing control mechanism was set for the organization as a whole, which gave the management team substantial competitive freedom. BT was able to increase its charges to domestic customers (where it has a monopoly) by much more than inflation but, at the same time actually reduce its charges to its business customers (where it faced increasing competition). In order to support future such relative pricing shifts, the company has undertaken a massive cost apportionment exercise to try to show the relative cost, and profit, levels of its various business segments. It has recently tried to use this accounting analysis to justify why certain charges should be changed dramatically. In the domestic segment BT wants to increase the rental charges for the actual telephone line but to decrease the charges per call. The justification is based on the very high investment needed to construct the national telephone infrastructure, but the logic may be helped by the fact that BT has a monopoly of domestic telephone lines but now faces competition on call services for domestic subscribers. Unfortunately, its published financial analysis is falsely based as it has been done as a full apportionment of historic costs, including the chairman's salary and related costs, which has no relevance to the decisions which are being considered.

What is interesting is the substantial change in the management accounting systems now being developed in this organization. It is also interesting to note the learning curve of the government in terms of the problems of privatizing total monopolies and subsequently curtailing their potential abuse of these monopolies by regulations. In the cases of the electricity and water industries, the government has tried to create some element of competition within the industry; albeit by creating regional monopolies where the major element of competition is through the comparison of their relative financial performances.

The changes in strategic focus by these privatized organizations have been dramatic, with the removal of the previous 'socio-political' emphasis and its replacement with financial criteria including the issues of both new areas of business potential and risk diversification. Despite this volume of privatization the UK public sector still consists of a very large number of businesses, which do not focus on profit as their principal objectives.

Thus in the UK the National Health Service, the Armed Services, Education in all its forms, law enforcement and the legal system, and government itself, should all be viewed as non-profit organizations. In addition, there are a vast array of trade associations and voluntary groups (such as Boy Scouts, Girl Guides, National Association of Youth Clubs) which must be included. Indeed with the current government driven trend towards creating many much smaller financially semi-autonomous organizations, such as schools, doctors' practices and hospital trusts, the non-profit sector can be regarded as rapidly growing.

It is obvious that many of the accounting problems facing this vast array of organizations will be significantly different and that much of the material discussed in other parts of the book should be applied as appropriate. The only unifying characteristic is the absence of the 'profit incentive' which is so important to more obviously commercially focused businesses. Profit is measured as the excess of sales revenue over expenses incurred in achieving that revenue, and this could be used as a measure of the efficiency of the operation of any organization. However, in many large diversified commercial companies this measure of financial performance is the *most* important concern of the shareholders in the company. For most non-profit organizations this is not true, particularly where there are no 'shareholders' in the normal sense. The organization has been established to achieve specific goals and objectives, in accordance with its mission statement, and its success should be judged against these strategic targets rather than just in terms of its achievement of a financial surplus, or profit.

Effectiveness not just efficiency

This requires the measurement of the effectiveness of the organization not just its financial efficiency. Establishing criteria to measure the effectiveness of management is important for all businesses but, for a commercially oriented company, a continuous record of increasing profits would be taken by many shareholders as a clear indication of effective, as well as efficient, management. A similar record for a regional health authority might not indicate an effective performance if waiting lists for operations were growing or other standards in patient care were declining. Thus for non-profit organizations, the financial performance must be considered completely in the context of the overall objectives of the organization; this can therefore be viewed as one of the best areas for the implementation of strategic management accounting.

Many of these overall objectives will not be expressed in financial terms and therefore non-financial measures of performance are very important. However, as for other businesses, there is an important role for management accounting in linking these strategic objectives into appropriate controls over the financial decisions made by the organization. Financial decisions on capital investment must be made by the regional health authority and these evaluations must reflect the main non-financial objectives of the organization. This must be done by careful integration of the non-financial goals and the financial evaluation and control techniques involved. If a key objective of the health authority is to reduce waiting times for operations, the financial evaluations of alternative projects must be conducted in terms of their impacts on this key objective. Thus, the most obvious financial technique is to identify the key limiting factor which constrains the hospitals at present, and to concentrate expenditure on removing it. This will then introduce a new critical constraint, and resources will then be directed to resolving this problem; this analysis is basically the same as for a production line in any manufacturing plant, once the key strategic objective has been identified. For example, the health authority may be considering several potential projects ranging from increasing the number of operating theatres and hospital beds, through hiring more professional medical staff, to changing the post-operational care programme conducted in the hospital. The relative cost-effectiveness of these programmes must be assessed against these key objectives of reducing patient waiting times and this could be expressed in terms of cost per thousand days of saved time.

The challenge for the role of management accounting in the non-profit organizations is to break down all the main strategic objectives into financially controllable elements. If this is not done, the organization may implement a sub-optimal strategy based much more on the personal desires of the senior managers. In a commercially focused business, the need for generating profit and the direct agency link to the shareholders normally operate as a reasonable constraint on the actions of managers. However, where there is no overt financial measure of the performance and where the link to the 'owners' of the organization is often much more vague, there is a risk that the personal strategy of the managers takes precedence over the original goals and objectives of the organization. If these goals and objectives can be made specific and measurable, the risk is significantly reduced. If these measurements can be linked into the financial evaluation, monitoring and reporting systems of the organization, the risk is not only reduced but almost removed. Unfortunately, there are still far too many instances of individuals abusing their positions of power for their own ends in non-profit organizations (particularly charities), including straightforward fraud and theft, which can be blamed on the lack of adequate financial controls.

One of the major results of this excessive managerial power can be an undue emphasis on increasing the size of the organization, irrespective of the impact of this growth on the effectiveness of achieving its objectives.

Revenue generating controls and efficiency of cost controls

Most professional managers prefer to control a larger organization and consequently, given a free hand, growth strategies are often implemented. For commercially driven businesses, the market place acts as a limiting factor on such growth because it may not be possible to generate additional sales revenues without reducing the overall profitability of the business. However for many non-profit organizations this economic sanction is not so obviously available. It may also appear that increasing the scale of the enterprise is 'a good idea' as the overall goals and objectives can be more comprehensively achieved.

A good example of this problem is any large charity where an increasing flow of donations may appear to enable more beneficial charitable projects to be undertaken. However an underlying, often implicit, objective of any charity is to do good in a cost-effective manner and this is often not achieved without sensible financial controls. Fund raising on a national or international scale is a massively complex and expensive process, irrespective of the fact that many people will freely give up their time to collect money, sell flags, etc. The charity should establish financial objectives for fund raising not only in terms of the total required funds but also in terms of the relative cost effectiveness of the different possible methods which can be employed. There is an increasing trend towards using external professional fund raisers, who receive a proportion of the total funds which they raise. When this cost is added to the internal costs incurred by the charity, a very high proportion of the gross donations are being spent on raising the money. Indeed there are occasions when the *net* funds generated for the charitable projects are *negative*, even though the apparent scale of activity of the charity has increased significantly.

Charities are also good examples of the need for financial controls on the various costs incurred by the non-profit organization. Administration costs are a necessary evil for charities as they are incurred to enable the worthwhile charitable projects to be undertaken. Consequently they should be regularly monitored to ensure that they are kept to a minimum. This may mean establishing a minimum scale of project which can be cost-effectively managed by a particular charity, due to its organizational structure. Financial controls can indicate the relative differences in the cost-effectiveness of alternative ways of running projects, such as using in-house management teams, locally based managers, bought-in professionals, etc. Once again these financial controls must be integrated into the real strategic objectives of the charitable projects. For example, if the charity is undertaking irrigation projects in less-developed countries, it should be evaluating the least cost method of irrigating each hectare of land, and these comparative costs should include all the relevant attributable costs of the alternative methods. In the context of a charity, neither fund raising costs nor administration costs are actually doing good; they are simply enabling the charity to do good and hence their cost-effectiveness must be monitored. So must the cost-effectiveness of the particular method adopted for each actual project, as this monitoring process can prove to be a valuable learning process for the evaluation of future projects.

Re-investment of surpluses or 'profits'

This logic of using management accounting techniques to evaluate and monitor effectiveness as well as efficiency should be applied to all non-profit organizations. However, there is another common feature which is really a major factor in differentiating these organizations from more profit focused businesses. Most non-profit organizations do not have traditional shareholders or owners who expect a direct financial return on their investment. Hence, these organizations are normally able to re-invest any remaining funds into their businesses. This re-investment can include any surpluses generated by previous projects and this can help the organization to grow over time. A good aspect of such a no dividend payout financial strategy is that the organization can make longer term investment decisions without unnecessarily being constrained by producing short-term returns to shareholders. Unfortunately, this is not true for the wide range of UK government controlled organizations which receive a large proportion of their funding in the form of annual cash allocations. Due to the absurdity of still using annual cash budgeting systems, next year's budget allocation depends on having fully spent the current year's budget. This goes against the logic of taking a longer term view, which may possibly entail building up funds for a larger project in the future.

However a more general and more significant result of the re-investment ability is that the non-profit organization tends to implement a growth strategy, whether this is appropriate or not. This is particularly true for many organizations as it fits with the desired strategy of the senior managers involved. Very few mission statements seem to envisage that the organization can be wound up once it has achieved its aims or these have become obsolete. The organization simply seems to move its attentions on to other, sometimes vaguely, related areas and invests its residual resources in these new areas. Over time, this can lead the non-profit organization to become involved in a very diverse set of activities on a global basis. In other words, it has become a non-profit conglomerate, which often suffers from all the associated problems discussed in Chapter 11, or a global company, as described in Chapter 12. Unfortunately, the sophistication of the management accounting system within many of these complex non-profit organizations leaves a lot to be desired, in terms of its contribution to both efficiency and effectiveness.

Part Four

Changing Strategies as Businesses Develop

14

Common problems of control

Introduction

In Chapter 3, the concept that all products follow a product life cycle was considered. The inevitability of these changes from stage to stage over any product's economic life and their consequences for the appropriate competitive strategies, which should be employed at each stage, were briefly discussed. This part of the book considers in more detail the implications for the strategic management accounting systems of companies of these changing competitive and corporate strategies, as businesses develop through their life cycles. Thus Chapters 15–18 inclusive deal with the individual stages of the product life cycle and the specific issues relating to financial decision-making and financial control, which are summarized in Figure 14.1. In this chapter the broader issues are considered as well as developing the discussion raised in Chapters 6 and 7 concerning the applicability and relevance of the product life cycle to brands and customer needs.

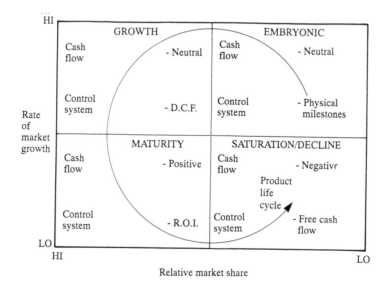

Figure 14.1 Product life cycle and financial control parameters

'Products have life cycles, brands do not'

This well-known marketing adage is based on the principle of the separability of brands from their underlying products. It is true that, with proper marketing support, a brand may flourish for many years and may outlast many generations of underlying products. Nevertheless, any brand has limitations and eventually the financial justification for continued support for the brand may become untenable. The brand should then be allowed to mature and decline as is the case for any product; thus it is argued that brands do follow life cycles, albeit sometimes very long ones. This can be further complicated by the use of umbrella brands, sub-brands and the combining of the corporate name with the brand name.

These different branding strategies can alter the way in which marketing expenditure is targeted and should correspondingly be financially evaluated in different ways as well. In many industries where the individual product life cycles are becoming ever shorter (such as the individual model life of motor cars), the ability to carry over to new models the sizeable marketing investment in the brand is clearly important. However, over a longer period this brand image will itself become outdated and the company then has to decide whether to attempt to reposition the existing brand or to launch a new brand image which will eventually replace it.

In some cases, the basic product may change many times over its life but the branding and the underlying customer value proposition may be maintained. Indeed, the original branding may even be used to encompass other newer, but related products. For example, Colman's English Mustard has undergone many changes to its ingredients, packaging and presentation over its life of more than 100 years but the same basic brand image and value propostion have been retained. Even the brand's original main limitation of a strong association with red meat consumption, which is now declining, has been attacked by using the overall brand image to support a range of new products, targeted at different market segments. In this case, the company had to balance the savings from not having to develop a separate brand image for the new products from scratch, against the potential negative associations of identifying the new products under an older brand image. As the new products were speciality mustards designed for use with foods other than red meats and were aimed at younger, more affluent customer groupings (eg one new product was an organic mustard) who were not users of traditional mustard products, there was an obvious danger of these new customers not wanting to buy a product with, in their eyes, an old, outdated image. Thus the company combined these two aspects by using the very strong consumer association of 'Colmans' and 'mustard', but effectively tried to reposition the brand through a completely changed marketing presentation for the newer products.

Obviously there is always some form of economic trade-off, which must be financially evaluated, when a decision is to be taken regarding the continued use of an existing brand on a new or replacement product. When considering this type of financial evaluation, it is important that the overall marketing expenditure has been analysed between development and maintenance activities, as discussed in Chapter 4. Maintenance expenditure on marketing is designed to maintain a marketing asset, such as a brand, at its existing value, while development expenditure should increase the asset value. This increased value can be achieved by developing either the overall market size, or by increasing the market share obtained by the particular product. This development type of marketing activity often has a long-term time-frame and so should be appropriately financially evaluated using the DCF technique.

If it is to be argued that a brand asset does not decline eventually it follows that, while its development marketing support may be withdrawn, it will always receive an adequate level of maintenance marketing support to ensure no decrease in the asset value. Intuitively this does not seem a reasonable proposition, given that this maintenance marketing activity must itself be financially justified and must include, over time, a series of transfers of the brand from product to product.

Brand investment strategy

However, it is possible to demonstrate the illogicality of this premise by applying a similar analytical model to brands as has already been used for products. Figure 14.2 shows a matrix with market share on the vertical axis and the relative level of brand investment in cash terms on the horizontal axis. As with the launch of a new product, a new brand requires substantial initial investment which, combined with the low, early sales revenues, means that the overall cash flows for the brand will be negative; as shown in the bottom, right-hand box.

The financial justification for this initial marketing investment in launching the new brand should be carried out over its expected useful life using the DCF techniques, as is explained later in the chapter. However, the discount rate used in this financial evaluation should reflect the relatively high business risk associated with launching new brands, due to their high proportionate failure rate. If the launch is successful, the brand will increase its market share and so move up the vertical axis. The resulting higher sales revenues will generate higher cash inflows, but during this growth phase the brand still requires a high level of investment through both development and maintenance marketing support. The net effect of these cash flows should be a much more balanced position for the brand, as is indicated in the top, right hand box of Figure 14.2. Although the brand should, by now, have developed a strong relative market position it has not yet started to repay the funds invested in its development during its initial cash negative phase.

However, eventually the law of diminishing returns sets in and makes further attempts to improve the relative market share of the brand uneconomic. This marks the end of the growth phase of the brand and the major marketing thrust for the brand should change from development to maintenance. It is clearly important that the business identifies this point as

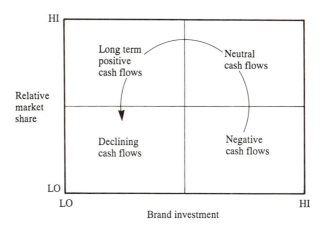

Figure 14.2 Market share/brand investment matrix

accurately as possible as it requires a fundamental change in the marketing strategy for the brand. The consequent reduction in the level of expenditure on development marketing activity is not matched by an equal increase in the required level of maintenance marketing activity, as this activity has of necessity been building up as the strength of the brand accumulated. Therefore, the brand now becomes cash positive, but the business still needs to take a long-term view of the financial returns from the brand if the substantial investment is not to be rapidly destroyed.

All brands are developed on the assumption of becoming cumulatively cash positive over some finite period, as it is ludicrous to start investing in some kind of intangible marketing 'black hole', which is to be allowed to absorb large quantities of cash to infinity. The major problems with brand management seem to be created by the differing views of functional managers over what this finite period should be. Many marketing managers appear unwilling ever to admit that the transition points from development to maintenance have been reached for their particular brands. Equally, some short-term focused financial managers seem to want to generate large immediate profits from brands with strong market positions. If these brands are harvested too quickly, the strength of the brand may rapidly be lost through a sharp decline in market share. Short-term cash flows may be generated, as shown in the bottom left-hand box, but these will be inadequate to justify the initial investment in the brand. It is critical therefore that adequate levels of marketing support are provided, particularly during this transitional phase, as it can seem very attractive, in the short term, to reduce discretionary levels of marketing activity for a brand which has strong awareness and loyalty attributes. This problem is exacerbated because, in many cases where such marketing cuts are made, there is no immediate impact on sales revenues. Consequently, the profitability and cash generation of the brand are improved in the short term, but its long-term positioning may be disastrously impaired.

A more sensible longer term marketing strategy is gradually to reduce the total level of marketing expenditure on the brand to a stable maintenance level where the brand does not decay, but equally does not increase its market share either. Logically this requires that brand management decisions are treated as an integral part of the long-term strategic management process of the business and that they be financially evaluated accordingly. Thus brand investment and dis-investment decisions should be driven by the future cash generation capability of the brand and this will, to a large extent, be dictated by the position of the brand in its life cycle.

Relevance of types of brand

If a brand image is strong enough, the customers' perception of the brand (and consequently their loyalty to the brand) may be unaltered even though the product may have changed dramatically in terms of design, packaging, technology, etc. Such a strong brand image can enable a company to stand aloof from the fierce price competition which often takes place during the shake-out period of the life cycle, before supply and demand are once again balanced as the product enters maturity. These strengths can be particularly beneficial in the case of large value, infrequently purchased items such as cars and consumer durables.

However, this very strong customer identification can itself prove a limitation to the future development of the brand. IBM developed a very strong brand image in its commercial computer business. This created a high degree of customer loyalty but these loyal customers were not directly relevant to its move into selling personal computers to individuals and neither was its strong commercial computer brand image. These individual customers had built up loyalties to suppliers of other complex electronic products, such as Amstrad, and these companies were able to take very high initial market shares in this new area even though they were unknown as computer manufacturers. IBM had to develop a new marketing programme to reposition its brand strengths more appropriately to this market and its particular customer needs.

Thus another limitation on the life cycle of brands is the changing nature of customer needs, which are supported by the particular brand. It is important that the business understands whether the critical limiting factors for any brand are the customer needs or the product attributes which are developed by the branding process. This can easily be determined by distinguishing functional brands from representational brands, as was discussed in Chapter 7. A functional brand is one where the branding says something about the physical attributes and performance of the product and enhances the expectation on the part of the customer. The value of the brand is normally represented by excess value added (ie premium pricing) over the cost of the brand's packaging and marketing compared to an unbranded version of the same product. Such a set of brand attributes can, as previously illustrated in Chapter 7, be transferred to other products where similar factors are important and will be identified by the same or similar customers.

A representational brand says more about the self-image of the customer than about the particular functionality of the products, and hence representational brands are more common in consumer products. This type of branding can be transferred to a wider range of less closely associated products, provided that the consumer image of the new branded product is likely to be similar. The company has to be very careful not to damage the customer association with the brand, by adding in new products which weaken this overall brand strength of representing specific consumer attributes.

Relationship to key strategic thrust of business

The management of brands as part of the overall strategy of the business is clearly very important, but this must be seen in the context of the key strategic thrust, as discussed in Part Two. Each transfer of, or addition to, a strong brand to a new product must be regarded as a risk, in that the existing brand value may be damaged if the transfer is unsuccessful. Also, the alternative marketing strategies of either developing a new brand to support this product or of selling the new product in an unbranded form should be financially evaluated.

The transfer is most likely to be successful when there is both a common link between the main competitive advantage of the business and the key characteristic of the brand, and when the timing of the transfer is appropriate. Thus, if the business is concentrating on developing the strength of its existing products by seeking new markets for these products, strong existing functional brands can be used to launch these products into these new markets. The brand attributes have to be appropriate for the stage of development of the new market which is, by definition, likely to be at an earlier stage of the life cycle. This can mean that the company should adopt a strategy of waiting for the new markets to start to develop before launching its product, rather than trying to create new markets when its mature, more sophisticated, product focused brand strengths may be irrelevant.

Alternatively, the key strategic thrust could be to build on existing customer loyalties by increasing the range of products offered to these customers. If so, appropriate existing representational brands could be used to accelerate the acceptance by existing customers of these new products. This type of branding can also be used to develop certain consumer products in new markets where the critical objective is to differentiate the brand by selling the concept of an attractively different way of life. This approach has been used in the global marketing strategy of Coca-Cola and Marlboro' cigarettes, where the same branding is done in all markets irrespective of its direct relevance to the customer's local way of life.

The common thread running through these branding strategies is that they all represent significant long-term financial investments. As such, proper financial justifications must be carried out and regular monitoring of actual and projected future performance is also essential.

Financial control mechanisms over the product life cycle

Any long-term investment is likely to produce a variable stream of future cash flows over the life of the asset. The financial evaluation of such investments requires the estimation of these future cash flows and the valid comparison of them against the cost of the required investment. This valid comparison can only be made by making all the cash flows directly equivalent. This requires converting all the future cash flows to their equivalent present values by using an appropriate exchange rate (this is the discount rate or negative interest rate). This discounted cash flow (DCF) technique is therefore converting cash flows of different time-based currencies into money of a single time period, where relative values can be directly compared. There is a valid comparison to the conversion of different foreign currency values (eg US dollars, Yen, Deutsche Marks, Francs, etc) into a single currency so that they can be directly compared. In the foreign currency case it does not matter which currency is chosen, but any company would normally convert back into its home-based currency, because its management have an immediate sense of relative values in this currency. Similarly for DCF analysis, the future cash flows can all be converted into equivalent values in any particular year but it is most logical to bring them back to their present values today, because managers can again compare relative values more easily in today's money terms.

This process hinges upon the selection and use of an appropriate discount rate, which is applied to all these projected future cash flows. As well as reflecting the time-value of money, the discount rate should also include the risk associated with these future estimates of cash flows. This can be assessed by considering their projected volatility over the life of the project. (A zero risk cash return must be absolutely certain both as to its timing and amount; thus it has zero volatility.) The use of DCF analysis is now very widespread as the main method of financially evaluating long-term investment projects, prior to making the investment. It should be clear that this technique can be validly applied whether the investment is in tangible fixed assets, such as plant and machinery, or in intangible assets such as brands. However, many companies do not yet apply the same rigorous financial evaluations to large marketing-based investments.

Even more importantly, although the DCF technique is a good way of carrying out initial project financial justifications, it is not necessarily a good way of either controlling these projects once they are started, nor of comparing the performance of different projects within a large diversified business. The overall business can, as discussed in Part Three, be regarded as a portfolio collection of projects (brands and products sold in specified markets) or SBUs, which are likely to be at different stages of development. Thus a company with a diversified product range is likely to have some products in the embryonic phase, with consequent negative cash flows, and some mature strongly cash generating products. In order to exercise proper financial control, each product should be considered in the context of its position in its product life cycle. It may be appropriate to compare directly the performance of two products which are both at the same stage of development, but it will almost certainly be disastrous to do the same direct performance comparison between a new developing product and an established mature product.

Consequently, it is very dangerous to apply *any* single criterion as the basis for assessing financial performance, even though it is valid to use DCF analysis as the initial evaluation process of *all* long-term investment projects. It is particularly dangerous to try to use a short-term financial performance measure if the financial performance is expected to be relatively volatile over time. Thus, the very popular ROI performance measure should only be used during the stable period of a product's life cycle; this is normally the mature stage of development. Unfortunately, research surveys still indicate that most companies use some form of Return on Investment criteria for assessing divisional financial performance irrespective of the relative stage of development of the business. The issues surrounding the appropriate use of ROI as a financial control measure are, not surprisingly in this book, considered in Chapter 17 in the context of mature businesses. The more appropriate methods of financial control for each individual stage of the product life cycle are discussed in detail in the following chapters. However, even where the most appropriate method of control is employed, there is still an underlying danger of managers 'managing the performance ratios' rather than managing the business. This means that business managers, eg divisional managers, can place a disproportionately high emphasis on making sure that the measurement (whatever it is), by which they are judged, is right even if this is detrimental to the overall or long-term performance of the business. This should not be regarded as surprising, as it is simply human nature to try to succeed; it is the fault of the central managers of the group if this measure of managerial success is inappropriate.

No single financial measurement can ever be adequate to control properly a complex business or operating division. It is vital therefore that the financial controls discussed in the succeeding chapters are applied intelligently. They should also be used alongside other managerial and economic indicators, which reflect other aspects of the desired performance of the managers and the particular business unit.

15

Launch strategies

Overview

In the embryonic stage of the life cycle, the company obviously has to invest in the technological development of the product, but it should also spend funds on marketing to see whether the product is likely to be successful in the marketplace when, and if, it is eventually developed. Marketing expenditure also plays a crucial role in identifying appropriate new target markets and new product opportunities which can be exploited by using the existing and potential competitive advantages of the company. Thus, market research is needed to establish not only that the proposed product will be successful but also that the likely key customer 'buying issues' can be exploited by this company. Otherwise there is a serious risk of creating a new market demand which is subsequently satisfied by a competitive product.

For many new products, a key competitive success factor is the time-scale before similar products can be launched by competitors. This element needs to be included as part of the initial financial evaluation process, if relevant, and this can often be affected by the overall development and launch time required by the particular business, when compared to its competitors. Indeed, a frequently voiced competitive disadvantage of many British companies is that they are very good at developing new, innovative product ideas but very bad at translating these ideas into marketable products before their overseas competitors, despite their initial advantage in having developed the concept.

Clearly, the use of any form of ROI as the financial control measure at this stage of development would be completely disastrous as the business should be investing in the product and the market rather than trying to make an accounting profit. It is even more important that the business does not try to manage the financial performance ratio by reducing the level of investment at this stage, as was mentioned in Chapter 14. The initial decision to invest in the development of the new product should be evaluated using the sophisticated DCF technique for the perfectly valid reasons also discussed in Chapter 14. However, this embryonic stage is normally characterized by a very dynamic and rapidly changing internal and external business environment. Thus the estimated cash flows which are used as the basis for the initial financial evaluation will not prove sufficiently accurate to serve as a base against which to try to measure and control the subsequent financial performance.

It is strongly believed that there is no soundly based financial control system which can be used at this early stage of a product's development. In particular, the common use of expense, or cost, centres as a means of controlling research and development type activities is falsely based. The business objective for the research and development department is not to spend up to a pre-set budget or allocated expenditure level, but to assist the business to achieve its overall objectives by developing and bringing to launch the desired new products. These objectives are normally much more clearly expressed by reference to specific, measurable milestones which may not themselves be measurable financially. As already stated however, the original project evaluation would have included the projected ultimate financial benefits of a successful outcome to the development programme.

Consequently, it is argued that this embryonic stage can most sensibly be controlled by reference to the achievement of previously identified milestones, and by regular reference back to the original project evaluation as the project develops so as to ensure that the projected benefits are still potentially attainable. Given the key issue for many such businesses of the relative timing of launching new products, an external financial comparison which normally is worthwhile is to compare relative expenditure levels on research and development with relevant competitors. This information can be obtained using the techniques discussed in Chapter 5.

It is also important that this critically important expenditure on research and development is regarded internally as an investment in the long-term future success of the business, irrespective of the accounting treatment of such expenditure. If this is done, it is much less likely that the frequent short-term expedient of cutting research and development expenditure in periods of profit pressure will be taken by senior managers.

Introduction

The financial information implications for a business of planning and implementing a strategy of launching new products have to take account of both the genuinely new business venture, ie a green field start-up, and an established organization, which decides to launch a completely new venture. Clearly there are many common issues, but examples of both types are considered in this chapter so that the differences can also be clearly seen. In the case of the completely new start-up, there should be very little problem of matching the corporate goals and objectives to the original vision and/or mission statement, but there may be very little historical evidence on which to base any financial forecasts. The established business may have already developed some quite sophisticated financial data collection and processing systems, which can give a better view of the prospects for the new venture. However the relevance of the new project to the overall corporate goals may be more tenuous; it is also often important for such an established group to define very clearly the product/market boundaries for the new business idea, if demarcation problems in the future are to be avoided.

This launch stage of the life cycle is almost always a period of significant net investment (ie negative cash flow) for the business. Expenditure is needed on research and development and market research and, if this is successful, more expenditure is needed on fixed assets, working capital and launch marketing. All of this has to be spent before any significant cash inflows are generated; indeed, if the eventual launch proves to be unsuccessful, no such cash inflows may be received. There is consequently a relatively high level of business risk associated with almost all such new product launches, as is shown in Figure 15.1. This risk must be taken into account in the initial financial evaluation, which is done to justify this up-front investment. DCF techniques should normally be used for such new product developments, as the eventual returns are often projected well into the future and the relative impact of the time value of money can be reflected in the computation. Also the discount rate can be adjusted to reflect the perceived risk associated with the project. This point highlights an interesting issue in the

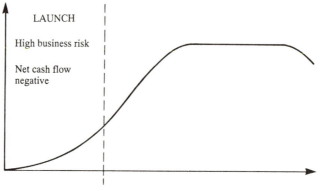

Figure 15.1

accounting systems of many companies. The degree of rigour in the financial evaluation and approval process is often proportional to the scale of the investment involved, ie large value projects are subjected to a much more intensive financial analysis. This is not necessarily the optimal use of the company's limited analytical resources, as some of these very large projects may have very predictable outcomes; such as in the case of an efficiency improvement project, using existing technology, for a well-established stable volume product. Contrastingly, the strategic importance of some much smaller value projects may be much greater. Launch projects can often fit into this classification. The relative value of the project also depends on the time-scale for including expenditure in a single project. Launch projects for major new products may involve several phases of expenditure over a number of years; some businesses consequently split this total expenditure into a series of projects, each of which may be relatively small by corporate standards. This technique may completely invalidate the financial evaluation process, as the eventual returns from high product sales can only be achieved if all the expenditures included in the series of projects are incurred. The financial evaluation must be done in total, over the expected life of the product and with the overall risk of the project taken into account.

However this overall financial evaluation is often based on some very tenuous and vague estimates of future sales and net cash flows, particularly if the new product is highly innovative. This is true for both the major examples which will be considered in this chapter.

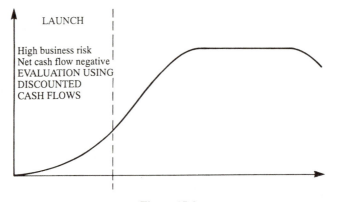

Figure 15.2

The completely new business was set up to develop and market computer based training (CBT) products, where the computer system responds interactively to the specific answers input by the student. At the time of starting this company, the CBT markets for sophisticated, truly interactive products hardly existed. Therefore the future sales revenue stream was likely to be, to say the least, volatile, since the potential sales volumes at different selling prices were highly speculative. So were the forecast costs of developing each particular courseware product, as such developments had never been done before. The profit margins on any eventual sales were almost certain to be very high; the actual 'product' consisting only of a 'floppy' disk and an instruction manual. The new company also intended to provide consultancy services, which could generate a more predictable source of sales revenue. Despite these uncertainties, the new company developed a business plan, which was sufficiently credible that it enabled the business to raise substantial funds from venture capitalists, in order to start trading.

The established business was a very large multinational food company which was evaluating the prospect of developing and launching an artificial meat product, made out of soya protein using technology which had been developed from the nylon spinning process. Here again the development costs were uncertain although the overall potential market could be estimated. However, since this potential market was viewed as the global market for all meat products, this did not really help; particularly as the company had no idea as to what presentation format any eventual product might take. Thus future sales revenues and profit margins were highly speculative, but the financial return, from taking even a minute share of this vast potential market, was sufficiently great that the group decided to go ahead with the project.

Information needs

Having carried out the initial financial evaluation and come to a positive conclusion, the business needs to consider how the project should be financially controlled. Both the detailed examples, and many similar new product developments, will be carried out in a very dynamic business environment with a vast number of unknowns.

The business is likely to need to respond to significant changes in this environment, caused both by internal and external issues, as the project unfolds. Consequently the accounting systems needed to cope with such an environment have to be flexible, informal and capable of rapid responses to these changes. This can only be achieved if there is a lack of bureaucracy and formality, both in the organization structure and in the method of financial reporting. This need for flexibility and informality may not be a problem in a completely new company, but can often cause problems in an existing large business, such as our multinational food company, which has well-established management accounting systems in the more mature divisions. These businesses need to develop new forms of financial reporting and control to cope with the higher business risk associated with these new product development projects. The more volatile external environment, caused by the lack of knowledge of these new areas of activity, is also likely to generate more one-off questions, which require answering rapidly.

One of the first objectives should therefore be to collect information which reduces the high risks associated with this lack of knowledge. Part of this will obviously be achieved by the research and development activity, but the business should also consider spending funds on market research to try to refine the initial estimates of the potential market size. Marketing expenditure can also be used in a more general way to try to identify new product opportunities, which utilize the existing competitive advantages of the company. This was, in

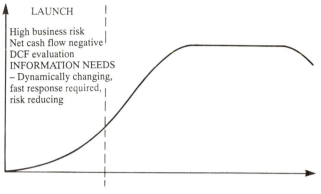

Figure 15.3

fact, how the idea for the artificial meat project was generated. The group already had successful brands in the processed meat market and had a good track record for innovative product development. These factors, when allied with its international branding and distribution capabilities, indicated the type of new product programmes which could be of interest.

It is always important to ensure that there is a good match between the new product opportunities and the internal capabilities of the company. If not, there is a good chance that the market, if subsequently created, will be taken away by a more compatibly placed competitor. Market research should endeavour to establish, not only that there is likely to be demand for the proposed new product, but also that the likely key customer 'buying decision issues' can be successfully and sustainably exploited by this company. In many cases this marketing expenditure may need to be carried out before any significant funds are 'invested' in research and development, as the results of the marketing activity may reverse the initial decision to go ahead. (The research and development expenditure has deliberately been described as an investment and this is how it should be treated for internal decision-making, irrespective of the externally presented accounting treatment.)

This aspect of reviewing the initial decision at stages through the project is of critical importance. The overall initial financial evaluation is always, of necessity, based on a whole series of estimates and assumptions. If any vitally important assumptions subsequently prove

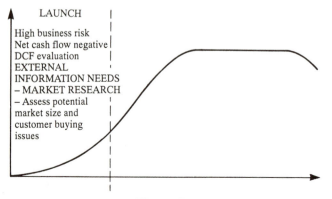

Figure 15.4

to be incorrect, there may be no point in continuing with the project; this is true no matter how much money has already been spent, as these funds should be regarded as a sunk cost. Therefore it is also very logical to try to validate these critical assumptions as early as possible, in order to avoid wasting expenditure on other areas involved in the project. In the artificial meat project, this was done by carrying out extensive market research on the most attractive type of final product, even before the initial basic product and process research had been successfully completed.

It is quite normal for much of this initial essential information to be externally focused, and this should be one of the strengths of using a strategic management accounting system in this area.

Critical success factors

As well as reducing the risks associated with any initial assumptions, the information collection process should identify the critical success factors for the particular product. These may relate to the achievement of a maximum selling price and this would indicate that emphasis must be placed on controlling the cost structure of the final product. Alternatively, the market research may indicate the need for a strong branding image to ensure the success of the product launch. The cost justification for such a marketing led launch strategy must be financially evaluated and the overall project evaluation should be updated as required. Thus the initial project evaluation is revisited and refined as more specific information is collected; at each such stage, the initial decision to go ahead is checked. In other words, the initial decision should not be regarded as committing the business to spend all the funds identified in the overall project. Rather it is a decision to commit the funds needed to get the business to the next logical review point, and then the whole project's financial viability is reviewed again. The implications of this are discussed in the next section.

For many new products, a key competitive success factor is the time-scale before similar products can be launched by competitors, and whether the business can erect adequate entry barriers in this period. An assessment of this factor is obviously essential to the initial project financial evaluation, and this assessment should be updated as more information is collected. In many cases there is the added risk that competitors may actually launch a similar product before the initial company's product is ready. Here the critical success factor is clearly the time taken to get a new idea to market. The car industry is a good example of this critical success

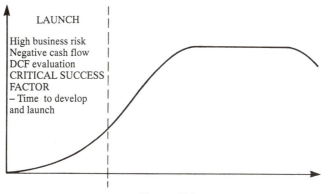

Figure 15.5

factor in action. When a car manufacturer decides to develop and launch a new model, the design is based on the latest market research available. However, if there is a three or five-year time lag between developing the design and producing the first actual new car off the production line, there is a significant risk that the requirements of the market may have changed in the substantial intervening period. Further, if a competitor can develop its new models much more quickly, it can base its designs on more up-to-date market information. As increased development time normally leads to increased total costs, these competitors may also use their competitive advantage to change their models more frequently; thus increasing the pressure on the already stretched research and development resources of the other car companies. This strategy has been used very effectively by the Japanese car manufacturers.

It was also a serious risk for our CBT company, as other companies were known to be investing heavily in this area. There are a number of ways of trying to reduce the time taken to develop and launch a new product, and these should be financially evaluated if this is a critical success factor. One obvious alternative is to avoid the delay caused by the research and development process by buying in the product from someone else. This is most commonly an option when the product is already available in another market, and the originating company seems to have no plans to go international. Acquiring product rights in this way can be done in different ways as the product can be bought outright or a licence to sell the product can be arranged. Licences can be agreed on a fixed fee basis, as a percentage of sales revenue generated, or as a mixture of the two.

If the market is very new and highly innovative, the total risk can be reduced by negotiating a licence fee which is mainly based on the sales revenue generated in the licenced market. This was the approach taken by the CBT company, which acquired the European licence for a USA-developed computer authoring system, designed specifically for CBT applications. The licence allowed the company to buy copies of the authoring system at very large discounts for onward sale to customers or for inclusion in its own training programme packages, with a licence fee also being payable on the end sales revenue value. Unfortunately, the deal included a commitment to buy a minimum number of authoring systems in the first three years, with the risk of losing the licence if this target was not met. This had the effect of making some of the variable cost into a deferred payment *fixed* cost with a consequent increase in the overall risk associated with the deal.

Another way of acquiring product technology is by buying it outright from the company which developed it. Some companies specialize in developing product ideas, process improvements, etc and can be regarded as research and development factories. They do not intend to develop the product themselves, but prefer to sell out once a successful prototype, or similar, has been proven. They then go on to develop the next idea. Other companies find that they have created a new potential product but do not have the skills or inclination to take the product to market. Perhaps it is suitable for a market where they have no expertise, or the rest of the production process requires manufacturing skills which they do not possess. This sort of opportunity became available to the artificial meat company, when its own research and development effort was well developed. A large company had developed a similar, although as it transpired inferior, process technology but had started from the basis of being a large nylon producer. Hence this company had no expertise in the food industry, although they had tried to go into manufacturing and sales on a limited basis. As part of their strategic decision to refocus on their core businesses, several of these peripheral businesses were put up for sale. Our artificial meat company decided to buy the business, primarily to avoid a better placed potential competitor from getting access to the technology. This could have significantly shortened such a competitor's time-scale in launching a rival product.

Such acquisitions of new products are relatively rare and most companies develop them internally, albeit over very prolonged time-scales. Indeed a frequently voiced criticism of British companies is that they are very good at developing new innovative processes and product ideas, but are far too slow at turning them into successful products available in the marketplace. Consequently other companies, which are far more focused on the product development phase are able to steal these markets by being quicker in launching the final product. The traditional way to segment research and development is to break it into three segments, which are respectively pure research, applied research and product development. Pure research is the blue skies stuff principally carried out by universities. When done by companies it requires a great act of faith, on the part of senior management, that there is a large potential future market for the type of products which may eventually be developed. A good example would be where a pharmaceutical company decides to put resources into investigating in depth how the brain functions, in the hope that this research may lead to product breakthroughs for any one of a wide range of illnesses. Such pure research activities are almost always very long term, and many companies now prefer to fund university based researchers to do such projects, with the company having the rights to any commercially worthwhile outputs.

Applied research is the process of trying to turn the outputs of pure research projects into such commercially viable products, and is often the first type of research undertaken by company research and development departments. This classification could be applied to the artificial meat company, while the CBT business really started life at the product development stage. This represents the stage of research and development where a fairly clearly defined product has been established, but it does not yet perform to its desired specification. Thus, product development normally occurs after the target market has been agreed and the main product attributes are also in place. Under this segmentation, British companies and universities are regarded as being good at pure and applied research, but as having a competitive disadvantage in terms of product development. This may be, at least partially, caused by the lack of emphasis on time as a critical success factor in the research and development process.

It also may be exacerbated by the absence of external focus in these companies' accounting systems and the application of incorrect financial control measures for their research and development activities.

Financial control measures

Throughout the book, the idea of linking financial control measures into the business strategy and, particularly, the critical success factors of that strategy has been emphasized. This is especially true of new product development, because the application, in this area, of the traditional, very common methods of financial control, such as Return on Investment, can be totally disastrous. Encouraging managers to emphasize short-term profits from such a strategically critical long-term investment project is obviously inappropriate. The use of ROI can also lead to managers trying to improve the performance ratio by minimizing their investment in such new products; this is also normally counter-productive.

Also, although the initial investment decision should have been evaluated using a full DCF analysis over the estimated economic life of the project, DCF is not recommended as a suitable means of financially controlling the project. The future cash flows are extremely volatile and will change dramatically as the project unfolds; consequently such a sophisticated technique should not be used as a regular control measure. However it has already been argued that the DCF analysis should be updated, whenever improved financial information is received on any of the key assumptions or forecasts. This up-dated financial evaluation should be used to review the original decision to invest, but this is not the same as applying it as a financial control measure.

There are two main practical reasons for not using DCF to control new product development projects. The first has already been mentioned earlier in the book, and is caused by the wide range of potential future cash flow levels from this type of project. In order to carry out a financial evaluation it is perfectly acceptable to use the expected value of these wide-ranging cash flows. Thus probabilities are assigned to the possible levels, and the weighted average expected value is calculated. Unfortunately this expected value may never be achieved in practice and hence is useless as a control measure. Suppose the new product could generate either £10 million p.a. in net cash flows if very successful, or £2 million p.a. if only just surviving in the market. If these events are each given a 50% probability of occurring, the expected value is £6 million p.a., and this can be used to justify the decision to invest in the project. However, as a financial control measure, either actual event will lead to an expected variance of £4 million p.a., which is not a good method of exercising meaningful financial control.

The second reason is that the financial investment decision is not necessarily helped by the use of the technique. The initial investment proposal is justified by reference to the positive net present value generated by the future cash inflows over the forecast investment required. Unlike many other investment projects, in research and development based projects the required level of investment is often very difficult to forecast. Thus for financial evaluation purposes, the best estimate is obviously used. However, when the first tranche of this investment has been spent, even if it has not worked as planned, the potential future benefits are still likely to be available with the same net present value. Consequently, the business can financially justify spending the same amount of money again, in order to try to achieve these benefits. This exercise in investing over and over again to receive the same financial benefits has been a problem for many businesses, which have confused the role of DCF analysis in this area.

DCF analysis provides the basis for the economic evaluation of the overall investment decision, but there need to be more specific financial control measures used on the specific areas of the project as expenditure actually occurs. Many companies try to achieve this by controlling the research and development department as a cost or expense centre, as discussed in Chapter 14. Unfortunately this creates more problems than it solves, because companies do not want their research and development departments simply to spend up to, or just below, their budgets. The research and development department's role is to develop, in accordance with the strategic plan, the required flow of new products which can be launched into the market. These products should be developed in a cost effective manner but, in many cases, the timing of the launch may be more critical than the total cost of development. In other words, it may be financially worthwhile to increase the expenditure if it accelerates the speed of development, thus enabling the business to create a sustainable competitive advantage by launching its product before the competition. If the department is treated as a cost centre, its managers may have an incentive to reduce overall costs, possibly by deferring particular activities rather than accelerating developments.

Another major problem of trying to use purely financial means of control, during this launch stage, is that the financial impact of delays in product launches are only reflected when the planned levels of sales *don't* occur. By then it is normally too late for the company to respond

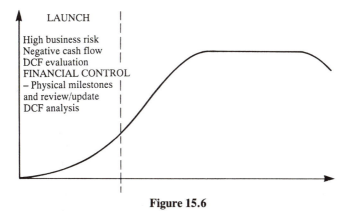

Figure 15.6

effectively to the problem, as a competitor may have taken a significant lead in the market. It can be argued that there is no really viable method of financially controlling this area because of the high volatility in both the potential returns and the expenditure levels.

However, the projects and the individual areas of activity can be controlled by using physical milestones. A physical milestone represents a key decision point in the project, such as proving the technical feasibility of a particularly important process, which has to be achieved before the project can move on to the next stage of development. These depend on the project being broken down into definable segments, each with their own measurable objectives. This enables the total forecast expenditure to be similarly analysed so that the required resources can be identified. The actual level of costs to achieve the milestone can be monitored against the budgeted level, as this is a very useful learning process for up-dating the overall expected project costs, and for estimating the costs involved in future similar projects. If the milestone cannot be achieved, the project may need to be abandoned unless an alternative way of solving the particular problem can be found. This highlights that normal project management techniques can be applied to this area very successfully, particularly where time is identified as a critical success factor for the project. Critical path analysis (CPA) and project evaluation and review technique (PERT) are well-established ways of identifying what items are the limiting factors in terms of the total time, which the project is estimated to take. The company may be able to reduce this total time by applying more resources to, and accelerating the expenditure on, elements of the project which lie on this critical path. These techniques can also indicate the areas of the project where expenditure should not be committed, until certain key earlier milestones have been achieved.

The commitment of expenditure therefore becomes a logically phased process, which can significantly reduce the risk level associated with the total funds forecast for the project. This is because large parts of the total budget may not need to be committed until some of the earlier high risk parts have been successfully achieved. However, this sequential process must not be allowed to delay the overall product development unnecessarily, as this could destroy the economic justification. As the milestones are achieved, the project is reviewed and the financial evaluation is updated to ensure that it is still justifiable to continue. Thus the review of projects is driven by events affecting genuine decision points rather than, as is done in many companies, where projects are reviewed on a time (say, every three or six months) or expenditure (say, when the expenditure reaches £100,000) basis.

Financial control should lead to action where necessary, and useful action can only really be taken at these key milestones. Obviously a draft timetable and budget should be agreed for achieving this milestone, and a brief progress review may be necessary during this period to ensure that the budget and time allowance are still realistic. If they are not, the project may need reviewing in detail to see if major changes are needed.

For some very long-term, complex research and development projects it may not be practical, at first, to break the complete project down into detailed segments. The important financial control issue is that funds are not allocated and committed to these, as yet, unspecified later stages of the project. Only when the first stages have been successfully achieved, will it become possible to describe in detail the objectives, required resources and expenditure forecasts for these stages. Consequently, only then should financial commitments be authorized.

These mixed physical and financial controls should, if used together with the review of up-dated financial evaluations, enable good, relevant control over research and development based projects to be exercised. Relevant means helping this area to achieve its objectives within the overall business' objectives. However, there is another piece of external financial information which may be helpful if time is considered a critical success factor. The time needed to develop new products is a relative measure as a two-year time cycle may seem quite fast, but is relatively very slow if a competitor can do it in one year. This relative speed may be a function of many things including organization structure, the emphasis of senior management on this area and its consequent level of profile, but an important factor is likely to be the relative level of expenditure on research and development. This information can be obtained using all the techniques discussed in Chapter 5, and disseminating the comparative information internally should highlight the relative strength or weakness of the company's position.

It should also remove the common temptation to reduce expenditure on research and development, when short-term profits are under pressure. If competitors are maintaining their expenditure, the long-term competitive positioning of the business can be weakened by such short-term profit motivated action. Research and development must be regarded as an important long-term investment in the future of the business, irrespective of the financial accounting practices used. If this is not done, the company may not launch the new concepts, which will develop into the growth products of the future.

16

Accounting for growth businesses

Overview

It was stated in the previous chapter that, before and during the launch of a new product, detailed financial control measures were not relevant. However, once the product is successfully launched and the market begins to grow, financial measures become more appropriate. The cash flow model on which the product was initially justified can now be up-dated, and the new cash flow forecasts used should have a greater level of reliability due to their lower degrees of volatility.

Marketing activity is the key success factor during this growth phase of development. Marketing expenditure should be directed both at making the market in total grow as rapidly as possible and at increasing the market share held by the particular product. There is a great deal of research which supports the strategy of expanding market share during the rapid growth phase of the product life cycle. Competitors may still experience quite rapid rates of growth in both sales revenue and sales volumes, even though they are losing relative market share. Indeed they may be capacity constrained from growing fast enough to maintain their market share, so that there is no logic in a severe competitive response. If a similarly aggressive growth in market share strategy is implemented during the maturity phase of the life cycle, the competitive response is frequently very rapid and equally aggressive, often resulting in a very expensive price-cutting war.

In this growth stage, a common competitive strategy is that of product differentiation through either branding or emphasis on particular product attributes. This differentiation strategy normally requires a high level of marketing support during its development stage and this can lead to still higher levels of total marketing expenditure. It is vitally important that this marketing expenditure is financially evaluated as a long-term investment by the business (in the same way as research and development activity should be regarded as long term during the embryonic phase of the life cycle). Any undue emphasis at this stage on short-term financial performance by using ROI based financial performance measures can easily damage the long-term success of the business, by causing lower than optimum investments in marketing activities. The financial return for this marketing investment is achieved during the maturity phase of the product life cycle. It comes from the higher profits created due to the larger overall market, and the combination of greater market share and higher margin levels made possible by the strong marketing platform created during the growth phase.

Thus the financial justification for these increased marketing expenditures should be carried out using DCF analysis of the projected future benefits, as was done for the embryonic phase.

However, as the forecasting accuracy levels should now have improved considerably, it is possible to use a combination of physical and financial measures as methods of establishing ongoing financial control of the business. The key physical measures during this growth stage are the overall growth rate of the market, and the change in relative market share for the particular product and its main competitors.

The overall growth rate of the market needs to be monitored to assess the relative impact of the different types of marketing expenditure designed to stimulate this overall growth. It can also be used to look for any early signs of maturity in the market, so that the competitive strategy can be appropriately altered before additional marketing expenditure on further growth is wasted. The changes in relative market share must also be regularly monitored so that the relative effectiveness of alternative forms of marketing expenditure designed to increase share can be assessed. Given this emphasis on marketing expenditure, it is not surprising that monitoring the relative levels of marketing expenditure by competitors is a key piece of competitive accounting information which is required during this growth stage of the product life cycle.

In addition to these physical measures, it is now practical to use the regularly up-dated cash flow models (ie including both actual and revised forecast levels of cash flows) as both an evaluation technique and a tool of financial control. The use of the long-term focused DCF technique helps to avoid any managerial tendency to concentrate on the short-term financial results of the product to the detriment of its longer term financial performance. However it is vitally important that the marketing investments to stimulate both market growth and increased market share are financially monitored as it is always possible to try to increase either or both by spending more money on marketing. At some point, the law of diminishing returns sets in and the extra expenditure cannot be financially justified, even against the long-term benefits. Regular monitoring should enable the changing relationship between expenditures and the consequent impact to be modelled so that the point of optimum expenditure can be estimated, albeit approximately.

Introduction

If the launch of a new product is successful, the business hopes for, and should plan for, a rapid transition to the growth phase of the life cycle. Some of the initial business risks will have been removed before this stage of development, because the technical feasibility of the product will have been proven and its acceptance by the market will have been indicated by the initial rate of sales. However the business risk is still relatively high, as is shown in Figure 16.1. This is because the initial investment in the launch will have been financially evaluated using the high level of sales, and corresponding cash flows, expected to be achieved during the maturity phase of the product life cycle.

This indicates the key strategic issues for the growth stage, which are to optimize the growth of the market and the product's share of that market. A large share of a very large market should produce very strong positive cash flows when the product matures, and this will generate a very healthy financial return for the business. However, this period of high positive return is still in the future and, therefore, profits should not be the primary focus of the strategy during the growth phase. During this time of rapid growth in sales volumes, marketing should be regarded as an investment, in the same way as research and development expenditure was considered an investment during the launch period. Although the increasing levels of sales will start to generate increasing cash inflows, the business should be re-investing

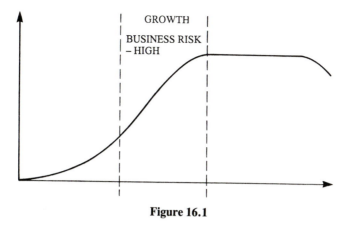

Figure 16.1

those funds in making both the market and the product's sales grow, while the opportunity to do so exists. Thus the net cash flow may still be slightly negative or broadly neutral at this stage, as is shown in Figure 16.2. If the company tries to make a rapidly growing product become cash positive, the market share of the product will normally decline as competitors invest more heavily in developing their own products.

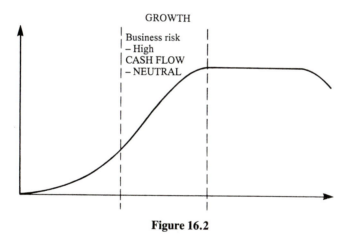

Figure 16.2

The objective of this concentration on marketing is, as has been stressed throughout the book, to create a sustainable competitive advantage. This can be achieved in a number of different ways, as discussed in detail in Part Two, and the marketing expenditure should be appropriately focused. One of the most common strategies employed during periods of rapid growth is to create significant barriers to entry for potential competitors. This can enhance the financial returns to the business substantially but, once again, the particular entry barrier must be appropriately selected and the relevant strategy effectively implemented. Development of some form of product differentiation can be attempted at this stage by either branding or emphasizing particular attributes of the product. If branding is the preferred route, a well-established company may have the choice of either developing a new brand to support this growth product or of using an existing brand. The existing brand may be transferred from another product, where the brand attributes are no longer as appropriate, or the new product may be marketed using an umbrella branding strategy which is still applied to the existing products. All of these alternatives need to be financially evaluated if the best strategic decisions are to be taken, and this indicates the main needs for information during the growth stage.

Information needs

Marketing is the key to success in the rapid growth phase of development. There is much evidence to indicate that it is financially most attractive to gain market share while a product's overall rate of sale is increasing. Competitors may not even notice that they are losing share, because their own sales volumes may still be increasing quite rapidly. Even if they do, they may be unable to respond as their capacity is already fully utilized. However the rapid growth by the market may also act to attract in a number of late entrants, who may increase the capacity of the industry beyond the mature, stable level of demand. This could drive down selling prices significantly in an ensuing price war, fought to try to regain volume shares of the market. The marketing strategy should therefore be designed to dissuade such late entrants, by creating effective entry barriers.

Marketing expenditure should be split into distinct categories at this time. One element is designed to help the overall market to grow to its full potential, by ensuring that all the possible customers are aware of the attributes of the particular product. This benefits all the players in the market and, consequently, this type of expenditure is normally undertaken by the leading companies in the industry (and only when they are confident that their position is sufficiently strong that they will receive the majority of the benefit). A major aspect of marketing activity by all companies during this stage is aimed at increasing the share of this growing market held by the company's range of products. This developmental expenditure must be treated as an investment, because it is creating a marketing asset. The financial return from this asset should be received from increased cash inflows when the product matures. Hence the financial evaluation should be done by using DCF analysis. This technique should also be used for comparing the alternative marketing strategies, discussed earlier in the chapter, which can be used to achieve this increased share.

One of the most important aspects of this analysis is to predict when the law of diminishing returns sets in. As marketing expenditure is increased, market share should also grow, and the financial justification can be calculated. Unfortunately, this type of relationship is not linear. Once a critical mass of expenditure has been reached (for example, in terms of the product's share of voice in the market), the increase in market share may be quite rapid. However, beyond a certain level of market share, the company will find it increasingly difficult to gain still more. Not only is it more difficult, but this makes it significantly more expensive. It also becomes more difficult *and* expensive to hold on to this increased share. This is normally caused by competitive reaction in the market; not least because, above a certain rate of share growth, the competition is actually experiencing a decline in their sales volumes, despite the continued growth in total demand. If the product had matured and the company then tried to increase its market share, it would normally face very rapid and severe competitive responses, which often invalidate the original decision to go for share growth. Similarly during the growth phase, there is a point where the return from incremental marketing expenditure declines and it is no longer financially justifiable.

The financial analysis system should try to predict this point but, more importantly, the financial control system should be designed to monitor the actual returns from incremental

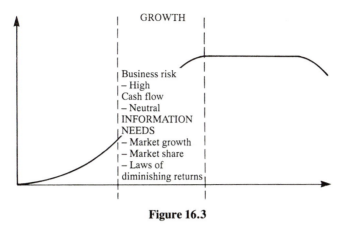

Figure 16.3

development marketing expenditure. This enables the company to avoid wasting a great deal of money on uneconomic marketing expenditure. A good strategic management accounting system can also provide very valuable information for future marketing strategies for the next generation of high growth products; another example of the system acting as a learning process.

As the demand for the product increases, expenditure is required for other purposes than marketing development. In the marketing area, an increasing amount is needed to maintain the share of the market which has already been achieved; if this is not done, the original financial investment has been wasted. Major investments are normally also required in fixed assets, as the capacity of the company must keep pace with the growth in demand. This increased level of output leads to increased investments in working capital to finance the inventories and outstanding receivable balances needed. These funding demands may present a major constraint on a rapidly growing business and the accounting system should highlight any such potential problem well in advance. (A very common cause of business collapse is a lack of available funding during a period of rapid growth.) This can be done by developing a financial model which shows the maximum rate of sustainable growth for the business, given its existing and future financing capabilities. If this model shows that the company cannot fund the expected investments needed to maintain, or increase the company's market share, during this growth phase, an alternative strategy should be considered. It may be very undesirable to allow market share to decline during this period, as the company may be at a significant competitive disadvantage when the market matures. Consequently, the company may decide to bring in extra funds by either looking for a partner or, if it is part of a group with a portfolio of products, the group may decide to alter the strategy of another product in the portfolio, so as to increase its cash generation. Alternatively, the company may decide that it is better to sell off the product and its associated technology to someone who has the required resources to develop the product and the market to its full potential.

The assessment of the marketing expenditure needed to increase market share and then to maintain the new level cannot be taken in isolation. As usual, the strategic management accounting system requires information from outside the business. For the growth stage, with its emphasis on marketing, the most important external information is obviously related to the rate of growth of the market and the marketing activities of competitors. Before finally deciding on the most appropriate strategy for increasing market share and creating effective barriers to entry, the business needs information on the marketing strategies and relative

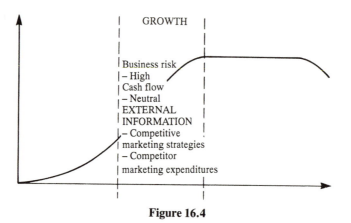

Figure 16.4

product positioning of competitors. The detailed information required will need to be tailored to the particular alternative strategies which are being considered, but there are some general points which will always be of interest.

Information on competitors' relative levels of marketing expenditure, and the nature of that expenditure, is of great interest during this period. Also the level of utilization of their existing capacity is important as it will indicate the type of competitive response which can be expected, if the company tries to increase its market share. As well as understanding the existing capacity utilization, the company should be aware of any committed or planned expansions to this capacity which will affect such competitive responses. The need for an external focus in a good strategic management accounting system is shown yet again for high growth products.

Critical success factors

The relative comparison of marketing expenditures is of great importance at this stage of development but, as in the previous chapter's discussion on research and development comparisons, the company needs to identify more specific critical success factors, which can be used in the financial control process. A key success factor for the long-term financial return from any product is the attainment of a strong relative market share before the product matures. Thus, monitoring the changes in relative market share should be part of the control process during the growth phase. However, the marketing strategy would normally have established this increased market share as the end objective of its very specific plans. These plans might aim to increase customer awareness, stimulate trial, raise rates of usage by existing customers, or lift levels of effective distribution for the product, as ways of achieving such increased market share. The management accounting system should focus on the most important of these marketing objectives and then integrate the specific objectives into the financial reporting process. This should enable the effectiveness of the relevant expenditure (eg advertising expenditure designed to increase customer awareness) to be monitored more directly. It also assists in relating these detailed objectives to the overall marketing objectives, so that alternative ways of attacking the overall strategy can be financially compared. As well as helping the current product, a major advantage of such a system is in the learning process which can be used to improve the financial evaluation of future growth products.

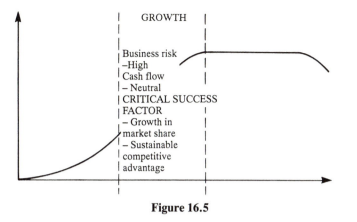

Figure 16.5

A critical element in any strategy for a growth product is positioning the product properly at the end of the growth period. The whole purpose of the investments in research and development, launch costs and the subsequent development marketing, as well as the more tangible assets, is to enable the business to earn a more than acceptable rate of return over the economic life of the product. This return is primarily generated during the mature phase of the life cycle but, as repeated deliberately throughout the book, added value is only created from a sustainable competitive advantage. Such competitive advantages can take many different forms (branding, lower costs of production, control of a channel of distribution, technology breakthroughs), but they should normally be developed before the growth stage ends. Consequently, the strategic management accounting system should be carefully monitoring the development of the sustainable competitive advantage, both internally and externally by reference to actual and potential competitive responses.

Financial control measures

These critical success factors involve spending money now, in order to increase the financial return in the future. Consequently, any short-term focused ROI based financial control measure would be totally inappropriate. This is particularly true if the normal financial accounting measures are applied, under which all expenditure on marketing is written off in the period in which it is incurred. Such a convention means that short-term profitability can be improved by cutting back on development marketing during the rapid growth phase. The business must guard against such strategically unsound actions by using a more appropriate long-term control measure.

The investment decisions will be based on the financial evaluations made using DCF techniques, because of the long-term nature of the resulting increased cash flow benefits. In the previous chapter, it was argued that using DCF analysis as a control measure was not appropriate due to the high volatility of all the cash flows. Once the product is successfully launched and the market has started to grow significantly, the cash flows should be capable of being forecast with some more relevant degree of accuracy. Inevitably they will be wrong, as all forecasts always will be, but the errors should now be explainable and an updated revised forecast can be used to control the following period. The objective of using the latest DCF analysis as the main financial control measure is to ensure that managers take account of the

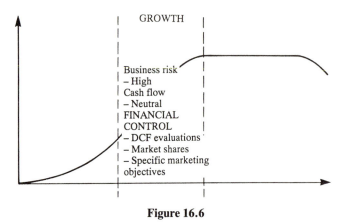

Figure 16.6

long-term financial impact of their actions. It also gets over the problem caused by the different accounting treatments of tangible and intangible assets, as the balance sheet presentation is subordinated to the more relevant cash flow impact. This is particularly important when major expenditures may be made in the form of relatively long-term investments in intangible, but very important, marketing assets.

However this stage of development cannot be adequately controlled using a single financial measure such as Discounted Cash Flow analysis. Therefore relevant non-financial measures must also be used to ensure that the key success factors are being properly achieved. During the rapid growth phase, the critical success factors are measures of relative market share and rate of overall market growth. These factors can be monitored regularly and compared back to the planned levels; any significant differences must be explained by analysing the changes in the more detailed underlying factors. This can obviously be done most easily and comprehensively, given the number of underlying factors and their degree of interaction, if a suitable modelling system has been developed. Any such model should include major competitors since their unexpected actions are the most common explanation of deviations from the strategic plan. As with any predictive model of such a dynamic situation, the model will not be right but the regular monitoring and analytical process should allow it to be updated and modified, so that future decisions can be based on better supporting financial information.

A major objective of any strategic management accounting information system is to highlight, as early as possible, the need for a change in strategy. At this stage of development, this means identifying when the law of diminishing returns sets in, in terms of increasing market share by extra marketing expenditure. This early warning signal should help to optimize marketing investment in market share, but such signals can also be of great value in terms of changing the overall competitive strategy of the business. If the accounting system monitors the rate of growth of the market, it can identify when the market growth starts to slow down. This may enable the company to predict when the maturity stage of the product will start. It can consequently change from a growth strategy to the more appropriate strategy for the more stable, mature phase of the life cycle.

Illustrative example

Before moving on, in the next chapter, to consider the management accounting issues involved in this maturity stage, it may be helpful to consider a numerical example which draws together

Capacity invested in – 50,000 units per year.

Investment required – Plant £500,000.

(It is assumed that this product is neutral in terms of working capital investment.)

Plant life is estimated to be 10 years with *nil* residual value. (All companies use straight line depreciation.)

		Per unit £		Per year (£000's)
Selling price		10		500
Variable cost		4.50		225
Contribution		5.50		275
Fixed costs – exc. depn.	1.5		75	
– depreciation	1	2.50	50	125
Profit		3		150
Investment at cost				£500

Year 1 Accounting return on investment = 30% (using cost of fixed assets)

DISCOUNTED CASH FLOW ANALYSIS (@ 20%)

YEAR	CASH FLOW	DISCT. FACTOR	PRESENT VALUE
0	(£500k)	1	(£500k)
1–10	£200k	4.192	£838.4k
		NPV	+£338.4k

(Note:– The DCF analysis uses the cash flow generated each year, ignoring any time lags, as being profits plus depreciation. Nil residual value for the plant at the end of 10 years has been assumed.)

Figure 16.7 Company A's initial cost structure and project evaluation

many of the issues covered in both this and previous chapters, regarding financial decisions during the growth phase.

This example has deliberately been set in a fictitious environment, as it makes it possible to keep the numbers relatively simple, while still illustrating the key issues. The logic can be applied to many industries and the simplifying assumptions do not destroy the underlying soundness of the financial analysis. Thus taxation and inflation are ignored throughout the example.

Company A, a diversified large business, develops a new product idea and decides to invest in plant and equipment to produce the product. In order, in its terms, to minimize the associated risk it only invests in capacity for 50,000 units p.a. initially (taking the view that it could subsequently invest in additional capacity if demand for the product takes off). Its cost structure is set out in Figure 16.7 and its effective cost of capital is 20%. In order to create added value for the shareholders the company consequently needs to achieve a return of over 20%, which the project apparently does (as shown in Figure 16.7).

This project has a high net present value due to the strong financial return forecast to be achieved over its ten-year life, and hence the stock market value of Company A should increase when the project is announced. At least, this should happen if the stock market believes that Company A will be able to sustain this high level of return over the ten-year period. However, in this example, Company A has not developed any sustainable competitive advantage as the process technology is generally available and their product is not strongly branded. Once the high level of 'super profit' becomes known, other companies are likely to

	Per unit £		Per year £000's
Selling price	9		450
Variable cost	4		200
Contribution	5		250
Fixed costs – exc. depn.	2.00	100	
– depreciation	1.00 3	50	150
PROFIT	2.00		100
Investment at cost –			£500

Capacity invested in – also <u>50,000</u> units per year (Year of Entry – Year 2)

Investment required <u>£500,000</u>.

First Year Accounting ROI = <u>20%</u>

DISCOUNTED CASH FLOW ANALYSIS (@ 20%)

Year	Cash flow	Disct. factor	Present value
0	(£500k)	1	(£500k)
1–10	£150k	4.192	£628.8k
			NPV +£128.8k

(Note: This positive net present value is based on the important assumption that the selling price remains at £9 per unit throughout the 10 years; or that it only reduces in line with efficiency improvements.)

Figure 16.8 Company B's cost structure

be attracted to this market, particularly as demand is forecast to grow rapidly. Indeed the marketing director of this division of Company A is soon hired by some outside investors to start a direct competitor. The new company, Company B, is started, one year later, specifically to produce this product, and A's ex-marketing director decides to replicate exactly the plant laid down by Company A. As a new small focused company, B is able to keep its manufacturing costs down below those of A, but its fixed cost base is slightly higher than A's as it is completely stand-alone; its cost structure is set out in Figure 16.8. The increased volume, now totalling 100,000 units, drives the unit selling price down to £9 so as to increase demand sufficiently, and Company A has no real choice but to reduce its price to this new market level.

Even with the reduced selling price, Company B's financial evaluation predicts a positive net present value on its investment over the ten-year life of the project. Consequently, if its investors also demand a 20% return, they will be pleased with this higher forecast overall return. This is despite the accounting ROI (which includes the depreciation expense) being reduced to 20% in the first year. One of the problems associated with accounting ROI measures, when they use net book value of assets in the denominator, is that the return automatically appears to increase over time, as the fixed assets are reduced due to the impact of accumulated depreciation. Both these return calculations, for A and B, assume that the cash flow generation can be maintained at the same rate over the economic life of the assets. In a growth market, this is not a logical assumption as market prices tend to reduce as the market expands. However, in many industries, the reduction in selling prices is more than offset by an even faster reduction in variable costs within the industry. If the rate of increase in capacity

		Per unit			Revised
		Original		Revised	per year
Selling price		10		9	450
Variable cost		4.50		4*	200
Contribution		5.50		5	250
Fixed costs – exc. depn.	1.5		1.5		75
– depreciation	1	2.50	1	2.5	50	125
Profit		3.00		2.5	125

*The variable cost per unit has reduced due to the experience curve effect, eg learning curve benefits gained during the first year of production.

Figure 16.9 Company A's revised cost structure (after the entry of B, ie Year 2 of production)

levels is dynamically increased by the entry of new competitors, this relative rate of reduction may be reversed, with selling prices reducing faster than costs come down as a consequence of the effect of the experience curve. This has happened in the illustrated industry because, although Company A's variable costs have been reduced due to efficiency gains, the reduction in selling prices has adversely affected the returns achieved, as is shown in Figure 16.9.

As can be seen in Figure 16.9, A's variable cost base has reduced to the same level as B's due to the learning curve advantage of being first into the industry. Thus, due to their lower fixed cost base, Company A still has a better net profit margin than B at this stage. However, the initial assumption made by A at the time of the initial investment is no longer valid and the financial evaluation should be up-dated. There are two main purposes in doing this. First, the company should consider whether any supplementary decisions need to be taken in the light of the new information. In this case, Company A cannot undo what has been done in terms of the original investment, but it may consider if an exit decision is now appropriate. The reducing cost base and the relatively small decline in selling prices do not make this sensible, as it is still showing quite a good return. Indeed, even if this drop in selling prices had been forecast originally, the project would still have been marginally financially attractive as is shown in Figure 16.10.

However, the changed competitive environment may make the Company want to review its future strategy and such decisions should always be based on the latest available financial information. More specifically, the entry of one new competitor may make Company A concerned about the possibility of further new entrants, particularly given the rapid increase in product demand for a small decrease in selling prices (volume demand having doubled for a 10% decrease in unit selling prices).

The second reason for updating the analysis is related in that the financial review highlights the sensitivity of such projects to subsequent changes in selling prices and profit margins,

Year	Cash flow	Discount factor	Present value
0	(£500k)	1	(£500k)
1	£150k	0.833	£125k
2–10	£125k	3.359	£420k
			NPV +£45k

Figure 16.10 Updated project evaluation for Company A's investment (@ 20%)

Capacity invested in – <u>200,000</u> units per year

(Year of entry – Year 3)

Investment required – <u>£1,000,000</u>

	Per unit £		Per year £000's
Selling price	7		1400
Variable cost	<u>3.2</u>		<u>640</u>
Contribution	3.8		760
Fixed costs – exc. depn.	0.8	160	
– depreciation	<u>0.5</u>	<u>100</u>	
	1.3		260
Profit	<u>£2.5</u>		<u>£500</u>

Investment at cost – £1,000,000

First year accounting ROI = <u>50%</u>

DISCOUNTED CASH FLOW ANALYSIS (@ 20%)

YEAR	CASH FLOW	DISCT. FACTOR	PRESENT VALUE
0	(£1,000k)	1	(£1,000k)
1–10	£600k	4.192	£2.515k
			NPV +<u>£1,515k</u>

Note: This DCF computation also ignores the prospect of reducing variable costs and selling prices over the life of the project.

Figure 16.11 Company C's cost structure

particularly due to unexpected entrants to the industry. In future projects, the Company may try to develop entry barriers more quickly. The company should also use the updated analysis to review its future launch pricing strategies, when experience curve benefits may be available. A lower, more aggressive penetration pricing policy at the time of launch may have discouraged Company B from entering the industry so rapidly.

However, in this example, neither A nor B reviewed their competitive strategies quickly enough, as Company C entered the industry at the beginning of Year 3. This new entrant focused on the rapid growth in demand caused by small price reductions and, consequently, went for a strategy of economies of scale giving it a lower cost base. This cost base is shown in Figure 16.11. It indicates that the combination of lower costs per unit and lower relative capital costs (quadrupling the output only doubled the required investment) produced a very high predicted financial return on the investment over ten years, despite having to reduce the unit selling price to £7.

This more substantial decline in selling prices affects Company A, and it once again reviews its strategic options by up-dating its cost base, as shown in Figure 16.12. Clearly the financial return is now unattractive and, if this position had been forecast before making the initial investment, the original decision should have been reversed. However, Company A cannot go back in time, and must now make the best decision for the future. If it is considering exiting from the industry by closing down its plant, the original cost of the investment is irrelevant and the Company should use the net realizable value of the plant instead. In this example this is only its scrap value, which is £50,000, and the Company should include the opportunity cost on this scrap value in its computation of its exit price. A has already decided to try to further

	Per unit		Per year £000's
Selling prices	7		350
Variable cost	4		200
Contribution	3		150
Fixed costs			
– exc. depn.	1.5	75	
– depreciation	1.0	2.5	50	125
Profit		0.5		25

Figure 16.12 Company A's revised cost structure (after C's entry)

reduce its costs by combining this product's fixed costs with some other existing products so as to achieve economies of scale. It also takes into account the further reductions in variable costs which will be achieved by efficiency improvements over the next year.

These restated costs are shown in Figure 16.13 in terms of the exit decision financial evaluation, which shows that A is no longer happy, but is better off staying in the industry than leaving. However, worse is to come as Company D enters the picture at the beginning of Year 4, with a new patented method of making the product, thus creating a potentially sustainable competitive advantage. This technology reduces variable costs and capital costs through large

	Per unit £	Per year 000's
Selling price	7	350
Variable cost	3.6 *(1)	180
Contribution	3.4	170
Fixed costs	1.2 *(2)	60
Net Contribution	2.2	110

Exit evaluation

Present value of opportunity cost of salvage value = £50,000

Benefit of future cash flow by staying in industry
  Years 1–7 £110,000 p.a. × 3.605 = £396,000
                        (Annuity factor)

Decision is clearly to stay in the industry

*(1) The variable cost will reduce due to the experience curve effect.

*(2) Fixed costs are included at their avoidable level only, some costs are now shared with other products.

Figure 16.13 Company A's exit decision computation

economies of scale; hence D decided to go for high volume with an initial investment in 250,000 units of annual capacity. Its cost structure is shown in Figure 16.14, which also shows that the selling price is now driven down to £5 per unit. This reduction has dramatic impacts on all the existing companies in the industry, none of whom could have justified their initial investment if this prospect had been foreseen.

Capacity invested in – 250,000 units per year

(Year of entry – Year 4)
Investment required – £750,000

		Per unit £		Per year £000's
Selling price		5.00		1,250
Variable cost		3.00		750
contribution		2.00		500
Fixed costs exc. depn.	0.70		175	
– depreciation	0.30	1.00	75	250
Profit		1.00		250

Investment at cost – £750,000

First year accounting ROI = 33.3%

Discounted cash flow analysis (@ 20%)

Year	Cash flow	Disct. factor	Present value
0	(£750k)	1	(£750k)
1–10	£325k	4.192	£1,362.4k
			NPV +£612.4k

Figure 16.14 Company D's cost structure (new patented technology)

Companies A and B should now rework their exit options using the latest selling price data and these computations are shown in Figure 16.15. Company B should leave the industry because of its higher fixed cost base, which is dedicated to its only product and is hence fully avoidable if the business closes down. This would be the best financial decision even if the plant had no residual value at all; however, in some industries, there is a net cost associated with closing down and where this is true it may still be financially justifiable staying in an industry even though the cash flow is negative.

Company A now faces something of a dilemma because, if B leaves the industry, it may just make sense for A to stay in. This is despite the fact that, by now, Company A is wishing it had never heard of this particular product. Company A decides to stay in for another year to see what happens; Company B leaves and the selling price rises to £5.50, thus temporarily vindicating A's decision to stay in.

However at the beginning of Year 5, Company E enters the industry with another large scale investment. This time, it is using a new cheaper version of the original technology. Also, as an overseas based company, it has a lower production cost base than even the patented technology of Company D. Company E is prepared to take a longer term view than the locally based companies and believes that its plant will last for 15 years (as opposed to the previous estimates of 10 years). It only requires a 15% return on its capital, as it has access to cheaper sources of long-term funds; the resultant cost structure is shown in Figure 16.16. As is shown, the increased volume drives the selling price down to £4 per unit. At this price, Company A must follow Company B in leaving the industry as its net cash flow generation is now negative as well. A's departure does not affect the selling price as it had already been predicted by Company E in deciding on the scale of its investment.

	A			B	
	Per unit	Per year		Per unit	Per year
Selling price	5	250		5	250
Variable cost	3.6	180		3.2	160
Contribution	1.4	70		1.8	90
Fixed costs	1.2	60		2.0	100
Net contribution	0.2	10		(0.2)	(10)

DISCOUNTED CASH FLOW @ 20%

Scrap value – Present value now £40,000.
Benefit of future cash flows Years 1–6 £10,000 × Annuity
factor of 3.326 = £33,260

On this cash flow analysis, A is also better off leaving the
industry,
HOWEVER:

  (1) Its variable cost will continue to decline.

  (2) If B leaves the industry, the capacity will be reduced
  and the selling price will rise – thus giving A an incentive
  to stay in.

B is clearly better off
leaving as it is
generating a negative
cash flow at a £5 selling
price.

Figure 16.15 Companies A and B – exit options after D's entry

Capacity invested in 250,000 units (Year of entry – Year 5)

Investment required – £750,000

(Life of assets assumed to be 15 years)

		Per unit £		Per year £000's
Selling price		4.00		1,000
Variable cost		2.50		625
contribution		1.50		375
Fixed costs – exc. depn.	0.8		200	
– depreciation	0.2	1.00	50	250
Profit		0.50		125

Investment at cost – £750k
First year accounting ROI – 16.67%

DISCOUNTED CASH FLOW ANALYSIS (@ 15% – lower cost of capital)

YEAR	CASH FLOW	DISCOUNT FACTOR	PRESENT VALUE
0	(£750k)	1	(£750k)
1–15	(£175k)	5.847	£1,023.2k
			NPV +£273.2k

Figure 16.16 Company E's cost structure (cheaper version of original technology and longer term view)

COMPANY		C		D		E	TOTAL
Capacity (000s)		200		250		250	700
Per unit data (£s)							
Selling price		4		4		4	
Variable cost (inc. learning curve for C & D)		2.75		2.8		2.50	
Contribution		1.25		1.20		1.50	
Fixed costs							
– exc. depn.	0.8		0.7		0.8		
– depn.	0.5	1.30	0.3	1.00	0.2	1.00	
NET PROFIT		(0.05)		0.20		0.50	

Figure 16.17 Relative cost structures (after departure of Companies A and B)

The remaining companies have to review their strategies in view of the new competitive structure, and their relative positions are shown in Figure 16.17.

Although Company C is shown making a net loss, it should not leave the industry until its plant requires replacing. The opportunity cost decision should exclude the depreciation on the historic cost of the existing plant, and substitute the net realizable value at the Company's cost of capital. This would show a reduced but still positive return for staying in when compared to the alternative of leaving the industry as soon as E enters the industry.

Although C and D are now making reduced returns they will both stay in and, consequently, Company E has selected a strategy which should create a period of stability for the industry. Its return is above its cost of capital and so the project should create shareholder value over the estimated life. Even if the assets only last ten years, there is still a positive net present value; the break-even period is approximately 7.5 years. However, for an existing competitor to have made the investment, using their previous criteria, would not have made financial sense; at a 20% cost of capital, the net present value, over ten years, is negative.

This illustrative example should have highlighted, not only the complexity of these strategic investment decisions, but also the critical importance of including potential competitive responses in these financial evaluations. The first four companies into our industry based their financial evaluation on the status quo immediately after their entry, rather than looking at the potential response of an existing or completely new player. As discussed in the body of the chapter, a critical success factor for a growth industry is to develop and maintain an entry barrier, which enables the company to retain the added value created by its *initial* competitive advantage.

17

Strategic management accounting on reaching maturity

Overview

As the rate of market growth slows and the market can be seen to be moving into the mature stage of the life cycle, the strategic thrust of the business should shift towards realizing the financial benefits which have been invested for during the embryonic and growth stages. The product should now become highly profitable without needing to re-invest all those profits to fund further growth. Hence, the cash flow now becomes highly positive on a period-by-period basis and, hopefully, the cumulative cash flow of the product also rapidly becomes positive on a net present value basis.

Consequently, the financial control process should start to concentrate on the shorter term performance of the business, with the emphasis on improving profitability levels and cash flow generation. Normally the level of long-term investment projects decreases during this stage and the type of project also changes. In place of the growth orientated investment projects, which are now less financially attractive in view of the declining growth opportunities, the major projects tend to be concerned with improvements in the efficiency of the existing level of operations. The thrust of the competitive strategy may also change with the onset of the maturity phase as price competition frequently becomes more important. This can be caused by the difficulty in maintaining a differentiated position in a marketplace where the product and its attributes are now well understood by customers. For many products, the maturity stage is reached when all potential customers have not only been attracted into the market but have also established their ongoing levels of product usage. Thus sales volumes are dictated by the repeat purchases of a stable mass of regular, and increasingly knowledgeable, customers. This frequently reduces the basic product to the nature of a commodity and highlights a key strategic thrust for companies in true commodity product markets, which is to be a low cost supplier.

The only viable alternative competitive strategy is to try to create customer loyalty to the company's product, by emphasizing its differentiation either through product attributes (eg quality or service, etc) or through branding. This strategy therefore focuses on a more restricted segment of the market, such as customers who are prepared to pay premium prices. These higher prices are required to generate the enhanced returns needed during the maturity phase to justify the extra investment in this differentiated strategy. It is often too late to try to develop a brand or other differentiation basis when the product has reached the maturity stage, and it is much more likely that the successfully differentiated business will be realizing a financial return on an investment made at an earlier stage in the life cycle.

If the strategy is based on price competitiveness and, hence a critical success factor is being *the* low cost supplier to the selected target group of customers, the emphasis of the strategic management accounting system should be appropriately altered. Comparative product cost information on competitive products is vitally important, so that the competitive strategy can be based on a strong factual analysis, rather than incorrect assumptions regarding the areas and sizes of competitive advantage. As discussed in Chapter 4, it is important to remember that it is relative cost differences which are needed, and quite small cost differences can create significant marketing opportunities during this maturity phase. The competitor cost analysis should also highlight sustainable cost advantages rather than temporary differences, which will automatically be eroded over time. A significant distribution cost advantage which is created by the particular location of production facilities should be used in the marketing strategy of the business, as it is difficult for competitors to remove such an advantage.

The financial control measures which can now be applied to the mature business are the commonly observed ROI criteria, but these should be enhanced by monitoring levels of profit margin and operating cash flows. It should be a strategic objective of the business to maintain the product in this mature, profit and cash generating phase of its life cycle for as long as possible. Indeed from the purely financial perspective, this maturity phase is the only attractive period of a product's economic life and thus the time spent here and the total cash flow generated should be maximized.

Introduction

As mentioned in the previous chapter, a key issue for any company is deciding when a change in competitive strategy is required. This is particularly true as the rapid growth phase of the life cycle comes to an end, because this required change in strategy is one of the most important. However, there are great dangers for any business which adopts the appropriate competitive strategy for the maturity stage before the product has really matured. A resurgence of rapid growth could lead to the company losing market share, particularly if the major competitors are still implementing a growth strategy. Consequently, it is important for the business to identify whether any decline in the role of market growth is a temporary or permanent feature. This can be particularly difficult when the market demand is heavily influenced by the ups and downs of economic cycles. Short-term sales volumes of some rapidly growing products can decrease substantially during a severe recession; however, the longer term trend for the product is still for strong growth and this should be reflected in the competitive strategy.

Another important and common issue towards the end of the growth phase is the question of overcapacity in the industry. The continued high growth in demand, and the good profit margins frequently seen in growth markets often attract a number of new companies to enter the industry at a relatively late stage. If this is combined with substantial investments to increase capacity by the existing competitors, so as to maintain or try to increase their market shares in the expanding market, the total result can be to create a very significant level of overcapacity in the available supply of the product. This overcapacity can eventually be taken up by the continued growth in demand for the product but, if this increase happens as the market starts to mature, there is no further growth to absorb the spare capacity. When this happens, the industry enters a period of intense competitive activity which, in the end, reduces the total capacity. This can result from some companies being forced out of the industry due to the severity of price competition, or by a series of mergers and acquisitions which enable the fewer, larger remaining companies to rationalize their total capacities, so as to restore a reasonable balance between supply and demand. It is only when this shake-out period is completed that the stability of the maturity phase of development can start properly.

Consequently, it is important that a business is aware of the relative costs associated with entering the industry and with exiting from the industry. As indicated in the example at the end of the previous chapter, when there is a large difference between the investment needed to enter the industry and the subsequent net realizable value of that investment, it can be very difficult to force out existing competitors. The development of effective entry barriers can therefore assist in the smooth transition from growth to maturity.

Another issue when growth starts to flatten out, is to make sure that the company understands whether it is the product or its associated brand which is starting to mature. As discussed before in Chapter 14, products and brands follow different life cycles, with the brand life cycle often being much longer than any individual product. However, if the brand has already been transferred from product to product several times, it may be approaching the end of its life cycle before the currently associated product is ready to mature. This would normally be indicated by a declining market share, despite a high relative level of marketing support. If the total market is still growing, the business may need to consider changing its marketing strategy for this product, before the decline in share makes it very difficult to maintain competitiveness in the future.

Once the company is sure that the market has matured, the competitive strategy must be changed away from trying to increase market share by re-investing all the operating cash flow back into the business. The mature stage of the life cycle is the period used to justify all the previous investments in launching and developing the product. Consequently the cash flow for the product should turn strongly positive at this stage and, indeed, the cumulative cash flow should become positive during this period. If the previous competitive strategies have been successfully implemented, the business should be well-positioned to achieve this with a strong relative share of the maturing market. The business risk of the product has now reduced, as shown in Figure 17.1, because the level of stable sales volumes has now been established. The main risk now concerns the duration of this relatively stable period of high sales volumes.

From the financial perspective, this cash positive period is the most important stage of the product life cycle, and the business should try to spend the maximum period possible generating these strong positive cash flows. Since the appropriate management style is now

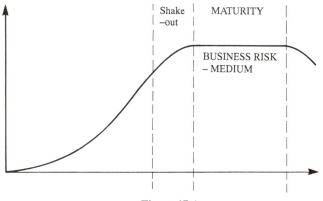

Figure 17.1

that of the controller which is the most stable and, some would say, boring of the main alternatives, many companies seem to spend as little time as possible in this mature phase of development. However, it is important that the business now focuses on producing positive cash inflows in order to justify the original investment and, if this product is part of a large group's portfolio, to provide the funding for investments in a new range of development projects.

The positive cash flows are generated by the high volume of sales at relatively good profit margins, but normally the gross profit margins are now lower than during the growth stage due to the increased level of price competition. A major difference is that now there is a lower requirement for re-investment back into the business and, consequently, much more of the operating cash flow is available for use elsewhere in the business or for distribution to the shareholders. Net profit levels are now increased because the proportionate rate of marketing support should decrease significantly. The business should no longer be trying to grow the market, as this expenditure would be wasted if the market has genuinely matured. Neither should the business try to increase its share of the market, as such a strategy is likely to be immediately met by fierce competitive responses. Increases in market shares in a mature market mean that the competitors are suffering decreased sales volumes, which severely affects their profitability without there being any long-term prospects of improvement: hence, they respond rapidly and aggressively.

Marketing expenditure is therefore now predominantly aimed at maintaining the existing market share, and the level of support required to achieve this is already being incurred at the end of the growth phase. Consequently the removal of the need for growth based expenditure represents an improvement in both profit and cash flow. Cash flows are also improved because there is no longer a need to invest in increasing capacity. Thus investments in both fixed assets and working capital are now mainly for replacement of existing assets, which represents no real drain on operating cash flows.

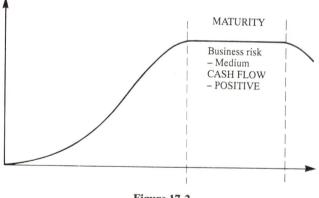

Figure 17.2

Although the emphasis is now on maintaining market share, the business may feel at a competitive disadvantage due to its lack of critical mass in some area. Rather than trying to increase its share of the market by organic growth, it may now be more economic to make an acquisition; the economic justification for the acquisition being the economies of scale which can be achieved as a result.

Information needs

This question of feeling at a competitive disadvantage highlights the key information requirements during the mature phase of the cycle. The business is now focusing on profits and cash flow generation, and therefore managers require financial information to ensure that these can be maximized. This does not mean maximizing the profits over the next accounting period, because this might be achieved at the expense of the current level of market share, or by not maintaining critical assets properly. As already stated, the business wants to stay in this cash positive stage for as long as economically justifiable. Therefore a long-term view of profit maximization needs to be taken and appropriate financial control measures need to be implemented.

Also the appropriate competitive strategy has to be implemented and this should take account of the relative competitive advantages of the company's product. Unless a clear differentiation strategy has already been established during the growth stage, it is normally difficult to develop one successfully once the product has matured. In fact, it is often impossible to maintain an existing differentiation strategy profitably at this time. Customers are becoming much more knowledgeable about the product's attributes. Thus they may be unwilling to pay the price premium needed to finance the higher level of marketing support required to sustain the product differentiation. Interestingly, many of the most successful mature product brands are highly representational in their characteristics. Obviously if a company intends to maintain a strongly branded competitive strategy, it must obtain regular market research information to check on the brand attributes which are important to customers' buying decisions. Also the relative price premiums and the associated additional marketing expenditures should be carefully financially evaluated, using market research testing to validate some of the assumptions wherever possible.

If the product has now developed into a virtual commodity, the only logical competitive strategy is to be *the* low cost supplier of the commodity. A large relative market share should enable the maximum economies of scale to be obtained, but the company's cost position must be checked out as fully as possible. Being the low cost supplier is a relative position. It is therefore vitally important that the company develops a comprehensive system for assessing and monitoring competitors' cost structures and actual cost levels. It is important to remember that these cost comparisons are relative, and that it is differences in costs which should be emphasized. Not only does this make the exercise much more practical, but it indicates which elements should be highlighted in the competitive strategy. If a company has a major cost advantage in one area against its competition, it should focus on this area in its marketing strategy.

This is a good way of determining if it is possible either to maintain an existing differentiation strategy or to move the product away from being a commodity, by retaining or creating a differentiation which emphasizes the specific competitive advantage. It is important to establish that this competitive advantage is sustainable. Basing a strategy on a temporary advantage which will automatically erode over time is financially unsound. Thus, if the company's product quality, or some associated service quality, is significantly better than the competition's, the business has to be sure that this superiority can be maintained, before building its competitive strategy around an image of better quality. Not surprisingly therefore, many of the most sustainable bases of differentiation tend to be centred on physical advantages which are more difficult, if not impossible, for competitors to match. The physical location of factories or distribution facilities close to major customers may give the company a significant advantage, if distribution or storage costs are a material cost item and consequently

consequently affect the buying decision. The company should ensure that it achieves the maximum benefit from this advantage; for example, by offering its conveniently placed customers the greatest possible flexibility and level of service in terms of distribution, which will be much more expensive for competitors to replicate.

Therefore an alternative strategy to being the low cost supplier may be to focus on one particular aspect of the total product package, such as service. If this area of concentration represents an area of significant competitive advantage, the company may not even require to charge a price premium for giving the customer such a better overall package. In some other cases, it is possible to segment the market and find a group of customers who are prepared to pay a premium to receive this higher level of service, or whatever other form of customer 'added value' which the focused strategy takes. However, as previously mentioned, it is normally very difficult to develop this type of differentiated strategy once the market has matured. Competitors will have established their own positions in the market and there are now very few new customers coming into the market. In many mature markets, the majority of sales are replacement purchases by existing customers and it can be very difficult to attract them to buy a newly positioned product, unless the 'added value' proposition is extremely attractive. Creating this highly attractive offering can be very expensive to the company involved, and its competitive strategy should now be focusing on profitability.

Also, even if these segments of the market can be identified, the company has to consider whether they are large enough to be financially viable and to keep its capacity fully occupied. The mature, slow growth phase of development is one where the cost/volume/profit relationship, discussed in Chapters 3 and 7 can be applied to great effect. During the previous phases of high growth and great volatility in sales demand, it was inevitable that levels of capacity utilization would fluctuate substantially. Once the product matures and the industry's overall supply and demand levels are more balanced, an important factor for financial success is to maintain a high level of capacity utilization. Thus the company needs information on its own cost structure, in terms of breaking costs down into fixed and variable and analysing the contribution rates generated by different products. However, it is even more important to obtain this information on competitors, because their relative cost/volume/profit relationships will determine their competitive responses to changes in the competitive environment. If a particular competitor has a very high proportion of fixed costs, it will be very keen to maintain its level of capacity utilization even if market demand drops temporarily. Therefore it may reduce its effective selling prices by implementing promotional activity during this downturn, because a lower contribution per unit on a higher volume of sales may be preferable to losing the volume.

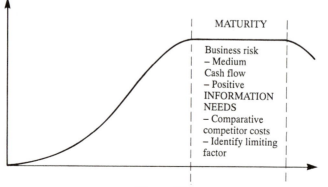

Figure 17.3

Indeed it is very common to find companies investing in more capital intensive processes during the maturity phase. This increases their fixed cost bases and consequently increases their financial risk levels. However, this may be acceptable as the business risk has been reduced due to the lower degree of volatility in sales volumes. As profitability is now a key objective, the company is looking for ways to improve its efficiency levels and thus reduce its total costs. In many cases this can be achieved by reducing labour costs through automation; these investment projects should be financially justified by the cost savings achieved rather than forecasting increased sales volumes. Thus, although the company is no longer increasing total capacity, it may still be investing in new fixed assets which improve its operational efficiency. These assets tend to increase the operational gearing of the business, as the proportion of fixed costs increases.

This can present a problem to some maturing companies if its major source of sales is replacement purchases by existing customers. During an economic downturn, these customers may defer their replacement purchases, and this can dramatically increase the economic cyclicality of sales volumes. A good example is in the area of consumer durables such as the USA car industry. In the 1990/91 recession, the demand for new cars fell dramatically as existing car owners decided to defer the purchase of their replacement cars. Such rapid volatility would not occur in a recession if the largest group of customers were new entrants to the market, as they would still need to buy the product. Companies need to be aware of this potential problem, as they should not increase their operational gearing excessively if sales levels can fluctuate violently about the steady, long-term trend level. The reaction of the USA automobile industry was discussed in Chapter 3.

As can be seen, the key strategic thrust during this stage of the life cycle is to improve the efficiency of the business as far as possible. This is the focus of capital investments as the overall capacity does not need to be continually increased as in the past. In order to achieve maximum cost efficiencies and the consequent enhanced levels of profitability, the company must allocate its resources as effectively as possible.

Critical success factors

If this allocation of resources is to be appropriate, it is essential to identify the limiting factor which is constraining the business. This could be one element in the production process, such as the available time on a critical machine, or it could be the resources available in the sales-force or the distribution network. Unless the utilization of this critical limiting factor is optimized, the company cannot maximize its profitability. As discussed in Chapter 10 in the context of transfer pricing, the way to optimize this utilization is by maximizing the contribution generated by each available unit of this limiting factor. Thus, where the limiting factor can be applied to several products, as is the case of a shared production facility, the contribution rate per unit of limiting factor must be the same for each product. If this is not the case, the overall profitability of the business can be improved by re-allocating resources appropriately.

It must be remembered that the limiting factors may change, due either to internal management action or to external circumstances. Thus managers may invest to increase the availability of this scarce resource, eg increasing the capacity of the particular machine or by hiring more sales people, and the business will now face a new constraint. Alternatively sales demand may decline so that the full output potential of the limiting machine is no longer needed; once again the business will face a new constraint. This means that the potential

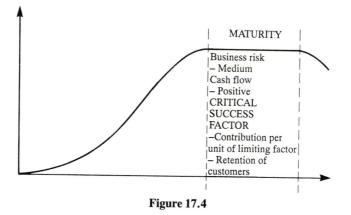

Figure 17.4

limiting factors must be regularly monitored to see not only which is currently applying to the business, but also at what point will alternative constraints come into operation. If this is done, the company is capable of responding very quickly and appropriately to changes in its environment.

However profits should be maximized over the long term, and therefore it is important that the business retains the market share, which was developed during the growth stage. Given that the overall market is no longer growing rapidly, the most cost effective method of achieving this is by retaining its existing customers. However, the company is also supposed to be increasing its total profits and cash generation capabilities. This means that the business needs a good system of customer account profitability (CAP) analysis to highlight the most important customers, which must be retained at all costs. As discussed in Chapter 6, most of a business' profitability is normally generated by a relatively small proportion of its customers. A critical success factor for this profit generating stage is therefore to retain, and even develop, these profitable customers. The company must remember that these customers will form important *potential* customers in the strategic plans of their competitors.

Another advantage of a good CAP analysis system is that it will highlight those customers who are not making an adequate contribution. During periods of rapid growth, companies should be prepared to invest in various categories of customers, because they may become profitable when the market stabilizes. If this has not happened, the company must take action either to reduce the costs incurred in servicing these customers, or to increase the gross contribution generated from sales to them. Should this prove impossible, the company should look at ways of re-allocating these resources which would improve the total contribution. It may be necessary to stop servicing these customers and reduce the total resources accordingly but, during the maturity phase, this is not normally the most appropriate response.

Financial control measures

The key strategic thrust during this mature stage of the life cycle is clearly to produce the maximum financial return possible. Thus it now becomes appropriate to use a profit measure to control the business financially. Return on Investment (ROI) can now be used in one of its several guises, but it is important to remember that any such accounting measure has a short-term focus, whereas the main objective is to maximize the financial return over the whole of the maturity period.

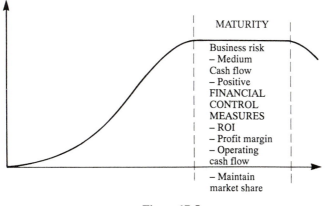

MATURITY

Business risk
– Medium
Cash flow
– Positive
FINANCIAL
CONTROL
MEASURES
– ROI
– Profit margin
– Operating
cash flow

– Maintain
market share

Figure 17.5

Therefore, in addition to ROI, the company needs some other control measures, some of which will be non-financial. A key issue is maintaining the relative market share, as long as this can be financially justified, and this can be used as an appropriate control measure. Any adverse changes should be investigated rapidly and the financial analysis should indicate the impact of the alternative available courses of action. As with many things, it is normally more expensive to carry out remedial work, ie to regain lost market share, than it is to pay for proper preventive maintenance. Therefore, the company should ensure that adequate maintenance marketing support is provided to retain its existing market share.

As well as using the overall ROI financial measure, the business should monitor the level of profit margins achieved during this period. This is important because managers can show an improved ROI performance by either increasing profits, or reducing the level of investment. The level of investment can be reduced by not replacing capacity as it wears out and, in the short term, the ROI will increase. However the long-term total cash generation capability of the product is being destroyed, and it is the long-term financial return which is important. This can be safeguarded against by including profit margins and the level of operating cash flows as part of the financial control process. It is never a good idea to use a single financial ratio as a method of measuring performance; managers can then concentrate on managing the ratio, rather than managing the business.

There are several other problems which can be created by an excessive emphasis on accounting measures, and particularly Return on Investment. ROI normally only includes tangible assets in the investment used as the denominator. This can cause problems if the main strategic thrust of the business has been to develop branded products during the growth phase of the cycle. As previously mentioned, the increasing degree of price competition, which is common as products mature, can put a strain on such a marketing led strategy. This can be particularly true when the customer base is dominated by a few, very strong companies. However this problem has been exacerbated in some instances by the way the financial control measures have been applied.

A good example is any manufacturer supplying the major supermarket retailers, initially with branded products. Once the product matures, the supplier wants to achieve the maximum profitability and for manufacturers this requires a high level of plant utilization. If its sales of its mainstream branded products do not completely fill its available capacity, it may look for additional ways of increasing its utilization rates. As its fixed costs base is, by definition, already there many such companies were willing to sell additional output at marginal prices, as long as a reasonable contribution was generated over its variable costs. The large retailers were very happy to buy such products, produced under the retailer's name rather than the existing brand, and the manufacturer saw it as a way of increasing its ROI.

Unfortunately, of course, these own label products often competed directly with the manufacturer's branded output, particularly in mature product areas where consumers were becoming more knowledgeable about product characteristics. Consequently, the sales of branded products were adversely affected and the overall long-term financial performance of these manufacturers did not improve as planned. This strategy clearly reduces the value of the intangible branded assets which have been invested in and developed in the past. It is vitally important that these intangible assets are properly taken into account in the strategic decision making process.

Companies can also run into other strategic problems if they over-emphasize one aspect of financial performance. This can be illustrated by considering the common treatment of freehold land and buildings in terms of assessing financial performance. The main financial reason for owning freehold land and buildings, rather than leasing them, is to achieve a capital gain through their appreciation in value. Indeed, because of this substantial potential capital gain, it is normally possible to lease buildings at a lower rental cost than the interest costs of financing the freehold purchase of the same buildings. This is because the landlord, in the leasing transaction, keeps the potential capital gain and is, consequently, prepared to discount the rental yield below the full financing cost for the property.

In this situation, it makes sense for any managers, who are judged exclusively on their ROI performance, to want to lease all the buildings occupied by their businesses. The operating costs will be lower and so will the asset base used for the ROI calculation. If the business does not want to forego the potential capital gain from owning the building, it should change the way the managers' financial performance is assessed. It is not logical to expect managers to behave altruistically, if they are given specific performance targets. The business must ensure goal congruence applies; this is even more important when the product leaves the maturity stage and goes into terminal decline.

18

Coping with old age and decline

Overview

In the last chapter it was argued that the maturity stage was the most attractive from the financial point of view and, consequently, companies should try to maintain products as high net cash producers for as long as possible. Unfortunately, it is inevitable that the product will eventually move into the saturation, declining or ageing stage as the total sales volumes start to be eroded, either by replacement products or due to a change in customer needs.

At this stage, there should be no question of trying to justify financially any long-term marketing investments in branding or differentiation strategies. Indeed the implicit assumption of the maturity stage, that the existing level of investment in both tangible assets and intangible assets (ie products and brands) should be maintained, should now be challenged. Therefore, re-investment in all assets should be rigorously financially evaluated before the funds are tied up once again in a dying business. There is a significantly increased risk that a sudden change in the business environment could almost immediately destroy any future sales potential for this already declining product. Consequently, the business should be seeking to minimize its residual investment in the product at this time.

This means that the use of accounting ratios (such as ROI) or even profits, which can be significantly affected by the timing impacts of the matching conventions in such areas as depreciation, are not appropriate methods of financial control. Even more inappropriate would be the long-term oriented DCF analysis as the main emphasis should now be placed on liquidity and short-term cash generation. Therefore 'free cash flow' generation is regarded as the best measure of financial performance during the old age stage of the life cycle. Free cash flow represents that level of funds generation which is available for distribution outside the business unit (ie either as dividends or as capital distributions to Head Office). Thus it is not needed by the declining business to support its future projected level of activity. As this level of activity reduces, the free cash flow can considerably exceed accounting profit levels due to funds being made available from declining requirements for working capital investment and from depreciation expenses on fixed assets which are not being replaced.

A key question for this decline stage is when should the product be closed down, and this should obviously be done when the product ceases to be cash positive. However, it may be sensible to cease production, even though the product is still making some net positive contribution in cash flow, but if the liquidation value generated by the product's closure exceeds the present value of these expected future cash flow contributions. This can be particularly true if there are other opportunity costs involved in the decision, such as freeing up limited resources which can be used in producing other products. As discussed in Chapter 14, the involvement of brands can further complicate the decision as to whether and when to close down a declining product. Although the particular product may be in decline, there may still be considerable potential value in the brand and this value may be realized by transferring the brand to a new or replacement product. Transferring the power of the brand away from the old product may result in its earlier demise, but there is a danger of killing, or severely damaging, a brand asset by maintaining its association with a declining product for too long.

Introduction

There is sometimes a danger of managers wanting to continue with a growth strategy after the market has matured. The business would be far better served by concentrating on profitability, rather than investing heavily in development marketing activity. If this is so, the risk of the managers trying to implement an inappropriate strategy when the product finally moves into the saturation and decline phase of the life cycle must be far greater. This final stage in any product's life is unattractive to most professional managers, as overseeing the orderly death of their business' main product does not seem like a good career move. However, it is very important that the appropriate competitive strategy is implemented during this stage, as the continuation of the maturity stage strategy can prove very expensive. There should be no automatic re-investment of funds when existing assets require replacement, as is normally done while sales volumes are still high and relatively stable. All such re-investment decisions must be financially justified in the light of the now declining sales levels.

It is, therefore, essential that a large group, which has a portfolio of products, ensures that its managers are properly motivated to manage a declining product appropriately. This can be achieved, as long as there is a clear separation between the assessment of the economic performance of the business unit, which will inevitably be getting worse, and the assessment of the manager's performance during these final phases of the product's life. If the managers are judged appropriately, they will want to implement the optimum competitive and financial strategy at this time.

Interestingly, the business risk reaches its lowest levels during the decline phase, because everyone knows the product is dying and the only real uncertainty is how long it will last. This reduced business risk means that the company could increase its financial risk correspondingly, as was discussed for the maturity stage in the previous chapter. However, it would not be sensible to increase the operational gearing of the business, by increasing the proportion of fixed costs, when sales volumes are expected to be declining steadily in the future. In this old age stage, the increased financial risk is better achieved by raising any required funding in the form of debt rather than injecting fresh equity funds. In fact, because the relative cost of debt is always less than the comparable cost of equity due to its lower risk perception by the provider, it is normally sensible at this time to increase borrowings and pay out very high dividends to the shareholders. This is not necessarily exposing these lenders to any excessive levels of risk should the company cease trading earlier than expected, because they should only lend money which is properly covered by the final realizable value of the remaining assets in the business. Such a financial strategy merely allows the shareholders to receive their capital earlier than would otherwise be possible.

This emphasis on cash flow is critical to this declining stage. No business should be thinking of making long-term investments in a declining product, which may not be financially viable if there is any additional deterioration in the business environment. Consequently, the use of

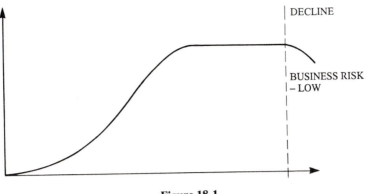

Figure 18.1

DCF analysis either for project evaluations, or as a financial control measure, is inappropriate, as the long-term future is too uncertain to be included. The company's investment strategy should be much more geared to reducing its residual investment in this product as quickly as possible. This also means that using accounting ratios, such as ROI, are no longer sensible, because there is an implicit assumption in such ratios that the business should maintain the investment base. Indeed, a key non-financial measure for the maturity stage was to monitor the relative market share of the product, so as to ensure that it did not decline while sales of the product were still high. Once the industry sales start to fall, the marketing expenditure needed for the maintenance of the existing market share should be financially justified using a short-term financial evaluation technique. As the major associated risk is that sales volumes may suddenly decline dramatically, or disappear altogether totally unexpectedly, the most appropriate financial decision-making technique is pay-back period. This quantifies the risk that any investment of funds will not have been recovered if the product dies more rapidly than is currently predicted.

Another reason for not using a profit based financial control measure is that profits rely on the accrual, or matching, concept. Thus, depreciation expenses are spread over the expected economic life of the assets, but these assets need to be realized in the near future if the product is closed down. Consequently, the realizable value of the asset may be more relevant than its net book value, based on the undepreciated portion of its original cost. If an asset, used with a declining product, has a high realizable value, the business may consider closing down the product in order to realize the proceeds from selling the asset. In many cases a high proportion of these funds may be obtained by borrowing against this net realizable value, but this type of decision indicates a key issue for the business at this time.

Once a product is in decline, it is only a question of time before it should be closed down. The business wishes to optimize the timing of this closure. This can only be done by reference to the total net future cash flows, which can be generated by the product. Once the product net operational cash flows turn negative, the product should be closed down as no business wants to *invest* in a dying, declining product; during the launch and growth phases, such negative cash flows are accepted because they will generate higher returns during the maturity stage. Thus, if the declining product becomes cash negative, its cost base must be reduced in order to make the cash flow at least neutral. These cost cutting exercises may result in reducing the level of marketing support, and this can lead to a reducing market share for the product. As stated earlier, during this phase, all expenditures on the product should be financially justified.

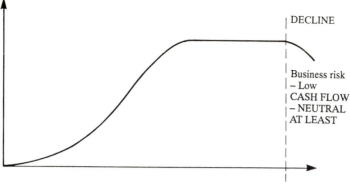

Figure 18.2

Information needs

Given this emphasis on cash generation, it is clear that forecasts of future cash flows are the most important elements of the required financial information. These cash flows can be dramatically affected by changes in the external environment, and the strategic management accounting system should try to identify the key external influences on the continued survival of the product. These will differ depending on the reason for the product moving out of the stable, mature phase into the old age stage, with declining sales volumes. If this was caused by the launch of replacement products with better ways of satisfying the same customer needs, the decline of the old product will be driven by the rate of development of its replacements. Thus, if new entrants arrive in the industry and significantly expand the capacity of the new products, the decline phase will be rapidly accelerated.

Another key element in the critical exit decisions facing the business at this time is the realizable value of the assets employed in producing and marketing the product. Clearly, the original historic cost is irrelevant, as is the net book value. An exit decision will result in the closure of the product, and the realization or transfer of these assets. Thus the net realizable value needs to be estimated, and this may only be the salvage value for some of the dedicated tangible assets. However, some of these tangible assets, such as freehold land and buildings, may have a realizable value far in excess of their costs or book value. In these cases, the opportunity cost associated with continuing to produce the declining product must be included in the financial evaluation of whether or not to close it down. For many of these assets, their value will be reducing over time, due to the lack of financial re-investment in the business. This can also be true for the intangible assets tied up with this declining product, such as brands. Quite often at this stage, the intangible asset values outweigh the realizable values of the more tangible assets. This is frequently because the brands can be transferred to new products, thus extending their life cycles as discussed in Chapter 14.

However, if this transfer is delayed too long, the value may be reduced significantly due to the brand being tainted by this prolonged association with failure. Consequently, the timing of the transfer of any such intangible assets away from the declining product is critical. This depends on the comparative forecasts of future cash flows from the various alternatives. The removal of these supporting assets may make the continued sale of the product uneconomic and lead to its immediate closure. The financial implications of these subsequent results of the original decision must be included in the evaluation of the decision to transfer the brands.

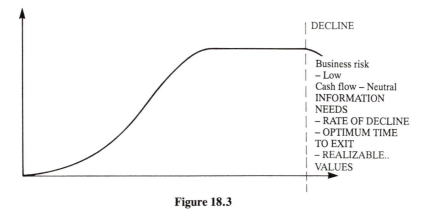

Figure 18.3

There are other alternatives to transferring these assets to more appropriate products. These may include their sale to an outside third party, as well as leaving them to run down with the declining product. However a more aggressive option can be to make acquisitions of other similar products, so as to increase the company's market share above the critical mass needed to continue to generate positive cash flows. The logic of this acquisition strategy is that other competitors will be facing the same relatively unattractive strategic choices regarding their similarly declining products. The aggressive company may be able to buy the complete business at an attractively low price, particularly if the realizable value of the assets is low. If some of these assets have significant realizable values, the buyer may either be able to exclude them from the deal or sell them on later, if they are not essential to the product's continued sale. It may even be possible to buy only the rights to the product, rather than having to buy the whole business. The strategic objective is to create, by a number of such competitive product acquisitions, a dominant position in this declining industry. This dominant position is then used to improve the financial return, ie make the operational cash flows positive again, from the product during at least part of its remaining life. This can be achieved in a variety of ways, including rationalizing the total productive capacity in an attempt to increase selling prices or reducing the cost base by economies of scale from the increased scale of operations. However, the most common method is to use the newly acquired dominant market share to change the relative power bases in negotiations with customers, thus increasing the share of the value chain retained by the product. This type of strategy has been very successfully implemented by a number of companies in a range of declining industries.

Financial control measures

The emphasis on cash flows during this declining stage indicates the most appropriate method of financial control. If re-investment is no longer automatic, the operating cash flows may be much larger than the profit streams due to the non-re-investment of depreciation expenses. The reducing tangible asset base may still be quite adequate to supply the reducing sales volumes. Indeed, these lower sales levels should require lower levels of working capital investment, and this also frees cash for other purposes.

This 'free cash flow', which is no longer required by the product, is a good financial control measure for a declining product, as it encourages the managers to concentrate on generating

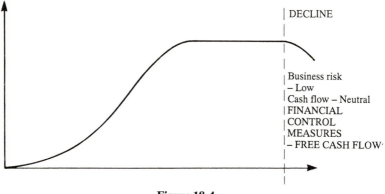

Figure 18.4

short-term cash flows. Thus, they may sell any assets which are not essential to the continued sale of the product. Indeed they should take into account the opportunity cost involved in retaining the product, if any high value assets are essential.

By using free cash flows, which can be invested elsewhere by the business, or repaid to the shareholders in the form of dividends, the vital exit decisions automatically focus on the relevant avoidable and severable costs associated with the product. Thus any unchanging apportioned costs will be ignored, and the business should take account of any discontinuities in fixed costs as the sales volumes decline. As volumes reduce, the fixed costs, which have to be increased if volumes increase substantially, do not necessarily decrease proportionately. Quite frequently, these fixed costs do not reduce at all once they are committed. For instance, in the case of a property lease, under which the rent must be paid even if the space is no longer required, there may be no avoidable cost should the product be closed down. Concentrating on future cash flows ensures that only the relevant cost elements are taken into account.

Part Five
Information Requirements for Strategic Management Accounting

19

Designing strategic management accounting systems

Overview

Strategic management accounting systems should be aids to decision-making, not historical reporting systems. Strategic decisions are taken in the context of the goals and objectives of the business. Consequently, the more specific the objectives, the more precise can be the decisions. If the decisions are precisely defined, the financial information needs can also be accurately specified.

However, this introduces a fundamental problem for designing such accounting information systems; most strategic decisions are one-off, non-repeatable decisions. Therefore, the information needs are likely to be similarly unique.

The design of the information system must take account of the significant potential communication gap between accountants and less numerately focused strategic decision-makers (eg senior marketing managers). The system must *communicate* the necessary financial information to the manager making the decision. The adage of the right information to the right manager at the right time is even more true and relevant for strategic decisions.

These issues require that the accounting system identifies those decisions which are likely to be required and which need financial supporting information. These decisions can be characterized as either entry or exit type decisions. Entry decisions include expansion of existing businesses, and both of these decision types require the use of incremental costs and revenues. Exit decisions include staying in a current area of operations as well as completely closing it down. These decisions should be based on the avoidable or separable cost concept, including the assessments of the opportunity costs involved. Unfortunately, none of these decisions require the financial information produced by most management accounting systems, which are dominated by apportioned historic costs.

As well as supporting strategic decisions, the well-designed strategic management accounting system should also identify appropriate financial performance measures. As discussed in Part Four, these performance measures must change as the key strategic issues facing the business develop over time. There must also be different financial performance measures used to evaluate economic and managerial performance. Economic performance of the organization must be assessed using all the relevant financial information, whether or not it is directly controllable by the managers. This relative overall financial performance of any business should be derived by using the opportunity cost comparison of a similar risk profile alternative. The alternative return will change with the external business environment, thus automatically making the economic evaluation dynamic. It also makes the economic assessment more objective and independent of the associated managerial performance. In other words, in a deep recession, the best managers in the world will lose less money than the worst but even they may not be able to generate a positive return. More importantly, the presence of a very good management team should not necessarily dissuade a company from exiting from an economically unattractive area of business. If possible, these good managerial resources should be re-allocated to a more attractive segment of the group's operations.

The evaluation of managerial performance should only take account of elements which the managers actually exercise control over. These evaluations should be referenced to pre-set objectives, but these objectives may need flexing to reflect changes in the external business environment, over which the managers have no control. These managerial performance measures should not normally be wholly financial, and the financial elements should be carefully integrated into the competitive strategy of the business.

The management accounting system should be designed from the perspective of the strategic decision-makers, so that only relevant information for the particular decision is provided. This is particularly relevant when subdivisions of a group are being considered, as many management accounting systems confuse decision-makers with irrelevant accounting neatness. For example, in a segment profitability analysis where *all* the costs are apportioned to products and/or customers. Such a design requires a high degree of teamwork and the close involvement of the decision-makers.

This design process should distinguish between committed and discretionary costs. Control cannot be exercised over committed costs even though the expenditure has not yet actually taken place; thus the financial control process should concentrate on those costs where discretion or choice can still be exercised. Discretionery costs should also be analysed into various categories. An important distinction for a strategically focused system would be between maintenance and development activities. This is normally automatically done for expenditure on physical assets such as plant and machinery, but should also be done for marketing expenditure as well. Marketing development activities can be further split between expenditure designed to grow the total market, and that specifically aimed at increasing the share of that total market held by the particular business. Maintenance type marketing activities are designed to retain the existing market share. All these categories of expenditure should be assessed by comparing actual achievements against planned, and these comparisons will, once again, include non-financial objectives.

Discretionery costs can also be distinguished from engineered costs. An engineered cost has a clearly definable relationship between the level of inputs and the outputs achieved. Normally this input to output relationship is defined in physical units rather than in financial terms, and can be used to measure relative efficiency. These engineering costs are by no means restricted to the production and operations areas of the business. The technique can be very successfully applied in the marketing, research and development, and administrative support areas as well; all that is required is a physical relationship between inputs and outputs.

This physical relationship can be used as the primary method of exercising control over efficiency, but a financial value needs to be overlaid so that comparative evaluations can be made. However, this does enable the proper use of standard costing to be implemented throughout the business. This type of standard costing requires a good understanding of the physical relationships involved, which must be monitored over time and, where necessary, modelled. In order to be of the greatest strategic value, the corporate and competitive objectives should be set in the context of these relationships, rather than purely in financial terms, so that their subsequent monitoring can be a meaningful learning process. The financial control system should always be regarded as a learning process rather than as a means of apportioning blame.

Where these physical relationships are used as part of the strategic management accounting system, it must be remembered that both strategic objectives and the physical relationships may change over time. The well-defined system should therefore not only be flexible enough to cope with such changes, but also be able to indicate the likely consequences of such possible changes. This can be done by using simulation and modelling techniques, and by incorporating sensitivity analysis into both the strategic planning process and the subsequent financial control system.

Introduction

Throughout the book, the role of management accounting within the context of the competitive and corporate strategies of an organization has been discussed. This role has important implications for the design of strategic management accounting systems, which are considered in this chapter. There are a number of general issues which need to be addressed in such designs, irrespective of the particular type of business under consideration. These have been refined and developed through application in a number of strategic management accounting projects in a wide range of companies. Consequently, this chapter considers them in the form of ten critical success factors for the design of such strategic management accounting systems.

Critical success factor (1) – Aid to strategic decisions

There must be a clearly established link between the overall goals and objectives of the organization, and the strategies selected to achieve them. These strategies must be broken up into overall corporate strategies and the tailored competitive strategies needed by the separate subdivisions of the business, which actually sell products in specified markets. The strategic management accounting systems must recognize these links and ensure that the selected strategies will, if successful, achieve the desired objectives. It should also check that the various competitive and functional strategies are mutually compatible with the overall corporate strategy of the business.

More importantly the management accounting system should highlight the key strategic decisions, which will have significant impact on the successful outcome of these strategies. This is the real emphasis of this first critical success factor; the strategic management accounting system must be much more than merely a historical financial recording and reporting process. It should be an aid to strategic decision-making, but this objective raises a number of key issues. As discussed in Part One, strategic management is a much more continuous integrated approach to managing the business than is conveyed by the alternative phrase, strategic planning. As companies adopt the strategic management approach, their accounting systems have to be able to assist not only in strategic planning decisions but also in monitoring, up-dating and, quite possibly, revising those decisions as their strategic plans are implemented.

If appropriate financial information is to be supplied in time to support this continuous round of potential strategic decisions, it is important that the likely types of decision can be identified so that the required information can be provided. These decisions are taken in the context of the key goals and objectives of the business. Therefore, if these goals and objectives are clearly expressed and can be broken down into specific areas, it is easier to predict what raw financial data is necessary and how that data needs to be analysed in order to enable a future decision to be taken. For example, if the business sets itself a very vague and general objective such as 'to get better at what it is currently doing', it is very difficult to know what financial information will be needed to support the future decisions required to achieve this objective. However, if this objective is expressed in terms of 'increasing its market share by 5% over the next 5 years while maintaining its profit margin at a minimum of 6% of sales revenue, and achieving a Return on Investment ratio in year 5 of 25%', the requisite financial analysis and comparative data can be specified quite accurately.

Some of this information will be needed to assess the current position of the company relative to these specific objectives, so that the required strategies to achieve the plan can be developed. Other information will be needed to monitor the achievement of these objectives over the five years of the plan. This monitoring will need to include changes in the external business environment, as the whole concept of strategic management is that it is not a static planning process but is a dynamic developing method of managing the business. Thus, as the business environment changes, the key strategic thrusts of the business may need to be altered. Indeed the objectives of the strategic plan may need to be reviewed as they may be made irrelevant due to external events.

These aspects of strategic decisions add another problem to the design of strategic management accounting systems, because most strategic decisions are one-off, non-repeatable decisions. Most traditional management accounting systems are designed to process large volumes of data on a regular, routine basis. This is fine to support the day-to-day operational decisions which can be relatively easily predicted, and where frequent historical financial analysis can provide a sound basis for future decision-making. However, if the future decisions are unique, the supporting financial information is likely to need to be appropriately tailored to each of these unique situations. It is, therefore, unlikely that extrapolating from past situations will be satisfactory, particularly if the key strategic thrust of the business is to change the way the product market interface reacts. This issue is considered in more detail in the next chapter.

Critical success factor (2) – Closing the communication gap

If the management accounting system is designed to function as a decision support system, it is important that it provides financial information which is helpful to the strategic decision-makers. This means the accounting system must produce information and not raw financial data which needs additional processing by the recipients. Such additional processing may unnecessarily delay the decision and, if done by non-experts, may lead to incorrect conclusions being drawn from the data, with potentially disastrous implications for the resulting strategic decision.

Equally importantly, the accounting system must produce this 'helpful' financial information in a format which is readily understandable and usable by the strategic decision-maker. It is still quite common to find that internal financial management reports are produced in formats designed by accountants for accountants. In other words, there is no real effort to present the financial information in a more readable manner, even if the key decision-maker is not financially trained or particularly numerate. This clearly makes it more difficult for the non-financial manager to make the best decision for the business based on the available information. Somewhat cynically, this can be regarded as a good way for financial managers to maintain or expand their power base within the organization, as they are essential to the decision-making process if no one else can understand or interpret the financial information. As discussed in Chapter 1, accounting is the common business language, but this should not be used to elevate the financial manager to the role of main strategic decision-maker. The role of language is to aid communication and, therefore, management accounting systems must be designed to present financial information in the most suitable and most easily comprehensible form. Given the power and flexibility of modern computers, particularly if a relational data-base system is in use, it is perfectly practical to provide all strategic decision-makers with individual tailored reporting formats. Thus, the less numerate manager can receive the relevant information in the form of graphs, pie charts, histograms or other visually based layout. The important elements in designing the format of communicating the financial information are to remove the risk of misunderstanding by the decision-maker, and to reduce the time required to assimilate the information before the decision can be taken.

If this communication gap between the accountant and the non-financial decision-maker can be closed, the business is likely to benefit from better strategic decisions. This will be enhanced because decision-makers will now be able to request additional information to support future decisions, as they become more used to incorporating such financial information in their decision-making processes.

Criticial success factor (3) – Identify types of decision

This tailored communication process is based on the simple but immensely useful logic of providing 'the right information to the right manager at the right time'. This requires ensuring that the strategic decision-maker receives relevant, useful financial information in time for it to be incorporated in the decision-making process. Given the frequent 'one-off' nature of strategic decisions, it may be very difficult to achieve this unless the accounting department can predict in advance what types of decision are likely to be required and, consequently, what financial information is likely to be needed.

Fortunately, it is relatively straightforward to characterize financial decisions into four main types. Financial decisions basically involve changing the allocation of the resources of the business. One obvious such decision involves *increasing* the allocation of resources to a particular area of the business. The financial evaluation of this type of decision should be based on the costs which would be incurred, compared to the benefits which would be derived, by the business. Both costs and benefits should be assessed on an incremental basis, ie ignoring the existing allocation of resources, but the cost should take account of any opportunity costs associated with alternative areas of the business which cannot be developed as a direct result of this decision. A similar, strategic decision is to consider *entering* a new area of business. This could involve launching new products, going into new markets or, possibly, both. Once again, the financial evaluation should be based on the net incremental impact on the business of the costs and benefits involved. In the case of an 'entry' decision, there is often a substantial delay before these benefits are received and, therefore, the financial evaluation must take account of this timing impact by using some form of the discounted cash flow technique.

The two other types of financial decision are forms of exit evaluations; in that, if the business environment turns against one part of the company's operations, it may need to consider whether to stay in this business segment, to close it down, or to sell it to somebody else. The financial evaluation should be carried out by comparing the financial cost or benefit which is expected to derive from staying in, with the best alternative method of closing down (ie either selling the business as a going concern, or liquidating any residual assets). It should be remembered that both of these returns can be negative so that the least *cost* alternative should be selected. This can occur in a business where it actually costs money to close it down (such as mining), so that it may be cheaper to stay in business, even though the operation is loss-making, rather than having to spend far greater sums of money to close it down. The benefits of closure are clearly the realizable values of any assets which can be sold, together with the savings which can be achieved by ceasing to pay for certain costs. Thus, the relevant costs can be defined as the avoidable or severable costs, which will be saved as a direct result of the closure decision. [It should be clear that these exit categories include any decisions to reduce the level of activity from its current level.]

The problem created for the strategic management accounting system by these categories of decisions is that they should be based on incremental or avoidable future cash flows. Most management accounting systems concentrate almost exclusively on analysing historic, accounting based costs, not the future cash flows which are relevant to financial decisions. Also, these systems tend to include sophisticated bases of apportionment, which spread the historic costs across the organization. Incremental and avoidable costs include only those elements which will change as a direct consequence of the particular decision under consideration. Thus, these attributable costs do not include the apportioned shares of costs which will not be affected by the decision. These differences mean that the design of a decision support focused strategic management accounting system must not be based on traditional historic accounting principles, as these will not provide the decision-makers with the appropriate financial information.

There is a further issue raised by this question of using cost/benefit analysis for financial decisions. It is clear that designing and implementing this type of decision focused accounting system can have a significant cost. These incremental costs must themselves be justified, before they are incurred, by comparing them to the expected benefits which will result from the enhanced information system. These benefits should accrue from the better decisions which will be taken by the strategic decision-makers in the light of these improved supporting financial reports. Unfortunately, like the outcomes of almost all business decisions, these benefits are not guaranteed and the costs have to be incurred before the benefits can be achieved.

Critical success factor (4) – Selecting suitable financial performance measures

Strategic management has already been defined as a continuous management style. This requires that the well-designed strategic management accounting system assists in the monitoring of the business strategies as they are implemented. In order to do this, the system should identify appropriate measures of financial performance. As discussed in Part Four these financial performance measures must be tailored to the particular strategies being used by the business. Most importantly, they must be appropriate to the key strategic thrusts of these competitive strategies as the businesses develop. This clearly requires that the performance measures change over time, and a critical feature of a good strategic accounting system should be to indicate when this should happen. Such changes can be very useful early warning indicators that the strategic thrusts should also be changing in response to the developing business environment. Failure to respond quickly and appropriately can be a very expensive mistake, and this is frequently caused by not receiving sufficiently clear signals through the internal accounting system.

It is also important that these performance measures are not exclusively financial and that the financial measures are properly integrated into the specific competitive strategies, as indicated in Chapter 14.

Critical success factor (5) – Economic versus managerial performance

These tailored financial performance measures must differentiate between the economic performance of the business, and the financial performance of the managers. Both of these are relative performance assessments, but it can be extremely demotivating to judge managers' performances by reference to elements over which they have no control. However, these uncontrollable elements can have a significant impact on the overall financial results achieved by a business. Therefore, they have to be taken into account when strategic decisions are being financially evaluated.

Thus, the assessment of economic performance includes everything that has an impact on the financial outcome, whether or not it is controllable by any level of management. These strategic decisions must select the option which brings the maximum economic benefit to the business, even if the best choice only results in making a smaller loss than under all the other alternatives. The selection of this maximum economic benefit can only be made in the context of the strategic goals and objectives of the business and the current business environment. As already mentioned, the business environment may have changed considerably since the current goals and objectives were agreed, and they may no longer be relevant or obtainable. Consequently, this overall evaluation of economic performance must be done using the opportunity cost logic of what alternative financial returns could have been achieved at a similar level of overall risk.

However, strategic decisions are taken by senior managers and it may be dangerous to assume that any particular manager is motivated to achieve these corporate goals and objectives. The corporate strategy may have a relatively high risk profile, which is considered acceptable to the shareholders due to the correspondingly increased expectation of return. To a particular manager, the resulting increased career risk may not be matched by such an increased return, so that there is a lack of goal congruence between the manager and the organization.

If the manager's performance is measured by how well the company meets its objectives, this need not reflect the manager's relative contribution at all. In a booming economy, the company may exceed its previously set objectives. Even if, as they should be, these objectives are up-dated to take account of the positive changes in the external environment, the resulting economic performance may still be impressive. This may still not represent a good managerial performance, but may simply reflect an extremely favourable business environment. Conversely, in a similarly adverse economy, the best set of managers in the world may not be able to avoid sustaining a loss; they are likely, however, to lose less than the average or bad management teams. For example, a large UK-based bank may find it very difficult to sustain or improve its economic performance in a very severe recession, which creates record levels of business failures.

However, the managers of the bank can take various actions to reduce the impact of the recession, and to position the bank for the inevitable economic recovery. In order to motivate these managers to do this, their performance should be primarily judged on areas over which they can exercise control. Managers can be held responsible for their forecasts of the external environment, if their forecasts lead the company to take certain strategic decisions which affect other areas of the business. The managers who were affected by, but were not responsible for, these forecasts would not be held personally accountable for this element of their overall performance. This deviation from the strategic plan can be allowed for by flexing the plan where necessary, so as to incorporate the revised external environment. If this is properly done, the manager's performance is compared to what it should have been, had the other uncontrollable forecasts been made accurately.

The main objectives of managerial performance evaluations are not only to motivate the managers to try to achieve the group's goals and objectives, but also to highlight good managers. These good managerial resources should be recognized so that they can be retained by the business, and allocated to the most beneficial areas of the group. In many cases this may mean putting these managers into some of the least profitable business segments, as they may be able to turn the businesses around. If this proves impossible using a good management team, the best economic solution may be to exit from that area of operations. This does not mean getting rid of the incumbent managers, as they can be re-allocated to a new business. Unless appropriate managerial performance measures have been incorporated into the accounting system, the best managers will tend to want to be involved in those areas of the business producing the highest levels of economic returns; this may not result in the optimum allocation of management strengths.

This highlights that managerial performance measures should not be exclusively financial, and the financial measures should not focus totally on profit or even contribution levels. The financial elements must, as always, be carefully integrated into the key strategic objectives of the business and, as these will change over time, so must the managerial performance measures.

Critical success factor (6) – Provide relevant information only

If the goal congruence objective has been achieved, senior managers will be properly motivated to achieve the strategic objectives of the business plan. They will, therefore, be looking at strategic decisions from the organization's viewpoint and this should be considered when designing the strategic management accounting system. The strategic decision-makers will not have time to sort through masses of unnecessary financial data. First, it is important, as already mentioned, that financial information, not data, is supplied to the decision-maker in a form that can be readily understood. Second, it is critical that only *relevant* financial information is supplied to the strategic decision-maker. This means producing specific tailored reports to support particular decisions. Clearly this requires a very rapid data processing capability, but a lot of this can be achieved by the combination of a good computer data-base and the previous analysis of the potential types of strategic decision, which identified the type of financial information which would be required. Consequently, the management accounting system is already collecting much of the raw data and carrying out the preliminary analysis to produce the basic financial information to support forthcoming strategic decisions.

This can be illustrated by considering strategic decisions which affect the subdivisions of a large group. Many of these decisions will have an impact on the allocation of resources to specific products, and specific markets. Therefore, financial information will be required on the relative current and future profitability of these products and/or markets. This can be supplied by preparing regular segment profitability analyses, but these must be prepared with the forthcoming decisions in mind. If the traditional accounting logic is used so that all costs are apportioned to both products and markets, the answer is, as shown in Part Two, very neat but completely useless.

Such an accounting system merely confuses the decision-makers with its obsessional neatness, rather than adding value through its relevance. The decision-makers require supporting financial information which shows how the economic returns of the business will change as a consequence of any particular decision. This clearly requires the use of incremental or avoidable future costs as previously indicated, and not the apportionment of irrelevant historic cost levels.

Critical success factor (7) – Separate committed from discretionary costs

Designing a strategic management accounting system which can respond so quickly to the demands of specific one-off strategic decisions, requires the close involvement of the actual decision-makers. Only they will know the types of decision which are likely to be faced in the future, and even more importantly, what possible alternative strategies should be evaluated for each such potential decision. Thus the design process needs to be a team effort, as the financial managers must ensure that the right information for each of these options is provided.

The involvement of the key strategic decision-makers also highlights the level at which, and the time-scale over which, choice can genuinely be exercised. Costs should be separated, within the strategic management accounting system, into committed and discretionary costs. Most accounting systems bring costs in when they actually occur, in the sense of the event to which they refer having taken place. This is the fundamental basis of accrual accounting and the matching principle; but it does not, in reality, reflect when the cost is normally committed. The company may enter into a legally binding agreement a long time before the actual event takes place and the accounting entries are recorded. For example, if the business takes on a 25-year property lease agreement, it is *committed* to pay the lease payments for the full lease period, even if it no longer wanted to occupy the property. The only point at which control can be exercised over the decision to spend money therefore is before the commitment is made. Prior to this time, the business has the ability to exercise its discretion over whether it spends the money or not; after commitment, the subsequent accounting entries are inevitable.

Thus, for strategic decision-making purposes, the company must focus on discretionary costs, as there is no point in considering committed costs even though the actual date of payment may be a long time in the future. Financial control can only be exercised over these truly discretionary costs, but even this distinction is inadequate for strategic analysis. The goals and objectives of most businesses are normally expressed in target levels of improvement from the existing position of the business. Indeed, an essential initial element in any strategic planning process is a detailed review of the current position of the organization within its particular business environment. This review, and the subsequent strategic plan, should indicate what activities are necessary merely to maintain this existing, starting position. Virtually all companies will include a plant and machinery maintenance budget in their financial plans, but this should be extended to all the key aspects of the company's strategic plans.

In other words, if the relative levels of market share and brand awareness by customers are key elements in the strategic plan, it is important that the expenditures needed to maintain the current levels of these items are identified within the business plan. This is because the real level of discretion which can be exercised by the company over these areas of expenditure is relatively small, unless the managers are prepared to see such key elements deteriorate during the period of the plan. On top of this maintenance level of activity, the strategic plan may aim to improve the company's relative marketing positions. This development level of expenditure should be identified and linked to the specifically associated objectives, eg to increase market share by 5% over the next five years. If this is done, the financial monitoring process can be designed to report on the developing relationships between this marketing expenditure and changes in relative market share. In the area of marketing, this development expenditure can be split still further into activities designed to increase the total size of the market, and those which should develop the company's share of that total market. Clearly the methods of financial evaluation and subsequent monitoring should be tailored to the needs of each particular type of development or maintenance activity.

Critical success factor (8) – Distinguish discretionary from engineered costs

By breaking discretionary costs down into further, more specific elements it is possible to concentrate analytical resources on those areas of the business where the true exercise of strategic choice is possible. This can be further aided by distinguishing discretionary costs from engineered costs. As its name implies, an engineered cost has an input to output relationship which is relatively predictable. In other words, for any given level of input resources, the resulting predicted level of output can be calculated and vice versa, eg the tonnes of sand needed to make a given output of glass. These fixed relationships are normally physical rather than financial, as changes in relative input prices will change the output values but not the physical volume of outputs. However, for a given set of input prices, the comparison of actual results against the plan is really being done using this physical relationship.

Using such an input–output relationship it is possible to adjust the level of activity in the original plan to the actual level, so as to see what should have happened under the up-dated situation. It is important to emphasize that this comparison only measures the efficiency of the operation, and this does not necessarily reflect the relative effectiveness involved. For example, if a distribution costing model has been developed for a business, even though the actual sales volumes differ from those included in the strategic plan, it is possible to use the model to calculate what the distribution costs *should have been* for that actual level of sales. This revised planned level of expenditure can be compared to the actual costs incurred so as to measure the relative efficiency of the distribution function. However, this comparison makes no comment on the effectiveness of this distribution function in terms of contributing to the strategic goals and objectives of the company.

If our company sells and distributes short shelf life, fresh products to retailers, the effectiveness of its distribution function may be measured by its ability to minimize the delay in delivery to the retailers so that the maximum shelf life is available during the period for which the goods are on sale in the shops. This factor may be more important than a small improvement in the relative efficiency in the cost performance of the distribution function. The problems of measuring and controlling both efficiency and effectiveness are critical to the design of a good strategic management accounting system. Engineering type input–output relationships limit the discretion which can be exercised by the organization, and this helps in controlling the efficiency of the operations. As before, the control over effectiveness depends on linking the accounting system very closely to the corporate objectives and strategies. If this is done, then critical success factors can be identified for each area of the business, which really do mean that if each area achieves these 'critical success factors' then the business should hit its overall strategic objectives. In many cases these effectiveness measures will also be largely non-financial, and some of these measures can be very good ways of assessing managerial performance, as well as the economic performance of the business, if financial values are added to make comparisons easier.

Input to output relationships are by no means restricted to the production areas of the business, as many such predictable physical relationships can be established in other areas. A good example is the field sales-force, where real discretionary control is exercised by the sales director over the number of sales people rather than over the total sales-force costs. This is because there is a logical cost relationship for any industry determining the cost of having an effective operational field sales-person; thus this cost can be regarded as an engineered cost. The decision-making process should consequently concentrate on the issue of considering how large the sales-force should be, once the validity of the input–output model has been verified. The performance of the sales management team should therefore be assessed on the *effectiveness* with which the available sales-force personnel were utilized, and on the *efficiency* with which the previously established cost model was managed. If the right sets of performance indicators were used, the managers should themselves be able to resolve correctly any potential conflicts between being more efficient but less effective, and vice versa.

Consequently, engineering type costs can be used wherever there is a predictable input to output relationship and this frees strategic decision-makers to concentrate their time on their discretionary ability to use these resources most effectively.

Critical success factor (9) – Using standard costs strategically

These physical input–output relationships enable close controls over the efficient use of resources to be maintained, even when the levels of activity deviate from those expected. By using a standard price per unit, these physical measures can be turned into standard costs; thus enabling more general comparisons to be made. As discussed in Chapter 4, it is possible to use standard costs as a key element of a strategic management accounting system. However, using standard costs strategically requires a very good understanding of the way in which the various physical relationships interact, as strategic decisions can often involve significant differences in the way in which the company operates. For example, in the earlier illustration of developing a standard relationship for the cost of a field based sales-person, the organization may wish to consider the relative effectiveness of servicing certain groups of customers through an alternative sales method, such as direct mail or third party sales-force. The comparison should be based on applying the cost models for each sales alternative to the relevant customer groupings so that their relative cost-effectiveness could be assessed, but the impact of any such changes on the efficiency of the remaining internal sales-force should also be taken into consideration.

Modelling these physical and financial cost relationships is a great advantage as it allows externally caused changes to be incorporated very easily. Staying with the field sales-force, several significant elements of its costs are driven by external factors and forecasts of these costs have to be made at the time of doing the strategic plan. As with all forecasts, these cost estimates for petrol prices, hotel rates, etc are likely to be wrong with the result that the comparisons of actual to budget become relatively meaningless. However if a model has been developed, it is quite easy to 'flex' the budget by including the new correct actual costs per unit and applying these costs to the planned usage levels. This allows the relative efficiency of sales managers to be fairly evaluated but, more importantly, it enables the business to consider any changes to the organization of the sales-force which could make it more effective, in the light of the revised actual cost levels.

Another benefit of using these physically driven cost relationships is that it helps the strategic management accounting system to be used as a continuous learning process, rather than as a negatively based method of apportioning blame. This becomes possible if the strategic objectives are stated in terms of these engineering style relationships, so that the objectives can be split into improvements in the efficiency of managing the relationship and the effective use of the resources involved.

Critical success factor (10) – Allowing for changes over time

Where these physical relationships are used as part of the strategic management accounting system, it must be remembered that both strategic objectives and the physical relationships may change over time. This is particularly true where the input–output relationship is not a true engineering one, as there may be many possible changes in the method of doing things which can affect the relationship over time. Strategic decisions can be long term and can have dramatic impacts on the nature of the organization (eg by exiting completely from one area of business). Therefore the use of physical standards needs to be monitored to ensure that they are still relevant to the business as it now is, and will be in the future.

The well-designed accounting system should not only be flexible enough to cope with the impact of these significant changes, but should also be capable of indicating in advance the likely consequences of such changes. In this way, the system can be a major decision-making aid. This can be achieved by incorporating sensitivity analyses into the strategic planning process and the financial control system and by using computer-based simulation and modelling techniques in the standard costing area.

20

Operating strategic management accounting systems

Overview

Managing accounting in many companies has failed to keep up with developments in corporate and competitive strategies. Indeed many other areas of management practice, eg marketing and information technology, have been far more responsive to the challenges presented by the increasingly competitive business environment. This is particularly strange since the advances in information technology have created a dramatic opportunity for companies to revolutionize the way in which they plan and control their organizations. The reducing cost and ever-increasing processing power of information technology have made this quite practical. Unfortunately, many companies have responded by simply doing the same things more quickly.

This increase in speed is not sufficient if the faster financial information is not tailored to the specific needs of the organization. The key strategic thrusts of businesses are becoming increasingly focused, and can rapidly change in the light of new environmental conditions. These strategic thrusts have highlighted a variety of different critical success factors, such as time, which must be incorporated into the strategic management accounting system. It is not logical to try to achieve this by using management accounting techniques and practices which were appropriate forty years ago, and in a completely different competitive environment.

Therefore, the opportunity to use information technology (IT) strategically must be seized by management accountants, in the way in which it is by other areas of the business. The development of genuine financial data-bases is a critical start point for many companies, but the value of such a relational data-base hinges on having thought through all the information which needs to be collected and how it needs to be coded. If the necessary data is not included, or is inadequately cross-referenced, it is not possible to access the required financial information rapidly in a relevant format. This can provide a number of problems for strategic accounting information. Strategic decisions tend to be one-off decisions, which require specific supporting financial information. This information is unlikely to be have been collected through the normal historic recording of the individual financial transactions, which form the input to most accounting data-bases.

Part of the solution to this problem is to use computer processing power to automate the repetitive accounting functions so as to minimize the time and effort required in these areas. This frees up financially skilled resources to concentrate on the one-off strategic decisions, where using historic analysis of trends, etc is of less value.

Another part of the solution can be provided by the accounting system identifying the types of strategic decisions which are likely to be needed and highlighting the relevant supporting financial information. Much of this information will be forward-looking or externally based, but the collection of the essential base data can still be automatically triggered in many cases. Such a comprehensive financial data-base makes it much easier to respond to urgent requests for a unique piece of financial analysis to support a critical business decision.

Truly automating data collection is not possible in most cases, and the next best alternative is to ensure that the data is input once only, as early as possible in the business transaction cycle. This often means that much of the data is input as part of the normal clerical recording function. The financial decision supporting information is subsequently obtained by processing this raw data. If this means, as it normally does, that the data is produced by one area of the business but is subsequently processed for use by another area, there is a risk of the adage 'garbage in, garbage out' coming true. Such a risk is particularly high where the data input represents an extra workload for the clerical staff involved, yet they do not see the eventual output, and they may well have no idea as what the data is eventually used for. It is important to motivate these critical employees positively, so that they understand how important it is that their input is done correctly and at the right time. Where possible, control checks over any particularly vital data should be automatically incorporated into the management accounting system.

These changes in the operation of management accounting systems in companies, so as to make them really effective as strategic decision support systems, represent the major challenge to management accountants in the years ahead. However, as these major changes are developed and implemented, the basic support functions of the accounting area must not be allowed to collapse. What is needed is a process of evolution, not revolution, but the business needs to create a positive climate for change within its accounting function. This can most effectively be achieved by selecting a few relatively quick and easy changes which will be visible to other managers, particularly the strategic decision-makers, within the organization. When they have seen the beneficial impact of these simple improvements, they are likely to become very supportive of more substantial changes in the way in which management accounting supports the business; and the management accountants are likely to be more confident of making these changes.

Introduction

In the previous chapter, the critical success factors for designing a strategic management accounting system were discussed. This chapter considers the issues arising from the implementation and operation of such an accounting system. However, there is an initial major concern which must be raised which is that, so far, relatively few companies have made any significant progress towards the type of strategically focused accounting system which was outlined in Chapter 19.

Many companies use several of the techniques discussed throughout the book, but they mainly still do so alongside a relatively traditional management accounting system. These traditional systems are generally internally focused, and very often still concentrate on apportioning responsibility and blame; rather than having an external focus, and acting as a learning process in order to improve the quality of future decisions. The lack of initiatives for, and progress in, developing these new management accounting systems seems to stem from the accountants' view that it is very difficult and complex, and may not really be needed by their fellow managers. This view does not seem to be shared by their colleagues; indeed, senior line managers in some large organizations regard management accounting as outdated and largely irrelevant to the modern day needs of their business. Such an extreme view casts the management accountant in the old fashioned role of 'scorekeeper', with the added criticism that, now, even the historic score is provided too late to be of any relevance.

A more moderate and balanced view may be that management accounting in many companies has been left behind by the increasingly rapid rate of change in other areas of business. The nature of management has changed dramatically in response to an increasingly competitive environment and the managers, themselves, have become ever more professional. This new environment places greater emphasis on the manager's ability to make decisions more frequently and more quickly. These managers' increasing professionalism is leading to a demand for better financial information to support these decisions. Better does not, in this context, mean greater volume, but more specifically relevant and more timely for each particular decision. The impact of these decisions is also magnified by the intensity of competitive pressures so that any wrong decision, which is not rapidly corrected, can have disastrous implications for the whole business.

Technology advances have created the capability for management accounting to respond to all these needs, but the information technology (IT) revolution needs to be used much more creatively than it is at present in many companies. Possibly because accounting systems were one of the first major commercial users of the early computers, there is a tendency still, in the accounting area, to regard the only benefit of computer power to be its ability to process large volumes of data very rapidly. The additional benefits of selectivity, analysis, prediction, accuracy, storage with retrieval on demand, are often largely ignored. Yet it is these features which have been used by several other areas of the business as the basis of their strategic applications of IT.

This has been largely caused by the increasingly focused competitive strategies employed by businesses, which are built upon very specific competitive advantages. Unfortunately, some of these developments have completely outstripped their associated financial control systems. For example, the recent revolutions in manufacturing practices have not always been matched by changes in the management accounting area. Many sophisticated businesses still use production costing systems, which are driven by direct labour as the key controllable, ie variable, cost. The introduction of automated flexible manufacturing systems, just-in-time inventory management programmes, computer-controlled and robotically resourced warehouses have changed the manufacturing environment dramatically in the forty or fifty years since these costing systems were developed. Direct labour is now a relatively minor, but also relatively fixed, part of the total cost structure for many companies; however, they persist with the logic of *recovering* all these other costs as a proportion of this direct labour element.

Flexible manufacturing systems (FMS) enable companies to tailor their output to the changing needs of their markets, without dramatic decreases in operating efficiencies. These sophisticated, computer-controlled, engineering installations are relatively expensive; the additional investment should be financially justified on the basis of the increased added value which can be generated as a result of this flexibility. The management accounting system has to be able to evaluate this type of investment.

Even more importantly, once installed, the critical success factor for a FMS layout is completely different to a traditional, more labour intensive, single product, process production line. The expensive, largely automated plant generates no financial return when it is not operating. Consequently, there is great pressure to keep these automated plants going 24 hours per day, 7 days per week. The costing system should highlight this new critical success factor of machine utilization, and contributions per hour of machine time should be available for all products. Comparative alternative costings for the major volume products produced in a more conventional way should also be prepared, in order to ensure that the enhanced sophistication, and correspondingly increased investment, of FMS is properly justified.

The key issue from this, for all strategic management accounting systems, is that they must be tailored to the specific critical success factors of the particular strategic thrusts being employed by each business. Moreover, as these strategic thrusts are likely to change over time, and with the dynamics of the competitive environment, the accounting system must be sufficiently flexible to adjust to each new set of critical success factors. The most logical way to achieve these aims is to harness the ever increasing power of IT.

Information technology impact

For many innovative companies, their key strategic focus is to change the way the product/market interface operates and, by so doing, to introduce a new critical success factor into the competitive arena. Not surprisingly, these companies just happen to have a significant competitive advantage in this new critical success factor.

A good example of this is the increasing use of time as a key strategic thrust by many companies, whose strategies emphasize being quicker, in some way, than their competitors. This competitive advantage can take the form of shortening the operational cycle of the business in some way, or even taking decisions faster than competitors. This demands better, quicker financial information. If the main element in the strategy is saving time in the operational, selling and distribution chain, there are a number of ways in which management accounting can add value. Time must be treated as a critical limiting factor in the financial analysis process, and the duration of each area of operations should be measured. Clearly any strategic initiative aiming to reduce the elapsed time for any function should be financially evaluated in terms of this critical success factor. This can only be done if a value is placed on time saved, and this valuation is critically important to the overall evaluation of this type of competitive strategy. The strategy is driven by the objective of delivering the product more quickly than the competition, and the business may need to invest considerable funds in order to achieve this. The economic justification for such an investment must be that creating such a sustainable competitive advantage will result in a higher financial return over time. This higher financial return must have a present value greater than the present value of the incremental investment. This can be illustrated in the area of fresh produce, eg fruit and vegetables. If one company can get its produce to the end customer more quickly, and hence in better condition, it should generate a greater financial return. It may be able to charge a premium price for its goods due to their better quality or earlier availability; alternatively, it could gain greater market share, by selling at the normal market price, and hence achieve economies of scale. Such companies should therefore concentrate on reducing the time lag between harvesting the fruit and vegetables, and delivering them to their customers (who may be consumers, wholesalers, retailers, or food processors).

However, this time advantage must have a minimum scale and be regularly sustainable if it is to have a financial value; a 'five-minutes fresher product today only' does not create an impressive competitive advantage. Even then, the law of diminishing returns is likely to set in once a significant time advantage has been achieved; having 'even more significantly fresher products' may not increase the added value very much. Only when the competition have almost caught up with the existing positioning does it become economically attractive to invest, so as to move significantly ahead again. This illustration shows that the financial analysis of the value of time must be done on a relative basis, ie the competitive advantage is created not by being fast, but by being *faster*. This relative analysis must be regularly up-dated so as to ensure that the relative advantage is being maintained.

What constitutes a significant time advantage depends entirely on the specific competitive environment. In the extremely competitive and time-critical world of financial markets, a few seconds advantage in receiving critical information can be very significant! This concentration on time as a critical success factor has led to a new way of apportioning costs across the business. Indirect costs are spread to products in proportion to the *time* spent by the products in each department. Not surprisingly, this method of apportionment is known as 'throughput' accounting, since an increase in the throughput of any product through a particular department results in a lower per unit charge to the product.

This concept of throughput accounting is only relevant if the critical limiting factor of the competitive strategy is time and, as mentioned earlier, both the strategy and the limiting factor can be subject to change. The business needs a flexible accounting system which can cope with the need for such changes in focus, and this is a major benefit of modern IT. A relational data-base enables the business to record data at its lowest level and to aggregate these individual data records according to coding references associated with them at the time of initial entry. As long as the coding references are sufficiently comprehensive, almost any inter-relationship between two pieces of data can be aggregated through the computer system, even if the relationship had not been identified during the initial system design process. However, this can lead to some ludicrously long coding reference numbers, which create significant administrative inefficiencies if they have to be input into the system each time. A more cost-effective approach is to spend longer deciding which inter-relationships are strategically important when the relational data-base is being designed. Alternatively, the storage power and cross-referencing capability of the computer can be used to increase the range of references which can be subsequently accessed, without needing the entire coding reference to be input each time.

At present it is fair to say that, for most companies, the critical constraint on the value adding capabilities of IT is management's ability to understand and utilize the full potential of the software and hardware at its disposal. Several years ago, people were talking about the prospect of a paperless office with all internal reports being made available on VDU screens and one company's computers talking directly to the computers of suppliers and customers. Some of this is happening but, for most businesses, there has been an explosion in the paper outputs generated by these increasingly powerful and faster systems. These management reports occupy a high proportion of many managers' time, often in order to find out if they contain anything of value. As stated in the previous chapter, this is completely wrong and is an abuse of IT; the computer system should be capable of delivering an individually tailored report to each decision-maker, containing the relevant financial information only.

However, this dominant use of IT can create several potential problems for strategic management accounting systems. Strategic decisions tend to be one-off decisions; such as whether or not to launch a new product, or whether or not to close down a particular factory. Once this particular factory has been closed, it clearly cannot be closed again, so in this way the decision is a one-off. This does not mean that there are no future benefits which can be gained from the financial analysis of such a decision, as it may be of great help if another factory closure decision is faced in the future. The use of all decisions as part of a learning process is therefore still valid, but this type of decision does create a data collection problem which must be resolved. Entry and exit decisions should not be based on the historic which will normally have been included in the computer data-base; each of these decisions should be evaluated using the relevant future cash flows which, of course, will not yet have been recorded.

The simplest solution is to automate as far as possible the repetitive type of financial transactions so that the limited, skilled accounting resources can concentrate on the strategically important one-off decisions. In far too many businesses, the management accountants spend the vast majority of their time on these routine, repetitive areas. Consequently, they are often too busy to get involved in the much more important financial analysis for strategic decisions. Many of these really vital strategic decisions are caused by sudden, unexpected dynamic changes in the external business environment, such as can be caused by the late entry of a major new competitor. Almost by definition in such cases, the historic financial data will be of very limited assistance, and the strategic decision-maker needs all the possible assistance which can be given by the experienced internal financial manager. As is discussed later in the chapter, it is possible for most of these situations to be anticipated to some extent, and for some financial information to be rapidly produced. Before considering this aspect, it may be useful to illustrate how financial expertise can be made available by increasing the level of automation for routine operational accounting problems.

IT has made it perfectly possible for companies to implement a 'peopleless payables' system, whereby nobody is actually involved in what is now normally regarded as the accounts payable area. An integrated computer system can link together the ordering department and the physical goods receiving area, without the need for any accounting personnel to become involved. Master files are held in the system, containing all the necessary details on all suppliers (including bank details for the eventual payment), the latest price data from each supplier for all products supplied, and a transaction file contains all outstanding, undelivered orders.

Upon delivery of an approved, live order (ie one on the transaction file), the prices are automatically accessed from the master file and the correct payment is calculated and stored in another transaction file. On the due date for payment, these funds are automatically remitted to the supplier's bank account and its computer is informed of the appropriate payment. All this happens automatically, without the human interference which creates the vast majority of the queries and errors in most accounts payable systems. The technology to achieve this has been available for some time, and some companies are now progressing well towards such a system. In most of the companies which are reluctant to take the first step, the major problems are either of trust (they do not seem to trust the computer, their own staff, or their suppliers) or of reduced flexibility in when the actual payments to suppliers are made. Many of these companies are implementing business strategies based on selling quality products, where the quality of the final product depends on the quality of raw materials and components received from these suppliers. Reducing the volatility of payment flows to these important suppliers, and working together more closely with them in the order/delivery/invoicing process would seem to be good ways of developing the trust necessary to ensure continuous high quality supplies, on a timely basis, from these suppliers. This is a classic way of demonstrating how many companies fail to follow through their competitive strategies and new strategic thrusts into the accounting area. Is it reasonable to expect a supplier to deliver, on four-hours notice a defect-free batch of components, if it hasn't yet been paid for the batch which it delivered, on the same terms, over 90 days ago?

An obvious essential element of this automated payments system is that the inputs to both the computer master files and the transaction file must be accurate and up-to-date. Thus, if the outstanding order file is not complete, the goods receiving area will not be able to accept delivery of certain items even though they are required by the production area. In a just-in-time manufacturing environment, the delays caused by such confusion can be extremely expensive. Also, keeping the master price file accurately up-dated is very important; if price rises are not included in time, suppliers may be very annoyed when they are subsequently paid at the old lower price. This sort of error can quickly destroy the increased feeling of trust developed by introducing such a system in the first place. The way round this potential problem is a good illustration of how to solve many of the data collection problems associated with a strategic management accounting system.

Data collection problems

In many companies, one of the major issues involved in implementing these new systems is which area of the business should be responsible for maintaining the integrity of the computer master files. Historically, this has tended to be the responsibility of the accounting department when it involved financial records, because these records were held by them and used by them almost exclusively. With modern data-base systems, this same record is accessed and used by a wide range of departments, but it is vitally important that one area has responsibility for the accuracy of this data. The accounting department cannot be held responsible for the accuracy of buying price files, except to the extent of accurately inputting the price data given to them by the buying department. In other words, their responsibility is for the clerical function, while the buying department are responsible for the prices actually negotiated with suppliers.

It seems logical therefore to avoid the unnecessary double handling of this important data, with the concomitant level of associated errors, and to make the buying department directly responsible for inputting all new supplier price details into the computer master files. As they are going to have to resolve any queries resulting from the wrong payments (due to price errors) being made to the supplier, they have a strong reason for ensuring that the price data is input accurately and on time. In fact, the system should allow for new prices to be input as soon as they are negotiated even if they do not take effect for some time. A trigger date can be fed into the system showing when the new price should be used for payment purposes.

If this is done, it can also provide very useful decision support information. These future prices really indicate replacement costs which, of course, are needed for many financial decisions. The strategic management accounting system can therefore access this file of supplier prices and select the most appropriate price for the particular decision. If no such future price is included and replacement cost data is required, the system should automatically revert to the latest actual price held in the system. This actual price may be for a current, outstanding order and thus may not yet have been actually incurred by the company.

Clearly, such a system has major advantages in that it automatically accurately collects some of the data needed for future strategic decisions, and it does so without increasing the workload for any area of the business. Indeed it frees up financially skilled resources to concentrate on the analysis of the consequently generated financial information. However, it has another significant advantage in the functional areas of the business, if this logic is also applied to the transaction part of the system. The buying department should input the orders into the system, as they can then check that the correct price file data is included in the master files. They must be made fully aware that once the goods or services have been supplied under this order, the subsequent payment will be made automatically in line with the agreed terms of the order. This concentrates managerial attention on the financial commitment by the company (ie the placing of the order) rather than on the subsequent payment of the invoice.

As discussed earlier in the book, managers only have true discretion before they are committed to pay for the product, and this is where the decision analysis and financial support must be focused. In too many businesses, it is still far easier to raise an order for something, than it is to get the resulting invoice actually paid; the relative authority levels for authorizing invoices and signing cheques versus signing orders are often completely illogical.

The data collection process for the strategic management accounting system should be as automated as possible, and fed by these types of inputs, where no extra workload is created as the data is required for other purposes. Unfortunately, because much of the necessary financial data is not the normal transaction-based accounting input, this cannot always be the case. This is further complicated by the external focus of strategic decisions which require the input of comparative data on competitors, the external marketplace, etc.

However, much of this required data already exists within the business, but is not necessarily recorded in one system, or in a form where it can easily be accessed and processed into relevant, decision support focused, financial information. For example, part of the normal financial evaluation process for all major new investment projects would involve an assessment of the net realizable value of the assets involved. Values would be assessed both at the end of the expected economic life of the project (the terminal net realizable value) and earlier, if the project failed so badly that it had to be aborted (this should be done as part of the project's risk assessment). In most companies, these net realizable value estimates are lost once the decision to go ahead has been taken, but they could easily be input into the system alongside the actual cost of the asset. If this was done, these estimates would be readily available for use in any subsequent evaluation of a potential exit decision; obviously the estimates may be up-dated as better information is received over the life of the assets concerned.

In the area of replacement costs, most businesses have a full review of their assets carried out for insurance purposes every three years or so. This review could also be used as the basis for inputting replacement cost estimates into the data-base, with index-based adjustments being used for the intervening years. Again these estimates can be up-dated if better information comes to light as the result of particular investigations or other sources, such as through analyses on competitors' investments. It is obvious from this discussion that these inputs will not be exact or precise, but this should not be used as a reason for not trying to collect the data. All financial decisions, particularly long-term strategic decisions, are based on estimates of the future, in terms of the benefits which *may* flow from the decision. Any data collection process which provides readily accessible and regularly up-dated estimates of the relevant financial data needed to support these decisions, such as replacement costs and realizable values, should be regarded as a significant improvement on relying on out-dated, irrelevant historic costs.

Even with respect to externally generated information, many companies already have considerable existing levels of comparative data on competitors, customers and suppliers. The issue for operating a strategic management accounting system is, therefore, to draw together these separate sources and to integrate them into a usable, overall data-base. Once again, one of the major obstacles to be overcome tends to be the ownership of the basic data which is already being compiled. Many areas of the company, eg the marketing department, will be collecting data on competitors on a regular basis for their own purposes. Making this available for more general analysis within the business may be seen by them as potentially dangerous. They may believe that it could be used to judge their relative performance, or they could be held responsible for any errors contained either in the data or in their extrapolations from this data. This can be resolved by allowing the inputting area to retain ownership and control over their raw data, by still feeding it in to the system themselves. More importantly, the culture within the organization should be changed to one where the accounting system is seen primarily as a learning process rather than the apportioner of blame. Essential co-operation can also be stimulated by demonstrating that an integrated system will give all parties better information than they can currently generate from their stand-alone analysis. This is normally possible in a fully integrated system because changes in relative market shares can be linked to alterations in product quality, or competitive price changes can be related to changes in relative cost structures, etc.

Thus the aim is for all the potential sources of external competitive data, outlined in Chapter 5, to feed into the single strategic management accounting system. A single system obviously avoids the costs involved in the duplication of data collection and analysis, but it should also improve the integrity of the base data, as the appropriate 'expert' area of the business can be made responsible for inputting the required data. This often means that the data will be input in one area of the business, while the benefit of the resulting financial analysis is felt in a different area.

Data input problems

These problems of separating data input from the resulting benefits are already occurring in many businesses, due to the divisions of labour now required to gain maximum efficiency through economies of scale, etc. For example, many sales information systems depend for their various segmented analyses on the coding references input by the clerical staff responsible for processing sales orders and invoices. The whole range of these very useful sales analyses require additional codes to be added to both the products' and the customers' reference numbers, which are used by the system to identify individual products or customers, and groups thereof. These increased reference numbers obviously add to the workload of the clerical staff involved and yet, in many cases, they have no knowledge of how important the subsequent financial analysis can be. Unless they realize the need for accuracy, or the system has built-in checks on the accuracy of the coding inputs (which normally further increases the length and complexity of the reference number), there is a risk of the subsequent financial analysis being based on false base data.

This problem is particularly apparent when the input required by another department is not part of the essential data fed into the system by the initiating area of the business. A good example of this occurred in a large insurance broking company which was having trouble collecting its premium income from its customers, before it had to pay the funds over to the insurance companies. As with many such intermediary service businesses, a critical success factor in today's competitive environment is ensuring that the business manages its working capital effectively. This company was having to invest substantial resources in chasing customers for overdue outstanding balances. It was also damaging its reputation with the insurance companies, as it tried to delay the payments to them until the funds had been received from its customers. The existing sophisticated computer system had anticipated the problem, and included an input field for the required payment date of premium to the insurance market. This date was supposed to be input by the broker at the time of arranging the insurance cover and entering the transaction into the system; the system then automatically set up a monitoring process on the receipt of the premium, triggering reminder letters to the customer, and issuing management reports on the status of the outstanding accounts. None of this system worked properly unless the required payment date was accurately fed in, but this required additional effort on the part of the broking clerical staff as they had to find this date out. Nobody had bothered to tell them why this data was needed or how it was used, and the computer system allowed them to leave this input field blank; so, they did!

A very limited amount of management effort was needed to improve their motivation and consequently to improve the operation of the whole system. This example can be compared to the earlier illustration of 'peopleless payables', where one of the strengths of the system development is to make the department, which is actually responsible for the particular data (eg price files and actual orders), also responsible for inputting the data into the system.

Evolution not revolution

As illustrated many of the existing systems in business are not being used as effectively as they could be, in the light of the current competitive strategies being implemented by the businesses. If the best possible strategic decisions are to be taken, the management accounting systems must make a significant contribution in their role of decision support. This represents the major challenge to management accounting in the years ahead, as too many such systems still function primarily as an historic analytical and reconciliation service, rather than in a forward-looking, decision oriented, strategically focused way.

However, financial control of the existing business is still an important function for management accountants and, implementing too many drastic changes too quickly, could lead to a loss of control, with potentially disastrous consequences. Progress should be evolutionary, but the evolution will be accelerated if wide-ranging support is given from other areas of the business. Such support can be stimulated if the accounting area propose, then rapidly and successfully implement, a few relatively straightforward improvements to their existing systems. Once other managers, particularly the strategic decision-makers, start to see what can be generated by the accounting area, and how useful it can be, they are likely to become far more positively demanding of further improvements. Such positive peer group pressure is always a good thing for stimulating innovation and change but, equally importantly, the management accountants should be more confident of making these changes, having successfully implemented the initial developments and had them favourably received.

For most companies the easiest area to attack is the presentation of the existing financial information. If the current communication gap, discussed in the previous chapter, can be closed, the other areas of the business will be able to understand what is already available in the way of financial information. They should consequently be able to discuss what else they need and want, and may be able to help in achieving many of these objectives, by taking over responsibility themselves for the required data collection and input. After all, strategic management accounting is really concerned with turning this raw data into strategically relevant, financial information, rather than collecting the data.

Index